FUNDAMENTALS OF
Developmental Psychology

Second Edition

Peter Mitchell and Fenja Ziegler

 **Psychology Press**
Taylor & Francis Group

HOVE AND NEW YORK

To Otto, who brought joy and light (F. Z.)
To Hugo, an eternal beacon of inspiration (P. M.)

Fundamentals of Developmental Psychology Companion Website:

The *Fundamentals of Developmental Psychology* companion website offers supplementary materials for both students and lecturers.

The Lecturer Resources include a PowerPoint presentation for each chapter, which can be used to support lectures. The presentations clearly summarise the material for each chapter and are illustrated with diagrams from the book. There is also a testbank of 25 multiple-choice questions per chapter which can be used in formal or informal testing situations.

For students there is a separate bank of chapter-by-chapter multiple choice questions to assist with learning and revision. There is also a comprehensive glossary of key terms used in the book.

Please visit www.psypress.com/cw/mitchell for more details.

First edition published 2007
Second edition published 2013
by Psychology Press
27 Church Road, Hove, East Sussex BN3 2FA

Simultaneously published in the USA and Canada
by Psychology Press
711 Third Avenue, New York NY 10017

Psychology Press is an imprint of the Taylor & Francis Group, an informa business

British Library Cataloguing in Publication Data
A catalogue record for this book is available from the British Library

Library of Congress Cataloging-in-Publication Data
Mitchell, Peter, 1959–
   Fundamentals of developmental psychology / Peter Mitchell and Fenja Ziegler. — 2nd ed.
      p. cm.
   Rev. ed. of: Fundamentals of development / Peter Mitchell and Fenja Ziegler. 2007.
   Includes bibliographical references and index.
   ISBN 978–1–84872–050–3 (hardback) — ISBN 978–1–84872–051–0 (softcover)
1. Developmental psychology. 2. Piaget, Jean, 1896–1980. I. Ziegler, Fenja, 1972–
II. Mitchell, Peter, 1959– Fundamentals of development.   III. Title.

BF713.M582 2012
155—dc23   2012014135

ISBN13: 978–1–84872–050–3 (hbk)
ISBN13: 978–1–84872–051–0 (pbk)

Typeset by Newgen Imaging Systems (P) Ltd
Cover design by Andrew Ward

Contents

Illustration credits

About the authors

Peter Mitchell is Professor in Cognitive Development in the School of Psychology at the University of Nottingham. His main research interests are the development of an understanding of the mind in typical and atypical development and visuo-spatial abilities in autism. He has served as Chair of the Developmental Section of the British Psychological Society (2004–2006) and since 2007 he has served as editor of the *British Journal of Psychology*.

Fenja Ziegler is a Senior Lecturer in Psychology at the University of Lincoln. Fenja received a BSc (Hons) in Psychology from City University, London, and a PhD in Psychology and Philosophy from the University of Nottingham. Prior to moving to Lincoln, Fenja worked as post-doctoral Research Fellow and Lecturer in Psychology at the University of Nottingham. Fenja's main research interest is the imagination and its role in social decision-making, mentalizing and perspective-taking in narrative and space, which she studies in children and adults.

Foreword

This is the second edition of our introduction to developmental psychology. The original idea for the first edition was borne out of a desire to share our excitement and fascination with developmental psychology in a comprehensive but reasonably concise introduction. As lecturers on developmental psychology courses ourselves, we had a pretty good idea of the kind of book we wanted to have as a course text and then set about writing it.

It has been about five years now since we published that first edition, and there have been many exciting discoveries in the field in this time, which made it sensible to update the text. In recent years, abilities in infants have become an especially burgeoning field of study and we have incorporated more of this work into this new edition. We have also added chapters on methodologies for studying development, developmental disorders, and number development. We could easily have added more chapters on other fascinating topics, but we wanted to keep this book manageable in size and avoid a chapter explosion. In this we also listened gratefully to the very helpful comments of reviewers of this second edition and of the first edition, who helped tremendously with identifying aspects of the first edition which were successful and should be kept, and which should be changed. We hope to have got this balance right and have kept much of the structure of the first edition, by trying to make the chapters self-contained, so that the book can be read from cover to cover, or by dipping in and out of chapters and referring to other places in the book where appropriate.

It is exciting to look at the way children grow and develop a range of astonishing skills, going from very little detectable ability in many areas to learning language, showing empathy, getting into other people's heads and adhering to morally sound behaviour. The guiding principle of developmental psychology is to examine changes that occur in these cognitive, emotional, social, and motor abilities across time. Many of these changes happen particularly during childhood, which is why developmental psychology is often concerned with studying children, but studying children alone does not define developmental psychology, it is the change that is the central focus of study. Developmental psychology has to go beyond a mere description of the changes we observe and offer theories and mechanisms that may explain these observed changes. We are also particularly keen to place these skills and developments in the context of theories, because without having a theory to explain what drives the development, we have little more than description; and description does not offer explanation. We examine the skills and developments by focusing on central topics and abilities contained in each chapter, and each topic will cover aspects of cognitive, social, emotional, and motor development, which combine to form the skills described.

What then can this study reveal? Developmental theory and observation can tell us much about adult psychology. By tracking the emergence and change of key faculties and skills we can better understand these concepts in their matured form in adults and understand the complex interplay between nature and nurture in defining our humanity. How do we form friendships? How do we connect with other people? How do we view the world? How can we be so moral on one hand but show aggression on the other? Do we learn to be good (or bad) or are we born this way? We hope that you will find the answers to questions you have been pondering in these pages and perhaps discover some other questions that are also worth asking and answering.

Peter and Fenja would like to thank the editorial team at Psychology Press for their expert guidance and help and continuing support throughout. We would also like to thank Camilla Gilmore for sharing her infectious enthusiasm and expertise on numerical development, which has inspired and shaped the chapter in this book.

Fenja Ziegler would like to thank her fantastic colleagues and students, both at the University of Nottingham and the University of Lincoln, who are a continual inspiration and motivation. Thank you to my family, for keeping me warm *and* on my toes. And to Susan, thank you, for everything.

Contents

Themes and perspectives in developmental psychology

Chapter Aims

- To introduce the idea of stages of development, versus gradual development.
- To introduce the idea of nurture combining with nature.
- To introduce some of the historical figures in developmental psychology.
- To introduce the various research traditions.

INTRODUCTION

Everyone knows that we are born with potential to become adult human beings. But just because we eventually grow up, it does not necessarily follow that we start out essentially as simplified adults. By analogy, tadpoles do not start out essentially as simplified frogs. Yet, if we applied the frog analogy rigidly to human development, it would be tempting to suppose that we are born as mini adults. After all, unlike tadpoles and frogs, babies and adults have a similar physical form and share precisely the same habitat; frogs and tadpoles don't even have the same process of respiration, and while one kind of creature must live in water, for the other a lot of time is spent out of water.

Although adults and babies have similar form, their mental processes might be quite different; and the question of whether or not they are different has long been a matter of debate in developmental psychology. Some theories effectively posit that the only difference between babies and adults is that babies don't know much because they have had relatively little experience of the world. In

Are children mini adults?

a way, these theories regard babies as being mini adults located at the starting point along a continuum of growth, psychologically as well as physically. These theories thus assume continuity between childhood and adulthood; an adult is essentially the same as a child, except bigger, stronger, and with more knowledge.

The opposing view maintains that actually babies are far from being mini adults. Although children visually resemble adults in a general sense, at least psychologically they are very different. In order to become adults, children would need to undergo a psychological metamorphosis, one that is monumental and profound, as with the transition from tadpole to frog. Advocates of this perspective regard development as discontinuous, insisting that children must progress through developmental stages en route to adulthood. Children are not viewed as being like adults with less knowledge; rather, they are presumed to have completely different thought processes. No matter how much knowledge a child possessed, according to this view, a child's knowledge would never have the *quality* of an adult's. That is, children and adults are considered to be qualitatively different from each other, at least in psychological terms.

Whether development is continuous or discontinuous is a pervasive theme that relates to many of the prominent perspectives on developmental psychology. Although the continuity debate is sometimes not acknowledged explicitly in these perspectives, an awareness of the debate's existence can provide useful insights and indeed can assist with comprehension of theories in developmental psychology. Knowing where a theorist stands with respect to the continuity debate can tell us where he or she is coming from, so to speak.

Another pervasive theme surrounds the nature–nurture debate. Some theorists think that psychological processes and abilities are largely the product of our genetic inheritance (nature), whereas others think they are largely the product of our environment and experiences therein (nurture). Everybody agrees that psychological processes and abilities are the product of nature and nurture in combination, and so the debate focuses on the relative contributions of nature and nurture in development. With these general themes in mind, let us now turn attention to some major perspectives on development.

BEHAVIORISM

The behaviorist perspective stresses the importance of nurture in which children are effectively regarded as mini adults. B.F. Skinner had by far the most influence over this approach. Born in 1904 (died in 1990), Skinner was captivated by the pioneers of conditioning, such as Ivan Pavlov (1849–1936) in Russia and John Watson (1879–1958) in the USA. Pavlov documented what he colorfully named "psychic learning" in his laboratory dogs. Having noticed that his dogs were salivating before they began eating, he started to reflect on the factors that might be at work. An obvious explanation surrounds the smell of the food, and the consequent salivation would be quite natural. However, the dogs seemed to salivate even before they were able to smell food, and hence Pavlov's musing that they seemed to be psychic. Apparently, the dogs had made associations between various sequences of events, such as the sound of the food containers being opened, followed shortly after by their subsequent access to

it case, why not use the
use we normally think of
positive or negative. So,
the child had completed
rtable and upright chair,
a *negative* reinforcer.
duct of the individual's
in how new actions are
count for this, Skinner
ssive approximation. He
ing the simple repertoire
mplex and sophisticated
a case in point. Skinner
bout the age of 8 to 10
resemble language, with
its excitedly respond to
fter a while, the parent's
ocalizations that sound
emit sounds like words
are extinguished from
infant will emit many
on't resemble language.
as learned to talk. One
of the infant's limited
d retort that we should
temptation to consider
he mind. Admittedly, it
t to avoid talking about

ings infants are capable
re capable of learning,
And he presumed the
me that apply to adults,
r thus regarded infants
rather than qualitative
here adults possess the

(born in 1928) who,
lanation of language
x that infants learn to
ded input of language.
only minimal levels of
ly. This seems all the
guage is an impressive
lt to learn a second
nably they have less
aded linguistic input,

Pavlov and staff during his study of conditioning with dogs.

und could stimulate
nded a bell just prior
of food were reliably
ll was not sounded at
ot presented at times
ase, although the bell
omptly and carefully
ult was positive—the

stimuli that naturally
ociation between two
ell and taste of food)
ry that is now known
, humans, mice) learn
ted at roughly the same
xplain how individuals
as about conditioning,
nd responses (whereas

Key Term

Reinforcement:
Any stimulus that, when
following behavior,
increases the probability
that the organism will
emit the same behavior in
the future.

Diagram of the apparatus used by Pavlov for his study of conditioning with dogs

Burrhus Frederic Skinner,
1904–1990.

encouraged the child to do more homework. In th
word *reward* in place of *reinforcer*? The reason is beca
rewards as being positive, whereas reinforcers can be
for example, if an aversive stimulus disappeared when
his homework, such as having to sit in an uncomfo
then this too would be considered a reinforcer, albeit

Skinner demonstrated that behavior is the pro
reinforcement history. However, this does not expla
incorporated into an individual's repertoire. To ac
introduced the concept of *shaping* via a process of succ
proposed that selective reinforcement is capable of sha
of reflexes available to us in early infancy into the co
behavior typical of adults. Take language learning as
acknowledges that babies babble quite naturally at a
months. This is the production of vocalizations that
a combination of vowel and consonant sounds. Pare
these vocalizations, which encourages the child. But a
excitement wanes, except when the infant produces
like words. Consequently, the infant is more likely to
in the future, while sounds which are not like word
his or her repertoire of vocalizations. Eventually, the
vocalizations that resemble language and few that d
At this time, Skinner would claim that the infant ha
might skeptically enquire, though, about the level
understanding and comprehension, but Skinner woul
concentrate on observable behavior while resisting the
the imponderables of what may or may not go on in
does seem rather ironic that a psychologist should war
the mind!

In summary, Skinner effectively claimed that the th
of learning are largely the same as the things adults a
notwithstanding various physiological differences.
principles of learning that apply to an infant are the sa
are the same that apply to rodents, and so on. Skinne
as mini adults: He saw development as a quantitative
process, as continuous rather than discontinuous, wl
same kind of knowledge as infants, but more of it.

NATIVISM

The champion of this perspective is Noam Chomsky
understandably, reacted against Skinner's radical ex
development. Chomsky drew attention to the parado
speak despite being subjected to a grammatically degra
Indeed he cites examples of infants who experienced
language but nevertheless learned to speak proficien
more remarkable when considering that learning a lar
intellectual feat. After all, adults find it very diffic
language. So, how do infants manage, when presu
intellectual capacity than adults, are subjected to deg

*Critically evaluate the
behaviorist account
of developmental
psychology.*

have no frame of reference (i.e. start out with no knowledge of language), and usually have no formally trained language teacher on hand to provide assistance?

Chomsky tried to resolve the paradox by suggesting that infants are born with innate knowledge of language. Now, it cannot possibly be the case that, for example, the distinctive characteristics of Chinese are transmitted genetically. If that were the case, then we would find that a Chinese baby adopted into an English home would spontaneously begin speaking Chinese. Chomsky argued, instead, that we are born with knowledge of language on a more general level. This would presuppose that on a deeper level, all languages have something in common. Chomsky claimed that this is indeed the case, and asserted that underlying the surface structure (i.e. the grammatical structure of the particular language in question) there is to be found a deep structure. This deep structure is supposed to be universal and innate. So, when we interpret language, we do so by translating into the deep structure; and when we utter a sentence, we do so by translating from a deep structure. By proposing an innate capacity, Chomsky felt able to explain the apparent miracle of infants learning something as complex as language.

Noam Chomsky, born 1928.

Being a linguist by training, Chomsky laid emphasis on innate capacities in the sphere of learning language. However, this example provocatively raises questions about the role of innate processes in other capacities. For example, are intelligence, motivation, temperament, and personality largely the product of genetic inheritance? Is the ability to walk innate? What about the ability to interpret a 2-D projection onto the retina of the eye as 3-D space in the world?

Evidently, Chomsky leaned towards nature in preference to nurture as an explanation for abilities, but where did he stand with respect to the continuity–discontinuity debate? Did Chomsky regard infants as mini adults? The answer is probably *yes* in the sense that he assumed that the core faculties that underlie sophisticated adult behavior are actually innate; and being innate, these faculties exist in infants just as they exist in adults. The principal difference between infants and adults relates to proficiency in utilizing innate capacities, but this proficiency can be thought of as something that changes quantitatively with age: The kind of processing carried out by an adult is essentially the same kind as carried out by an infant; it's just that an adult does it better. It thus seems ironic that despite taking radically different views on how much competence to attribute to infants, Skinner and Chomsky might actually be united in their perspective of continuity between childhood and adulthood.

Can nativism provide a comprehensive theory of developmental psychology?

MATURATION AND ETHOLOGY

It is reasonable to assume that humans have an innate ability to walk and yet typically they do not begin walking until about a year old. The innate knowledge of walking therefore must remain dormant until the baby has the level of strength and balance to make use of this capacity. Humans are also innately programmed to shed their milk teeth and develop secondary teeth, something that happens well into childhood. And they are also innately programmed to become sexually mature, something that happens during adolescence. In these instances, we see examples of innate characteristics that do not present

Key Terms

Deep structure: An innate grammatical structuring of language that is both universal among humans and unique to humans as a species.

Innate: An ability or trait that is with us from birth.

themselves at birth; just because a characteristic is innate, it does not necessarily follow that it would be active or indeed evident from the outset.

On the face of things, it might appear that a baby learns to walk through experience, is coached by adults, and improves through trial and error. Actually, though, walking might in fact be the product of an innate capacity, one whose expression results from maturational unfolding. The noteworthy point here is that just because a capacity develops after several months or even years, it does not necessarily follow that this development depended on learning or experience. To illustrate, imagine a scenario in which a baby did not have the opportunity to practice walking or even to practice moving about under his or her own volition until the age of about 12 months. Would the baby need a further 12 months to learn to walk? No. In fact, even this baby would probably begin walking shortly after gaining the opportunity to move around independently.

Although maturational stages in humans are not as radical as in frogs, recognition of the role of maturation inevitably alerts us to discontinuity in development. We thus speak of *maturational stages*. The maturation of certain capacities and faculties transforms us, step by step, from being a baby to being an adult. A baby therefore would be seen as qualitatively different from an adult, because an adult is exponentially more sophisticated thanks to various capacities having matured. In short, a maturational view is seated within the nativist tradition and it rejects the notion of babies as mini adults.

Maturation could have an effect in at least two ways. One way is the obvious, which is that a capacity, such as for walking, unfolds maturationally perhaps almost independently of experience and learning. A less obvious effect would be in terms of readiness to learn. So, for example, Chomsky proposed that we are innately equipped with a "language acquisition device," a special mechanism located in the brain that helps us to learn the particulars of our native language, whether it is Chinese, Dutch, Russian, or English. This device is supposedly under the control of a maturational clock and hence we witness babies finding it much easier to learn language at 18 months than at 12 months. We might say that the infant is *biologically prepared* to learn language.

Many of the actual details of language learning remain speculative, including the role of biological preparedness, and therefore another example would be more informative: attachment. We say that children are attached to their parents but we could also talk about attachment between geese and their hatchlings. Goslings attach themselves to their mothers, which is evident from the fact that they follow their mothers around. How do they know who their mother is? Why don't they erroneously follow a goose who is not their mother? Stimulated by these questions, the Nobel-Prize winning ethologist Konrad Lorenz (1903–1989) devised some ground-breaking experiments. Following careful observations of the behavior of newly hatched goslings, he began to suspect that they attach themselves to, or imprint upon, the first conspicuous moving object they see. To investigate further, he hatched some eggs in an incubator and then moved his wellington boots around them in the ensuing hours. Sure enough, the goslings attached themselves to the boots, which became apparent in that they followed Lorenz whenever he wore them.

Subsequent research revealed the circumstances and scope of the goslings' learning. The attachment began to be formed about 10 hours after hatching

and was at a peak at 30 hours. Thereafter learning did not occur so readily. Importantly, after the gosling had formed an attachment, the capacity for learning switched off. For example, in attaching to Lorenz's boots, the gosling lost the capacity to attach to its biological mother or indeed to any member of its own species. Evidently, a maturational clock set the temporal limits on this attachment learning. It was not that the gosling was in an intellectually heightened state at 30 hours after hatching, whereby all kinds of learning were facilitated; rather, specifically attachment learning was switched on. Hence, Lorenz introduced the notion of biological preparedness to learn something very specific, the timing of which is under maturational control. He added that there is a critical period when learning optimally occurs.

Konrad Lorenz, 1903–1989.

Being highly influenced by Lorenz's research, John Bowlby (1907–1990) began to consider the implications for human development. He suggested that humans also form a bond of attachment with their parents and that because this is a natural process under maturational control, any disruption could be seriously detrimental to emotional development. Not surprisingly, the time scale is quite different for humans. Bowlby and his colleague Mary Ainsworth (1913–1999) noted that the onset of separation distress seems to be around 8 or 9 months of age. Prior to this time, the baby typically is unfazed by their mother's departure from the room, but at the age of 8 or 9 months the baby typically shows a very strong reaction. The baby's distress is not assuaged by the comforting attentions of an unfamiliar adult and it seems the baby can only gain satisfaction from the mother's return. Bowlby regarded separation distress as a sign that the baby had formed a bond of attachment, something that would only be possible when the baby is maturationally ready, namely at about the age of 8 or 9 months.

Bowlby proceeded to study the plights of babies who were separated from their mothers for long periods, for example, as in the very unfortunate but thankfully rare case where the mother dies. In some cases that Bowlby documented, babies were reared in an institution in which there was no opportunity for the baby to form any attachment. This terrible circumstance had a profound and devastating effect on the babies' development. They failed to thrive and exhibited serious developmental delay physically, intellectually, and emotionally.

The concepts of maturation and biological preparedness help us to understand how innate factors combine with learning and experience as a driving force of development. Learning is steered by innate processes and the timing of this steer is maturationally determined. But the way in which the process comes to fruition depends on the environment and one's experiences. In an environment that is not conducive to satisfactory development, as for example when there was no moving object shortly after the gosling hatched, the biological preparedness to attach would come to nothing. In short, innate factors combine with learning and experience in allowing the individual to achieve developmental milestones. These milestones could be regarded as a kind of watershed: After achieving the milestone, the individual might be qualitatively different in some sense than before. For example, a baby who has formed a bond of attachment might be regarded as being qualitatively different in some psychological sense than before having formed a bond of attachment. Accordingly, it would not be psychologically valid to think of a baby as a mini adult.

In what sense, if any, do children progress through stages of development?

STAGE THEORIES: FREUD AND PIAGET

Stage theories maintain that children undergo a succession of psychological metamorphoses in their odyssey to adulthood. We can try to understand these stages as the product of the combined influence of, on the one hand, innate factors such as maturation and biological preparedness, and, on the other hand, experiential factors associated with learning opportunities and characteristics of the environment.

Sigmund Freud (1856–1939) was one of the first stage theorists. He set himself the challenge of explaining personality development and suggested that this largely depends on sexual fixations. He suggested that babies start out in the oral stage, in which the focal erogenous zone is the mouth. The baby supposedly gains a kind of erotic gratification from feeding. This is followed by the anal stage whereupon the focal erogenous zone is the anus and the baby gains gratification from the sensation of withholding and then expelling excrement. This is followed by the phallic stage, in which the child gains gratification from touching the genitals and from contemplating differences between the anatomy of males and females.

Freud's theory had tremendous influence, perhaps because it somehow resonated with the repressed sexual ethos that prevailed in the late nineteenth and early twentieth centuries. Conceivably, Freud's great popular impact inspired Jean Piaget (1896–1980) also to formulate a theory based on stages. It is probably fair to say that Piaget was preeminent in developmental psychology. His theory had a radical influence on the discipline across the world in the second half of the twentieth century and the legacy of his influence continues to this day.

Piaget was born in Switzerland in 1896, and died in 1980. His early interest focused on biology and, amazingly, his first publication on that subject appeared when he was only aged 10. A few years later he was invited to take up the elevated position of curator of shellfish at a natural history museum in Geneva. This was an offer he had to refuse, since he was still attending secondary school! At the age of 21, several years earlier than is usually the case, Piaget was awarded a doctoral degree. At this point he concentrated attention on cognitive development, whereupon he began working on the idea that intelligence is a crucial factor in determining how creatures adapt to their environment. In order to acquire insight into intelligence, he focused on the most intelligent creatures of all: human beings. Furthermore, Piaget believed that insight into the nature of intelligence could best be gained by studying its development. Hence Piaget became a cognitive developmentalist. At the time of his death, Piaget had written over 40 books on cognitive development, and over 100 articles on the subject.

Piaget suggested that children pass through a series of stages on the way to adulthood. He championed the idea that cognitive development is not a continuous process, dependent upon the accumulation of more and more information and skills; he thought that cognitive development proceeds not by gradual evolution, but rather by way of cognitive revolution. As the child shifts onto a new and more sophisticated plane of intelligence, she sheds many of the old cognitive limitations in a single sweep. In this respect, Piaget did not regard young children as mini adults. He did not think that children have the same

Key Term

Erogenous zone:
An area of the body that has sexual focus.

kind of thought processes as adults but with a smaller quantity of knowledge. Rather, Piaget considered that children's thought is qualitatively different from that of adults; and their long journey to full competence would only be possible by progressing through a succession of stages.

According to Piaget, intelligence is a faculty whose purpose is to help us adjust to the environment. We can broadly divide the environment into two. On the one hand there is the human, social, or psychological environment, while on the other hand there is the physical environment. Adjusting to both kinds of environment is very important. So, we can think of an individual adapting to (or perhaps changing) their physical environment to allow them to function optimally: how to build a shelter, to forage for food, to cultivate food, how to develop skills to be able to afford a good style of life. And similarly, we can think of an individual coming to terms with problems in the human environment: How to find a mate, how to be liked, how to be influential.

Jean Piaget, 1896–1980.

Piaget assumed that a singular factor stood in the way of good adjustment—namely, egocentrism. By this term, he did not mean that people are selfish; rather he meant that people see the world from their own perspective and setting aside their own particular viewpoint is achieved only as a monumental intellectual feat. He suggested that egocentrism presents such a formidable challenge to adjustment that overcoming it is something that could only be possible through a series of stages. Each successive stage confers better adjustment to the environment, along with a concomitant reduction in egocentrism.

During infancy, egocentrism is claimed to be most severe; so severe, supposedly, that the baby does not even discriminate between self and the rest of the universe. In other words, the infant cannot distinguish between the subjective and the objective. The individual then progresses to early childhood and, in doing so, sheds the severe egocentrism of infancy. Now the child understands that she herself is different from the rest of the world but she is still hampered by a milder form of egocentrism. Specifically, the child finds it difficult to acknowledge that her perspective on reality is relative to her vantage point and to her framework of knowledge. In middle childhood the individual manages to overcome this more subtle form of egocentrism, but nevertheless is still mentally trapped in the here and now. Only during adolescence can the individual break free of the shackles of the world as it is and imagine how things might have been different depending on key events in history.

If Piaget were correct about the form development takes, then it would have important implications for education. The material presented would need to be adapted to the intellectual level of the child. For example, it would be pointless to expect the child to engage in a mode of hypothetical reasoning if she had not yet reached adolescence. Does this mean that we should abandon attempts to introduce children to the Harry Potter or Lord of the Rings books? Clearly, many children love these stories and seem to have no difficulty comprehending a depiction of an imaginary world. Indeed, we see signs of an aptitude for make-believe in early pretence, which appears from about the age of 18 months. But just because children have imagination, it does not necessarily follow that they can easily apply that to the task of working out that their own perspective on reality is relative: It is relative to their location in space, to their position in society, to their framework of knowledge, and to a whole variety of accidents and events in history.

When Piaget talked about stages in development, did he suppose that these are maturational stages? Actually, no he did not: Piaget was a stage theorist without being a maturationist. While Piaget talked about his stages having biological significance, that is not the same as saying that the stages are under the control of a genetically determined maturational clock. He was also fond of the phrase "genetic epistemology," but in this usage *genetic* means something other than what most of us commonly take it to mean. In Piaget's sense, *genetic* means "origin" and *epistemology* means "knowledge." Hence, he was interested in the origin of knowledge—the knowledge that an individual acquires within a single life time.

If the stages are not maturational, then how do they come about? According to Piaget, each successive stage is an adaptation to a prevailing state of egocentrism. Thus, the individual's efforts of adaptation to the profound egocentrism of infancy culminate in a state where it becomes possible to distinguish between self and the rest of the universe. However, the new adaptation, although good in some ways, also has limitations with the consequence that a more subtle form of egocentrism survives. Eventually, the child finds an even better level of adaptation in overcoming this subtle form of egocentrism, and so on. The question, then, is why can't the individual move directly from the infant mode to the fully fledged adult mode in a single step? Why does the individual need to negotiate the intervening stages? The answer, we think, is that the adaptation the child hits upon early in childhood is specifically an adaptation to the egocentrism that is typical of infancy. The adult mode of functioning is an adaptation to the mode that preceded it (in childhood) but it is not directly an adaptation to the mode of egocentrism that dominates infancy. Hence, knowledge (or levels of adaptation) is built stage by stage, where each not only serves as a good adaptation but also provides a foundation for the next stage. Missing a stage would be akin to constructing a five-storey building without the third storey!

While Piaget assumed that the advent of a new mode of adaptation necessarily rendered a previous adaptation obsolete, such a view has been challenged by Siegler (1996). He suggested that when children formulate a new way of understanding the world, their old way of understanding can linger for a while and actually co-exist with the new adaptation. Siegler observed that at the point of transition, children vacillate between new and old kinds of strategies in solving problems, but the new way, being a better adaptation, eventually takes precedence. He calls this the *overlapping-waves theory*, in recognition that children have strategies that co-exist, or overlap in time. He uses the *wave* metaphor because as the prominence of the old strategy recedes, so the new strategy might swell. Siegler advocates a *microgenetic* approach to research, which involves repeated testing of children over a period of days or weeks at the time of transition. The technique reveals the co-existence of different strategies. If repeated testing had been separated by months, then we might have been fooled into thinking that one strategy had supplanted another with no overlap.

DEVELOPMENTAL PSYCHOLOGY

This chapter presented the various permutations of nature–nurture and continuity–discontinuity accounts, illustrated with ideas that were developed focal interest in the study of developmental psychology, and a flavor of some of these debates is presented throughout the book. Although we must not lose sight of the task of understanding children, and describing and explaining development, the controversy that surrounds the process of discovery is itself tremendously interesting.

m:
knowledge
erated by
rather than
another
ugh one's

Summary

- Different research traditions have been in ascendance at different points in the history of developmental psychology, ranging from behaviorism, to nativism, to constructivism. The latter sees development as a product of nature and nurture. Piaget's constructivist theory proposed that children progress through a succession of stages; in cognitive terms he asserted that we develop through radical revolution rather than gradual evolution, so to speak.

by figures who played major roles in the history of developmental psyc
In so doing, it sets a framework for the rest of the book. Researchers
take a stance with respect to the continuity of development and with res
the relative contributions of nature and nurture. Keeping this in mind co
digestion of the rest of the material we present.

Developmental psychology has many and varied facets. The foll
pages survey research into intellectual growth, social, emotional, a
artistic, perceptual, and aberrant development, along with the developm
language and numeracy. Not all research endeavors share the same tradi
and some areas of investigation have relied a great deal on the techn
of experimental psychology while others have employed survey metho
systematic observation. Much of the research is motivated by theory-testir
other words, investigators are not content merely to describe development;
actually want to explain development, especially the causes of developn
Explanations are provided by theories. Therefore, in order to decide whe
or not a theory provides a good explanation, we need to submit the theor
empirical test. This involves making predictions from theory. So, we cont
a suitable empirical test and observe whether the resulting data materia
in support of the theory. If they are not in support, then the status of
theory would come into question, along with the theory's explanation
development.

As an example, remember that Piaget explained the characteristics
young children by saying they are egocentric, meaning that they suppose th
perspective on the world is the only possible perspective. We could subr
this theory to empirical test by contriving a situation in which children ha
opportunity to reveal their egocentrism. To this end, Piaget showed children
model of three mountains. He allowed them to view the model from every ang
and then seated them so that they could survey the model from a particul
vantage point. Piaget then introduced the children to another person sittin
at the opposite side of the model and asked them how the model looked fro
where this other person was sitting. Because it would be difficult for children (o
anyone else for that matter) to give a verbal description, he presented an arra
of photos that showed the model from different locations. Piaget predicted tha
children below about 7 years of age would systematically select a photo of thei
own view (because they are egocentric) and this is precisely what he found;
only children above about 7 years selected a photo that correctly matched
what a person would be able to see when sitting at the opposite side of the
model. Consequently, there continued to be grounds for thinking that Piaget's
theory was satisfactory and useful. If young children had been able to correctly
identify another person's perspective on the scene, then Piaget's theory might
appear untenable and thus would have to be rejected.

The interpretations of experimental findings deserve to be critically
scrutinized, and it would be reasonable to contemplate why young children
selected their own view of the model. Is it because they are egocentric, as Piaget
suggested? Alternatively, is it possible that they are not egocentric but somehow
misinterpreted Piaget to be asking what the model looks like from their (the
child's) perspective? Perhaps younger and older children differ not in terms of
egocentrism but in their ability to interpret the experimenter's question. The
critical analysis of experimental findings and the ensuing debate thus assume

Key Term

Constructivi
A theory that
is actively ge
the individual
transmitted b
person or thr
genes.

Essay Questions

1. What factors should we consider when assessing whether the quality of thinking in children and adults is the same or different?
2. What is the nature–nurture debate?

Further Reading

To find out more about theories in developmental psychology you can turn to this excellent book:

- Miller, P. H. (2010). *Theories of developmental psychology* (5th edn.). New York: Worth.

Chapter 2

Contents

Methodological approaches

2

Chapter Aims

- To introduce some of the common techniques to investigation.
- To raise awareness of the challenges we face in interpreting data gathered from children, particularly in respect to children's verbal responses to questions.
- To give an idea of the changing constraints of collecting data as children develop from newborn babies to young adults.
- To identify various sources of information about children's mental functions.

INTRODUCTION

One of the main purposes of psychological research is to make discoveries on how the mind works; as far as developmental psychology is concerned, we are interested in the way these workings of the mind develop over the period spanning childhood. And yet any attempt to understand the development of the mind, paradoxically, was anathema to an earlier tradition. This is the School of Behaviorism, championed most notably by B.F. Skinner in the middle of the twentieth century. He and his followers were utterly dissatisfied with psychoanalysis as an approach to psychology and felt that the discipline should be more systematic, more technical, and most of all more scientific. They argued that research should be based on objective observation and measurement; since the workings of the mind cannot be observed and measured directly, they insisted that we should abandon the notion of "mind" altogether and concentrate instead only on understanding the principles of behavior. Subsequently, in the latter part of the twentieth century, we witnessed a "cognitive revolution," where researchers investigating cognitive processes started once again to believe that it was legitimate to make inferences about the workings of the mind so long as data were obtained from systematic and objective experimentation.

Research approaches, especially those that measure behavior, have to be adapted to the age of the participant. The kind of measures we use to investigate the performance of infants can be quite different from the kind of measures we use with children. This is because in the case of children we are able to issue instructions on how to perform the task that we have set, while the same would be quite impossible with preverbal infants. Techniques for investigating the psychological abilities of infants and children deserve to be considered separately.

DEVELOPMENTAL COGNITIVE NEUROSCIENCE

What are the strengths and weaknesses of cognitive neuroscience?

More recently, Psychology as a discipline has engaged with the idea that our understanding of the mind can be informed by discoveries of the structure and form of the brain, based on various imaging techniques. We no longer think of cognitive approaches only as something that can be adduced from measurable behavior. Now we are able to locate these processes within the architecture of the brain. Thanks to advances in cognitive neuroscience, the dichotomy between mind and brain is finally beginning to dissolve.

Perhaps the most well-known imaging technique is magnetic resonance imaging (MRI), developed at Nottingham University, UK, which is capable of generating exquisite and high-resolution images of the brain. These images are offered in two general forms, structural MRI and functional MRI. Structural MRI provides a snapshot of virtual "slices" of the brain. By working from the top to the bottom of the brain, we are thus able to create a three-dimensional image. This technology generates an image that has some features in common with X-ray, in that we can see structures beneath the skin, but unlike X-ray, the quality, resolution, and detail of the image can be quite exquisite. Functional magnetic resonance imaging (fMRI) gives an image of how areas of activity change within the brain over time. The scanner is capable of detecting concentrations of blood, and providing it is correct to assume that areas of activity draw larger volumes of blood, we can gain an impression of which areas or structures of the brain are responsible for which mental activities. For example, when a person is solving problems, the frontal lobe will be most active and will draw more blood than when less active. High concentrations of blood can be displayed graphically as "lighting up." Hence we can see an image of the brain where active areas "light up" as the participant is processing information.

Of course, all areas of the brain are supplied by blood at all times and the researcher has to take this into consideration when designing his or her study to find out which part of the brain is especially active during a particular task. For example, suppose we want to discover which part of the brain is responsible for language production and which is responsible for language comprehension. When the participant speaks, we would expect to see high levels of activity adjacent to part of the motor cortex, in the frontal lobe, which is known as Broca's area, but we would not expect to see strong activity in Wernicke's area, located in the temporal lobe. Conversely, when the participant is listening to speech, we would expect to see high levels of activity in Wernicke's area but not in Broca's area. We might then wish to conduct further investigations into the specificity of activity in Wernicke's area to be sure that it is responsible for processing language and not other kinds of auditory stimuli. Under one condition, the control condition, the participant

Key Term

Motor cortex:
A region of the frontal lobes of the outer cortex of the brain that is responsible for volitional control of the muscles.

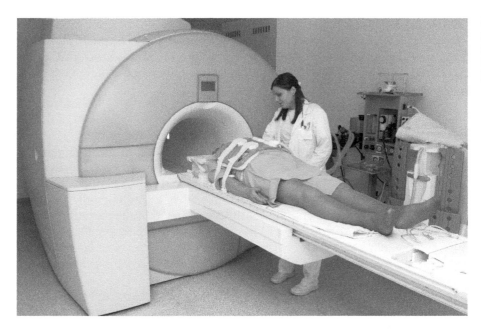

Functional magnetic resonance imaging (fMRI) scans have become an important source of data in psychology.

might hear nonspeech, which could include scrambled speech, music, sounds of animals, or other stimuli. Under the focal experimental condition, the participant would hear speech and nothing else. Under both conditions, we would observe general activity in the temporal lobe but if we subtract the level of activity observed in the control condition from activity in the experimental condition, there should remain a unique level of activity in Wernicke's area. This is a level of activity in the experimental condition existing over and above the levels of activity in the control condition. The convention would then be to graphically represent this finding by presenting an image of the brain with a "lit up" area corresponding with the activity that was unique to the experimental condition—in Wernicke's area.

Another method of brain imaging employs an electroencephalogram (EEG). This is a net of perhaps 128 or 256 tiny electrodes that the participant wears on their head. The electrodes are so sensitive that they are capable of picking up minute electromagnetic activity generated by the electro-chemical processes occurring at the surface of the cortex of the brain. Admittedly, EEG is not as precise as MRI in telling us where activity is located in the brain; however, it is even more accurate than MRI in telling us how neural activity changes over a very brief period of time. When a participant experiences the onset of a stimulus, this will evoke a characteristic cortical response, which will then decay over the ensuing milliseconds. This technique provides valuable information about attention at the level of the cortex, especially the speed of shifts in attention.

Imagine that we wanted to test the hypothesis that the cortex of a typically developing child is specially adapted to processing social information, while the cortex of a child who has autism is adapted to processing nonsocial information. When children see a person's face, the cortical response in those who are typically developing might be relatively quick, while the cortical response in those with autism might be relatively slow; conversely, when

Key Term

Autism:
A developmental disorder affecting about one per hundred of the population. Those with the disorder are impaired in socially connecting with other people.

A participant in an EEG experiment.

Critically assess the different types of brain-imaging techniques.

children see a physical object, the cortical response of typical children might be relatively slow and the response of those with autism might be relatively quick. EEG would be capable of identifying such a pattern and we could thus test a hypothesis about differences in attentional priority between children with and without autism.

One of the great benefits of imaging research is that it can help us understand how cognitive function is represented in the architecture of the brain. But how can that in itself be useful? We already know that cognitive activity is located in the brain—we know for sure it is not located in the heart, the kidney, or the liver. Does it matter that we know which part of the brain hosts a particular function? In some ways, knowing how form is related with function can indeed be valuable. For example, we might speculate that higher cognitive abilities, those not shared with our primate cousins, are located in the part of the brain that emerged most recently in evolutionary history—the frontal lobes; and sure enough, it seems that executive functions, some aspects of language and the mental processes involved in inferring what other people are thinking, are hosted by the frontal lobes.

Knowing about the particular location of specific cognitive functions can also allow us to test theories. A case in point relates to how we are able to infer what other people are thinking. One theory says that we acquire a set of rules and formulas that we apply to the task. For example, we observe that John did not see a thief steal his wallet and therefore we can infer that he continues to believe his wallet is in his pocket. We base this inference on the rule that if a person has not witnessed some event then he will not know and by default will maintain his prior belief. Another theory, conversely, says that people do not use rules to infer what other people are thinking but instead imagine themselves in another person's situation: If I were John and, like John, I did not see my wallet being stolen, then I would continue to believe that the wallet is in my pocket. John is rather similar to me so presumably he thinks his wallet is in his pocket, even though in fact his wallet was stolen.

The latter theory assumes it is easy to imagine being in the situation of another person; it assumes that we easily empathize with others and that effectively one mind resonates with another. As far as neural architecture is concerned, we might enquire whether there is any evidence for a center in the brain that holds the rules for inferring what other people are thinking. Alternatively, do we instead see evidence that one brain resonates with another brain? The evidence supports the latter possibility. For example, consider a person who is yawning. Using brain-imaging techniques, we can establish that a particular kind of neural activity is associated with the act of yawning. Now suppose that we see another person yawning. Imaging techniques reveal that the same region of the cortex is active in the person observing the yawn as in the person who is doing the yawn (Gallese, 2001). Presumably, this explains why yawning is contagious and the imaging shows that neurons in one brain resonate with those in another brain. This is known as the mirror neuron hypothesis (Rizzolatti & Craighero, 2004). For that reason, presumably it is quite easy for a person to imagine being in the same situation as another whom they are observing. Hence, the evidence seems to suggest we understand other people's minds not by applying rules but by imaginatively projecting ourselves into the shoes of another person (Mitchell, Currie, & Ziegler, 2009).

As we see in chapter 5, a large body of research in developmental psychology has addressed questions on how we acquire an understanding of the mind. This innovative approach in cognitive developmental neuroscience has allowed us to make strides in this endeavor.

Despite these exciting developments, there are limitations to cognitive neuroscience. Generally, as already mentioned, simply knowing where a cognitive process is located is unlikely to be particularly helpful in itself. Besides, recent research reveals that most cognitive processes are not located in any one particular place. Second, as

far as research with children is concerned, there are some practical difficulties. Sliding into the narrow bore of an MRI scanner is a claustrophobic experience and the apparatus makes loud mechanical noises that can be unnerving. Apart from ethical concerns about testing children under such conditions, it is unlikely that the neural activity that we observe will be representative of activity that occurs when the child is not in such a frightened and uncomfortable state. EEG is less of an ordeal but in order to obtain informative results testing needs to be conducted in a Faraday cage to screen for ambient electromagnetic activity. Again, testing conditions might not be representative of a real-world environment and this could affect the results.

The mirror neuron hypothesis dictates that the same region of the cortex is active in the person performing an action (e.g. the man yawning in this photo) as in the person who is observing it (you).

In summary, brain imaging has huge potential to advance our understanding of how the mind develops; but there are limitations associated with obtaining data that are generalizable to the real world and there are distinct ethical considerations. Using techniques like EEG and MRI can be very expensive and we have to balance the value of what can be gained in knowledge about the developing mind against how much it costs. One could collect a large amount of data using observation techniques for the same cost and it is not always clear which approach affords the best value.

RESEARCH BASED ON OBSERVATIONS OF BEHAVIOR: INFANCY

Two techniques that have been used to good effect with infants are nonnutritive sucking and preferential looking. This is an example of nonnutritive sucking: Imagine that we want to know whether or not a 6-week-old infant recognizes the same object presented at different distances. Imagine, moreover, that the infant has a pacifier in her mouth and that when she sucks she sees something pleasant and exciting (her mother doing a peek-a-boo) if and only if this stimulus is present. Now the questions we can ask are: Will the infant suck in the presence of this object irrespective of whether it is close or distant? Will the infant suck in the presence of a different sized object strategically located so that it produces the same retinal image as the object that the infant has come to associate with a peek-a-boo? If the infant sucks in the presence of the target object and not in the presence of a different object, irrespective of retinal size and distance of the objects from the baby, then it seems fair to conclude that the baby is capable of perceiving depth. This is because the infant seems to grasp that the retinal *size* of the image does not provide any clue on whether a particular object is associated with a peek-a-boo; only the true physical size of the object determines whether sucking will elicit a peek-a-boo. In order to be attuned to the true size, the infant must be capable of perceiving depth and effectively appreciate that the same object projects differentially sized retinal images at different distances. Such appreciation is tantamount to understanding about the effects of distance—that retinal size is relative to distance. In other words, if the baby sucks only in the presence of the object associated with a peek-a-boo, this tells us that he can perceive depth.

How could an infant's preference to look at certain objects be used to understand the behaviour of infants?

Recently, preferential looking is a procedure that has become more widely used than a nonnutritive sucking procedure on the grounds that it is a more simple and versatile technique of investigation. This approach is based on the principle that, all things equal, babies prefer to look at novel rather than familiar objects. Such preference indicates that babies are able to recognize novel objects. So, under what conditions do babies successfully recognize a novel object as such? Continuing with the example offered previously, if babies have been familiarized with a particular object, let's say a cube of certain dimensions, would babies prefer to look at a novel object over the familiar one even though the novel object projects the same retinal size (but is of different distance)? In other words, do babies, who we know prefer novelty, prefer to look at a novel object that projects the same retinal size as the familiar object, or do they prefer to look at the familiar object even though it projects a different retinal size owing to the fact that it is now placed at a different distance? The answer is that babies tend to prefer the genuinely novel object even if it projects the same retinal image as the familiar object presented during the familiarization phase. This tells us that babies encode objects according to their true size and not according to projected size. It effectively means that babies recognize a given object as being the same despite the fact that different retinal sizes are projected at different distances. In short, babies perceive depth.

Preferential looking is an investigative approach based on the principle that, all things equal, babies prefer to look at novel rather than familiar objects.

The preferential looking procedure can be applied to different problems of investigation: Do babies discriminate between faces belonging to members of their own culture and faces belonging to members of a different culture? What is the memory span of babies for faces? Do babies prefer to look at protagonists who are helpful and cooperative over protagonists who are obstructive and cause hindrance? If so, this could be evidence in support of early moral sensitivity. Do babies discriminate between familiar and unfamiliar angles in geometric shapes? If so, this could be evidence in support of early shape constancy.

The preferential looking procedure is versatile and sensitive for investigating babies' perceptual, cognitive, and emotional development. The biggest challenge it presents is in coding the data. One way to record looking preferences is for observers to watch discreetly and encode where the baby is looking while the task is ongoing. Another method is to film the baby from a point between the two objects that the baby could look at. On watching the video recording, raters could then make judgments on how many times and for what duration the baby looks to the left and to the right. If the raters are blind to what the baby is looking at and if they are ignorant of the hypotheses, then this is a particularly powerful procedure, for we could be sure that any expectations held by the raters do not contaminate or bias their coding. Moreover, if there are two or more coders and there is a high rate of agreement between their respective codings, then we can be confident that the coding method is accurate and reliable.

A method that employs modern technology is based on the recording of eye movements by an eye-tracker. This is a device that precisely measures the direction of the baby's gaze in relation to the scene that lies before him or her. Specifically, the eye-tracker will generate a recording of the scene that the baby observed and superimpose a succession of fixation points, coupled with a scan path. In other words, we will have a precise and objective recording of what the baby looked at and when. This technology thus tells us precisely which object the baby looked at and for what duration. The problem with this procedure is that calibrating a baby's eye movements can be difficult (though not impossible). Before we record any data, we must be sure that the apparatus is set up in such a way that it accurately records which part of the scene the baby is looking at.

Another challenge presented by the preferential looking procedure concerns extraneous effects associated with the positioning of objects and to remedy this problem we employ counterbalancing. In other words, we must ensure that the position of the object during familiarization does not predict its position during the preferential looking phase. If the object was presented on the right-hand side during familiarization, then in some cases it will be presented on the left and sometimes on the right during the preferential looking phase. This will allow us to be sure that babies' preference for the novel object is not really just a preference for objects that appear on the right-hand (or left-hand) side. Hence, the positioning of the novel and familiar objects during preferential looking is counterbalanced.

These systematic and objective methods of observation are rather different from techniques used in the past. Jean Piaget established a great tradition of researching children's intellectual growth using more basic and perhaps primitive procedures. Indeed, Piaget was content with simple observation. He watched his own three children as babies and then reported, for example, whether or not they retrieved a toy that was hidden under a cloth. On finding that the infant did not retrieve the toy, Piaget concluded that the baby was oblivious to the object's continuing existence when it was no longer visible. Piaget made similar observations about his three children that led him to conclude that being oblivious to the existence of an out-of-sight object is a universal phenomenon in infancy. Arguably, this conclusion is something of an over-interpretation, not least because Piaget seemed not to recognize the potential biases in his own observation and did not seem to appreciate that he might need a larger sample than three participants in order to generalize his conclusions to the world's entire population of infants. If other observers reported precisely the same behavior in many different samples and if the observations between different observers were in agreement then we could be more confident that the reporting was reliable. Also, Piaget did not seem aware of the possibility

How do the procedures used today to study the behaviour of infants by observation differ from the past?

| Key Term |

Counterbalancing:
A methodological technique for neutralizing order effects in a repeated measures experimental design. Imagine that the participant has to perform under two conditions, A and B. Half the participants will do A followed by B and half will do B followed by A. This manipulation of the order of testing is called counterbalancing.

that there could be other explanations for the baby's failure to search once the toy was out of view. This is not to say that Piaget's observations, or indeed his theory, are wrong; rather, in modern research we are rigorous in our approach to observation and we are a good deal more cautious in the conclusions we draw from those observations.

RESEARCH BASED ON CHILDREN'S ANSWERS TO QUESTIONS

When children become fluent in language and communication, it offers a rich source of information about developing knowledge and abilities. From casual conversation, we can gain much information about children's everyday use of language: We can estimate the size of vocabulary, the acquisition of grammatical principles, pragmatic ability, and so on. We might also want to investigate what they know and understand by asking questions in the context of a structured activity. Such a method was championed by Piaget and here is an example: Piaget wanted to know when children acquire the concept that quantity is conserved despite an irrelevant but visibly conspicuous transformation. He poured water into two glass beakers to the same level and made adjustments in each until the children agreed that they both contained the same amount. Piaget asked the children, "Is there more water in this glass, is there more water in this glass or are they just the same?" He then announced, "Now watch this," and poured the water from one of the beakers into a tall thin glass, whereupon the level of water was much higher. He repeated the question, "Is there more water in this glass, is there more water in this glass or are they just the same?" Unlike older children, those aged about 7 years and below incorrectly gave a nonconserving answer, usually by saying that the tall thin glass contained more water. In the light of this, Piaget concluded specifically that these young children lack a concept of conservation, and more generally he concluded that it was a sign that children were in a preoperational stage, meaning that they were unable to think logically.

In one sense, the approach to investigation seems appropriate and the resulting data seem revealing. In another sense, it all seems deeply problematical. First, consider the matter of interpreting the data—the child fails to say that the tall thin glass has the same amount as the short wide glass. In failing to conserve, there is no evidence to show that the child is competent; indeed, there is no evidence to indicate that the child possesses the concept of conservation. But absence of evidence is not tantamount to evidence of absence. Just because we failed to demonstrate the child's competence it doesn't necessarily follow that the child is incompetent. Perhaps the test was unsuitable for revealing competence in children aged 7 and below. Accordingly, we should question the appropriateness of the approach to investigation. Could some aspects of questioning lead children to underperform despite their having the requisite competent?

According to Piaget, children over the age of 7 years will give a conserving answer, by acknowledging that a taller, thinner glass contains exactly the same amount of water as the original wider glass.

Donaldson (1978) offers the following insight: Imagine a person asks you a question ("Is there more water in this glass, is there more water in this glass or are they just the same?") and imagine you answer correctly by saying, "Yes, they both contain the same amount!" The person then does something and repeats the question. Conventionally and conversationally, it would be strange if you replied the same as previously, for it might indicate that you had not been paying attention to the action of the questioner. Putting it another way, it goes without saying that there's still the same amount in the two glasses following transformation. And yet if the experimenter thinks it is worth asking you about quantity, it seems to imply that something extraordinary has happened and that you are supposed to give a nonobvious answer. In short, Donaldson (1978) suggested the inappropriate form and context of questioning led competent children to give a wrong answer—the conservation question is a leading question. Donaldson's critique of Piaget stimulated a large volume of research aimed at testing Piaget's theory with better methods and some of this is summarized in detail in chapter 4.

This problem, concerning how to ask questions and what conclusions to draw when children give the wrong answer, has been pervasive throughout the history of developmental psychology. It is a very frustrating problem for researchers who sometimes just wish that they could draw straightforward conclusions from the errors in children's replies and then get on with the job of developing a grand theory. Indeed, sometimes those who urge caution in how to interpret children's errors are maligned by peers for presenting obstacles in the quest to develop theories of cognitive development. Such criticism is akin to derogating the messengers of bad news. The fact of the matter is that researchers need to be aware of sources of bias in the way children answer questions.

What are the sources of bias encountered by researchers when studies require children to answer questions during the experiment?

The most basic source of bias is the yes bias (Ackerman, 1982), which is that if children are asked a question that requires an answer of either "yes" or "no," they are biased to answer "yes" irrespective of what is actually the correct answer. In other words, children like saying "yes." Another source is the performative bias (Ackerman, 1981). Among children aged 7 and below, there is a strong tendency to answer questions not verbally but by carrying out a relevant action, especially pointing at something. For example, imagine we show a child pictures of cartoon characters and we ask, "Does your friend Simon know which of these is Superman?" The child will almost certainly reply simply by pointing at the picture of Superman! We could then emphasize: "But I'm asking you about *Simon*. Does *Simon* know which of these is Superman?" Still, it's very likely that the child would once again point at the picture of Superman instead of addressing the question of what Simon knows. On the strength of this evidence, it might be tempting to conclude that the child is incapable of adopting another person's perspective. And yet if we did not have pictures in front of the child, then there is a much better chance that she will give an accurate judgment of Simon's state of knowledge or ignorance (Mitchell & Robinson, 1992). Hence, a performative bias is liable to mask children's competence in judging others' states of knowledge and this is something we should take into consideration when designing the study.

Having elicited a response, this needs to be recorded. One method is simply to write down the child's response or tick a box from a set of alternatives that represents the full range of the child's possible answers. Such a procedure

Key Terms
Yes bias: A bias to answer all questions that require an answer of either "yes" or "no" in the affirmative.
Performative bias: The tendency to respond to a question with an action instead of replying verbally.

is simple and practical but allows for a variety of different kinds of error. First, it might be that the experimenter simply makes errors in writing down what the child says or ticks the wrong box. Second, it might be that the child does not give a natural response because she is aware that the experimenter is writing down what she says. For example, the child might be tempted to say something unusual or strange in order to make the experimenter's report more interesting. Or the child might feel self-conscious and become taciturn. Less conspicuous methods of recording might help, such as video or voice recording, but the research will enter sensitive ethical areas if images of the child are archived.

In summary, being able to pose questions to children offers rich opportunities for collecting data on aspects of development, but considerable care is needed. Specifically, we need to be aware of various sources of bias in children's responses that could mask competence, including various conversational biases, such as question sequencing, a "yes" bias, and a performative bias. We also need to appreciate that if there is absence of evidence for children's competence, this could be due not to lack of competence but to error in performance associated with the questioning and testing context. We also need to be aware of the process of recording data. The very fact that children know they are being recorded can and probably will impact upon the character of their responses; and we need to be aware of our own fallibility as experimenters in making accurate recordings or in transcribing data.

| Key Term

Intellectual realism: The phenomenon of children drawing what they know rather than what they see.

BEHAVIORAL RESPONSES

Some kinds of research questions require children to make not a verbal but a different kind of response. For example, we could investigate intellectual realism by asking children to make drawings. At around 7 years of age, children's drawings tend to be stylized in a particular kind of way. Specifically, their drawings tend to be based on a stored schema or prototype of what they think the thing should look like rather than what they can actually see. It is tempting to interpret children's drawings not just as a sign of how they prefer to represent the world artistically but as a clue to the way they perceive the world. Perception is likely to be influenced by what we are expecting to see, based on previous experience and stored knowledge.

Consider this example: Looking at a dinner plate on the table before us, we think we see a round shape, but the shape that actually projects from the plate to the retina is elliptical because our perspective is slanted. Thouless (1931) asked adult participants to draw the plate precisely as it looked and found that while participants understood the instruction well enough to draw an oval, they nevertheless exaggerated circularity. Hence, adults' judgments of the appearance of a shape seem to be contaminated to a

At around 7 years of age, children's drawings tend to be based on a stored schema of what they think something should look like rather than what they can actually see.

matter of degree by their knowledge of the real shape. This suggests that perception is not a photographic record of reality but is rather an interpretation based on knowledge and experience.

How could children's drawings be useful in research?

If drawings could reveal something about perception in adults, perhaps by the same token some aspects of children's drawings could tell us how perception develops. The topic of children's drawings is covered in detail later in chapter 9 and all we are concerned about in the current chapter is the principle of what we can gather from children's drawings. We hope we can learn something about perception, but a barrier to such interpretation surrounds the development of manual skill in manipulating a pencil or crayon. It so happens that, like adults, children also exaggerate the circularity of a dinner plate that they view from a slanted angle (Mitchell & Taylor, 1999). But is this because they perceive the appearance of the dinner plate as being more circular than it really is or is it that they are good at drawing circles and not so good at drawing ovals? In other words, do they draw a circular shape due to the characteristics of perception or due to limitations in skill?

One way to answer this question is to adopt an experimental approach that includes a control condition. For example, suppose children were asked to draw an oval dinner plate that they were viewing squarely and not at a slant. In this case, there is no conflict between what the child can see (an oval) and what they know of the true physical shape of the object (an oval). If they exaggerated circularity in this case, it could not be because their knowledge of reality contaminated their judgment of appearance since there is no conflict between what they know and what they see. If they exaggerated circularity, it would thus seem to be due not to a characteristic of perception but due to a limitation in skill—perhaps it is easier for children to draw a circle than to draw an oval.

This would be a very important finding, for it would constrain our interpretation of children's exaggeration of circularity in the experimental condition, where they had viewed a slanted circle: We could not rule out the possibility that children simply find it easier to draw a circle than an oval due to limitations in their manual skill. Accordingly, we would have no grounds for concluding that children's perception is influenced by their stored knowledge based on past experiences. Hence the control condition provides an essential point of comparison, allowing us to make a meaningful interpretation of findings in the focal experimental condition. This principle applies not only to research on the topic of children's drawings but more generally to all kinds of experimental investigation.

In summary, children's drawings can give us various clues about how they see the world. Drawings surely can tell us something of their budding artistic talent, and they can tell us much more besides. In this example, we have concentrated on an aspect of children's perception, but drawings can reveal other things as well, such as how mentally mature the child is and whether or not the child has problems in the arena of emotional development. The systematic approach to investigation outlined here, comparing an experimental condition against a control condition, trades on the general principles of experimental psychology. The method has served well in the past and it continues to offer a valuable framework for ongoing research, irrespective of the kind of measure we are taking and irrespective of the age of participant.

Key Term

Experimental noise:
Sets of data arising from psychological research seldom or never are pure measures of the phenomenon of interest. Usually, the set of data is composed of a mixture of the thing we want to measure plus other factors that influence the way that research participants (e.g. children) respond. The aspect of the data that is caused by these other unwanted factors is called "experimental noise."

Summary

- There are various methods available for investigating mental development, ranging from question and answer sessions to advanced brain-imaging techniques. Each approach has strengths and weaknesses and it is not possible to champion a definitive or best technique. Some approaches are particularly well suited to gathering data from babies (e.g. a preferential looking procedure), while some are completely unsuitable (e.g. question and answer techniques). Some can be used with babies but better suit older children (e.g. brain-imaging procedures). One thing all techniques have in common is that the data they yield need to be interpreted very carefully. Data do not speak for themselves and usually they contain biases associated with **experimental noise**.

- Sometimes researchers feel frustrated by obstacles that stand in the way of gathering easily interpretable data, but this challenge is not confined to psychological research with children. Obtaining informative data that are interpretable in simple ways presents a challenge for all researchers, whether they are interested in psychology, biology, physics, or any other area of inquiry. This fact is not a reason to feel frustrated; rather it poses an exciting challenge and no doubt future generations of scientists will achieve breakthroughs in developing new methods that will lead to monumental discoveries in the quest to find out who we are and where we came from—the mission of Psychology as a Science.

Essay Questions

1. If children give the wrong answers to verbally presented questions about aspects of the world, does this imply that they are intellectually incompetent?
2. Are brain-imaging techniques better than behavioral measures for finding out how children's minds develop?

Further Reading

If you want to delve deeper into the methods specifically used to study development and the issues associated with them, then turn to the relevant sections in this accessible handbook:

- Laursen, B., Little, T. & Card, N. (Eds.) (2011). *Handbook of developmental research methods.* New York: Guilford.

Chapter 3

Contents

The development of thinking

3

Chapter Aims

- To introduce Piaget's theory of cognitive development.
- To detail Piaget's stages.
- To detail the evidence that lends support to Piaget's stage theory.
- To present the mechanism that Piaget posited as responsible for cognitive development.

INTRODUCTION

The discipline concerned with studying the development of thinking is cognitive developmental psychology. The word "cognitive" refers to knowledge, but not necessarily according to the common meaning of the word. When people talk about knowledge, they usually mean the kind of information useful for answering questions in games such as *The Weakest Link* or *Who Wants to be a Millionaire*, or in order to do college exams. In contrast, cognitive developmentalists think of knowledge as referring to *understanding* about things.

You might have noticed a child aged around 5 years speaking on the telephone about things only he can see: He seems to overlook the fact that the person he is speaking to is in a completely different location and cannot see the same things. Perhaps this is a sign that the young child is incapable of putting himself in someone else's shoes. In the broadest sense, it is tempting to suppose that the child does not understand that other people can have different perspectives. Cognitive developmentalists look at particular difficulties children have, such as poor communication ability, and then draw general conclusions about their underdeveloped knowledge of the world. An exciting aspect of cognitive developmental psychology concerns the things children say and do in various situations, and then speculating about the meaning of these in terms of what the child does or does not know about the world.

Not everybody is in agreement about the way children understand the world, and how that understanding develops. This is mainly because what children say and do is open to interpretation with respect to the implications for their level of competence. For example, a commonsense explanation for young children's difficulty in communicating on the telephone might simply say that their lack of experience has not allowed them to develop a suitable "telephone manner." If this were true, the problem would not be attributable to the child's immaturity, but to lack of practice. By the same token, an adult who had little experience of using telephones would be equally poor at communicating. Cognitive developmentalists thus look for independent evidence to support their suggestion of children's immature understanding. The result is that cognitive developmentalists who hold different opinions try to present evidence and argument to show that their theory is compelling.

The most interesting aspect of cognitive developmental psychology is, of course, making discoveries about how children understand the world. But there is also an interesting subplot surrounding the discovery process itself. The interest in this process is stimulated by some ingenious tasks which have been presented to children in order to investigate their thinking, coupled with some brilliantly insightful arguments that have been developed in support of particular ideas about the character of children's understanding. The purpose of these arguments is to persuade us to accept one view of children in preference to a competing one.

In the following pages, we begin by looking at some of the findings and ideas of the most influential cognitive developmentalist, Jean Piaget. We will consider some criticisms of Piaget's conclusions, and then examine subsequent findings and ideas that were offered in the post-Piagetian era. Piaget proposed that children negotiate a succession of stages en route to maturity, and the following provides a summary.

STAGES OF COGNITIVE DEVELOPMENT

According to Piaget, what mechanisms are involved in cognitive change?

Piaget indicated age ranges for the stages, but these were only intended to be approximate. The more important feature is that the order of stages is supposed to be fixed and invariant, based on the assumption that each stage served as the foundation for the next; so, according to the theory, it would be impossible to miss a stage. To Piaget, missing a stage would be akin to building the second storey of a house without first building the first storey. Consider an example more relevant to the development of thinking: It is very hard to imagine how you could do long multiplication without first being able to do addition. According to Piaget's theory, then, progressing through one stage is a prerequisite for progressing to the next. Still, if you enjoyed the benefit of appropriate experiences, it might be possible to progress through the stages more rapidly than someone less fortunate. Later, we will consider what kind of experiences might be beneficial. The stages are summarized in the table below.

Piaget's stages of development

Name	Developmental period	Characteristic
Sensorimotor	0–2 years: Infancy	Failure to differentiate between self and surrounds
Preoperational	2–7 years: Early childhood	Mental imagery without principled thought
Concrete operational	7–12 years: Middle childhood	Principled thought confined to real-life problems
Formal operational	12 years onwards: Adolescence and adulthood	Principled thought applied to abstract problems

Sensorimotor stage: Birth to 2 years

This is the stage of babyhood or infancy. The stage gets its name from the idea that the infant has sensory experiences (can see, hear, feel, taste, smell) and can move her limbs and other bodily parts (motor movements), but there is scant cognition mediating the two. For example, Piaget believed that the infant has no conception of the permanence of the world that she inhabits.

Piaget had a great many things to say about this stage, but we shall focus on his ideas about the development of the concept of object permanence, which is central to the suggestion that babies presume that the world profoundly lacks permanence. Piaget claimed that at birth we are in a state of solipsism. In other words, he was making the remarkable claim that babies cannot distinguish between self and surroundings. Infants supposedly have no understanding of the permanent existence of things (i.e. objects) other than self. In order to achieve that differentiation, the infant needs to progress through a series of substages, which we will take a look at in a moment. This progression is something that occupies the first 24 months, culminating in a capacity for mental imagery along with an understanding of symbols.

In all, Piaget listed six substages of infancy, but we shall just examine those most relevant to the concept of object permanence. The first relevant one is Stage 3, which is approximately 4 to 8 months of age. At this time, the baby is perfectly capable of grasping and picking up such things as rattles. Given this ability, we can play a game, in which we take the baby's rattle and put it in various places, just within the baby's reach. So long as the rattle is within easy reach (many babies of this age cannot crawl yet), the baby might enter into the game and retrieve it. However, if we put the rattle within reach but immediately cover it with a cloth, even though the shape of the covered object is conspicuous, the baby will not reach out. Instead she will lose interest and switch attention to something else.

Piaget claimed that the baby does have the dexterity to remove the cloth and grab the rattle. Therefore it does not make sense to argue that a lack of motor skill explains the baby's aborted search. Instead, Piaget suggested that when an item is hidden from view, the baby no longer conceives of its existence. At this stage, when the infant cannot sense an object directly, the object no longer has any existence for the infant. If we remove the cloth, the infant will then recognize the rattle and grasp it. So the infant can recognize objects she is familiar with, but when objects are no longer accessible to the senses, they cease to exist for the baby. According to Piaget, this is because the infant is unable to conjure an image of the object in its physical absence.

One implication of this radical claim is that although the infant recognizes and is familiar with her mother, when the mother leaves the room, the infant ceases to think she exists. To the young infant, the mother is just a manifestation that goes through a curious cycle of appearing and disappearing: "Out of sight" is quite literally "out of mind."

Object permanence is the term used to describe the awareness that objects continue to exist even when they are no longer visible. Following experiments with hiding toys under a cloth, Piaget held that infants do not build an understanding of object permanence until the age of 9 months. © Doug Goodman/Science Photo Library.

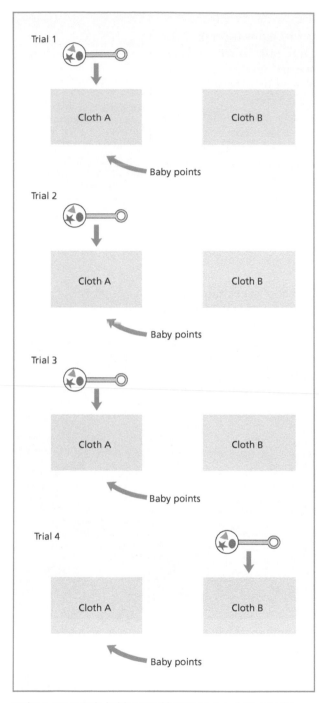

Trial 1

Cloth A   Cloth B

Baby points

Trial 2

Cloth A   Cloth B

Baby points

Trial 3

Cloth A   Cloth B

Baby points

Trial 4

Cloth A   Cloth B

Baby points

In the A not B task, babies aged between 8 and 12 months retrieve the hidden rattle successfully from underneath cloth A on the first three trials. On the fourth trial, even though the baby watches as the rattle is hidden under cloth B, she immediately searches under cloth A.

During Stage 4 of infancy (8 to 12 months), the baby's concept of objects develops to the point that the infant appears to hold a primitive notion that objects may indeed exist even when they cannot be sensed directly. At this age, the infant has no difficulty retrieving a rattle hidden beneath a cloth. On the face of it, you may think that if the infant searches for something hidden from view, this must mean that the infant continues to appreciate the existence of that hidden thing even when it cannot be seen. However, Piaget would have us believe that the infant is still dominated by what she senses, and in particular, at this stage of infancy, her actions (i.e. motor movements). An older child, in contrast, relies much more on mental imagery. According to Piaget, once the infant retrieves the rattle from under the cloth, she then understands its existence in terms of her very act of retrieving it.

Piaget demonstrated this with a simple test, known as the A not B task (see the figure to the left). Piaget spread two cloths side by side in front of the infant. He then hid the rattle under the left cloth (cloth A), and, as expected, the infant pulled away the cloth and picked up the rattle. Piaget repeated this two more times. Then, on the fourth trial, and in full view of the infant, he put the rattle under the right-hand cloth (cloth B). The infant searched under the left cloth, as before, and on failing to find the rattle there, ceased searching and switched attention to something else! What makes this finding especially odd is that the shape of the rattle remains visible under the right-hand cloth throughout the fourth trial.

In this task, according to Piaget, once the infant has brought about the reappearance of the object by the act of searching, she then understands the reappearance of the object purely in terms of the specific actions involved in the search. In other words, the infant has little notion of the existence of the object independently of her own actions. To the infant, the existence of the object means a series of hand and arm movements. Accordingly, Piaget suggested that perception is subordinate to action.

Between 12 and 18 months, the infant progresses to Stage 5. The infant now has no problem with the A not B task, and searches under the right-hand cloth as soon as the rattle is hidden there, even if it had previously been hidden under the left-hand cloth on several previous occasions. Clearly, the infant no longer understands the object just in terms of her own actions. However, Piaget suggests that infants still have difficulty understanding the existence of objects they cannot directly experience, since they apparently have no notion of the movement of an unseen object. To demonstrate, Piaget put the rattle under the left-hand cloth, and then, before the baby had opportunity to search, Piaget also put an upside-down bowl under that cloth, covering the rattle with the bowl as he did so. He then pulled the bowl from under the cloth, with the rattle hidden inside, and moved it under the right-hand cloth. He subsequently removed the bowl, and placed it in full view, where it could be seen to be empty, having deposited the rattle under the right-hand cloth. The baby, who had witnessed all this, was then allowed to begin searching. The baby searched under the left-hand cloth, where the rattle was put to begin with, but on failing to find it there, ceased searching, lost interest, and switched attention to something else.

During Stage 5, the infant is no longer dominated by her own actions in understanding the existence of objects. Nonetheless, it seems the infant continues to have lingering difficulty understanding objects that are not sensed directly, since she seems unable to comprehend the possibility of movement of the object when it is hidden from view. Older children presumably understand that if the rattle were not under the left-hand cloth, it must have traveled with the bowl to the right-hand cloth. This is an understanding that seems to be beyond a baby aged between 12 and 18 months. The reason, according to Piaget, is because the infant has difficulty imagining the object as an entity in its own right with its own independent existence; the infant struggles to understand that when the object is not directly experienced, it is still possible for things to continue happening to it, such as moving from one place to another.

At 18 to 24 months, the infant enters the final of Piaget's stages of infancy, Stage 6. At this stage, the infant at last is able to conceive of the existence of an object independently of self, and therefore is no longer in a state of solipsism. The infant now understands that on the one hand there is the external world, and on the other hand, distinct from that, is self. The infant achieves this, according to Piaget, by acquiring the faculty of mental imagery. The infant is able to generate a mental picture of things, along with what might happen to them, even if these events cannot be experienced directly. In consequence, the infant no longer has difficulty locating an object that is hidden and then moved, providing it is easy to work out where it moved to. That is, the child no longer has difficulty with the task she failed during Stage 5 of infancy.

As you will discover further in the book, there is dispute over Piaget's interpretation of the findings of his object permanence "tests." However, to our knowledge, no one disagrees about the way babies perform in these tests at roughly the ages Piaget indicated, and it is easy to replicate his findings.

The advent of mental imagery is revolutionary in the child's life, which heralds the transition to a whole new stage of development in the broadest sense. At this point the child is viewed as progressing from the sensorimotor stage of infancy to the preoperational stage of early childhood. We will explore the preoperational stage in some detail later, but first, we will take a further look at the implications of having mental imagery.

Perhaps the most important benefit of mental imagery is that it allows the use of symbols. A mental image need not be a mental replica of the thing it is associated with. If the image is about something in the world, but is not a mental replica of that thing, then it is a symbol. According to Piaget, it is no coincidence that at the end of infancy the child begins to develop proficiency in that most powerful of human symbols, language. The intellectual feats that become possible with language in its various forms are awesome. For example, consider some of the remarkable progress in technology and science over the past couple of centuries. Most of this would have been impossible without the mathematics and written language to work out and communicate ideas.

An important aspect of Piaget's thinking comes to light at this point. Piaget stressed that intellectual development underpins language development in important ways, not the other way round; a capacity for mental imagery permits proficiency in using symbols, one form of which happens to be language. It hardly needs to be stated that language affords more efficient problem solving. However, symbolic activity other than the use of a recognizable language may also facilitate problem solving. Piaget tells how his daughter, who was nearing the end of infancy, solved the problem of retrieving a chain hidden inside a matchbox. When given the matchbox, the girl made a clumsy attempt to open the box but failed. She then paused, opened and closed her mouth a few times whilst gazing at the matchbox, and then smoothly opened the box to retrieve the chain. According to Piaget, his daughter symbolically registered the way in which the matchbox opened with her jaw movement. Effectively, she simulated a solution from the analogy of opening mouth. After working out the problem in this way, she was then able to proceed and open the box with no further difficulty. This example shows that Piaget believed that symbolic problem-solving activity is not dependent on language. That said, no doubt Piaget would regard language as a useful medium in which to exercise symbolic thought.

Symbolic activity is most apparent in young children's pretend play. Here we find children pretending that bananas are telephones, that chairs are cars, that shoe boxes are television sets, and so on. Watching young children engage in pretend play gives the impression that they are exercising their newly acquired symbolic ability purely for the delight of it. There is good reason to suppose that the symbolic element of pretend play is not just a sign of having reached a developmental milestone. Some argue persuasively that pretend play actually promotes cognitive development in various important ways (e.g. Leslie, 1987).

Preoperational stage: 2–7 years

As the child enters this stage, she is capable of solving problems with the help of symbolic activity, and is rapidly developing proficiency as a user of language. You would be forgiven for thinking that most of the developmental milestones have now been achieved, and that things are downhill from this point. Surprisingly, Piaget argues that this could not be further from the truth.

According to Piaget, the young child is plagued with *egocentrism*. This term might seem a little confusing because Piaget did not use it according to its common meaning. In ordinary parlance, we might call someone "egocentric" to mean that they are selfish and inconsiderate of others. Piaget used the word in reference to a cognitive limitation that prevents the child seeing things from somebody else's point of view. It is not really fair to say the young child is

To what extent can the range of errors in thinking that are apparent in early childhood be explained as egocentrism?

inconsiderate, since it is claimed that she is not even capable of understanding that another person might have a viewpoint different from her own. In this case, "different viewpoint" is used both in a literal sense, as in failing to understand that objects look different from different perspectives, and in a conceptual sense, as in failing to understand that people may hold opinions, beliefs, and so on, that are different from her own.

Intimately linked with egocentrism is a profound inability to understand and apply principles to help understand the world. The young child's grasp of things is intuitive and highly subjective, rather than logical and objective. Consequently, the child's thinking is dominated by surface appearance, and not by underlying principles. The best way to illustrate this is with examples of tests that preoperational children fail. We will consider this in a moment, but first a note on the name of the stage.

By "operation," Piaget was referring to the process of following mental rules in solving a problem: in other words, a logical operation that is done mentally. According to Piaget, operational intelligence is necessary to rid the child of egocentrism, to rid the child of his highly subjective and overly intuitive view of the world. Hence, the preoperational child is egocentric.

Perhaps the best known evidence of failure to understand and apply principles during the preoperational stage lies in the failure to conserve. In this sense, "conservation" has nothing to do with preserving the earth's precious resources, laudable as that may be, but rather concerns the understanding that a change in appearance need not result in alteration of the underlying reality. The underlying reality remains constant, and therefore is conserved, despite the transformation in appearance.

In the conservation of quantity task (see the figure to the right), the child watches as we pour water into two short wide jars to the same level. We then carefully transfer all the content from one into a tall thin jar, and put this beside the remaining short wide jar. Of course, the level of water in the thin jar is much higher than in the wide jar. Very few people above the age of 7 would say that the thin jar has more water, but nearly all children below that age claim that it does. Young children's incorrect judgments seem even more striking because Piaget always got them to agree initially that there was the same amount of water in the two wide jars. Also, he took pains to ensure that the child watched carefully as he poured the water from one glass to another; the child could see that no water had been added.

Apparently, instead of using a principle (i.e. operation), such as "none was added or taken away, so the amount of water must be the same," young

Key Term

Operational intelligence: The process of solving a problem by working through logical principles.

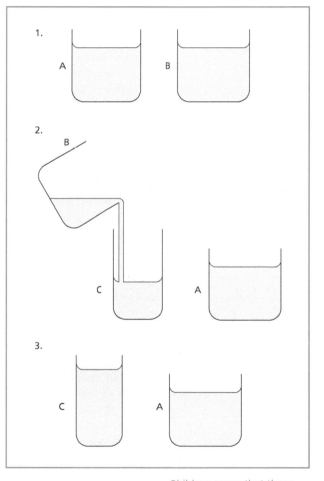

Children agree that there is the same amount in glasses A and B when the water is poured to the same level in each. Then the experimenter pours the contents of B into C and those below 7 years tend to judge wrongly that C contains more than A.

children were seduced by, and centered on (to use Piagetian terminology), the increased height of the water level in the thin glass. The child gives an intuitive answer instead of working out the correct answer on the basis of an underlying principle. Hence, the child fails to decenter.

Young children also display failure to conserve on a variety of other tasks, some of which we will now look at. In the conservation of length, we show the child two pencils, and begin by aligning the points so that their equality in length becomes apparent. After the child agrees they are the same length, we move one of the pencils slightly, so that its point protrudes above that of the other by about a centimeter. We then ask, "Are these two pencils the same size now, or is this one bigger or is that one bigger?" Preoperational children judge they are different in size, and point to one of the pencils, usually the one pushed further away, claiming it is bigger. In the conservation of mass, we make two balls of plasticine the same size, and, after the child agrees they are the same, we roll one into a sausage shape. Preoperational children usually judge that the sausage shape is bigger and has more plasticine. In the conservation of number, we spread two rows of, for example, five counters, in one-to-one correspondence. After the child agrees there is the same number of counters in each row, we expand one of the rows further by making spaces between the counters bigger. Preoperational children now claim that the longer row has more counters.

Piaget documented many errors young children make, which he claimed are symptoms of preoperational, nonprincipled, nonlogical thinking. We shall consider just two more of these. First is the difficulty young children have with class inclusion (see the figure below). We spread out, for example, seven Lego™ bricks, five red and two blue. In this example, the overall class of bricks includes the subclasses of red and blue bricks. The child knows that all seven items are in the class of bricks, because if we ask how many bricks there are, they have no difficulty saying "seven." We then ask, "Are there more bricks or more red bricks?" Preoperational children answer with, "More red bricks." According to Piaget, young children center on the greater number of red bricks compared with blue bricks, and fail to operate on the principle that the class of bricks must be bigger than the subclass of red bricks, because the class of bricks includes both red and blue.

Finally, we come to transitive inference. This is the test that gives most of us an attack of panic as we hear the problem: Jane is taller than Susan; Jane is shorter than Mary; who is the tallest, Susan or Mary? Piaget presented a task that involves the same problem in principle, but which to adults and older children seems absurdly simple. We show the child two towers made of Lego™, one a little taller than the other. Just by looking, it is impossible to tell which is the taller, for two reasons. First, the towers are in different parts of the

Children are asked how many bricks there are altogether and say there are seven. Then they are asked whether there are more red bricks or more bricks altogether. Those below 7 years tend to judge that there are more red bricks.

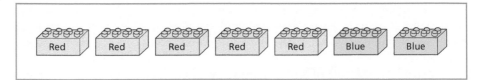

| Red | Red | Red | Red | Red | Blue | Blue |

room, so they can't both be taken in at a glance. Second, they are on different levels, for example, one on a coffee table and one on the floor.

We present the child with a stick of intermediate length, and ask him to compare each tower with the stick in order to find which is biggest. The comparison reveals that one tower is bigger than the stick, whilst the other is smaller. Preoperational children are poor at this task. They seem to have no idea what to do with the stick, and even if we do the measuring for them, they do not then reliably give the correct answer, that the tower taller than the stick is bigger than the tower shorter than the stick. According to Piaget, this is yet another example of young children failing to operate on a principle, which, in this case, would be, "If this tower is bigger than the stick, and that tower is shorter than the stick, then this tower must be bigger than that tower."

It is very unusual to find a young child who does not make the errors described in these pages, though some people, as you will discover later, disagree with Piaget's interpretation. The tests are very simple to carry out, and you can demonstrate the errors very easily by performing them on young children in your family. It is especially interesting to introduce modifications to the procedure of the tests to see if it helps or hinders children in getting the correct answer.

We began this section with a definition of what Piaget meant by "egocentrism." After that we looked in some detail at preoperational errors but little at the way in which the young child's thinking reveals itself as egocentric. A classic example of egocentrism can be found in the "three mountains task" (see the figure right). The child sits in front of a model landscape of three mountains located side by side. At the summit of each is a distinctive feature, such as a house, snow, and a cross. Another individual sits facing the child, from the other side of the model, and we ask the child to select a photo of what the scene looks like to the other person. In the set of photos there is a picture of the child's own view as well as the view from the other side of the model, in which the distinctive features on the top of the mountains are in left–right reversal. Preoperational children nearly always choose a photo of the model from their own vantage point, and claim this is how the person sitting opposite sees the mountains. Piaget claimed that because young children are egocentric, they only conceive of their own viewpoint, and fail to appreciate that from another perspective things may look different; they have no notion of alternative views of the world.

Children are asked to choose a picture that shows how the scene looks from the opposite side. Those younger than 7 years tend to select a picture showing the scene that they can see currently, instead of the one showing the mountains in left–right reversal.

Obviously, children are able to describe how a model looks different as they move around. They are also capable of recalling from memory how it looked from a different perspective. But this does not qualify as an understanding of multiple perspectives, according to Piaget. He suggested that children in effect are presuming that reality changes in accordance with appearance. In other words, the child thinks that as the model's appearance differs with changes in their viewing point, it has actually undergone some fundamental

Compare and contrast the signs of egocentrism that are characteristic of infancy, and those that are characteristic of early childhood beyond infancy.

transformation. In this respect, the child's putative misconception resembles nonconservation, where the child supposedly assumes that a change in the appearance of a column of water engenders a change in quantity.

Stage of concrete operations: 7–12 years

Children suddenly seem to appreciate that there is more to things than superficial appearances, and that their view of the world is but one of the many possible. They acquire a first grasp that an underlying more objective reality is accessible by following principles. When they do so, they are described as entering the stage of concrete operations in middle childhood. We take a look at some of these principles in a moment, but first a note on the name Piaget gave to this stage. In this context, the term "concrete" means "real or tangible." Piaget's idea was that the child in this stage can solve problems in a principled way, in other words using logical operations, so long as the problem is real or concrete. A child in this stage cannot handle imagined or hypothetical problems, according to Piaget.

The difficulties facing preoperational children, which we examined in the previous section, are not shared by the child in the concrete operational stage. The child gives a correct conserving judgment following transformation, that there is the same amount of water, that length, mass, and number are the same. The child gives a correct class inclusion judgment that there are more bricks than red bricks, and can reliably give the correct answer to the transitive inference problem, indicating which of two towers is bigger after measuring both with a stick of intermediate length. Also, the child no longer selects his own view on the three mountains task.

Not only do children give the correct answer, they provide the kind of justifications that seem to suggest they are using logical (operational) principles. Consider justifications children give for correct conservation judgments. Piaget identified three:

- *Compensation*—the child says that although the water in the thin glass is taller, the water in the wide glass is broader. The broadness makes up for (i.e. compensates) the tallness, so there is still the same amount;
- *Inversion*—the child says that although the water in the thin glass is taller, if you poured the water back into its original container (i.e. the inverse transformation), it would look just the same as the water in the comparison container, which shows that really the amount is just the same;
- *Identity*—you did not add anything or take anything away from the water in the thin glass, so it must be the same.

After these monumental achievements in thought processes, it might be difficult to imagine how the child's thinking could be refined much further. Although the concrete operational child has a radically different and better understanding of things than the preoperational child, chiefly because he is no longer seduced by surface appearances, the concrete operational child nonetheless is firmly ensconced in the real world. As a result, the child is no good at dealing with problems that are not situated in reality. He cannot handle the "just suppose ..." variety of problems. We will consider some examples of these in the next section.

Stage of formal operations: 12 years onwards

Before looking at these examples, as usual, a note on the name of the stage. In no sense does "formal" as used by Piaget have anything to do with well-mannered etiquette. Rather, it means systematic reasoning about things that take a hypothetical form and not necessarily a real, concrete form. The best examples of systematic reasoning can be found in the procedures for scientific investigation. Piaget evidently upheld the scientific method as preeminent, and as the highest form of known thinking.

During this stage, but not during the concrete operational stage, the youngster is able to solve the transitive inference problem on a purely mental level; no real items need to be involved. The adolescent can work out that if x is bigger than y and x is smaller than z, then the smallest altogether must be y. These characters need have no value in the real world for the adolescent to find the correct solution. In solving the problem, the adolescent can mentally manipulate the symbols in a way that is purely formal and logical.

Another classic example Piaget gave, which better illustrates the "scientific" aspect of formal operational thinking, is found in the pendulum problem (see the figure below). We show the adolescent a pendulum, and state the problem, which is to find what determines how frequently the pendulum swings back and forth (i.e. number of oscillations per minute). We show the adolescent how to vary four factors, which rightly or wrongly we may suppose affect speed of oscillation: weight of the suspended object, length of string, force of initial swing, and the height from which the pendulum is released. In case you don't know, it is the length of string that is the important factor, but giving the correct answer is not as revealing as the way the adolescent goes about finding the solution.

A concrete operational child approaches the problem apparently with no plan, in a haphazard manner. For example, he may first test a long pendulum with a light weight and then compare that with a short pendulum with a heavy weight. Whatever the result, it is impossible to tell whether any effect is due to the difference in weight, the difference in length, or a combination of the two.

In sharp contrast, the formal operational adolescent rigorously compares a short heavy pendulum with a short light one, and so on. In other words, the adolescent holds three factors constant whilst comparing the effect of different values of the remaining factor. Thanks to this systematic approach, the result of the adolescent's "experiments" can unequivocally be attributed to differences in values of just one of the factors.

To repeat, it is not getting the correct answer that counts. What is much more revealing is that the adolescent approaches the problem in a measured and systematic manner. According to Piaget, this says something special about the adolescent's thought processes. Adolescents understand that in order to make a sensible interpretation of the results, whatever the outcome, the experiment must be carried out in a systematic way. Therefore, the adolescent identifies the optimal conditions for interpreting the results even before any results have

Compare and contrast signs of egocentrism in early childhood, and those in adolescence.

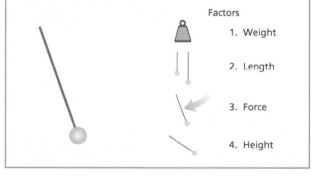

Factors

1. Weight

2. Length

3. Force

4. Height

The participant has to work out which of the four listed factors influences the speed of oscillation. Adolescents characteristically adopt a systematic approach by holding three factors constant while changing values of the remaining factor. Younger participants tend to change the values of two or more factors at once and as a consequence generate results that defy interpretation.

been obtained. In this case, the adolescent anticipates, and therefore reasons in a hypothetical manner. Putting it another way, before acting on the pendulum, the adolescent works out that altering values of two of the factors simultaneously would yield uninterpretable data. The fact that when the adolescent eventually begins her experiment she takes a systematic approach shows that prior to this she must have reasoned hypothetically about how to get the best from her investigation.

Piaget suggested that not everybody achieves formal operational thinking, and added in characteristically arrogant manner that such thinking may be scarce in some primitive "concrete operational" cultures. According to Piaget, the ability to reason systematically in hypothetical mode is a feat that is enjoyed by people fortunate enough to have experiences that aid progression through the stages of cognitive development. We shall now turn our attention to what these experiences might be, and how development takes place. Our guiding question will be, "What is the mechanism of development?"

PIAGET'S EXPLANATION OF COGNITIVE DEVELOPMENT

According to Piaget, what are the respective roles of nature and nurture in development?

Piaget identified the building blocks of thinking as mental units he called schemes. At birth, we are equipped with a set of action schemes, which develop and multiply. The descendants of those early schemes come to form intelligent thought processes. Piaget's account is a kind of mental analogue of Darwin's theory of natural selection, in the sense that he supposed that within each developing mind these schemes adapt and evolve according to the principle, "survival of the fittest." The schemes provided by our genetic heredity are commonly recognized as a set of reflexes, such as the grasping reflex: From the moment of birth, the baby will close its hand around any item which comes into contact with the palm. This is quite likely to be the mother's finger, at least in the first instance. What we now need to know is how these simple reflexes evolve into the grand semblance of formal operational intelligence.

A clue to Piaget's view of this development is provided by the fact that young babies grasp at things other than a finger. The infant generalizes the scope of application of the scheme in this way. Piaget called the application of a scheme to a novel context assimilation. It gets its name from the idea that the new application is taken into the overall scope of the scheme. However, the scheme, which may be thought of as a set of mental instructions to the hand on how to grasp the object, inevitably will not be suited to every item the baby holds. For example, the first time the baby holds her rattle, it may be necessary to adjust the position of the fingers and the extent to which the hand closes around the object. Information about these adjustments is fed back to the scheme, and in consequence the scheme is modified. Now the scheme is activated in one way if it is a finger that is being grasped, but in a slightly different way if it is a rattle that is being grasped. Piaget called the modification to the scheme accommodation. Assimilation and accommodation work in combination as a scheme is activated; it would be peculiar for one to occur in the absence of the other.

Piaget suggested that the ideal is when assimilation and accommodation contribute equally. If either dominates, then there may be a problem. An example of overassimilation is pretence. In this case the child displays little

Key Terms

Schemes:
A mental operation that guides action or allows us to work through a problem in a principled way.

Assimilation:
Applying an existing scheme to a novel task.

Accommodation:
Modifying a scheme to adapt it to a new application.

adaptation to the world, but instead interprets the world in her own highly idiosyncratic way. As mentioned earlier, some take the view that pretence may be cognitively beneficial, but presumably pretence to the exclusion of any acknowledgment of reality would be disastrous. An example of overaccommodation is imitation. Here, the child parrots somebody else, with little understanding.

According to Piaget, we are intrinsically motivated to exercise our schemes, particularly when they are newly acquired, and this process is not dependent on external reward. Therefore, there is plenty of opportunity for assimilation and accommodation to occur, and plenty of opportunity for schemes to develop. In other words, there is plenty of opportunity for the growth of intelligence, given the way in which development supposedly takes place.

An example of the dominance of assimilation over accommodation—pretending that hairbrushes are microphones.

As a scheme's breadth of application increases, so the demarcation in each mode of application increases. There comes a point when the modes of application of a scheme are so diverse that it is no longer a single scheme but rather a series of schemes within a certain genre. For example, the scheme for holding a paintbrush is in some respects quite different from the scheme for holding the steering wheel of a car, yet both are descendants of the innate grasping scheme. Schemes may also be coordinated, or brought together, into a giant scheme to perform complicated actions. Driving a car provides a useful example of coordination of schemes: Steering, gear shift, brake, clutch, and accelerator, just to name some of the individual schemes comprising the overall scheme of "driving."

At this point things seem reasonably straightforward, that schemes develop, and this is influenced in an important way by assimilation and accommodation. So how do the stages of development feature in all this? Piaget would have us believe that underlying each stage is a new breed of scheme. In the sensorimotor stage, we can only rely on motor schemes, as in throwing rattles, crawling, and so on. In the preoperational stage, the child has schemes that are not just motor, but may involve mental imagery also. At the concrete operational stage, schemes may proceed through a series of mental actions perhaps in the way a computer runs a program, to arrive at the solution to a problem in a principled and logical way. In the formal operational stage, the same applies, except the problem need have no physical basis.

How does a new category of scheme emerge? Piaget identified equilibration as one of the main factors. As an example, consider the acquisition of understanding conservation of quantity. The nonconserving child entertains the belief that tallness and quantity are intimately linked, so she will think that a tall column of liquid contains more than a short one. That seems like a perfectly reasonable belief to hold, and no doubt most adults think in a similar way. However, the child is different, because she thinks tallness is all that counts. We adults know that width is also important. At the age of about 6 or 7 years, the child begins to recognize, perhaps through observation and experience, that attention to width might also be useful in judging quantity. The trouble is that the child of this age does not bring together, or coordinate, these two beliefs, and so may vacillate when faced with a conservation judgment: After

Key Terms

Coordination of schemes:
Combining schemes to carry out an elaborate task, such as driving a car.

Equilibration:
A motivational process that compels us to strive for logical consistency.

the contents of one of two identical glasses is poured into a tall thin glass, sometimes the child judges that the tall one has more, and sometimes the same child judges that the wider glass has more.

This situation gives rise to a state of internal cognitive conflict, because the tall glass cannot both contain more and contain less than the wide glass. The cognitive conflict activates the motivational process, equilibration, which functions to remove that conflict, and in the process generate new schemes that function on a higher cognitive level. In the case of conservation, through equilibration, the child resolves the conflict by viewing the problem in an entirely new way. The child achieves reconciliation between the extant rival schemes by appreciating that although it is fair to think the wide glass contains more due to its extra width, and that the tall glass contains more due to its extra height, the tall glass has a corresponding reduction in width which cancels out any increase in quantity that might be expected from the extra tallness. Therefore, quantity has remained constant, and the pouring from one glass to another was irrelevant.

In this case, the motivational force of equilibration, stimulated by cognitive conflict, pushed the child onto a higher and more flexible cognitive level. In the previous stage, the child had made judgments on the basis of single dimensions, such as width or tallness. In the new higher stage, she can mentally handle both width and tallness simultaneously and compare the two in relation to the problem she was trying to solve. Having achieved that, the child is equipped to face novel tasks with increased mental flexibility, and so development enjoys a quantum leap at around the age of 6 or 7 years. The child's mental processes are then reorganized, or restructured, to use Piagetian phraseology, to take on board the new flexible thinking capacity. In the aftermath of mental reorganization, enormous potential for a mental growth spurt opens. The child can now view the world in a new light. For example, she has acquired the mental flexibility to examine the world from another viewpoint, and therefore no longer suffers the egocentrism characteristic of the preoperational stage.

Why, according to Piaget, does cognitive development progress through a series of stages?

TRADITIONAL LEARNING THEORY AS A CONTRASTING EXPLANATION OF DEVELOPMENT

At the time Piaget's theory first became widely known to psychologists, in the early 1960s, the "establishment" view was that learning, including all the learning that takes place during childhood, can be understood purely by looking at external rewards and punishment. The prominent figure endorsing this view was B.F. Skinner, who showed that any kind of behavior that is followed by reward is more likely to occur again in the future, whereas any behavior that is followed by punishment is less likely to occur in the future. On the face of things this claim seems absurd, but not so when we realize that Skinner meant something much more general than the common meanings of "reward" and "punishment." Skinner used these words not necessarily to imply money or rebukes. Rather, he meant that behavior that has pleasant consequences is likely to recur, whereas behavior that has unpleasant consequences is likely to be extinguished.

Statements like these would not be new to the circus trainers who have for centuries trained elephants to waltz and lions to balance on hind legs. Yet remarkable as it may seem, Skinner succeeded in persuading psychologists to accept his outrageous claim that all human behavior can also be understood in terms of reward and punishment. For example, a child achieves literacy by being rewarded with praise from teacher and parent "for doing the right thing," and by being punished with chastisement "for doing the wrong thing." Piaget's ideas flew in the face of this mainstream psychology, because his findings strongly suggested that there is much more to development than reward and punishment. In particular, Piaget argued that we need to consider whether a child is ready to acquire new information or a new skill primarily by identifying her particular stage in development. A child in the operational stages may be receptive to principles that require mental juggling and flexibility, whereas a child in the preoperational stage would not. Also, Piaget argued convincingly that development is partly driven by internal motivation, with the idea that humans find learning and development to be intrinsically pleasurable experiences. This was anathema to Skinner, who believed that all learning can be explained in terms of external rewards independent of the learning process itself.

A SUPPLEMENT TO PIAGET'S THEORY: SELF-CENTERED ADOLESCENTS

No doubt a random sample of middle-aged people would have many misgivings about adolescents, with comments such as "lazy, vain, self-centered . . . ." These negative features are not so obviously linked with cognitive development, but perhaps more related to personality characteristics. Yet many personality traits, such as extraversion, introversion, eccentricity, and neuroticism, seem to endure, spanning much, if not all, of the individual's life. In contrast, vanity and self-centeredness seem to have a peak in many people during adolescence, and therefore seem more to do with a stage of development rather than with enduring individual differences in personality.

Is it possible that an aberration in personality during the years of adolescence can be understood with reference to Piaget's theory? It cannot be illuminated directly by his writings, but it can be explained by the ideas of one of Piaget's disciples, David Elkind, who supplemented Piaget's theory about adolescent thinking in order to embrace some of the more noticeable aspects of adolescent behavior.

Recall that Piaget claimed that young children are oblivious to other people's points of view. In a sense, young children seem unaware of other people's thoughts and cognitions. Elkind (1967) suggested that although adolescents know about other people's thoughts, they very often egocentrically assume that their own preoccupations will be shared by others. That is, adolescents recognize that others have potential to think differently from themselves, but in the absence of strong evidence to the contrary, assume that their own interests, likes, dislikes, and so on are universally held views.

Elkind suggests that since adolescence is a period of radical physiological change, during that period it can be no surprise that teenagers become preoccupied with their own appearance. For example, because an adolescent

Adolescence—a period of egocentric self-examination. Elkind believes this behavior may be driven by a desire to satisfy the scrutiny of an imagined audience.

boy egocentrically assumes what is of interest to him is of interest to everyone, he wrongly thinks that everyone else is preoccupied with whether his facial hair is sufficiently prominent to require the use of a razor. Just as the adolescent spends long periods scrutinizing her own face, so she will assume others she meets will wish to examine her face in a similar way. According to Elkind, all this results from the adolescent becoming more sharply aware of others' thoughts, whilst failing to appreciate that her own interests are not necessarily universally shared. An adult, in contrast, recognizes her own idiosyncratic preoccupations for what they are, and appreciates that others have different personal concerns. The adult has a notion of being just one rather unexceptional person among the billions who inhabit our planet.

In order to help describe the adolescent failure to distinguish between topics of interest held by oneself compared with those held by others, Elkind introduces the idea of imaginary audience. The adolescent forever anticipates the reactions of others to herself, anticipations that are based on the wrong belief that others will be as admiring or critical as she is of herself. Therefore, the adolescent believes she will be the focus of attention, and hence the term "audience" used by Elkind. However, this "audience" is imaginary, because it is likely that people the adolescent actually encounters have much more interesting things to think about than contemplating whether a youth has dermatological problems. Of course, it might be that the adolescent engineers the situation so that she really does become the center of attention, but that is a different story.

Elkind suggests, then, that the imaginary audience is responsible for the self-consciousness typical of adolescence. Due to the belief that the audience is concerned with, and indeed enlightened about, the adolescent's cosmetic defects, the adolescent becomes overly shy and continually seeks privacy. This is an understandable reaction to a feeling of being under scrutiny. Further, Elkind claims that adolescents frequently experience a sense of shame, a characteristic reaction to a disapproving audience.

There is another side to this coin, which is that sometimes the adolescent plays to the audience, with the idea that others find the adolescent's "performance" deeply interesting. On such occasions, the adolescent actively takes a high profile by being loud, both in the literal sense of making lots of noise, and in wearing outrageous garments and hairstyles. The adolescent spends extended periods preparing for an appearance before an audience, partly imagining how others will find her features and qualities irresistible, and partly adding the final touches to those appearances by careful application of cosmetics. When adolescent members of the opposite sex eventually meet, in characteristically vain manner they are more concerned about being observed, and imagining the impact they make on the observer, than doing the observing.

Because the adolescent is the center of her own attention, and also assumes she is at the center of everyone else's attention, she develops an inflated notion of self-importance. Elkind tells us that adolescents believe their feelings, experiences, and ideas are especially intense and unique. They often believe that they have been specially chosen by divine decree, and in consequence believe they have a preferential relationship with a personal God. Altogether, these adolescent feelings lead the individual to think she holds a special,

Key Term

Imaginary audience:
A fantasy that people are watching your actions with great intrigue.

perhaps immortal, position on earth. To help describe this idea, Elkind used the term personal fable. This is a kind of story the adolescent tells herself about her gifted special status, which might be that no matter what, the adolescent always triumphs in the end. The adolescent experiences a fatalistic inevitability that she can gamble and win, and can dice with death with impunity.

Elkind points out that imaginary audience and personal fable are concepts that can help explain some deviant or delinquent adolescent behavior. Consider the case of soccer hooliganism, which is an almost exclusively male adolescent phenomenon. Soccer violence is an activity that is guaranteed the attention of an audience in thousands if not millions in the case of televised events, and it is an activity that involves considerable danger. Perhaps the adolescent relishes the opportunity to display courage and skill to such an audience, believing that onlookers will be immensely impressed. A risk is that the ensuing physical combat could result in serious injury. However, the adolescent's personal fable leads him to think he is immune to any harm inflicted by adversaries.

The personal fable also leads the adolescent to think that he can avoid reprisal from authorities. If he happens to be arrested, then he relishes the new source of attention from police, lawyers, jury, probation officers, and so on. After the event he may perceive himself to have achieved legendary status among peers for going on official record as having committed an act of horrible brutality. He may believe that this earns awesome respect and fear from fellow hooligans who have not yet graduated to star-status in this way.

Toward the end of adolescence, and during early adulthood, the imaginary audience begins to fade and eventually disappears. How does this development occur? Elkind suggests that imaginary audience is actually a prediction about how people react, based on the adolescent's own preoccupations. However, the actual reaction is frequently different from what was anticipated, when others treat the adolescent as a rather dull person who presents as new and unique, things that everyone else already knows. This sobering reaction of the real as opposed to the imaginary audience enlightens the adolescent as to her true position in the universe, which of course is usually that she is just another unremarkable person. It is the adolescent's capacity for making hypotheses that is responsible for the emergence of the imaginary audience, and her subsequent testing of those hypotheses against real experiences that is ultimately responsible for the dissolution of the imaginary audience. A by-product of the imaginary audience is the personal fable, and as the former dissolves, so does the latter.

Elkind's ideas about imaginary audience and personal fable possess very strong intuitive appeal, and most of us can comprehend aspects of our own behavior in terms of these notions. No doubt most of us would also acknowledge that these kinds of behaviors were prominent during adolescence. Theorists pay tribute to Elkind for the appeal these ideas have.

Despite this, Elkind's critics question whether it is sensible to suggest that imaginary audience and personal fable are manifestations of egocentrism. Lapsley and Murphy (1985) draw attention to an anomaly in Elkind's account. Recall that Elkind suggested adolescents appreciate that other people have thoughts, but fail to differentiate the content of their own thought from that of others. That is what Elkind meant by egocentrism. However, Lapsley and Murphy point out that even preadolescents are perfectly capable of

> **Key Term**
>
> **Personal fable:**
> A fantasy that you have a privileged position on earth and that you are being watched over and protected by a supernatural being.

differentiating the content of others' thoughts from their own. For example, concrete operational children have no difficulty selecting the appropriate photo on the three mountains task, when asked how the model looks to someone sitting at the other side of the table. Clearly, these children can differentiate between the content of their own thought (how the model looks to them) and that of another individual (how the model looks to the person opposite).

Lapsley and Murphy argue that imaginary audience and personal fable are not so much to do with failure to differentiate between content of own thought and that of others, but on the contrary that they stem from an acute enlightenment of the thought of others. During adolescence, the individual first becomes aware of others' thoughts on a big scale. Therefore, so far as the adolescent is concerned, a first awareness of others' views of oneself is akin to suddenly being thrown into the limelight. We all know from the well-documented cases of legendary pop and movie stars about the effect of overnight fame. Perhaps adolescents experience the same to some degree when suddenly becoming aware of the thoughts others might have about them. This could provide a better explanation for imaginary audience and personal fable than the concept of adolescent egocentrism.

Lapsley and Murphy suggest that imaginary audience and personal fable could fade for the following reason. Knowing that others think about us is quite harmless in most cases. As a result, young adults come to terms with the fact that they feature in the thoughts of others, and begin to pay less attention to the thought as a consequence.

Summary

- This chapter focused mainly on Piaget's stage theory of cognitive development. Instead of assuming that the intellect develops gradually during childhood, Piaget proposed that the quality of thinking develops through a succession of stages, where the character of thought is quite different in each stage. Piaget viewed each stage as an adaptation to a natural tendency to be egocentric. In its most profound form, in infancy, egocentrism represents a failure to distinguish between oneself and the rest of the universe. Piaget formulated a detailed theory of the mechanisms that lead to stage-like development. He proposed that the foundations given to us by nature are complemented by the processes of nurture, enabling the individual effectively to construct an intelligent adaptation to the world. His theory was supported by a variety of ingenious tasks designed to reveal how young children think differently about the world. Before Piaget's theory, it would have been easy to suppose that children and adults think in much the same way (except adults have more knowledge).

Essay Questions

1. Does children's intellectual development progress through a succession of stages? If so, how does it happen?
2. Are children aged around 6 years egocentric?

Further Reading

There are several texts summarizing Piaget's theory. Our favourite, for its detail coupled with easy prose style, is:

- Ginsburg, H. & Opper, S. (1979). *Piaget's theory of intellectual development*. London: Prentice-Hall International, Inc.

Alternatively, or additionally, you may wish to look at Piaget's summary of his own theory. Piaget's writing is notoriously difficult to understand, and is usually targeted at a highly specialized audience. However, the following book was written for people new to the subject, and as such is not quite so daunting:

- Piaget, J. & Inhelder, B. (1969). *The psychology of the child*. London: Routledge and Kegan Paul.

Chapter 4

Contents

Does Piaget's theory stand up to examination?

4

Chapter Aims

- To review studies that challenge Piaget's claims about infants being in a state of solipsism.
- To review studies that challenge Piaget's claims about egocentrism in early childhood.
- To examine Piaget's claim that formal operational thinking is not constrained by the type of problem being tackled.
- To introduce Vygotsky's social constructivism as an alternative to Piagetian theory.

INTRODUCTION

Piaget's ideas of cognitive conflict stimulating complete cognitive reorganization embody qualities that excite many people. Also his observations of infant behavior and reports of children's judgments on various logical tasks are undoubtedly fascinating, whatever the status of the theory created to explain them.

In some quarters, though, there are serious misgivings about Piaget's theory. The eminent American developmentalist John H. Flavell, who was responsible for popularizing Piaget in the early 1960s, has expressed some of these in a book he published approximately three decades ago. Flavell (1982) argues that Piaget did not clearly or consistently define the mental activities that constitute the thinking involved in such things as conserving quantity. Indeed, he suggests the thinking for solving conservation problems may bear no resemblance to what Piaget proposed. Flavell further points out that findings obtained by other researchers indicate that young children may have cognitive limitations that are completely unexpected on the basis of Piagetian theory. Also, it seems the logic Piaget developed as he formulated his theory could be seriously flawed. Braine and Rumain (1983) analyzed the components and structure of the theory, and concluded on logical grounds that it simply does not hold water and moreover that it does not hang together properly. If these critics are right, we may find that we are left with some interesting findings on how children answer questions about certain problems, but with an incomplete or inadequate account of what these findings mean. However, as we see in the following pages, the reliability of Piaget's findings has also been questioned.

INFANT COMPETENCE

Piaget proposed that infants are born in a state of solipsism, meaning that they fail to distinguish between self and surroundings. An implication is that infants do not understand that objects have an existence independent of self. Consequently, so the story goes, the infant is merely aware of a series of images, without understanding the continued existence of things in their perceptual absence. The development of an understanding of object permanence, and therefore an understanding that self is but one of many relatively permanent entities in the world, supposedly progresses through a series of stages during infancy. In Stage 4, which occurs roughly between 8 and 12 months, the infant fails the A not B task. Recall that we hide the rattle under cloth A three times, and the infant retrieves it without difficulty, but then when we hide the rattle under cloth B in full view, the infant perseveres in searching under A.

Studies carried out by other researchers suggest that Piaget's tests underestimated infants. Bower (1965) reasoned that if Piaget were correct to claim that infants perceive the world as a series of images, and are ignorant about the stable permanence of things, then they would have no faculty of size constancy. In other words, they would not understand that an object moved into the distance is still the same object, even though the apparent size changes. That would require understanding that things have underlying enduring qualities which remain stable despite changes in appearance. If they understand this, presumably we could argue they understand object permanence. Bower trained 1- and 2-month-old babies to move their head only when he showed a box of certain size. Infants received a reward for moving only when that particular box was placed in front of them, and received no reward in the presence of boxes of other sizes. Bower then shifted this box into the distance and found that the babies continued to move their head on seeing it. In contrast, when he presented a box of different size, babies did not move, even if the new box was strategically placed so that it projected an image onto the eye that was identical to that of the original box. This suggests that these young babies could recognize the original box, despite changes in its apparent size with changes in distance. Bower argues that this shows that even young babies understand that objects have stable and enduring properties that transcend changes in appearance.

Key Term

Size constancy:
A perceptual mechanism that enables us to appreciate that an object remains the same size even though it appears smaller as it recedes into the distance.

A further study demonstrating a consistent result was conducted by Baillargeon, Spelke, and Wasserman (1985). They familiarized 5-month-old babies with a board pivoted at one side that swung back and forth through 180 degrees like a drawbridge (sees the figure to the right). Once the babies were well acquainted with this stimulus, the researchers introduced an ingenious modification such that the board appeared miraculously to pass right through a solid object that was standing in its path. The trickery was so convincing that adults who witnessed the spectacle regarded it with amazement! If babies had no notion of the permanence of things, then this impossible event should not cause the infants to experience surprise. After all, Piaget would have us believe that they inhabit a world that lacks the kind of permanence that prevents one object passing clean through another. Would the infants show any sign of surprise? Actually, they did and it took the form of prolonged gaze at the impossible event. Their gaze was sustained for a longer period than in a control condition when the movement of the board seemed to be arrested by the obstacle in its path.

A demonstration using a similar technique to record surprise yielded consistent results. Wynn (1992) presented two balls to 4-month-olds and then erected a screen that temporarily hid them from view. Subsequently, the infant watched as an adult reached behind the screen and took away one of the balls. The screen was then removed to reveal, under one condition, that only one ball remained, but under another condition both balls still remained (see the figure to the right). Infants reacted to this "impossible event" by looking at the pair of balls for a prolonged period, as if it had provoked surprise. And yet why should the infants be surprised? If they have no conception of the permanence of objects then they should have no thoughts about what happens to them when out of sight and should have no expectations about their reappearance. This finding, together with Baillergeon's, offers a convincing demonstration that young infants do have more grasp of object permanence than Piaget supposed.

Butterworth (1981) argues that early object permanence is surprisingly sophisticated. He suggests that not only do infants know that

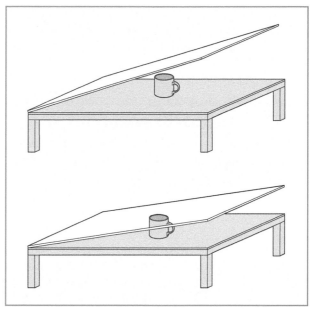

The pivoting and apparently solid drawbridge passed right through another solid object. This impossible event provoked a reaction of surprise from babies, suggesting they understand that the world is solid and stable.

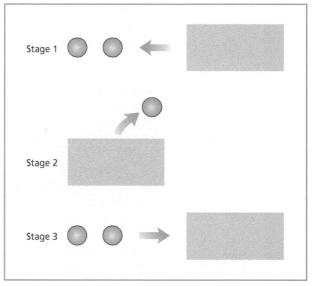

In Stage 1, the infant saw two balls on the table that were then hidden from view when a screen was moved in front of them. In Stage 2, an adult reached behind the screen and removed one of the balls. In Stage 3, the screen was removed to reveal that two balls were still present. This apparently impossible event provoked a reaction of surprise in babies, suggesting that they had made assumptions about what was behind the screen. This indicates that they understand more about the world than they can currently see or touch, contrary to Piaget's claims.

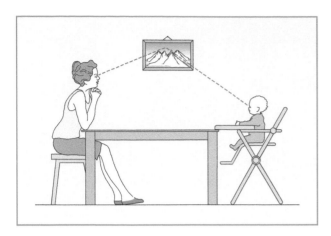

After securing eye contact with her baby, the mother suddenly looked to one side at an object on the wall. Babies demonstrated a surprising level of proficiency in coordinating their gaze to fixate on the same object. This finding is difficult to explain for anyone who holds the opinion that babies are profoundly egocentric.

things have a stable and enduring quality, they appreciate that there are other people in the world who hold perspectives different from their own. Following earlier work by Scaife and Bruner (1975), Butterworth arranged for the infant, aged between 6 and 8 months, to sit facing her mother. At a certain moment, as arranged with Butterworth, the mother was to break eye contact with her baby and look to a specific point in the room. When the mother did this, the infant promptly looked to the same point (see the figure to the left). It was not that the infants were just imitating the mother's head-turning, failing to look at any point in particular. A detailed video analysis of the babies' eye movements revealed that they were accurately fixating on the same point as the mother. Butterworth argued that this shows the infants understood that something might be going on that the mother could see, but that they could not yet see, and turned their heads to find out what it was. If this interpretation is correct, it implies the infants did know about a stable enduring world that was not always visible to them.

Do these findings indicate that the A not B error is unreliable or unreal? On the contrary, the tendency to search in location A when the object is hidden at B is so strong that infants continue searching at A even when no covers are involved. Harris (1974) arranged two ramps "back-to-back," each of which terminated in a toy garage. On the first three trials, he rolled a toy car down ramp A, and the infant retrieved it without difficulty each time from garage A. On the fourth trial, he rolled the car down ramp B, and the infant continued searching in garage A, at least initially. Bizarrely, the infant searched in garage A even though the garage was more like a carport, with open sides, and therefore was visibly empty. Initially, the child seemed to ignore the visual presence of the car in garage B. This finding shows that the tendency to search in location A is so strong that the child continues even when searching in an empty space.

Bremner and Bryant (1977) succeeded in prompting infants to search in location B in a study that nonetheless further demonstrated how infants rely on their past actions. After three trials with the rattle at A, Bremner and Bryant would swiftly move the infant to the opposite side of the table, and place the rattle at B. This time, infants always succeeded in searching at B, but note that the infants searched at B making the same reaching movement they had made whilst searching at A on the first three trials. In another test, Bremner and Bryant did the same, except after shifting the infant round the other side of the table, they once again, for a fourth time, hid the rattle at A. The infants searched wrongly in location B, using the same hand movement as they had previously!

These findings strongly suggest that when infants aged 8–10 months handle an object, they subsequently understand that object in terms of their previous reaching movement. They only searched in location B if that could be achieved with the same reaching movement involved in searching at location

Why do infants give incorrect judgments on the "A not B" task?

A on the first three trials. These findings suggest, then, that Piaget was partly right and partly wrong. It seems that infants have potential to show that they can distinguish between themselves and other things in the world, a potential which is demonstrated by findings suggesting they do not think things are just a series of changing pictures, but recognize that things have a stable and enduring quality. This is evident in their understanding that an object is the same even if it moves nearer or further away. It is a potential which is evident as awareness that other people may be privy to things going on that they cannot see, which prompts them to gaze in the same direction as another person.

Nevertheless, it seems infants are dominated by their own actions: if a reaching action led to retrieval of an object, then no matter what goes on outside in the world, they repeat that action when they want to retrieve the object. The object's visible absence seems not to deter the infants. This finding suggests that in some respects the infant has not come to terms with the idea that the world exists independently of self. The infant seems to assume that the existence of things in the world, such as a rattle, depends largely on her own actions. In this respect, Piaget seems to have been right, suggesting that perception is subordinate to action.

How compelling is the evidence in support of Piaget's claim that infants lack a concept of object permanence?

COMPETENCE IN EARLY CHILDHOOD

We shall now direct attention to the errors made by children Piaget would judge to be in the preoperational stage. Margaret Donaldson and colleagues investigated many of the findings reported by Piaget concerning the inabilities of young children. In a classic book entitled *Children's Minds*, Donaldson (1978) argues that Piaget's findings tell us next to nothing about children's immature or absent logical abilities, but instead tell us simply that children misunderstood what Piaget was asking. She argues that Piaget's tasks made no human sense, so children imposed their own meaning and answered according to what they thought Piaget wanted to hear. The unfortunate consequence, according to Donaldson, was that children gave "the wrong answer" as defined by Piaget—but not for the reasons Piaget suggested. In a nutshell, Donaldson claims Piaget wrongly concluded that the young children he tested were incompetent. We shall examine Donaldson's claim by looking at the studies she either carried out, or cited, in support of her argument.

Beginning with conservation, consider number as an example. We show the child two rows of seven counters, arranged in one-to-one correspondence so the two rows are the same length. We ask, "Is there the same amount of counters in these two rows, or is this one more or is that one more?" Children reply by saying that each has the same amount. We then say, "Now watch," and further spread the counters in the top row. We then repeat the question we asked at the very beginning: "Is there the same amount of counters in these two rows ... ?" Most 6-year-olds answer by saying that the rows do not have the same amount, and that the longer row has more. According to Piaget, the child's lack of conservation logic is responsible for this error, just as in quantity, length, and mass nonconservation, described in the previous chapter.

Donaldson argues that the repetition of the question makes the young child think she is supposed to give an answer that relates to the alteration we made to one of the rows, thinking, "He asked me that question before, and I gave

Key Term

Human sense:
A term coined by Margaret Donaldson. A task that makes no human sense is one in which children misinterpret the purpose of the experimenter's questions.

the answer. Since he's asking the same question again, he must want me to say something different. What shall I say? He spread out the counters to make this row longer, so he probably wants me to say that it has more; why else would he spread out the counters and then ask the same question?" That is, Donaldson argues that the repetition of the question, coupled with the change the experimenter makes to the length of one of the rows, makes the young child think that the answer to the repeated question has to be about that change. Donaldson reasoned that if either the first question were omitted, or if the change to one of the rows was accidental, and done by someone other than the experimenter, the young child would give a correct conserving judgment that the two rows still had the same amount of counters in each.

Rose and Blank (1974) presented a conservation test that excluded the first question, resulting in no repetition; children were asked about equality only after the experimenter had made the superficial change. Just as Donaldson expected, under this condition more 6-year-old children gave the correct answer that the two rows were the same, even though the counters in one had been spread out. The occurrence of correct answers under this condition stands in stark contrast to the procedure used by Piaget, involving repetition of the question.

Donaldson, in collaboration with her colleague James McGarrigle, carried out a study that also supported her argument. McGarrigle and Donaldson (1975) repeated the question, but made the change in length of one of the rows of counters appear to be accidental. In their study, they introduced a character called "naughty teddy." They told children that naughty teddy was always trying to spoil games, and that he might interfere with the game the experimenter was playing. The experimenter spread out the two rows of counters in one-to-one correspondence, and the child agreed that there was the same amount in each. Then the experimenter said, "Oh no! Look, here comes naughty teddy, and he's going to try to spoil the game!" The experimenter moved the delinquent teddy over the counters and made him kick those in one row, resulting in the counters being spread more widely compared with the row not disturbed by naughty teddy. Naughty teddy then returned to his base, and the experimenter asked if there was the same amount of counters in each row, repeating the initial question.

What do the findings of the "naughty teddy" experiment tell us?

Under the "naughty teddy" condition, the great majority of children aged between 4 and 6 years gave the correct conserving answer, saying that the two rows had the same amount of counters in each. Under the standard Piagetian condition, the great majority gave an incorrect nonconserving answer. Donaldson argued that because it was naughty teddy, and not the experimenter, who disturbed one of the rows of counters, the child no longer felt compelled to answer the repeated question by focusing on the change in length of one of the rows of counters. In this case, the experimenter's repeated question made "human sense," Donaldson claims, because the experimenter ostensibly wanted to establish whether naughty teddy had spoiled the game to the extent that the two rows no longer contained the same number of counters.

Donaldson's argument, therefore, is that in fact young children can conserve, but Piaget's questioning led them to answer incorrectly. If Donaldson is right, then Piaget's idea that cognitive development progresses through stages, from nonlogical to logical thinking, is seriously wrong. Light, Buckingham, and Robbins (1979) conducted an experiment similar to McGarrigle and

Donaldson's, and obtained consistent results. Instead of "naughty teddy" bringing about an accidental change, the change appeared incidental. In a conservation of liquid task, after the child agreed that there was the same amount in the two identical glasses, the experimenter "noticed" that one of the glasses had a crack. He therefore had a legitimate reason for pouring the liquid into another glass, which just happened to be taller and thinner. The experimenter then asked the child if the two glasses contained the same amount, one being an original glass and the other a tall thin glass. Again, the question seemed a reasonable one to ask. Children were more likely to judge that the two glasses contained the same amount, compared with a standard Piagetian condition. However, Light *et al.* proposed that often children were not answering the question as a question about conservation. Their argument seems to be that because the change and question were incidental, the children were giving the answer in an incidental way too, rather than in a serious and reflective way. In sum, they suggested that the disruption in the procedure resulted in children saying there was the same amount whilst really believing there was a different amount.

Evidently, some believe that Donaldson was a little hasty in claiming that Piaget was wrong about nonconservation. Moore and Frye (1986) brought into focus the dissatisfaction over Donaldson's conclusion when repeating the naughty teddy experiment with a simple yet ingenious modification. In principle, it could have been that naughty teddy's interfering did actually effect a change to the number of counters. This is precisely the manipulation that motivated Moore and Frye's study. Under a standard naughty teddy condition that was faithful to McGarrigle and Donaldson's procedure, teddy scattered the counters in one row but did not effect any change other than in the appearance of that row. Under a novel condition, teddy did not scatter the counters, but introduced an additional counter! Under one condition, then, teddy effected a change to appearance only, while under another condition, he effected a change to the underlying reality only (see the figure right). Otherwise, children were asked exactly the same conservation question, as asked by McGarrigle and Donaldson, and the result was that children aged around 6 years denied that the number of counters had changed under *both* conditions. Because children wrongly judged that number was not altered when it really was, it is impossible to know how to interpret their judgment of the same when number was not altered. Apparently, children's judgments had little to do with their appreciation of the invariance of the underlying reality, confirming Light *et al.*'s (1979) suspicion that correct judgments were merely false positives.

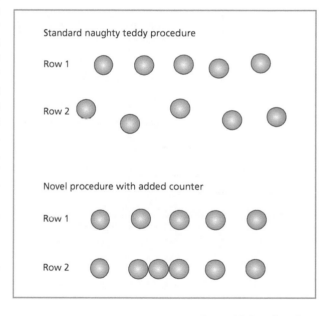

Naughty teddy interfered in a way that changed the length of the row without altering the number of counters in the standard procedure. In the novel procedure, he did not affect the length of the row but he did change the number of counters.

So what are we to make of all this? Perhaps we should conclude, as did Light *et al.*, that Piaget's procedure resulted in some children making nonconserving judgments when really they could conserve, and that McGarrigle and

Donaldson's procedure resulted in some making conserving judgments when really they could not conserve. In other words, is it possible after all that what Piaget said about conservation is roughly correct? Perhaps young children are incapable of the logical thought required for conservation, but that children come to acquire such thought at an earlier age than Piaget had supposed. Piaget said that children come to conserve at the age of about 7. Perhaps the truth of the matter is that children one year (but not two years) younger than this may be able to conserve.

Let us now consider the status of Piaget's findings on the three mountains task. Recall that Piaget showed children a model of three mountains, each with a distinctive feature at the summit. The child's task was to select a photo of what the mountain looked like to a person sitting at the opposite side of the model. Children below the age of 7 tended to select a photo of their own view, rather than a view showing the mountains in left–right reversal. Piaget claimed that children made this error because they are egocentric, and fail to imagine that other people have different points of view.

One of Donaldson's colleagues, Martin Hughes, challenged this claim with a study that seemed to have the same ingredients as the three mountains task, yet young children usually gave a correct judgment. On Hughes' (1975) task, young children apparently acknowledged that others do have views different from their own. The task drew on the child's knowledge of the game hide-and-seek, which the experimenters assumed children know and enjoy. Hughes prepared two intersecting walls from a doll's house, forming four quadrants, which we will label A to D to aid description (see the figure below). Hughes introduced two "policeman" dolls, overlooking quadrants A–B and B–D respectively. The child overlooked quadrants C–D. The child was told that a naughty boy doll was trying to avoid being caught, and the child was instructed to hide the boy doll where he could not be seen by the policemen. Ninety percent of children aged between 3 and 5 placed the boy doll in quadrant C. That is, the children recognized that a quadrant they could see was one that the policemen could not see. These young children seemed to understand that others, in this case the policeman dolls, have a view of things different from their own. On this task, children displayed no sign of the egocentrism we have come to expect on the basis of Piaget's theory.

Donaldson explains the success of the young children on Hughes' task by suggesting that it made "human sense." The children knew about hide-and-seek, and about the aim of trying not to be seen by the seeker. Donaldson claims that young children are not egocentric, contrary to Piaget's claim, and that this is demonstrated by the finding that they appreciate that something they can see may not be visible to another person. So why is it that children of this age fail the three mountains task? Donaldson acknowledges that the three mountains task not only involves understanding someone else's point of view, but also involves performing a difficult mental

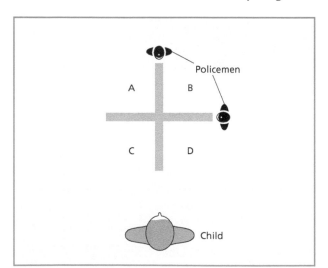

The hide-and-seek policeman experiment.

left–right reversal of the appearance of the mountains in order to identify what somebody opposite would see. That is, the policeman task involves determining what someone else cannot see, whereas the three mountains task involves working out how a scene will appear from a different vantage point, presumably by a complex process of mental rotation. Despite acknowledging this potentially important difference between tasks, Donaldson argues that the difference that really matters is that the policeman task made human sense to the children in that they could understand the motives and intentions of the protagonists involved. Also, Donaldson asserts that young children have considerable knowledge of the game hide-and-seek, which they can call upon in order to comprehend the problem Hughes presented to them. She suggests that in contrast, young children have no experience of an eagle's-eye view of mountains from differing perspectives, and made wrong judgments (selecting their own view) for this reason.

With the wisdom of subsequent research, we are now in a better position to assess the implication of Hughes' finding. There is little doubt Hughes' study poses a serious challenge to Piaget's idea, and it cannot be dealt with quite so easily as with the naughty teddy experiment. Light is shed on the issue by Flavell's suggestion about Level 1 and Level 2 perspective-taking abilities. At Level 1, the child thinks about viewing objects, but not about views of objects. There is a subtle but very important difference between the two, which is best illustrated with a simple test Flavell and his colleagues (e.g. Flavell, Everett, Croft, & Flavell, 1981) presented to children. They had a double-sided picture of a turtle, which showed the creature's back on one side, and its underneath on the other. The task began with the experimenter laying the turtle on the table on its back and then on its feet, to make sure the child was acquainted with the two sides of the picture. Flavell then oriented the turtle in space so that the child could see its back, whereas he, Flavell, could see its feet. Children then had to describe what they themselves could see, and also what they thought the experimenter could see. The picture was then turned around, so the child could now see the turtle's feet, and they had to answer the same questions.

Children as young as 3 years had no difficulty reporting their own view. Children also judged correctly that the experimenter could not see what they could see. That is, they understood that the experimenter did not share the same view (Level 1). However, a majority of children below age 4 were unable to specify what the experimenter could see instead. For example, children judged correctly that they could see the turtle the right way up but failed to judge that the experimenter could see it upside down. In contrast, nearly every child above age 4 judged correctly that the experimenter could see the turtle upside down even though they themselves could only see it the right way up (Level 2).

There is an obvious resemblance between Level 1 ability and success on Hughes' policeman task, and Level 2 ability and success on the three mountains task. Strictly, Piaget's account is wrong. Young children do know something about others' points of view in that they can recognize when another person can or cannot see something. Therefore, young children do not necessarily assume that others can see the same as they themselves and perhaps in this respect are not quite as egocentric as Piaget had supposed. However, young children do have difficulty imagining what another person can see from a different perspective. In this respect, Piaget's interpretation of the children's failure on the three mountains task seems to have some truth. Still, Piaget again seems to have underestimated children. Flavell's Level 2 ability is achieved by many 4-year-olds, which is much younger than Piaget would have expected, given that he had attached a great deal of significance to the finding that many 6-year-olds have difficulty with the three mountains task. Perhaps Donaldson is correct to argue that part of the reason children failed the latter was because they had difficulty interpreting what the experimenter wanted them to say.

A study by Borke (1975) provides converging evidence in support of such a conclusion. She presented children with a model like Piaget's three-mountain scene but asked the children not to select the opposite view from a photo but to rotate the model to show how it looks from the opposite side. Children as young as 5 years successfully rotated the model through 180 degrees, which Borke interpreted as indicating that the children were able to recognize the left–right transposition of the features as how it would be seen from the other side. An alternative interpretation, however, is that the children understood that to see the opposite side of something, either you have to walk round to the other side or you have to swivel the object through 180 degrees. It does not necessarily follow that children expected to see a difference in the scene on doing either of those things. In other words, Piaget was asking children how the model looked from the other side, while Borke was perhaps asking them effectively to judge how they should go about looking at the other side. Just because children know how to look at the other side, it does not follow that they expect to find a different view there. In the light of this comment, the conclusion drawn on the basis of Flavell's work probably is the most reliable.

Now consider young children's difficulty with class inclusion. An example of this task involves Lego™ bricks, say four red and two blue. Piaget asked, "Are there more red bricks or more bricks altogether?" Most children aged 6 years and below say there are more red bricks, apparently comparing subclass (red bricks) with subclass (blue bricks) instead of comparing subclass (red bricks) with total class (Lego™ bricks, which includes both red and blue). As usual, Donaldson claims that children's problem is not with the logic of class inclusion, but is due to misunderstanding what the experimenter means. Donaldson presents the case of failure on class inclusion as another example of Piaget intending one thing and children interpreting him to mean something else, which wrongly gives the impression that young children are logically incompetent.

Donaldson supports her argument once again by citing the work of McGarrigle. He supposed that children ignore the literal meaning of the words and focus instead on what they think the experimenter means: a comparison between the two subclasses. This seems a sensible argument considering that when we ask children a question, and specify alternatives, those alternatives are usually mutually exclusive. In other words, one alternative usually does not include the other: for example, "Are you a boy or a girl?" Therefore, in order to give children a fair chance to demonstrate their competence, McGarrigle strove to clarify the question. He attempted this by laying out four counters, which he called "steps," to a toy chair and a further two beyond this to a toy table, as illustrated in the figure on the next page. The steps to the chair were colored red, and those to the table were colored white. McGarrigle then asked children either, "Are there more red steps to go to the chair or more steps to go the table?" or "Are there more steps to go to the chair or more to go to the table?" Only 38% of 6-year-olds answered the first question correctly, whereas 66% answered the second correctly. Donaldson argues that in the case of the first question, which is very similar to the question Piaget asked, because it mentions color of items, it makes children think that color

A class inclusion task invested with more "human sense."

is the important feature: Are there more red steps or more white steps? When color is not mentioned, as in the second question, even though the problem still concerns class inclusion, children tune in to the correct way of thinking about the problem, so revealing that they can handle class inclusion. According to Donaldson, this is because the emphasis on subclasses as the focus of interest is reduced.

In order to deliver the coup de grace, McGarrigle carried out a further demonstration to show that young children thought Piaget wanted them to do a comparison between subclasses, rather than between subclass and total class. He arranged four cows facing four horses situated either side of a fence. There were two black and two white cows. There were three black horses and one white horse. McGarrigle asked 6-year-olds, "Are there more cows or more black horses?" The correct answer, of course, is that there are more cows. However, 86% judged that there were more black horses, presumably meaning "There are more black horses than there are black cows." As before, children were performing the comparison on subclasses (black cows/black horses), except this time the comparison was not between a subclass that was included in a total class, unlike the classic class inclusion problem set by Piaget. According to Donaldson, this shows that really the child's difficulty has nothing to do with class inclusion, but rather stems from their attempt to impose sense on the experimenter's question.

In the case of conservation and the three mountains task, it seemed that although Piaget had underestimated young children, it was also the case that Donaldson had overestimated their abilities. However, it seems that in the case of class inclusion, Donaldson is correct in judging the child to be competent, or at least not to have the kind of difficulty Piaget suggested. This led one eminent developmentalist, Howard Gardner (1982, p. 403), to conclude that "the class inclusion question does seem more of a trick than most other Piagetian puzzles."

Transitive inference is supposedly another difficulty for young children. In this task, you have to work out the relative length of two sticks, not by direct comparison, but by employing a stick of intermediate length. Stick A is smaller than stick B. Stick C is bigger than stick B. Therefore, C must be bigger than A. Importantly, there is no need to compare A with C directly because the preceding information allows the inference that C must be bigger. In other words, we can solve the problem logically without needing to make a practical comparison between A and C. Piaget claimed that children aged 7 years and below do not yet possess the logic to do this. Recall that Piaget showed children two towers and asked them to find which was tallest using a stick he supplied, which was intermediate in length. Children of 7 years and below failed, but older children succeeded. Although this finding is not in dispute, the interpretation is questionable.

What develops at age 7 that allows children to make a transitive inference? Is it, as Piaget claimed, acquisition of logical thought, or is it improved memory retention of the important information provided in the task? Regarding the second possibility, consider this: Suppose someone says, "John is heavier than Fred; John is lighter than Joe. Who is heaviest, Joe or Fred?" You may think, "What did he say? John is lighter than Fred, or was it that John is heavier than Fred? What did he say about Joe?" The point is that when we hear these problems, the panic we experience is usually concerned with trying to hold in mind all the important information we have to juggle in order to arrive at the correct answer that Joe is heavier than Fred.

According to Piaget, children fail because they cannot grasp the logic that Joe must be heavier than Fred if John is lighter than Joe but heavier than Fred. However, how can we be so sure this is the case, given that the problem does not just require understanding of logical relations, but also puts a massive demand on memory? What if it is the limited memory that really prevents young children giving the correct answer? Of course, the measuring problem Piaget presented to children seems a little more child-based than the verbal version of the task. Nevertheless, young children may find it difficult to give joint consideration to the facts that the measuring stick is both bigger than tower A, but smaller than tower B. If so, error on Piaget's transitive inference task may have a lot to do with limited memory capacity in young children, and little to do with lack of logical thought.

Bryant and Trabasso (1971) tried to devise a "pure" transitive inference test, one that could be used to assess understanding of the logic without putting a big demand on memory. They used five rods of differing length and

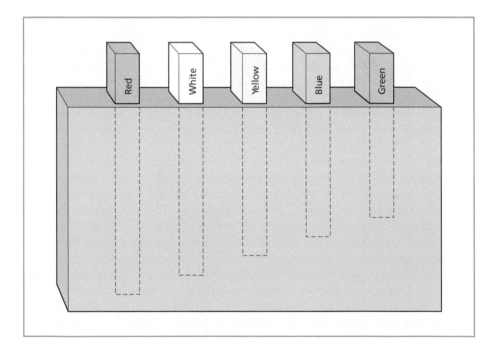

Bryant and Trabasso's (1971) transitive inference task.

color, held in a special box, shown in the figure on the previous page. The box had holes drilled in it to different depths, so that when the rods were placed in the holes in the appropriate sequence, each protruded above the surface of the box by 2.5 cm. The rods were in a left to right sequence, from big to small, though that was not obvious just by looking at the visible tops of the rods. The experimenter then went about training the children that the red rod (at the left end) was bigger than the white rod next to it, that the white rod was bigger than the yellow rod to the right of it, and so on. The experimenter questioned children about the relative size of pairs of rods situated next to each other, and then lifted the pair out of the box to show the child whether she was right or wrong. The experimenter continued with this laborious procedure until the child always stated which rod was the longer in any given neighboring pair.

At this point, Bryant and Trabasso could be sure that children retained all the relevant information, because they had "overlearned" which rod was biggest in each adjacent pair. They then asked children which was biggest in a pair not situated side by side. Bryant and Trabasso claimed that this time children had to perform a transitive inference to work out the correct answer, of the kind, "If the white one is bigger than the yellow one, and the yellow one is bigger than the blue one, then the white must be bigger than the blue." They found that children even as young as 4 years could give the correct answer on this task.

Bryant and Kopytynska (1976) conducted another study which also indicated that young children may be capable of transitive inference. They presented children with a block that had two holes bored into it, one to a depth of 10 cm, and the other to a depth of 15 cm. Children had to work out which hole was deeper, and were provided with a measuring stick for the purpose. The stick was not of a length intermediate between the depths of the two holes, for obvious reasons. However, the stick did have a yellow band round its middle section. When dropped into the shallower hole, the yellow band was in view at the top of the hole. When the stick was dropped in the deeper hole, the yellow band was submerged beneath the surface of the hole, and not in view. Bryant and Kopytynska found that a majority of children who had already failed on the Piagetian tower measuring task succeeded in working out which hole was deeper with the measuring stick.

According to Bryant and Kopytynska, the main difference between hole measuring and tower measuring was that in the case of the towers, since their heights were always in view, children may have formed a wrong impression, just by looking, as to which was the taller. In the case of the holes this was impossible, and children had to rely solely on the stick. When this was the case, children succeeded in giving a correct answer.

Impressive reasoning has been elicited from 4-year-olds using a completely different procedure. Pears and Bryant (1990) showed children four towers, each made of two colored building blocks. For example, red on top of green, green on top of blue, blue on top of yellow, and yellow on top of white. The child's task was then to make a tower out of blocks of five different colors used in the sample towers: red, green, blue, yellow, and white. Pears and Bryant had previously trained the children to build towers maintaining the relationship between colors in the sample towers. We can thus infer that the tower should be red at the top, followed by green, blue, yellow, and finally white at the bottom. In other words, from the sample towers we can make a transitive inference that in the tower the child was to construct, green would be at a higher position than yellow. Before allowing children to commence construction, Pears and Bryant asked the children which brick would be higher, the green or the yellow. Remarkably, a substantial majority of the 4-year-olds answered correctly with "green."

In that case, can young children do transitive inference? It certainly seems they can do some problems that appear to require the relevant kind of reasoning. However, perhaps we ought to give further consideration to children's failure on the Piagetian version of the problem, which requires a judgment about the relative height of two towers using a stick of intermediate height for measuring. Why is it that most children below age 7 fail, while most above this age succeed? To our knowledge, there is no suggestion in this case that children misunderstood what Piaget was asking them, unlike the cases of conservation, class inclusion, and the three mountains task. Is it, then, that the increasing success with increasing age is simply to do with a corresponding increase in the capacity of memory, as Bryant and Trabasso suggest?

On the face of things, it seems rather odd that at around the child's seventh birthday there is a sudden and dramatic increase in memory. Indeed, to some it seems unbelievable. Russell (1978) suggests that the more sensible explanation is, as Piaget claimed originally, that young children do not have the requisite logical thought to grasp that if tower A is bigger than the stick, and tower B is smaller than the stick, A must be bigger than B. Russell (1981) offered support to this argument when he showed that about a third of those who failed to give the correct answer had no difficulty recalling that the stick was shorter than tower A, but taller than tower B. Moreover, those who made the transitive inference were not much better at remembering this information! The onus was then on Russell to explain how children succeeded on Bryant's tasks, if not by transitive reasoning.

Piaget's idea was that young children understand things in terms of how they look, or how they can imagine them looking. Older children have a cognitive advantage over younger ones, because they can reason in a logical way, beyond mere images, which allows them to do transitive inference. Russell suggested that children could solve Bryant's tasks just by the appearance of things, or by imagining the way they appear. In Bryant and Trabasso's task, in which children thoroughly learned the lengths of all the rods, Russell suggests they developed a mental image of all the rods. When faced with the transitive inference problem, they merely had to do a direct mental comparison of the two rods in question. Accordingly, the problem would not require any logical understanding of the kind "A is bigger than B, B is bigger than C, therefore A must be bigger than C." The same argument can be applied to Pears and Bryant's findings. Perhaps a correct judgment of relative heights of differently colored bricks in a tower yet to be constructed could be achieved by a nonlogical process of imagining how the tower looks.

As for Bryant and Kopytynska's task, which required children to determine which of two holes was deeper, again children could short-circuit the problem by looking at how deeply the stick is submerged. Certainly the child has to remember how deeply it sank into the first hole when assessing the depth of the second hole, but once again the task does not seem to require the kind of logical reasoning that deserves to be called transitive inference.

Whether or not young children have a genuine difficulty with transitive inference, they certainly do have some logical competence of a kind that was not anticipated by Piaget. Robinson and Mitchell demonstrated that virtually all children aged 4 years find it very easy to make an inference by elimination

Key Term

Inference by elimination: Finding the correct answer by ruling out alternatives.

(Mitchell & Robinson, 1992). Children were shown a set of cartoon characters. Three were familiar, such as He-Man, Batman, and Spider-Man. Children were then asked to identify "Murkor," which actually is a name unknown to them. Nearly all pointed to the unfamiliar character without hesitation. They seemed to appreciate that since the unfamiliar name did not fit any of the familiar characters, it must belong to the character they had never seen before. They could not determine positively that it belonged to the unfamiliar character, but they could make an inference by elimination to that effect. Interestingly, it seems that from about 4 years of age, children begin to understand that other people can work things out by a process of elimination (Rai & Mitchell, 2006). This is an impressive feat because it suggests young children are so proficient that they grasp that the mind is a processor of information (people work things out) and is not just a receptacle for information that impinges on the senses.

Another example of early logical competence can be found in children's success with syllogisms. This refers to a category of logical problem in which a particular state can be determined from a general rule. For example, if the general rule is that all fish live in trees, and if we are told that Tiddles is a fish, then we can infer that Tiddles must live in a tree. Dias and Harris (1990) presented that kind of problem to children aged around 4 years. However, children adamantly denied that Tiddles lived in a tree and insisted instead that she lives in water. On the face of things, it seemed children lacked the logic needed to handle the syllogism. However, their underlying competence was revealed when Dias and Harris began with a preamble explaining that Tiddles lived on an alien planet where strange things happen. Children readily entered into the spirit of this make-believe and then were able successfully to apply the general rule to make correct inferences about particular cases. Evidently, children as young as 4 years grasp the form of syllogisms but have difficulty demonstrating this understanding when they have to set aside their knowledge of the real world.

Seemingly, young children are far more able than Piaget gave them credit for. Nevertheless, it seems there is also danger of overestimating the abilities of young children, and that perhaps they lack the requisite mental flexibility or perhaps the logic for solving certain problems, such as conservation. Even in the case of conservation, though, it seems children younger than Piaget had supposed are able to give the correct judgment if the problem is presented in the right way. Collectively, then, studies investigating Piaget's claims have blurred the distinction between preoperational and concrete operational thinking. Although we can argue that young children do appear to have difficulty with the logic of certain problems, it now looks very unlikely that these errors all fit together neatly to suggest an overarching characteristic of thought that we could call preoperational intelligence.

Besides refining our understanding on how young children think and solve problems, the post-Piagetian research provides a sobering lesson on the challenges posed by developmental investigations. It would be a great folly to suppose that young children comprehend a question in much the same way as an adult. Interpreting meaning amounts to much more than a literal decoding of the utterance. We interpret meaning in context, and the context includes the psychological environment as well as the physical environment. There is a distinct asymmetry in the power and knowledge relations between adults and children. Consequently, it would be foolish to think that the way an adult (or older child) interprets a question posed by an experimenter is the same as a young child.

▌Key Term

Syllogism:
All Xs are Ys. John is an X, therefore he must also be a Y.

CONCRETE THOUGHT IN ADOLESCENCE

What is the status of Piaget's claim about the existence of a stage of formal operational thinking? This time the moot point is whether Piaget overestimated rather than underestimated the abilities of adolescents and adults. If Piaget underestimated the abilities of children, and overestimated the abilities of adults, then this would seriously undermine his theory of development consisting of a series of distinct cognitive stages, each characterized by its own special way of thinking. Instead, it would suggest that the thought of children and adults has a great deal in common.

Piaget claimed that formal and scientific thought is a special feature of adolescent reasoning. Is that really true, or do people have more of an intuitive and practical intelligence? Everyday experience certainly seems to suggest the latter, but let us take a look at the evidence. We shall begin by considering Karl Popper's (1972) idea on the philosophy of science, which touches on something central to Piaget's belief about formal operations. One of the key facets of formal operations as described by Piaget is an ability to test ideas. It does not matter so much whether the problem is solved correctly or incorrectly, but whether the adolescent tackles the problem by deploying a formal operational strategy. In other words, does the adolescent display any understanding of a scientific way of thinking? This is where Popper comes in, because he had a great deal to say about the character of scientific discovery.

Consider the example of a glass beaker, which we are told is made of a special new kind of material that is quite literally indestructible. Let us say that because of a theory about the composition of the glass, we have the firm expectation that a beaker made from this material truly could not be broken. To test this, we situate the beaker next to an A-bomb, and then detonate the device. After the smoke has cleared, we search the area and eventually find the beaker intact. Does this mean the beaker is unbreakable? Probably, but suppose we tried an H-bomb instead, a device with the strongest known blast? We duly repeat the test and find the beaker still intact. Does this mean the beaker is unbreakable? Again, probably, but we could never be certain that a future device, let us call it a Z-bomb, with an even stronger blast, would destroy the beaker. If this came about, we would demonstrate that the theory that says the beaker is unbreakable is false. This illustrates, according to Popper, that it is possible to prove a theory wrong, but impossible to prove it right. For that reason, he continues, it is pointless trying to prove a theory; we could only ever hope to disprove it. It follows that if we want to assess the truth of something, we should not look for evidence confirming its truth, but look for evidence showing it is false. In essence, we have to engage a negative strategy.

Piaget's adolescents who succeeded on the pendulum problem, described in the previous chapter, appeared to adopt a suitably negative approach to reasoning. Considering they avoided varying the values of two factors simultaneously, such as varying both the weight of the suspended object and the length of the string all in one move, they must have realized that had they done this, the results would have been uninterpretable. Actually, the results would have been uninterpretable in principle, no matter what form they took. Therefore, it seems Piaget's adolescents' testing was based around an impressively negative strategy: If we vary the weight of the suspended object while holding the other factors constant, and this has no effect on speed of oscillation, then we will have refuted the hypothesis that oscillation is governed by weight. We proceed to test rival hypotheses until we are left with only one plausible explanation for variations in speed of oscillation. Although the pendulum problem may have elicited negative reasoning of the kind held as being fundamental to science, it now seems that in the great majority of situations adults are very poor at this. Wason and Johnson-Laird (1972) demonstrated as much in their classic book, *The Psychology of Reasoning*. They tested university students, figuring that if these people do not display proficiency in the kind of negative reasoning we suppose is at the heart of formal operations, we can assume that formal operations are not a central feature of adult intelligence. Wason and Johnson-Laird presented what is known as the selection task by showing students four cards, each displaying a letter on one side and a number on the other, as shown in the figure above. The students were given a rule, and had to find out whether or not it was true:

If a card has a vowel on one side, then it has an even number on the other.

If a card has a vowel on one side, then it has an even number on the other.

The students were instructed to turn over as few of the cards as possible to test the rule. Before reading further, spend a few moments choosing which cards you would turn. Think very carefully because the problem is not quite as simple as it seems!

We are not concerned so much with whether the students gave the correct answer, but which cards they chose to turn. This potentially reveals how they go about solving the problem. Now, remember that the correct approach, as discussed above, is to engage in a negative reasoning process, and thus treat the problem as "find out whether the rule is false."

Most intelligent adults wrongly choose E and 4, but in fact the correct pair is E and 7. If it turned out that E had an odd number on the reverse, that would show the rule was false; likewise if it turned out 7 had a vowel on the reverse, that would also show the rule was false. If there is an even number on the other side of E, and a consonant on the other side of 7, the rule has not been violated. Especially surprising was the finding that when professional logicians tackled the problem, even some of them, to their great embarrassment, included the 4 in their choice.

Everybody can recognize immediately that the E is a correct card to choose, but why is 4 incorrect? If there was either a vowel or a consonant on the other side of the 4 it would tell us nothing because the rule sets no condition concerning what should be on the other side of an even number. Whatever is the reverse of 4, as Popper could have told us, it is totally uninformative.

Why did the students choose the wrong pair of cards? It seems they were looking for instances of vowels being paired with even numbers in order to show that the rule was true. Wason called this erroneous strategy a confirmation bias, which is characteristic of adult thinking in very many diverse instances. What the students should have asked themselves is, "Supposing the rule were wrong,

Key Term

Confirmation bias: Inappropriately seeking evidence in support of a hypothesis instead of seeking evidence that might falsify a hypothesis.

which pair of cards would show that to be the case?" If students thought along these lines they would realize that if 7 had a vowel on the other side, the rule must be wrong. In other words, the students did not adopt the classic scientific problem-solving attitude described by Karl Popper.

Wason and Johnson-Laird's selection task neatly demonstrates that most intelligent adults do not meet the ideal of effective scientific reasoning proposed by Piaget. That is a blow to the status of Piaget's stage of formal operations, but an even more damning finding has emerged. Namely, it seems people have far less difficulty solving certain versions of the selection task. Cheng and Holyoak (1985) demonstrated this in an envelope version of that task, which appears in the figure below.

Participants saw four envelopes, two with their back in view and a further two with their front in view. Looking at the two with their back in view, participants could tell whether the envelope was sealed or unsealed. Looking at their fronts, the participants could see either that a 20-cent stamp was attached or that a 10-cent stamp was attached. They then heard the rule "if the envelope is sealed, it must have a 20-cent stamp," and had to choose which envelopes to turn in order to test the rule.

The participants were from the USA, where in fact there is no such postal rule. Presented like this, most participants committed the error we have come to expect, choosing the wrong pair of "sealed" and "20 cents" (the correct pair, of course, is "sealed" and "10 cents"). However, under a slightly different condition, nearly all participants succeeded in choosing the correct pair. The crucial difference responsible for the dramatic improvement was a simple justification, explaining why sealed envelopes should have 20-cent stamps on them. The reason given was that the mail company knew that personal mail is nearly always posted in a sealed envelope, and that the company sought to elevate its profits by demanding higher revenue from personal mail. Thus, if the sender has a personal message and therefore wishes to seal the envelope, then he should pay an extra ten cents!

Now the participants could easily recognize that the rule would be violated if an envelope with a 10-cent stamp was sealed. In other words, so long as the participants could grasp a reason for the rule, and particularly the implications for violating the rule, they no longer exhibited the confirmation bias described by Wason. To borrow a phrase from Donaldson, when the selection task made "human sense," the participants could engage in the appropriate reasoning required for a successful choice.

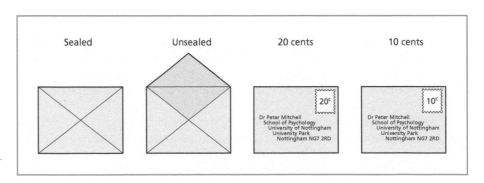

The selection task with real-world content.

The finding that some versions of the selection task are easy, whereas others are hard, poses a serious problem for Piaget's stage of formal operations. Piaget proposed that formal operational reasoning is not entrenched in specific tasks; otherwise it would deserve to be called concrete operational reasoning. The whole point behind Piaget's idea of formal operational reasoning is that it is a general reasoning strategy, which works much the same no matter the content of the particular problem in question. Cheng and Holyoak's findings strongly suggest that in the great majority of cases, adult reasoning is content-specific. The clear implication is that a stage of formal operations does not exist, and that perhaps there is no real difference between the quality of a 9-year-old's thinking and a 16-year-old's thinking.

Critically evaluate evidence that has been put forward in support of a stage of formal operational intelligence.

THE IMPACT OF POST-PIAGETIAN RESEARCH

Taking stock, the evidence compels us to accept that Piaget's theory requires modification. Indeed, the evidence suggests that perhaps some aspects ought to be rejected. For example, the idea that cognitive development heads toward formal operational thinking patently seems wrong, and, for that reason, perhaps the whole idea of formal operations as a typical feature of adult cognition should be rejected.

Studies on infants suggest that babies may well be sensitive to the existence of a stable and enduring world, contrary to Piaget's claim. As for young children, it seems that some things Piaget claimed they could not do, in fact they can do. Class inclusion is a case in point. Also, many conceptual difficulties young children have may not be quite as severe as Piaget supposed. Conservation and three-mountains perspective taking are examples.

Nevertheless, it seems wrong to argue that babies and young children are like mini adults, with the main difference being that they have less knowledge. Studies continue to suggest that babies and young children think in quite different ways from those of adults. Although we may accept that some details of Piaget's account are wrong, is it still possible that young children and babies are egocentric in a fashion? For example, do they only know about their own views, feelings, and so on, and fail to imagine other points of view? This very important issue is covered in the next chapter.

Are young children egocentric?

CONSTRUCTIVISM AND SOCIAL CONSTRUCTIVISM

One of Piaget's central contributions was to suggest that knowledge is constructed as we develop. He supposed we are born with minimal knowledge, but also that there is not much we can glean directly from simply looking at the world, or for that matter being told about it. Instead, according to Piaget, we construct a kind of mental model of reality. He thus claimed that formation of knowledge consists of a process of personal discovery and creation. Piaget thought that we gain little knowledge directly from others by way of instruction. An implication is that the traditional teaching method of chalk and talk is largely useless! What is eminently preferable, according to Piaget, is an activity-based method of instruction, where direct involvement with the study matter will stimulate the individual to create a scheme for understanding the problem. In other words, knowledge would be created if the mechanism of equilibration were stimulated.

An example to illustrate how equilibration works was presented in the previous chapter. It is activated when there is cognitive conflict, as when the child holds two conflicting schemes, like tall columns of water are "more" and wide columns of water are "more." When deciding whether a tall thin glass or a short fat glass has more, such a child would experience a state of cognitive conflict, which might stimulate her to coordinate these two conflicting schemes on the road to discovering or creating the concept of conservation.

Piaget suggested that although it would be impossible to teach something like the concept of conservation, experiencing a clash of opinion with another person could promote new understanding of this kind. Inspired by this suggestion, Russell (1982) had a brilliant idea on how to engineer a situation in which children experienced a clash of views that might promote their acquisition of the concept of conservation. Children participated in pairs in a study on length conservation. They faced each other across a table on which there were two pencils of identical length, as shown in the figure below. It so happens that nonconserving children are not content simply to judge that once misaligned the two pencils are different in length; they characteristically judge that the one moved further away from where they are sitting is longer. By having children face each other in this way, Russell was able to provoke a clash of opinions in the sense that children would be in disagreement over which pencil was longer! He left them alone in the testing room under the surveillance of a hidden camera and instructed them to come to an agreement over which pencil was longest or whether they were they same.

Russell hoped to find that the inevitable disagreement between children would stimulate equilibration in each of them, which in turn should generate a correct conserving judgment. Ironically, then, it could be a case of two wrongs making a right! The results were not quite so simple, however, and it turned out that social dominance played an important part in the proceedings. Fortuitously, Russell had sufficient foresight to make an assessment of the social dominance of each participant using an independent measure prior to testing conservation. When the two children were nonconservers, their agreed verdict was usually in accordance with the view expressed by the socially dominant child. Analysis of the video record showed the children initially expressing different views, but the submissive child subsequently yielded to the dominant one following implicit or explicit threat! Interestingly, when a conserving child was paired with a nonconserving child, then they usually agreed on the conserving answer, *even if this happened to run against the initial judgment of the socially dominant child*. In other words, nonconserving children seemed to recognize the force of a conserving argument, even if they were socially dominant. Despite those interesting results, it was very seldom the case that a couple of nonconserving children arrived at a grasp of conservation purely from a clash of incorrect opinions. Accordingly, there was no evidence of equilibration being aroused by cognitive conflict.

The results of Russell's study seem to lend more support for Vygotsky's social constructivism than Piaget's constructivism. Vygotsky advanced a theory

Child A   Child B

Children faced each other across a table. Each judged that the pencil further from them was longer, meaning that they were in conflict. Would this promote deeper understanding of conservation?

that was similar to Piaget's but he laid much greater stress on social experience and artifacts of culture, such as language and numeracy, as tools of the mind that might facilitate intellectual development. Apparently, children were able to learn about conservation from a more competent child, but were unable to hit upon a conserving judgment unless it was offered to them explicitly. This is precisely what Vygotsky would have expected.

Let us venture further into what Vygotsky had to say about development. His view was that the intellectual profile of individuals reflected the culture they belonged to. In other words, he saw intelligence as culture-relative, not just across the globe but across history also. He was claiming that the intellect of individuals a couple of thousand years ago was quite different from the typical modern intellect, even though the physiology of the brain is essentially identical. Effectively, he was claiming that an individual reared in a culture with a sophisticated language in a social environment where complex ideas are routinely considered, would inevitably develop an intellect of high caliber. While Piaget saw the intellect as personal property that belongs to an individual, Vygotsky saw intellect as something in the social ether that was bigger than any one person. To understand intellectual development, then, it is not sufficient just to focus on the individual.

Disciples of Vygotsky's ideas, Wood, Bruner, and Ross (1976), introduced the metaphor of scaffolding in order to express the sense in which the intellect is situated in the social context. They suggest that more competent individuals, such as parents and teachers, are disposed to support the skills of the apprentice child thinker by providing routes to the solution of problems. As the child develops, these more competent individuals remove the scaffolding of intellectual support piece by piece until the child is able to stand alone as a fully-fledged thinker in a given domain of problem.

The extent of scaffolding will depend upon what Vygotsky called the child's zone of proximal development. He supposed that it would not be possible to teach a 6-year-old child about Einstein's theory of relativity, but that it might be possible to teach her about conservation. Vygotsky suggested that acquiring a new concept is not all or nothing, but that the mental framework had to be in place in some form or other. A child who has the mental framework for accommodating the concept of conservation thus has that concept within his zone of proximal development. In other words, whilst the child might not currently possess the concept, it would be within his receptive grasp. Hence, in Russell's study, the nonconserving children who recognized the force of a conserving argument when it was put to them by their child partner might be said to have conservation within their zone of proximal development.

As mentioned, Vygotsky emphasized the role of language as a tool of thought. While Piaget saw language as an expression of symbolic competence, Vygotsky saw language at the hub of intellectual growth. At around the age of 6 years, children characteristically mumble to themselves in a way that is not particularly communicative. Piaget regarded this "egocentric speech" as further evidence of preoperational thought, and nothing more. Vygotsky, in contrast, saw this mumbling as vocalization of thought, and therefore as a symptom of language having assumed a prime position in the intellectual functioning of the individual. Vygotsky referred to this as inner speech or private speech. Apart from absorbing the concepts inherent in the language, Vygotsky saw private

Key Terms

Scaffolding: Support provided by adults (or more competent other individuals) that helps children to construct knowledge.

Zone of proximal development: A period in which the child is cognitively ready to acquire a certain kind of new concept.

Private speech: Privately talking through a problem in order to arrive at a solution.

Left to her own devices, could this little girl make her sister a birthday cake? Her mother uses scaffolding to create a situation in which she can begin to move into a zone of proximal development.

Compare and contrast Piaget's and Vygotsky's theories.

speech as a medium for internalizing thought that can occur between individuals where the development of ideas occurs through dialogue and debate.

Putting psychology into perspective, we see that Vygotsky has massively influenced many of Piaget's detractors. His theory was adopted and promoted by Jerome Bruner, whose influence was greatest in the 1960s and 1970s, and who in turn inspired Margaret Donaldson. Hence we turn full circle and we now see Donaldson's enterprise not just as an attempted demolition of Piaget but as a promotion of Vygotsky. Instead of trawling for evidence directly in support of Vygotsky, her approach was to undermine the rigidly individualistic account of development put forward by Piaget. The moral of the tale is that it is very much easier to unearth evidence that challenges Piaget than to find direct support for Vygotsky. Actually, it seems there is definitive support for neither Vygotsky nor Piaget. Ultimately we are left to reason about which theory offers the best approach. Common sense surely says that intellectual growth is enhanced and promoted by the social context. In any case, Piaget and Vygotsky were not wildly in disagreement, but rather just had different emphases. Piaget seems to have underestimated the role of language and social context in development.

Summary

- Some of Piaget's findings have been called into question, but some seem to stand up fairly well to scrutiny. During infancy, it seems babies do have understanding at least on one level that the world continues to exist even when they cannot see aspects of it. While this finding challenges some of Piaget's claims, it seems Piaget was nevertheless correct to say that babies relate to the world in terms of their own previous actions, such that perception is subordinate to action in infancy. During early childhood, it seems children are a good deal more competent that Piaget had claimed, though the errors children make still seem to be present, only at a younger age. With respect to formal operational reasoning, it is very difficult to identify supporting evidence; rather, adult reasoning seems to resemble what Piaget called concrete operational thinking. Piaget generally underestimated the role of language as a tool of thought and consequently he underestimated language as a driving force in development. Vygotsky, in contrast, stressed the value of language, not just as a tool of thought but as a vehicle for cultural transmission. This view seems a good deal more plausible than Piaget's overly individualistic perspective.

Essay Questions

1. Compare and contrast constructivist with social constructivist theories of intellectual development.
2. Is it fair to say that Piaget underestimated the role of language and communication in his research on intellectual development?

Further Reading

Margaret Donaldson's book is excellent in many respects. It is highly readable, outlines many educational implications, and provides a neat summary of Piaget's theory:

- Donaldson, M. (1978). *Children's minds*. Glasgow: Fontana/Collins.

Another book with a similar theme is:

- Siegal, M. (1997). *Knowing children* (2nd edn.). Hove: Psychology Press.

Contents

What children understand about the mind

5

Chapter Aims

- To introduce a definition of "theory of mind".
- To introduce the test of false belief as a method of investigating children's understanding of the mind.
- To examine the claim that children undergo a radical change in their understanding of the mind at about 4 years of age.
- To examine evidence that children understand about the mind from 15 months old.
- To examine developments in understanding the mind beyond early childhood.

INTRODUCTION

Piaget was driven by the quest to understand how we achieve a logical understanding of the world. Incidental to this endeavor, he described young children as egocentric, meaning that they find it impossible to assume another individual's mental or visual perspective. In Piaget's opinion, young children's lack of logical understanding is regarded as the principal cause of their lack of social understanding. In the past three decades, there has been a concerted effort to systematically document what children understand about the mind and establish when and how that understanding develops.

Understanding other people's mental states is a formidable and possibly uniquely human intellectual feat. Humans are fundamentally social creatures, and a history of our species would no doubt reveal that those who thrive in a social group probably stood the best chance of enjoying longevity and probably enjoyed the most privileged mating rites. Hence, we are the benefactors of the wealth of genetic inheritance of social competence. It would not be surprising if an understanding of other minds was something that developed very early indeed, given such background, and perhaps a good deal earlier than Piaget might have supposed.

Certain philosophers (e.g. Dennett, 1978) say that the basic element of an understanding of the mind rests on the insight that people hold beliefs and that these beliefs govern behavior. In this context, we are not so much concerned with religious or political beliefs but with simple factual beliefs. For example, if we wanted to predict where John will search for his chocolate when he feels hungry, we can base this on where we think he thinks the chocolate is located. If we think he thinks the chocolate is in the fridge, then we can predict he will look there. In other words, we can use John's beliefs to predict his behavior. The reverse is also true, in that we can explain observed behavior by inferring beliefs. If we observe that John is looking in the fridge for his chocolate, we can explain his behavior by saying that he thinks his chocolate is there. We can immediately see how powerful this understanding of others' mental states (like beliefs) is in explaining or predicting behavior and thus making sense of the social world and the actions of people in it.

Why is the test of false belief regarded as a good tool for investigating children's developing understanding of the mind?

Although very young children seem competent in predicting how another person will behave according to their assumption about that person's beliefs, we have to exercise great caution. Perhaps it is just an illusion that young children understand anything about beliefs. Perhaps after all they simply judge that John will look where they themselves would look and judge that John thinks what they themselves think. This is how an egocentric child would perform. Effectively, we need to ask whether young children are capable of understanding that John holds a *false* belief.

Suppose that earlier in the day, John had left his chocolate in the kitchen drawer. Unknown to him, the plot developed when his mother moved his chocolate to the fridge. At this point, we know that the chocolate is in the fridge, but John still thinks it is in the drawer because he did not witness his mother's actions. If we ask the child participant to predict where John will look for his chocolate, they ought to mentally set aside the place they know it is, and just concentrate on John's false belief, which would lead them to predict that he will search where he last saw his chocolate. A child who successfully made that judgment could not be accused of being egocentric for he would effectively acknowledge that the content of his own mind is different from that of another person. The test resulting from this logic dominated developmental research into understanding of the mind for over 30 years after its conception, and we will chart an overview of those productive years in the following sections before moving on to investigate some new directions in this research area.

YOUNG CHILDREN'S UNDERSTANDING OF BELIEFS

Wimmer and Perner (1983) enacted a story with playpeople to investigate young children's ability to acknowledge false belief. Their aim was to identify at what age children begin to take into account the fact that people hold beliefs by investigating their ability to acknowledge that a false belief could lead to a fruitless search. Nearly all children aged 5 years and above correctly judged that John will search in the place he last saw his chocolate. In contrast, not many children aged 4 years and hardly any aged 3 made a prediction that took into consideration John's belief. Instead, they simply pointed to the current location of the chocolate when asked where John will search. The developmental progression seemed very sharp indeed, as if it were typical for children aged around 4 years suddenly to gain a new insight to the effect that people's behavior is governed by beliefs that are specific to them.

Wimmer and Perner concluded that children aged 5 years and upward have acquired a fundamental insight into the mind, one that equips them to predict behavior according to their assessment of an individual's belief. In making correct judgments, children demonstrated an ability to distinguish between beliefs held by themselves and those held by other people. Evidently, they cannot be egocentric in the way suggested by Piaget, given that they are capable of crediting others with different conceptual perspectives. On the other side of the coin, Wimmer and Perner suggested that children below age 4 or 5 have very little insight into the existence of mind, considering that they fail a test of false belief.

Although the early competence is much greater than Piaget would have anticipated, perhaps some might object that children are still being underestimated. One problem with Wimmer and Perner's unexpected transfer test, as it has come to be known, is that children are invited to make a judgment about the belief held by a doll. Perhaps children who failed to take into account the doll's belief were acting on the rather sensible assumption that dolls do not actually have minds! To deal with this obstacle to straightforward interpretation, Perner, Leekam, and Wimmer (1987) developed a new test known as the deceptive box task, as shown in the figure below. In this, children were shown a Smarties™ tube or any other familiar container and asked to guess the content. After they had said "Smarties," the experimenter opened the lid to reveal the unexpected content of pencils. The experimenter returned them to the tube, closed the lid, and then asked the child to predict what another child, who had never seen the tube before, would say or think was inside. Younger 4-year-olds and 3-year-olds simply reported the content of the box (pencils). Older children, in contrast, correctly acknowledged another person's false belief by replying with "Smarties."

Perner *et al.*'s findings thus offered converging evidence in support of the conclusion articulated several years previously by Wimmer and Perner. An interesting feature of Perner *et al.*'s article is that the authors evidently assumed quite understandably that while young children had difficulty acknowledging other people's beliefs, they would easily be able to acknowledge their own beliefs. However, Gopnik and Astington (1988) adapted the deceptive box task to show that 3-year-old children experience just as much difficulty acknowledging their own as they do acknowledging others' beliefs. After the experimenter had shown the pencils and returned them to the tube, she asked a modified question: "When you first saw this box, before we opened it, what

Does the finding that young children have difficulty with tests of false belief suggest that they are egocentric?

Stage 1

Stage 2

Stage 3

The deceptive box task has three distinct stages. In the first, the child sees the box initially unopened. In the second stage, the experimenter opens it to reveal the unexpected content of the pencil. In the third stage, after the pencil has been returned and the lid closed, the box appears as it did initially. At this point, either the child is asked what another person would say was inside, or they are asked what they themselves had thought was inside when they first saw it.

did you think was inside?" In answer, a large majority of young children wrongly reported their current belief. Indeed, Gopnik and Astington found that children who had difficulty acknowledging another person's false belief in the unexpected transfer test were the same who had difficulty acknowledging their own belief in the modified deceptive box task. This striking result leads to a rather interesting conclusion. It seems that young children not only lack understanding of other people's minds but perhaps are not even aware of the existence of their own mind!

Gopnik and Astington presented the same children with a third test, to investigate whether they understood the difference between appearance and reality, based on a procedure devised by Flavell, Flavell, and Green (1983). In the appearance–reality test children were shown an object that looked like a rock and asked what they thought it was. Not surprisingly, they answered with, "It's a rock." The experimenter then nonchalantly tossed the object to the child, whereupon it became apparent that it was not at all heavy like a rock but actually extremely light: It was a sponge disguised to look like a rock. At this point, children were asked about the real identity of the object and they readily acknowledged that it was a sponge. Finally, children were asked what it looked like and what it was really. The young 4-year-olds and virtually all the 3-year-olds gave the same response to both questions, usually "sponge" and "sponge." Once the children knew the true identity of the object, they seemed unable to acknowledge that it could have an illusory appearance.

There is close similarity between children's failure to acknowledge the difference between appearance and reality and their failure to acknowledge their own prior false belief. In judging that the sponge looked like a sponge, they were effectively denying that they had been deceived by the object's appearance. Indeed, the children who failed to acknowledge the distinction between appearance and reality tended to be the same who failed to acknowledge false belief, whether their own or that of another individual. This led Gopnik and Astington to argue that difficulty on the three tasks of the appearance–reality test is united by an underlying conceptual deficit that prevents young children understanding about the existence of the mind. These authors also noted the sharp developmental trend across the three tasks, which led them to suggest, in agreement with Wimmer and Perner, that some time around their fourth birthday children experience a radical conceptual shift akin to that described by Piaget, which equips children with a kind of informal theory of the human mind.

Does a child's understanding of the mind have theory-like properties?

HAVE CHILDREN BEEN UNDERESTIMATED?

After getting over the shock that even some children as young as 4 years seem to acknowledge the existence of the mind, several researchers were audacious enough to question whether the 3-year-olds who failed tests of false belief may actually have been underestimated. Among the first were Lewis and Osborne (1990), who, perhaps inspired by Donaldson, suggested that young children simply might misunderstand what they are being asked. Specifically, when presented with the deceptive box task, children might think that the experimenter is asking what is inside the tube right now. Similarly, Siegal and

Beattie (1991) suggested that children might misunderstand the time reference in the unexpected transfer test. When asked to predict where John will look for his chocolate, perhaps children assume they are supposed to say where John will look after he has first looked in vain in the empty place where he last saw the chocolate. Lewis and Osborne introduced a simple improvement to the deceptive box task, by adding to the question, "before we opened the lid": "What did you think was inside before we opened the lid?" Siegal and Beattie introduced a similar improvement to the unexpected transfer task when they included "first of all" in the question: "Where will John look first of all?" Both sets of authors reported that children aged 3 years stood a better chance of giving a correct judgment of false belief when the questions were modified, though errors were still common.

Despite that, an ingeniously simple experiment conducted by Wimmer and Hartl (1991) yielded results that were deeply persuasive in suggesting that young children really did have severe difficulty acknowledging false belief. First, they were keen to examine whether children's difficulty acknowledging their own prior false belief resulted from embarrassment over not knowing that the tube had contained pencils all along. Perhaps the children were attempting to avoid the loss of face that they would have experienced by admitting that they had not known the true content of the tube initially. To investigate the embarrassment hypothesis, Wimmer and Hartl commissioned Kasperl as a confederate in the experiment. Kasperl is a notoriously stupid puppet who appears on Austrian television (the participants were all Austrian). Kasperl's counterpart on British television is Sweep from the once popular children's program *Sooty and Co.* The hapless Kasperl is renowned for being mistaken about virtually everything, so surely he could be expected to think wrongly about the content of a certain tube. In the test, children accompanied Kasperl as he was presented with the deceptive box task! He stated initially that he thought there were Smarties™ inside, but this was disconfirmed when the experimenter opened the lid to reveal the pencils. Finally, observing child participants were asked not what they had thought was inside initially, but what Kasperl had thought was inside. In this case, there would be no loss of face in judging that Kasperl had wrongly thought the tube contained Smarties™. Indeed, it is to be expected that Kasperl would think the wrong thing. However, children aged 3 years fared no better when judging about Kasperl. They had just as much difficulty acknowledging Kasperl's false belief as they did their own. Evidently, the embarrassment hypothesis was not going to be good enough to account for children's difficulty acknowledging occasions when they hold a false belief.

The most important contribution from Wimmer and Hartl was not in their procedure with Kasperl, but in a new task they devised known as the state change, shown in the figure overleaf. The experimenter opened the lid to reveal the expected content of Smarties™ and proceeded to remove these from the scene, only to replace them with pencils. All this was done in full view of the child. Finally, the experimenter asked precisely the question presented in a standard deceptive box task: "When you first saw this tube, before we opened it, what did you think was inside?" In responding to the question, over 80% of children aged 3 and 4 years answered correctly with "Smarties." In

Key Term

State change:
A task employing a box that has characteristic content (e.g. Smarties™ tube) in which the normal content exists to begin with but is then replaced as the child watches with an atypical content.

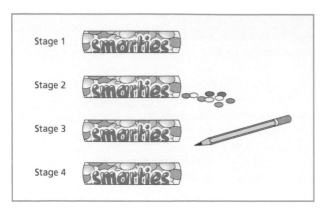

Stage 1

Stage 2

Stage 3

Stage 4

The state change task has an additional stage compared with the deceptive box task. After the child has seen the exterior in Stage 1, the experimenter opens the lid to confirm the expected content.

sharp contrast, members of the same sample who were tested on a standard deceptive box task, in which the tube contained a pencil all along, were much worse: Only around 40% gave a correct judgment; the rest reported the current content of pencils.

The beauty of the state change is that it helps to narrow down the exact basis of children's difficulty. As mentioned already, some take the view that children's wrong answers on the deceptive box task stem from a superficial misunderstanding of what they are being asked: Perhaps children misinterpret the experimenter to be asking what is inside the tube right now. If that were the case, then surely children would answer wrongly to the same extent in state change as in the deceptive box. After all, the current content is identical in both, and so is the question. It would thus be hard to explain why children interpret the question correctly on one occasion but misinterpret on another. Evidently, we need a more convincing explanation of why children have so much trouble with the deceptive box task. Another virtue of the state change is that it neatly demonstrates that young children's difficulty does not lie with poor memory. They easily remember Smarties™ in at least one of the tasks, so it seems memory failure cannot be put forward to explain errors in the other.

It still needs to be explained why children did find it so easy to give a correct judgment in state change. Wimmer and Hartl suggest that they give a correct judgment actually for the wrong reason. They argue that if young children really lack a concept of belief, then they would face a dilemma when asked a question that includes the word "think" or any other reference to thought. When asked what they thought was inside, they might thus be expected to assume a blank expression and remain mute. As we all know, that is not characteristic of young children! Indeed, it is quite striking that young children seem so highly inclined to talk and communicate, even though it must frequently be the case that they respond to utterances containing unfamiliar words making reference to unfamiliar concepts. In another sense, though, it would be just as surprising if they did not engage in communication with only partial understanding; if they did not, then presumably they would be destined to remain mute forever. Young children thus seem comfortable engaging in communication even with partial understanding.

If we accept that point, then the question to be asked of state change, and indeed the deceptive box task, is what form does their partial understanding take? Wimmer and Hartl had a simple answer to this question. They propose that young children who have no concept of belief would simply treat the question as if it did not contain the word "think." Hence, "What did you think was inside?" would be interpreted as "What was inside?" The answer to that question in a deceptive box task is "pencils," while the answer in state change is "Smarties." The contrast in the pattern of judgments between the deceptive box and state change, coupled with Wimmer and Hartl's clever argument, makes a compelling case in support of the suggestion that young children have a deep-seated difficulty with the concept of belief that cannot be explained as

Does a young child's understanding of the mind undergo a radical conceptual shift?

a superficial linguistic misunderstanding. Although misunderstandings might explain part of the difficulty, there is more to the story.

Yes, young children have been underestimated!

It turns out, though, that Wimmer and Hartl's argument is wrong. This was demonstrated in a test devised by Saltmarsh, Mitchell, and Robinson (1995), shown in the figure below. They showed children a Smarties™ tube and asked them to guess what was inside. After children had replied, "Smarties," the experimenter opened the lid to reveal the unexpected content of a toothbrush. As the child watched, the experimenter then removed the toothbrush right away from the scene and replaced it with pencils. Finally, the experimenter asked the observing child participant what she had thought was inside when she first saw the box. If Wimmer and Hartl had been right about 3-year-olds lacking a concept of belief, then they would answer this question with "toothbrush," because they would interpret "What did you think was inside?" as "What was inside?" However, the most common response was for children to report the current content of pencils. Under another condition, the children were asked explicitly to recall what was inside at the beginning, and nearly all replied correctly with "toothbrush." If Wimmer and Hartl had been right, then children would have given the same answer to both questions, but they did not. In sum, Wimmer and Hartl's prediction failed on two counts. First, it was uncommon for children to report the first content of the tube when asked a "think" question. Instead, they tended to report the current content. Second, they answered a "think" question quite differently from the way they answered a similar question that did not contain "think."

The problem facing us is how to explain children's success in giving a correct answer in Wimmer and Hartl's original state change procedure, now that it seems their account is inadequate. The most obvious possibility is that when children give a correct judgment in state change, they do so for the right reason. In other words, perhaps children genuinely give a judgment of belief. In that case, why should they have so much difficulty with a deceptive box task? An important difference between the two tasks is that in the state change but not in the deceptive box, children's initial belief of Smarties™ is made concrete and salient. Perhaps this makes it more accessible. Alternatively, is it simply that children's difficulty is confined to the case of false belief? Recall that state change is a test of prior true belief.

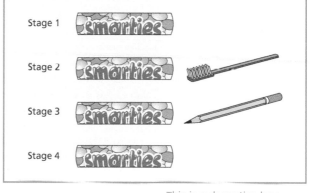

Stage 1

Stage 2

Stage 3

Stage 4

It seems we need a procedure that incorporates the crucial ingredients of state change that ensaliates the initial belief and makes it concrete, but that is actually a test of false belief. A test that fits the requirement is the mailing procedure, devised by Mitchell and Lacohee (1991) and shown in the figure overleaf. Children were shown the Smarties™ tube and as usual guessed that it contained Smarties™. They were then invited to select a picture of what

This is a deceptive box with a succession of two unexpected contents. It is similar to state change except for Stage 2, where an unexpected content appears instead of the expected content.

Key Term

Mailing procedure: A false belief test in which children mail a picture of the false belief into a mailbox before learning that the belief is actually false; the mailed picture serves as an aide memoir to the false belief.

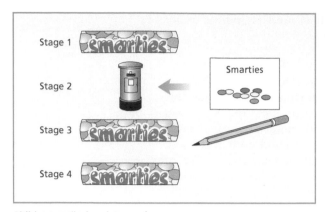

Children mailed a picture of what they thought the tube contained in Stage 2.

they thought was inside from a set of alternatives and all appropriately identified the picture of Smarties™. Next, the children were asked to mail this picture into a special mailbox, where it remained hidden from view until the end of the procedure. Meanwhile, the experimenter opened the tube to reveal that really it contained pencils and then returned them to the tube as usual. Finally, children were asked a modified question: "When you mailed your picture, what did you think was inside this tube?" While only around 20% of the sample answered correctly in a standard deceptive box procedure, over 60% answered correctly in the novel mailing procedure.

How did the mailing procedure help children? Is it possible they gave the right answer for the wrong reason? Perhaps they misunderstood the question, thinking the experimenter was asking not what they thought was in the Smarties™ tube, but to report what they thought was inside the mailbox. Why else would the experimenter make reference to the mailing if they were not supposed to say something about the mailed picture? If this was the basis of correct judgments, the findings would be totally uninformative about what they understand of beliefs. Fortunately, we are able to eliminate this explanation, thanks to a control condition. In the control, the procedure was the same, except children were not asked to select and mail a picture of what they thought was inside the tube, but to mail a picture of their favorite cartoon character. Children dutifully did this, and at the end of the procedure, they were asked exactly the same question posed in the procedure in which they mailed a picture of Smarties™: "When you mailed your picture, what did you think was inside this tube?" If children misinterpreted this to be a request for information about the mailed picture, a tell-tale sign would be a reply of "Mickey Mouse," or whoever was their favorite cartoon character! It so happens, though, that not a single participant answered that way.

Another possibility is that because the mailing question pinpointed the exact moment in time (when you mailed your picture), the time reference was sufficiently clear for children to understand precisely what they were being asked. The implication is that children do not have a deep-seated difficulty with false belief, but only a superficial linguistic misunderstanding of the kind suggested by Lewis and Osborne and also Siegal and Beattie. The time reference was equally precise in the cartoon mailing as in the Smarties™ mailing procedure, so if this explanation is correct, then children should have been helped just as much by the cartoon mailing. However, correct judgments were uncommon in the cartoon mailing and in fact were no better than in a standard deceptive box procedure that did not involve any kind of mailing. It seems we are left with the conclusion that having an evidential basis to their belief was sufficient for children to give a correct judgment.

Although the mailing procedure seemed to help children give a correct judgment of belief for the right reason, performance seemed not to be as good as in the state change procedure, where over 80% of children made a correct judgment. This could be due merely to sample differences, but another possibility is that the state change is more potent in helping children, perhaps because it requires a judgment of true belief. That question motivated Saltmarsh *et al.* to conduct further studies to investigate whether true beliefs really are easier to acknowledge than false ones. The research involved two steps, the first of which was a small modification to Wimmer and Hartl's basic state change. Children participated alongside Daffy Duck, and as in the classic state change, the tube contained Smarties initially, but these were swapped for pencils as the child and Daffy watched. Finally, children were asked what they thought was inside and also what Daffy thought was inside. As would have been anticipated by Wimmer and Hartl, they answered both questions correctly with "Smarties."

Although introducing Daffy in this first step of the research did not generate any new findings, it did create an opportunity to carry out a further step that had potential to provide a very important insight into the basis of children's success in state change. In this next step, Daffy departed from the scene after initially seeing the pristine and apparently unopened Smarties™ tube. The child participant then saw that the tube did indeed contain Smarties™, which were subsequently replaced with pencils. Finally, Daffy returned and children were asked what Daffy thought was in the tube right now. Due to Daffy's absence, of course, he had not seen the usual content exchanged for pencils, so he held a false belief. Interestingly, children found it just as easy to acknowledge Daffy's current false belief as they did to acknowledge his past true belief. Under another condition, the procedure was the same except that the tube contained pencils all along. This time, very few children gave a correct judgment; they either wrongly stated that Daffy thought there were pencils inside first of all or that he thinks there are pencils inside right now. Hence, it was not the truth of the belief that counted, and neither did it matter whether the belief concerned oneself or another individual. Rather, what mattered most was whether the belief was seen to have an evidential basis in reality.

IS DEVELOPMENT STAGE-LIKE?

A survey of the findings from a large number of articles published on children's difficulty acknowledging false belief confirms that most children below the age of 3 years wrongly tend to report what they know as reality, while children aged 4 years and above stand a better chance of setting aside what they know of reality (Wellman, Cross, & Watson, 2001). Modifications to the task sometimes help young children, but these modifications do not eradicate errors altogether. Clearly, acknowledging beliefs is extremely difficult for young children, perhaps not because they lack the requisite concept but because false beliefs in particular seldom have an evidential basis. If that conclusion is correct, then it has very serious implications for the character of development. As mentioned at the beginning of this chapter, some researchers had assumed that the sharp improvement in correct judgments over a fairly narrow age range implied that a new concept of belief is acquired at around the age of 4 years. If it turns out to be wrong, however, and if children simply come to rely less on physical evidence in making judgments of belief, then it seems development is not stage-like after all. If development is not stage-like, then two indications to this effect might be apparent. One is that young children would be able to acknowledge false belief under the right conditions, and the evidence presented already is consistent with that. On the other side of the coin, we might expect to find too heavy reliance on the evidential basis in the judgments of belief made by older individuals and even adults in some circumstances.

Surprisingly, evidence to this effect has been around for a long time, but its significance has not been fully appreciated. The seminal work was done by Fischhoff (1975), who investigated the intriguing phenomenon of hindsight bias. Adult participants were told about a historical battle between British and Gurkha armies that took place a couple of centuries ago. The participants were apprised of various factors that might advantage one or other army. For example, the Brits were well disciplined, well organized, had excellent equipment, and good logistics. On the other hand, the Gurkhas knew the terrain intimately, had numerical superiority, and were renowned for their bravery and courage. The participants had to weigh up the advantages that favored each army and then make a judgment on who they thought would have the best chance of winning. Additionally, participants were told of the actual "outcome" but were instructed to put that information out of their minds when arriving at a judgment. Despite the instruction, it became apparent that the participants simply were unable to ignore what they were led to believe was the true outcome. Those told that the Brits actually won tended to judge on balance that they thought the Brits had the best chance. Those told that the Gurkhas actually won tended to judge that the Gurkhas had the best chance.

In another investigation, Fischhoff presented the same information but asked participants to assess how another person would predict the outcome of the battle. Supposedly, this other person too was apprised of all the information pertaining to factors that advantaged one side or the other. Crucially, only the participants themselves were told the privileged information on which army was victorious. Participants advised that the Brits actually won judged that the other person would predict a British victory, while participants advised that the Gurkhas actually won judged that the other person would predict a Gurkha victory. Seemingly, participants were not merely suffering from a hindsight bias; rather, they were having difficulty acknowledging false belief because their knowledge of reality contaminated their judgment of belief. This was true when estimating their own belief as well as when estimating another person's belief.

Converging evidence in support of this conclusion was obtained by Mitchell, Robinson, Isaacs, and Nye (1996). They showed adult participants a video about a couple of protagonists, Kevin and Rebecca. The scene was their kitchen. On the shelf stood a conspicuous jug and Kevin noticed that it contained orange juice. A little later in the day, Kevin and Rebecca were together in their kitchen preparing lunch, whereupon Kevin volunteered to prepare the beverages. Rebecca then announced that there was milk in the jug. At this point Kevin was the victim of conflicting information. He had seen juice in the jug but now was told that it contained milk. The observing participants were invited to judge what Kevin now thought was inside the jug. Obviously, there is no right or wrong answer. Although we might suppose that people believe what they see in preference to what they are told, in this case things were not equal. Rebecca's utterance was the most recent information, so it is

Key Term

Hindsight bias:
Believing that you had known something all along even though in fact you only made the discovery recently.

possible that although the jug used to contain juice, it now contained milk. Nevertheless, a large majority judged that Kevin thought the jug contained juice. In itself, this finding is hardly newsworthy, but it assumes considerable significance when considered in the context of the strikingly different judgments made by participants in a comparison condition.

In the comparison condition, participants were told precisely the same information, plus they were told that Rebecca had poured out the juice and replaced it with milk. Effectively, these participants were told that Rebecca's utterance was true. However, it was made abundantly clear that this was privileged information, available only to the participants and not shared with Kevin the protagonist. Despite that edict, participants simply could not help but be influenced by their knowledge of the true content of the jug. Nearly all in this comparison condition judged that Kevin would believe the jug contained milk. Effectively, their judgment of the believability of Rebecca's utterance was massively contaminated by whether they knew it was true. Putting it another way, it seems participants were inclined to report their own knowledge of the current content of the jug when asked about Kevin's belief.

It is almost bizarre that adults have difficulty making objective judgments of belief in some contexts, while children aged 3 years in other contexts succeed in acknowledging belief. In the light of this possibility it seems inappropriate to say categorically that adults but not young children are able to distinguish between their own and other people's beliefs. Rather, it seems that children and adults differ in the context in which they need evidential support in order to set aside knowledge of their own belief. In most (but perhaps not all) contexts, young children tend to err by reporting their own current belief. Adults also are inclined to report their own current belief in contexts in which they are not equipped to determine for sure what another person believes. Interestingly though this may not be true for all cultures. In Mitchell *et al.*'s (1996) task participants are asked to judge whether someone else would believe what they saw in preference to a verbal message, in other words, it taps into the old adage that *seeing is believing*. A study by Mitchell, Souglidou, Mills, and Ziegler (2007) tested participants from rural areas who scored highly on a measure of interpersonal trust and those from urban areas who scored low on trust measures. Participants who scored highly on trust were more likely to judge that Kevin would believe the verbal message, but those who scored low on trust predicted that he would disbelieve the verbal message and believe what he saw. This difference between cultures in reasoning about the mind might reveal that we use our own disposition to make judgments about others' states of belief and suggests that culture is related with subtle aspects of understanding the mind and especially how people evaluate messages.

Further evidence that passing a test of theory of mind is not the endpoint of development comes from other studies with adults. Keysar, Barr, Balin, and Brauner (2000) presented participants with a shelf full of objects. Participants were asked to move some of these objects by a director who was positioned on the other side of the shelf. Whilst all the objects were in full view of the participant, the construction of the shelf meant that the director could not see some of objects and participants were fully aware of this, having even inspected the layout from the position of the director. On the critical test trials the director's instructions required that participants take into account which

Is the development of children's understanding of the mind stage-like?

objects the director can and cannot see in order to correctly identify the object he refers to. For example, if there are two tapes, one visible to both and one visible to the participant only, then the tape that should be moved is the one visible to both. Interestingly though participants made a high proportion of egocentric errors, by reaching for objects only they could see. Although all the participants could pass a test of false belief, this was not in itself enough to correctly reason about others' mental states on all trials. It seems then that having an understanding of others' minds and using that understanding are not the same thing!

WHAT CAUSES DEVELOPMENT?

It might be that development unfolds spontaneously, through a process of maturation, as in the development of secondary teeth and puberty. Although maturation might contribute to development, it would be strange if social experience did not figure in an important way. Understanding about the essential features of the mind is relevant only in the social arena, so it is to be expected that social experience would feed into this understanding. What kind of social experience in particular is likely to be significant? A child's first relationships are likely to be with parents and with siblings. What characteristics of the parent might be involved in children's development in understanding the mind?

How important are relationships in children's developing understanding of the mind?

Cole and Mitchell (1998) investigated environmental factors that correlate with the ability to pass tests of understanding about belief in children aged 3 and 4 years. Some of the children in the sample seemed to underperform, and they were the ones who had mothers who stated that they were experiencing a great deal of hardship and distress. The children of single parents who expressed such difficulties were most likely to be disadvantaged. It is possible that the social hardship experienced by these mothers might have affected the quality time they could spend with their children, which in turn might have put the children at a disadvantage in understanding about other people. Alternatively, it might be that hardship created a distraction for the mothers that prevented them from giving optimal attention to their parenting.

A fine-grained analysis of beneficial parenting was conducted in a longitudinal study by Dunn, Brown, Slomkowski, Tesla, and Youngblade (1991). They observed mothers interacting with their toddlers when aged 33 months. There were clear individual differences between the mothers in how they related to their children. Some provided a narrative on the actions of people or on the characters in pretend scenarios, embroidered with abundant references to psychological motives. For example, they might comment that Daddy is looking in the kitchen drawer for the chocolate because he thinks it is there and that he did not see it being moved to the fridge. In contrast, some mothers gave a commentary on Daddy's futile search for his chocolate but without making reference to what he thinks. It was not so much that these parents avoided using the word "think." They did use it, but not to explain behavior. In consequence, children of these parents did not hear much in the way of psychological explanations of human behavior.

When the observations of parental speech were made, the children were too young to stand any chance of being able to pass a test of false belief. Six months later, though, the researchers returned, this time to assess the children rather than the parents. The researchers presented a test devised by Bartsch and Wellman (1989), as follows. The children witnessed a story enacted with small dolls, concerning the protagonists John and Susan. Susan cut herself while playing, so John rushed off to get a Bandaid (sticking plaster). It so happened, however, that the Bandaid box was empty, and the contents had been put into a plain white box. The observing child participants had previously seen that the Bandaid box was empty and were privy to the true location of the Bandaids. They were also led to believe that the protagonist John had not been enlightened about this.

The enacted story continued with John heading to the Bandaid box. As he approached, and just before he opened the empty box, observing child participants were invited to explain why he was going to the Bandaid box. Some children, but not others, were able to give what was judged to be a sensible and coherent explanation of John's behavior with appropriate reference to his psychological states. For example, they commented that he is going to that box to look for a Bandaid. When asked explicitly what he thinks is in the box, these children replied with "Bandaids." When asked if there really were Bandaids in the box, the children correctly stated that the box was empty. Other children, in contrast, showed less fluency and insight by failing to give any coherent explanation of why John was going to the Bandaid box. When asked what John thinks is in the box, these children tended to say he thought nothing was in there.

The individual differences between the children coincided reliably with individual differences between the interactional style of their parents as observed 6 months previously. The parents who had been observed to give explanations of behavior to their children with reference to psychological causality had children who showed greatest insight into the psychological basis of John's futile search for a Bandaid. The parents who seldom referred to psychological causality had children who seemed at a loss to explain John's futile search. These results confirm the commonsense notion that parents, whether or not deliberately, can be effective tutors of their children's understanding about the mind. Dunn *et al.*'s study seems to present results that fall within the spirit of the Vygotskyan idea of scaffolding mentioned in the previous chapter. The parents of the most competent children created a framework to support the concepts of psychological causality, which the children apparently assimilated and then applied effectively to a range of tasks to explain behavior.

Dunn *et al.*'s (1991) longitudinal study showed that individual differences in the way that mothers related scenarios to their children would later impact upon the child's ability to comprehend psychological causality.

If Dunn *et al.*'s results lend support to Vygotskyan social constructivism, which does not necessarily rule out the possibility that development could profit from cognitive conflict of the kind suggested by Piaget, where would the opportunity for cognitive conflict lie? Children living in large families, with lots of siblings, face the formidable challenge posed by sibling rivalry in competing for attention and favor. It is little more than a statement of the obvious to say that sibling interactions can sometimes be heated. Coming to terms with siblings while not losing out in the share of available resources is a considerable feat that must be on a par with the most robust crash course in diplomacy! Intuitively, it thus makes sense to suppose that a child with several siblings would swiftly need to gain insight into the psychological working of his or her brothers and sisters.

Although a simple intuitive prediction is that having more siblings should promote understanding of the mind, the picture becomes complicated when considering the implications of a survey conducted by Zajonc (1983). He investigated the relation between the measured intelligence of children and the characteristics of their family. Two findings from this research are especially striking. The first is that children with few siblings tend to gain higher scores on tests of general intelligence than children with many siblings. Indeed, there is a reliable relation between the number of siblings a child has and the score they gain on a test of intelligence. The other interesting finding is that birth order is also related with measured intelligence. The first born tends to gain a higher score than the second born, who tends to gain a higher score than the third born, and so on.

To explain these provocative findings, Zajonc suggested that the cognitively beneficial effect of the parent's influence would be distributed ever more thinly as the number of children in the family increased. This suggestion might have serious implications for the effect of siblings in the development of an understanding of the mind. Since understanding the mind probably has its place in more general aspects of intelligence, we might expect that as general intelligence is given less opportunity to be expressed by having lots of siblings, so the intelligence needed to understand about minds in particular might be disadvantaged. This suggestion makes further sense when we consider Dunn *et al.*'s conclusion that parents who explain psychological causality to their children actually promote their children's understanding of the mind by doing so. Presumably, a parent with lots of children has little time to provide elaborate explanations of the psychological basis of human behavior to each and every one of her children.

Zajonc (1983) suggested that the cognitively beneficial effect of parental influence was inversely proportional to the number of siblings within the family.

In sum, there are some reasons for thinking that having siblings would benefit a developing understanding of the mind, and there are other reasons for thinking that having siblings might indirectly hamper such understanding. Perner, Ruffman, and Leekam (1994) carried out the much-needed survey to obtain the relevant evidence. The results suggested that 3-year-old children who had siblings were more likely to pass a test of false belief than those of the same age but without siblings. Moreover, those with several siblings stood a better chance of giving a correct judgment than those with just one or two siblings. A further study, by Jenkins and Astington (1996), clarified things a little further. The apparently beneficial effect of having siblings was narrowed to the older siblings. Children who only had younger siblings were no better at acknowledging false belief than those with none at all, but those with older siblings did show the kind of advantage reported by Perner *et al.*

At this point, with but a small qualification, the findings seem to provide support for the Piagetian view that a clash of perspectives is sufficient to promote development. However, a study by Lewis, Freeman, Kyriakidou, and Maridaki-kassotaki (1996) suggested that such a conclusion would be too simplistic. In a cross-cultural study that included Greek families, the researchers took into consideration a wide range of factors concerning family structure, and were not content just to have details of siblings. Lewis *et al.* confirmed that children with siblings were at an advantage in acknowledging false belief compared with those without. They also established that the advantage was stronger among those with older siblings than those with younger ones. The most important discovery, though, was that another social factor was even more strongly related with children's success in acknowledging false belief: The more adults that the child interacted with on a daily basis, the more likely it was that the child would acknowledge false belief. By coincidence, it also turned out that the more siblings a child had, the more he or she was likely to interact with many adults on a daily basis. The authors concluded that what really counted was contact with adults, and that, purely by coincidence, the number of siblings a child had happened to be associated with that. So it was not the siblings that were important, but the adults. On balance, it seems that the results support the Vygotskyan view that development best proceeds when there is beneficial support available from more competent others, maybe including older siblings but certainly including adults. There is little support for the possibility that experiencing a cognitive clash of the kind described by Piaget is especially profitable.

COMPETENCE IN DECEPTION

From a very young age, children have some insight into the mind. In particular, they seem to understand that people's simple factual beliefs feature in determining behavior. Children usually develop abilities for good reason, so we might ask what purpose an understanding of the mind serves. One advantage is that it helps us to communicate effectively, and especially to interpret what other people say. We shall consider this point in more detail in the chapter on the development of communication (chapter 13). Another spin-off from understanding about the mind is that it would give more insight into how to carry out deception.

Consider the common experience of a toddler playing hide-and-seek, covering her eyes and then declaring that she cannot be seen! It seems that such a young toddler is capable of confusing not being able to see you with you not being able to see her. Presumably, such a toddler would not be equipped to carry out convincing acts of deception. On the other hand, parents sometimes suspect, for good reason, that their toddler is telling lies. The trouble with investigations of deception is that if the deception is really effective, then presumably it would be impossible to detect! A study by Lewis, Stanger, and Sullivan (1989) was ground-breaking in exploring this aspect of deception. They led children aged 2 and 3 years into a room in which a large sheet shrouded a hidden object. The experimenter declared that there was a toy zoo underneath the sheet, but that the children were strictly forbidden to look until later. The experimenter then left the room for a few moments, ostensibly to attend to an urgent matter, but really to present children with an opportunity to disobey by peeping under the cloth. A hidden camera monitored children's surreptitious actions, and revealed that nearly all did take an elicit peep.

When the experimenter returned, she asked the children if they had peeped under the cloth. About a third admitted that they had, but two thirds attempted to conceal their misdemeanor: A third of the children resisted owning up by refusing to answer. The remaining third told a blatant lie by insisting that they had not looked when in fact they had. These lies would be worse than useless if they were transparent. If adults discovered every time the child told a lie, then presumably she would end up in very deep water indeed. It is one thing to tell a lie and quite another to do it successfully. Lewis *et al.* had the data to determine just how convincing those children were who told lies. They edited the video footage to isolate the children who denied that they peeped when they had not peeped and those who denied that they peeped when in fact they had. They then presented the resulting video to a panel of adults who were ignorant of the details of the study. Their briefing consisted only of a statement that all the children were denying having done a forbidden act and that some of them were telling lies. The panel's task was to assign a rating to each child on whether they thought he or she was lying. On seeing the varying degrees of nervousness of the children, the adults felt that the task was fairly straightforward and proceeded to assign scores with reasonable certainty. Each child thus accrued a score that represented the sum rating from the panel of adults. Surprisingly, however, the rating assigned to those who were telling lies was no different from that assigned to those who were honest. Although the adults may have felt they could decide who was lying and who was honest, in fact they could not. In sum, those who told lies were convincing.

Knowing how to deceive does not necessarily mean that one would be able to enact the deception in a convincing manner. Indeed, a child who had a deep understanding of how their mother is being misled on a serious matter might suffer hideous pangs of guilt that would be impossible to conceal. There are two components to deception, then. One rests upon an understanding that other minds hold beliefs, with the implication that those beliefs are manipulable by feeding misinformation. The other rests upon the ability to simulate a convincing expression of sincerity. Cole and Mitchell (1998) investigated the relation between these two abilities by testing children on a range of standard tests of false belief and a test of convincing acting. The acting involved telling another person that what they knew to be a nasty lion from the movie *The Lion King* was really a nice lion. Children were implored to persuade this other person as much as they could that the nasty lion was actually rather nice.

The children's efforts at persuasion over something they knew was untrue were videoed and the resulting footage was shown to adult raters. The raters were instructed to assign a score to children according to how sincere they appeared in asserting that the lion was nice. Interestingly, the children who were judged to appear most sincere performed least well on the standard tests of false belief. It might be that those who understand the psychological implications of their deception feel most inhibited, perhaps because of guilt pangs, in enacting deception. Presumably, those who did not understand the psychological implications of deception would, as a consequence, not be equipped to experience the associated guilt.

Being effective in deception depends not just on the insight that people can hold false beliefs and on convincing acting, it also rests upon having a repertoire of strategies for misleading. These strategies were explored by Chandler, Fritz, and Hala (1989). In their study, children aged 2 and 3 years witnessed a doll navigate to one of four plastic garbage bins where she deposited some loot. In doing so, her aim was to hide the treasure from a second experimenter who had left the room temporarily while the hiding took place. Unfortunately for the doll her effort was thwarted by the trail of tell-tale inky footprints left in her wake, revealing the actual garbage bin that she visited. The experimenter directed the child's attention to the conspicuous physical evidence of the doll's movements and reminded the child that the second experimenter would soon return to look for the treasure. Children were asked if they had any ideas on what could be done to prevent the second experimenter finding the loot. A cloth was conveniently placed nearby and very many children promptly picked it up and proceeded to rub at the footprints and thereby erase the evidence. The experimenter congratulated children on their clever idea and asked if they could think of anything further to prevent the second experimenter finding the treasure. Many proceeded to take control of the doll and led her from base to an empty garbage bin, so that she left a false trail of footprints. The authors concluded that because deception has a potentially useful value, this is an arena of functioning in which we are likely to be able to find especially precocious insight into the mind. Chandler *et al.*'s children seemed to hold the insight that manipulation of information can lead another person to think something untrue such that it would obstruct them in finding prized treasure.

Chandler *et al.*'s study has aroused a certain amount of controversy over whether young children are underestimated by standard tests of false belief. Chandler *et al.* insist that children have been underestimated, by pointing out that competence is more apparent in tests of deception, while others such as Sodian, Taylor, Harris, and Perner (1991) contest that claim. Sullivan and Winner (1993) also suggested that early competence might be revealed in studies on deception. In their procedure, children were shown a Smarties™ tube, and that it contained Smarties™ as expected. Children were then encouraged to remove the Smarties™ and replace them with a pencil in order to fool the experimenter's assistant who had left the room briefly. Under this "trick" condition, children were more likely to anticipate the assistant's false belief than under a condition in which the tube contained a pencil all along and there was no aura of trickery. Sullivan and Winner concluded that the element of trickery was sufficient to attune the children to the assistant's state of false belief.

"I can't see you, therefore you can't see me!"—Chandler *et al.*'s (1989) study suggested that toddlers have some competence in deception, more than we might have expected from their rather poor performance on a traditional test of false belief.

Their result is open to an alternative interpretation, however. Saltmarsh and Mitchell (1998) pointed out that it might have been the state change rather than the deceptive narrative that helped children to succeed in acknowledging the assistant's false belief. That is, the children saw the true content of Smarties™ initially only in the deceptive condition, so it might have been this, rather than the deceptive motivation, that helped them. To find out, they repeated Sullivan and Winner's procedure but had a state change with and without deceptive narrative and also an ordinary deceptive box with and without deceptive narrative. They found that when a state change was involved, children were advantaged in acknowledging the assistant's false belief, irrespective of whether it was accompanied by deceptive narrative. In contrast, the presence of deceptive narrative in itself did not help children. Although young children may be proficient in deceptive strategies, as shown by Chandler *et al.*, having a deceptive narrative in a deceptive box task seems to give no further advantage.

DO INFANTS ACTUALLY UNDERSTAND FALSE BELIEFS?

We asked earlier in the chapter whether young children's competence might have been underestimated when assessing their understanding of beliefs and the mind, and found to some degree that it had. However, in spite of many modifications that we make to the unexpected transfer test, or other tests of false belief and mental state understanding, it appears that children at 3 years old fail such tests and those over the age of 4 years old tend to pass. Most theories of how understanding of the mind develops and what it means to have such an understanding focused on the results from work with this very narrow age range. About the same time that research drifted away from this age range to test the higher end of competence in adults (e.g. Birch & Bloom, 2007; Keysar, Lin, & Barr, 2003) and older children (Friedman & Leslie, 2004), evidence also began to emerge that perhaps infants who are much younger than 4 years old actually understand beliefs. The false belief tasks used with children had been seen as a reliable test of children's competence, and lack thereof, with understanding beliefs. All of the tasks we have described so far in this chapter rely heavily on the verbal component, for example, telling a story about John and finding chocolate or having expectations on what containers may contain and being able to express something about our own mental states when we find that they have an unexpected content. As 3-year-olds failed these tests and seemed to reveal their lack of understanding of minds, there seemed little point in testing children even younger, especially as they clearly would not be able to cope with the verbal element. However, other methods can be used to test preverbal infant understanding, and we encounter these methods in other chapters in this book, for example the violation-of-expectation and anticipatory looking paradigms (for a detailed explanation of this paradigm see chapter 8). Using the violation-of-expectation looking paradigm, Kristine Onishi and Renée Baillargeon provided some of the first evidence of what looks like competence in mind-reading in infants who are only 15 months old. Onishi and Baillargeon (2005) created a version of a false belief test that does not rely on understanding stories or verbal messages or require an explicit response. In their nonverbal task, infants watched an agent put an item in one of two boxes. In the false belief trial an occluder appeared, which meant that the infant, but not the agent, could see that the object moved from the location it was put to the other location. The occluder is then removed and the agent reaches into the box that was the original location of the object and is thus consistent with their (false) belief, or they reach into the box that the object is now located in, which is consistent with what the infant knows, but not consistent with the agent's false belief. Onishi and Baillargeon found that infants looked significantly longer at scenarios where the actor reached for the object in its actual location. This indicates that infants *expect* actors to search for objects consistent with their beliefs about the object location. This seems a truly astonishing capacity in such young children, and we are now tasked with explaining such early competence. The first objection might be that this result is a blip, perhaps to do with the specific procedure used, and what we need to know is that infants will reliably show such patterns of performance in a variety of tasks. Since Onishi and Baillargeon's ground-breaking study, much converging evidence from other paradigms points at infant competence in 25-month-old infants (Southgate, Senju, & Csibra, 2007) and 13-month-old infants (Surian, Caldi, & Sperber, 2007) and the evidence might seem to point at early infant competence with understanding that behavior is motivated by beliefs and that the mind is a mediator of reality. However, it is extremely difficult to reconcile this early competence in nonverbal tests of belief understanding with the pattern of performance in later childhood when 3-year-olds fail a verbal test of false belief. Mitchell, Currie, and Ziegler (2009, and also Luo & Baillargeon, 2010) propose that the difference might be explained by the additional demands made in the verbal false-belief task of having to give an explicit response about where someone will look for an item, rather than reveal competence implicitly through eye movements. The extra demands of having to give a response can be managed by the 4-year-old child, but not the 3-year-old, nonewithstanding their implicit understanding of the task. This would still credit infants with competence to a degree, but not with a full understanding of beliefs. Other theorists have taken the view that nonverbal false belief tasks actually do not require infants to track an agent's belief and the content of that belief, but that infants only have to track object locations and the agent's attitude to those object locations (Apperly & Butterfill, 2009). This leads them to expect the agent to reach into the nonobject location, without having to represent the content or structure of the belief. Such representation of beliefs is, however, required when solving the more complex verbal false belief tasks. Apperly and Butterfill propose that infants have a minimal theory of mind, but only develop a full representational theory of mind later. This idea of two complementary systems is reminiscent of thoughts on number development which we will encounter in chapter 8, and offers a reasonable explanation of much of the infant literature. Time will tell whether it can explain new and emerging evidence.

Summary

- Children's early insight into the workings of the mind is striking and remarkable. They have a wealth of understanding that would not have been conceived by Piaget, and the evidence gathered over the past three decades refutes his claim that young children are egocentric. It is probable that children are born with the rudiments of an understanding of minds, but that early social experiences feed into this to promote a rapid development of surprisingly early competence. A widely held view is that children's development takes a quantum leap at about the time of their fourth birthday, whereupon they acquire an understanding that minds hold beliefs. However, some research suggests that development is probably gradual rather than stage-like, and that the kinds of factor that influence children's judgments of beliefs are probably the same that affect adults. It seems that beliefs that have an evidential basis are a good deal easier to grasp both for children and adults. Some of the earliest signs of competence are in the insights children have about the way people fall victim to deception. More recent research has shown that infants might understand something about the mind, whereas adults do not always make use of their theory of mind in social interactions. The debate on whether infants actually understand anything about the mind is far from resolved, but this debate, together with a focus on points later in development and adulthood, has given the research a much needed fresh impetus.

- We probably take for granted our insights into mind, just as we take for granted our ability to talk and to walk. We are quite wrong to take these abilities for granted, however. There are some individuals who find it profoundly difficult to understand other people's minds, and they are severely socially debilitated as a consequence. Those individuals are diagnosed with autism, a perplexing developmental disorder that forms the subject of Chapter 7.

Essay Questions

1. Assess the claim that children at the age of 4 years old undergo a radical conceptual shift in understanding minds.
2. How can we explain failure to pass a test of false belief?

Further Reading

- Doherty, M. J. (2007). *Theory of mind: How children understand others' thoughts and feelings*. Hove, UK: Psychology Press.
- Apperly, I. A. (2011). *Mindreaders: The cognitive basis of "theory of mind"*. Hove, UK: Psychology Press.

Chapter 6

Contents

Developmental disorders

6

Chapter Aims

- To describe features of various developmental disorders.
- To consider the extent to which developmental disorders have a genetic basis.
- To explore the prevalence of various developmental disorders.
- To examine the interrelationship between different kinds of developmental disorder.

INTRODUCTION

Developmental disorders might be apparent in some form in one out of every ten children (Boyle, Boulet, Schieve, Cohen, Blumberg *et al.*, 2011). This chapter describes but a selection of developmental disorders and is not in any sense exhaustive. Some of these disorders have a known genetic basis, such as Fragile X; some are inherited, like Williams syndrome, but some are not, like Rett's syndrome, Down's syndrome, and cerebral palsy. Some of the disorders have a *putative* genetic basis, such as autism and ADHD. In other words, researchers assume that these disorders are genetic because of circumstantial evidence: They run in families and your risk of having the same disorder when another member of your family also has the disorder depends on how closely you are related.

Even though these disorders have a genetic basis, the development of the child will depend considerably on the environment, which will include nutrition, quality of living space, and having socially and intellectually stimulating experiences. Probably we cannot claim to be able to cure the disorders but at least we can intervene to give the child the best possible chance of adapting to their condition and developing optimally.

How children develop depends a great deal on attitudes toward disability that prevail in society. Some decades ago, even in developed countries, parents felt a sense of shame and embarrassment at having a child who suffered a developmental disorder. Being unaware of the genetic or organic basis of

Key Terms

High functioning autism:
Autism with measured intelligence in the normal range.

Asperger's syndrome:
Having the features of autism but in the absence of language delay.

developmental disorders, these parents sometimes felt that their child's failure to develop typically was somehow a reflection of their inadequacy as a parent. Many therefore tried to hide the child from public view by keeping the child at home and by not taking the child out shopping or to the playground. On one level we can empathize with these feelings but possibly this action compounded the difficulties already faced by the child and made it even more difficult for them to thrive developmentally. Besides, it would be quite damaging to the child's self-esteem to be allowed to think that they were somehow not good enough to meet or be seen by other people.

Times have changed and modern society is much more accepting of developmental disability. Indeed, legislation was passed in 1995 in the UK (The Disability Discrimination Act 1995), dictating that education authorities have a duty not to discriminate, thus ensuring that disabled children have opportunities that are comparable to those who do not have disability. The greater openness, awareness, and willingness to engage with disability has coincided with an increase in the number of diagnoses of developmental disorders in recent years. It is unlikely that developmental disorders are more common now than they used to be; rather, the increased awareness of developmental disorders has probably resulted in the increase in clinical referrals and the consequent increase in diagnoses. The following sections summarize some of the more widely known disorders (as well as a few that are less well known) that are of particular psychological interest.

AUTISM

A fairly common and quite well known developmental disorder is autism and this is covered in some detail in the next chapter. The disorder is described in detail in Frith (2003), and the following is a summary. People with the disorder have core impairments in communication, social ability, and imagination.

They also tend to lack common sense and tend to develop a special interest and then focus on this to the exclusion of most other things. People with autism seem to prefer routines and seem not to like unpredictable events. Many with a diagnosis have learning disability, especially language delay, but some have measured intelligence in the normal range and no sign of language delay. These individuals are classified as having high functioning autism or Asperger's syndrome. According to a study published in *The Lancet* (Baird *et al.*, 2006), autism in its broadest sense occurs at a rate of about 1:100 of the population; previously, it was thought that autism was much rarer than this.

One of the characteristics of autism is the tendency to develop a special interest in something, and then focus on this to the exclusion of most other things.

Over the past three decades a substantial amount of research has investigated autism and we have gained a better understanding of its causes, its features, and methods of intervention. The research has also helped to dispel some myths about autism. For example, an early theory posited that the disorder is caused by an aspect of the social environment—emotionally cold parenting (Bettelheim, 1967). This is not true. Actually, it seems autism has a genetic basis, such that certain combinations of genes increase the risk that the child will develop autism. The environmental condition that interacts with the genetic predisposition is complicated and not fully understood (Pickles *et al.*, 1995). But at least there is no basis for saying that autism is caused by emotionally cold parenting. We also know that autism is not caused by combined measles–mumps–rubella (MMR) immunization. Only one badly controlled study suggested such an association. Subsequently, a large number of high quality investigations have been unable to detect any association between MMR and the development of autistic features (Goodlee, Smith, & Marcovitch, 2011). Because autism is a well known disorder that has been thoroughly researched, the following chapter is dedicated to it; the current chapter offers a summary of some of the other developmental disorders of psychological relevance.

ATTENTION DEFICIT HYPERACTIVITY DISORDER (ADHD)

ADHD occurs in around two or three percent of children, with twice as many boys as girls. Children with this disorder seem to have difficulty focusing their attention on a particular task; instead their attention shifts rapidly from one thing to another, thereby preventing concentration on any one thing. Many parents are inclined to think that such behavior is caused by diet, particularly food additives. Carefully controlled research corroborates this view (McCann *et al.*, 2007), in which children aged 3 and 9 years consumed a drink containing preservatives and artificial colors. Children often became hyperactive, and this was more evident than when they had consumed a placebo—a similar drink that did not contain any preservatives or artificial colors.

What are the core symptoms of ADHD?

Is it the case, then, that ADHD is caused by bad diet? No, not entirely. The features of ADHD have a genetic basis. We know this from studies in which the features of ADHD are measurable across members of a family. The closer you are genetically to a person with ADHD, the more likely you are to exhibit the same features of ADHD. The level of correlation between genetic relatedness and severity of the features leads to the estimate that ADHD is 75% heritable (Saviouk *et al.*, 2011). In that case, how can we explain the association between ADHD and food additives—an environmental factor? For sure, ADHD is not completely caused by genetic factors; rather, it seems that some children are genetically vulnerable to developing ADHD, and environmental risk factors, such as diet, might have greater impact on these children than on children who are not genetically vulnerable to ADHD.

Despite the genetic predisposition for ADHD, the condition is currently diagnosed not by analysis of the child's genetic complement but by behavioral features that are listed in the 2013 edition of the Diagnostic and Statistical Manual of the American Psychiatric Association (DSM-5). In this respect, the diagnosis of ADHD is similar to that of some (but not all) of the other developmental disorders, including autism, specific language impairment, and pragmatic language impairment. It is different from other developmental disorders, like Fragile X, Williams syndrome, and Down's syndrome that are diagnosed according to genetic analysis.

Key Term
Placebo: An inert substance that has no active ingredient.

The core features of ADHD are inattention, hyperactivity, and impulsiveness.

The core features of ADHD are inattention, hyperactivity, and impulsiveness. Inattention and impulsiveness can also occur in adults with frontal syndrome, which is caused by damage to the frontal lobes of the brain. The frontal lobes developed quite recently in evolutionary history and this part of the brain is notably well developed in humans compared with other species. It is a part of the brain involved in controlling mental activity, a process known as executive function. In consequence, it appears as though children with ADHD have underdeveloped executive functions (Barkley, 1997). It also appears that children with ADHD have difficulty with delayed reward or gratification, which could explain their impulsivity and unwillingness to wait patiently for their turn in games. This is different from the explanation that is based on underdeveloped executive functions, in that it explains the disorder at a motivational rather than a cognitive level. Evidence for cognitive impairments associated with executive dysfunction as well as evidence of impaired motivational processes can be measured in ADHD (Sonuga-Barke, 2005).

Inattention in ADHD presents itself in various ways, including lack of responsiveness when we talk to the child. A teacher or parent might feel that the child is rude in ignoring us. Apparently, though, the child does not have good aptitude for controlling his attention in order to be responsive to communication from other people. And yet paradoxically the child might easily be distracted by other stimuli, such as extraneous noise in the classroom. The child will also have difficulty maintaining attention to a task, will lack patience, and will rapidly switch attention to something else that impinges. Children with ADHD tend to be forgetful, perhaps because they are not processing information deeply at the time of encoding. This could work against memory traces being established in the sense that children with ADHD do not concentrate well on the tasks they are engaged in; as a result they are error prone and make careless mistakes.

Hyperactivity in ADHD is evident in various ways, perhaps most notably in that children seem to have an internal dynamo that compels them to constantly expend energy. They find it almost impossible to sit still: They fidget, run about the room, and climb on chairs, tables, doors, windows, and anything else that can be climbed. These children talk inexhaustibly, requiring a sympathetic, selfless, and patient listener.

Impulsivity manifests as severe impatience, for example unwillingness to wait in a queue or to wait for a turn in games. The behavior can appear quite insensitive to others who are waiting quietly and in an orderly way, but some with ADHD seem not to be troubled by this. Children with ADHD also tend to be poor at controlling emotions and might display levels of rage, fear, surprise, and euphoria that are uninhibited. Similarly, these children sometimes behave in ways that are dangerous to themselves, harmful to others, or seriously socially inappropriate, apparently because they are behaving without considering the consequences.

How should ADHD be treated? A medical tradition has been established whereby some children with ADHD are treated with Ritalin, a stimulant drug whose effects are similar to amphetamine and cocaine. Children with ADHD seem naturally over-stimulated and it is counter-intuitive that the symptoms are treatable with a stimulant drug. The basis of the drug treatment is not founded in theory and the drug's efficacy is hard to explain. Nevertheless, it does seem that Ritalin is capable of helping some children to become less rather than more active. The question of whether drug therapy is preferable to therapy based on changes in diet accompanied by behavior training is the subject of ongoing discussion.

TOURETTE SYNDROME

Several TV documentaries have famously shown teenage boys with Tourette syndrome barking profanities, lewd expletives, and racist utterances to nonplussed passersby. These cases are the most extreme forms of the disorder; the more common signs of Tourette syndrome are tics, such as repeated blinking, throat clearing, stereotyped facial movements, vocalizations, shoulder shrugging, shouting, and so on. As with ADHD, this developmental disorder is associated with impairment in executive function. In consequence, children tend to be impulsive and distractible. Indeed, children with Tourette syndrome are at risk of developing the broader features of ADHD (Denkla, 2006).

Tourette syndrome is assumed to have a genetic basis and is found in about 1% of the population. As with many developmental disorders, it is more common in boys than girls, with a ratio of about three-to-one. The onset of symptoms is usually early to middle childhood, averaging between 7 and 10 years of age. The most severe symptoms appear during adolescence and early adulthood, often followed by gradual decline in severity.

In addition to co-occurring with ADHD, Tourette syndrome sometimes co-occurs with obsessive-compulsive disorder (Baer, 2001). The disorder is diagnosed according to criteria listed in DSM, meaning that a clinician makes a diagnosis following her observations of the child's behavior rather than with a genetic test. The symptoms (tics) need to be present for at least one year for a positive diagnosis to be made. This is to ensure that any throat clearing, eye blinking, or other symptom is not caused by a different problem, such as atmospheric variations in the levels of pollen or the development of poor eyesight.

FRAGILE X

This disorder, occurring at the rate of 1 per 3600 males, has a genetic basis in the form of abnormality in the X chromosome. The normal composition of sex chromosomes in males is XY, and when there is abnormality in the X, there is no compensating structure in the Y to minimize the impact of the abnormal X. In the case of Fragile X, this causes underdevelopment in aspects of intellectual growth as well as a characteristic appearance (amongst other things). Boys tend to have a long, thin face and large ears. They sometimes are double jointed, have poor muscle tone, and an undeveloped foot arch.

Fragile X is associated with some aspects of impaired neurological development. This leads to difficulties in intellectual and social functioning. In many ways, the psychological features of Fragile X are similar to those of autism and indeed, children with Fragile X are at risk of developing autism (Brown, Jenkins, Friedman, Brooks, Wisniewski *et al.*, 1982). In particular, we see difficulty in focusing and holding attention, coupled with hyperactivity, as in the case of ADHD; associated with this, children with Fragile X have difficulty holding in mind verbal or linguistic information, more so than with visual information. Repetitive behavior is common, and so is sensitivity to

Key Terms
Obsessive-compulsive disorder: A clinical disorder associated with compulsive ritualistic behavior and obsessive cleanliness such as incessant hand-washing and aversion to touching things that have been touched by another person (e.g. coins).
DSM: Diagnostic and Statistical Manual of the American Psychiatric Association. This manual lists features of various psychological disorders.

tastes, sounds, touch, and visual stimuli. In some cases there is evidence of obsessive-compulsive tendencies. There is a distinctively uneven intellectual profile in Fragile X: Verbal intelligence lags behind spatial abilities, combined with impaired attention and heightened sensitivity to stimuli. Generally, Fragile X is associated with impaired executive function, suggesting that the frontal lobe of the brain is underdeveloped.

Social development in those with Fragile X is also impaired in various ways. Children typically experience high levels of social anxiety, have unusual and perhaps reduced eye contact, and they are impaired in interpreting facial expressions in some cases. Those with the disorder appear to be rather slow at processing emotional cues from other people, and they are generally slow in conversational turn-taking. In consequence, children with Fragile X have considerable difficulty forming relationships with other people. Partly, this is because they are neither comfortable nor effective in engaging with people and partly it is because other people sometimes find it not very socially rewarding to spend time with people who have Fragile X. This is similar to what happens in cases of autism and ADHD.

Fragile X cannot be cured at present, though effective schooling and sensitive parenting can help children to adapt to the disorder and to adapt to living in the community. This process of adaptation is also greatly assisted if the community itself is educated and understands some of the features of developmental disorders. Specifically, it is important to give children with Fragile X time to respond and not to hurry them in their social interaction. And it is important to be patient when the child seems not to focus or sustain attention as well as a child who does not have a developmental disorder.

RETT'S SYNDROME

This is a fairly rare genetic disorder in females, affecting one per 12,500 of the population. Despite being a genetic disorder, it is not inherited but rather occurs through spontaneous mutation on the X chromosome. The disorder is not normally seen in boys because the mutation in an individual who only has one X chromosome (i.e. boys) is not compatible with life. In the case of girls, the compensating characteristics of the intact X chromosome often enable the individual to survive. The disorder can vary from mild to severe, depending on the level of mutation on the affected X chromosome. The disorder is degenerative and progressive, meaning that the individual might develop more severe symptoms with increasing age. This is because the chromosomal abnormality affects the balance of the chemistry of the brain in a way that negatively impacts upon normal neurological growth. In consequence, girls with the disorder tend to have an abnormally small head, a symptom that becomes more apparent with increasing age.

Development in many cases will be normal until 6 to 18 months. Problems will then become apparent when the child is slow to begin walking and talking. Most notably, the child with Rett's syndrome is unlikely to develop socially as rapidly as a child without the disorder and will probably not make normal eye contact. An associated feature is lack of social responsiveness, including lack of imitation, lack of smile, and lack of gaze following. Other features include poor coordination and even loss of the ability to walk in children who had previously mastered the skill. Problems with the digestive system are also likely. With respect to delayed social development, children with Rett's syndrome tend to have poor communication, lack social responsiveness, and make eye contact in an unusual way.

What are the similarities and differences between Fragile X syndrome and Rett's syndrome?

DOWN'S SYNDROME

Like Fragile X, Down's syndrome is a chromosomal disorder. In this case, there are three instead of two chromosomes at site 21 and hence the disorder is also known as trisomy 21. It occurs in one per 1000 children and there is higher risk among children of older mothers. Children with the disorder tend to have thyroid abnormalities and in consequence stunted growth; they also have a small head with round face, small chin and large tongue. Health problems are common, including heart abnormalities, impaired lung function, digestive problems, and vulnerability to ear infections. In middle life, individuals with Down's syndrome are at much higher than average risk of developing neurological disorders associated with advanced years, such as Alzheimer's disease.

The social and intellectual development in children with Down's syndrome is quite distinct. It is common for children with the disorder to be affectionate and to relate effectively with other people and to show a fair level of interpersonal sensitivity and awareness; despite that, children with Down's syndrome typically experience delay in speech, language, and the muscle control involved in fine and skilful movement. While the IQ of children varies, it is common to see moderate to severe learning disabilities. The problem with language development could be secondary in some degree to problems with hearing and problems with speech production. Any child who cannot hear well and who is unable to discriminate speech sounds will be slow in learning language. The problem is compounded in Down's syndrome by a speech impediment caused by an abnormally large tongue and by lack of the fine control needed to form the sounds of speech. Despite hearing impairments, children with Down's syndrome tend to have much better language comprehension than speech production. While the same is quite often true in children who are developing typically, the disparity can be quite distinct in Down's syndrome.

It is common practice in many developed countries for children with Down's syndrome to be included in mainstream education, where they will probably be placed according to their chronological age. So long as teaching provision is adequate, such an arrangement seems to work well, especially in the early years of education. In the later years, the intellectual gap between typically developing children and those with Down's syndrome can widen. This is because children with Down's syndrome not only tend to have developmental delay but their rate of development also tends to be slower than that of their typically developing peers. Providing the teaching provision is adequate, there can be many benefits to including children

It is common for children with Down's syndrome to be affectionate and to demonstrate interpersonal sensitivity and awareness.

with Down's syndrome, and indeed children with other developmental disorders, in a mainstream classroom: It can foster understanding and adaptation among typically developing children; it can help the self-esteem of children with a disorder to find that they are accepted and understood by typically developing peers.

TURNER SYNDROME

This is a disorder found exclusively in girls that, as with Fragile X, is associated with aberration in the sex chromosomes. In this case, girls are endowed with one X chromosome instead of the normal complement of two. It occurs in one per 2500 females and is associated with various physical features. These include stunted growth but with relatively overdeveloped upper torso and in some cases a webbed neck in the form of a fold of skin from the shoulder to the head, giving the appearance of an unusually short neck. The syndrome is associated with infertility, heart disease, sensory impairment (especially hearing and vision), under-activity of the thyroid gland (which normally has a role in physical growth and development), diabetes, and general vulnerability to illness.

In most cases, girls with Turner syndrome do not have marked learning disabilities and can function well in a normal educational setting. Subtle impairments can be evident though, especially in spatial and mathematical abilities. In some girls with Turner syndrome there are signs of impaired social understanding, somewhat similar in kind, though very much milder, to what we see in autism (Skuse *et al.*, 1997).

WILLIAMS SYNDROME

This is a genetic disorder caused by truncation in one of the chromosomes (Chromosome 7), and occurs at the rate of about 1 per 10,000 of the population. The disorder leads to a distinctive appearance: Fragile and underweight, giving the impression of large eyes, coupled with a low bridge of the nose and widely spaced teeth. Children with the disorder are disposed to smile liberally, showing rather small teeth and large gums. These features combine to give an elfin-like appearance. The disorder is associated with an underdeveloped circulatory system and aberrations in the heart. Children with the disorder are also vulnerable to secondary disorders of the digestive system and there is evidence of hormonal abnormalities. Neurological problems are typical and these are responsible for general learning disabilities but the profile in some respects is quite different from that seen in other developmental disorders.

In many of the disorders we have considered so far, children have delayed language and social development, but spared functioning in the visuo-spatial arena. Williams syndrome seems to be the opposite. Children are distinguished by apparent sociability. They make sustained eye contact, even with strangers, they have a friendly and socially engaging disposition. But children with Williams syndrome are not known for being adept in their visuo-spatial abilities. They have very poor memory for the configuration of physical environments and little aptitude for finding their way around any place they happen upon, such as a school or supermarket. In short, they seem to have an affinity for the social world but not for the physical world.

How is Williams syndrome different from autism?

Williams syndrome is quite different, then, from autistic disorders, which are typified by affinity with the physical world but lack of affinity with the social world. A comparison between Williams syndrome and autism informs us that disorders that impact upon intellectual development (as is typical of both of these disorders) need not lead to the same kind of features. The human mind thus seems to be composed of a collection of faculties and we see instances of the social faculty being delayed or impaired, whilst faculties for understanding the physical world are spared—and we see the reverse of this pattern too, depending on the particular developmental disorder in question.

CEREBRAL PALSY

What are the features of cerebral palsy?

This disorder occurs at the rate of around two or three per thousand of the population. The most striking feature is very poor movement control, caused by damage to the cortex of the brain, especially the motor cortex which is located in the frontal lobes (Rapp & Torres, 2000). There is also likely to be damage to the connections between the motor cortex and the cerebellum, which sits below the base of the back of the brain. The disorder is not progressive, meaning that poor motor control does not become worse over time. Having said that, in one sense living with the disorder becomes more problematical because as we grow older we are expected to develop our skills quite considerably. Having cerebral palsy presents a considerable barrier to this kind of development and quite a big gulf develops between those with and without the disorder, especially in the teen years. Nevertheless, thanks to brain plasticity, spared areas are able to take on the activities that otherwise would have been served by damaged areas (Taft, 1995).

The most prominent feature of cerebral palsy is very poor movement control, caused by damage to the cortex of the brain. Therapy and walking aids, for example, can help improve motor control.

Although cerebral palsy is most notably a disorder of movement, it is also associated with problems with vision, especially depth perception. A person with this disorder might have other sensory problems as well, including hearing impairment and heightened sensitivity to touch (Fennell & Dikel, 2001). Speech impediments are also common, primarily due to poor motor control of facial muscles and lack of breathing control. Indeed language delay can be marked for these and other reasons, including hearing impairment and more general learning disability. But there is considerable variation in the intellectual functioning of people with this disorder and some are well above average (Jenks *et al.*, 2007).

Approximately a third of those who suffer with cerebral palsy are at risk of epileptic seizures (Zafeiriou, Kontopoulos, & Tsikoulas, 1999). The occurrence of these seizures is in itself a sign of cerebral damage. The seizures can begin from the first year of life and are more likely in children who have more severe cerebral damage. The seizures can be life-threatening but can be controlled to some degree with appropriate medication.

Unlike several of the developmental disorders described in this chapter, cerebral palsy is not genetic or chromosomal in origin. In many cases, it is caused by an event that led to shortage of oxygen in the brain (Nelson & Grether, 1999). This could be associated with problems with the blood flow in the placenta or it could be associated with trauma during birth. Premature birth is another factor that puts the baby at risk, where the lungs do not function so efficiently with the consequence that the supply of oxygen to the brain is

▍Key Terms

Cerebellum:
A structure located at the rear of the brain that has a role in generating fine movements.

Brain plasticity:
The capacity for unaffected parts of the brain to assume the activities of damaged parts of the brain.

insufficient. Following birth, various other factors can put the baby at risk, such as choking or nearly drowning.

The symptoms of cerebral palsy, especially poor movement control, can be treated with occupational therapy. Secondary problems can develop, caused by using the limbs in a way that is not well adapted. This can place strain on joints and can cause muscles to develop abnormally. Some of these secondary symptoms can be treated by surgery when appropriate. Generally, cerebral palsy can vary from mild to severe and the developmental outcome, and indeed the quality of life, will considerably depend on severity.

LANGUAGE DISORDERS

The most common disorders are associated with aspects of communication and literacy. *Specific Language Impairment* (SLI) occurs in about 7% of the population and is more likely to affect boys than girls. It is a disorder of speaking that is not explained by hearing impairment and is not explained by acquired brain damage. There could be a subtle neurological abnormality that accounts for the disorder. The disorder is apparent in children's delay in mastering basic features of grammar. For example, a child with SLI might have difficulty forming the past tense or the plural form of verbs. They might also have difficulty in using grammatical articles such as "a" and "the," where they might use the article wrongly or neglect using it altogether. In addition to difficulties in grammatical aspects of language production, children with SLI also have difficulty comprehending language spoken by other people. Hence the disorder affects receptive as well as expressive language.

Pragmatic Language Impairment (PLI), sometimes called "semantic-pragmatic disorder," presents as a disorder in the social use of language and occurs in about 7% of young children. Children with this disorder might talk excessively or talk about unsuitable topics. Eye gaze might be unusual, as well as body posture and gestures. The child is likely to have difficulty understanding the meaning of common words, and yet might be acquainted with obscure words in instances of hyperlexia. For example, the child might have a vast vocabulary of dinosaur names and yet have an underdeveloped grasp of common labels of emotion and psychological states like *desire*, *disgust*, *anxiety*, *fear*.

In addition to underperforming in the social and communicative use of language, children with PLI sometimes have difficulty in basic aspects of language production. Pauses are notable, while the child searches for words, even ones that are fairly common. There are instances of echolalia, during which children seem to automatically echo words or phrases that are spoken to them. We also see pronoun reversals, where children refer to themselves as "you" and to others as "me"; and similarly we see instances of word-order errors, along with word category errors, as in a child who confuses nouns with verbs. Echolalia and pronoun reversal also occur in autism and indeed PLI can co-occur with autism. But it does not necessarily follow that a child who has the core features of PLI will inevitably warrant a diagnosis of autism.

Developmental dyslexia is perhaps the most well known of the language disorders. Children who have this disorder have marked difficulty in reading and in spelling that is not explained by generally poor ability. Indeed, some children with dyslexia can have good abilities in other areas of functioning and

Key Terms

Hyperlexia:
An unusually large vocabulary, relative to developmental level, especially on a particular topic (e.g. species of dinosaurs).

Echolalia:
Meaninglessly repeating words or phrases that you just heard.

Pronoun reversals:
Confusion over whether *I* should be denoted as *I* or *you*.

yet struggle inordinately with written language. As with many developmental disorders, it is far more common in boys than in girls.

Developmental dyslexia is different from acquired dyslexia, sometimes called alexia. The latter results from specific brain injury and while developmental dyslexia also has a neurological basis, this does not result from specific injury. Rather, developmental dyslexia has a genetic basis and research is making progress in determining precisely which genes are involved. Despite having a genetic basis, dyslexia is also influenced by environmental factors, notably the characteristics of one's first language. To understand this, we need to distinguish between written languages that are transparent and those that are not transparent. A transparent language is one where the letters that form words have consistent pronunciation, allowing us easily to give the correct pronunciation of words that we have not seen previously.

Developmental dyslexia is marked by a difficulty in reading and spelling that is not explained by generally poor ability.

Italian and *Japanese* are both transparent languages. English, in contrast, is not. For example, the combination of letters *ch* is pronounced quite differently in the word *church* than in the word *yacht*. And the letters *gh* are pronounced differently in the word *cough* than in the word *through*. The incidence of dyslexia in a population differs depending on whether the language spoken by that population is transparent or not transparent. For example, there are few instances of dyslexia in Japan. In Italy there are some instances of dyslexia, but fewer than in countries where English is the national language, such as the USA. In a country where the language is not transparent, the incidence of developmental dyslexia might be around 10% of the population (Lindgren, Renzi, & Richman, 1985).

Is developmental dyslexia due to genetics or environmental factors or both?

There are various clues in the speech of children who are dyslexic. They struggle to learn the alphabet despite putting in lots of effort. They also might confuse left with right and before with after. They typically struggle to identify how many syllables are in a word and to find rhyming words. Also, they struggle to learn the sounds of individual letters, have difficulty identifying the constituent sounds in words, and have difficulty discriminating between the sounds of different letters. Many of these features might lead us to think that the child has hearing impairment and yet in dyslexia we see these various features even in children with good hearing.

Dyslexia is associated with stuttering and difficulty in recalling words, or word pauses. It is also associated with lack of fine control, especially in the form of poor handwriting. This is evident in the slow speed of writing as well as in the poor ability to form letters and words effectively. Indeed, some children with dyslexia can be quite clumsy generally, suggesting that the cerebellum, a part of the brain involved in the fine control of movement, is not working properly.

Are left-handed children at greater risk of having dyslexia than children who are right-handed? Folklore at least seems to say that handedness is associated with dyslexia and on one level one can understand why there might be such a

> ### Key Term
>
> **Alexia:**
> Dyslexia that is acquired, perhaps during adulthood, following neurological damage caused by accident or illness.

Are left-handed children at greater risk of having dyslexia than children who are right-handed?

link. The language centers of the brain are usually located in the left hemisphere, known as Broca's area (language production) and Wernicke's area (language comprehension). The left hemisphere is also dominant where handiness is concerned, in that most people are right-handed. Moreover, the part of the cortex that is responsible for motor control is located close to the area associated with language production. Hence, in the minority of individuals where the right hemisphere is dominant (leading to left handedness), one might wonder if that impacts upon the functioning of the area responsible for language production.

An article by Rodriguez, Kaakinen, Moilanen, Taanila, McGough *et al.* (2010) reveals that, in fact, things are not quite so simple. First, left-handed people are not at greater risk of having disorders associated with language development: When the language centers are established in the right hemisphere, this does not in itself make the individual vulnerable to developmental disorders. Most right handers and left handers are united in having unilateral hemispheric dominance—in one case the left hemisphere is dominant and in the other case the right hemisphere is dominant. In contrast, some people, maybe 1% of the population, are devoid of unilateral hemispheric dominance and these are also at great risk of developmental disorder, including language disorder but especially attention deficit hyperactivity disorder. The study by Rodriguez *et al.* revealed pervasive difficulties in such individuals, spanning childhood and adolescence.

Which developmental disorders are associated with impairment in the executive function?

Summary

- The material presented in this chapter summarizes the various features of different developmental disorders and shows how several disorders have some features in common. Some of the disorders have an established genetic basis while some have a putative genetic basis, but all disorders are bound to present differently depending on experiences and the form of the environment. Some of the disorders are rare and some are relatively common, and this chapter offers specific information about their prevalence.
- Many of the developmental disorders described here have overlapping features and as far as symptoms are concerned it is difficult to argue that they are truly distinct from one another. On a genetic level, one can identify the sense in which Fragile X is different from Rett's syndrome, but some of the behavioral features might be very similar. In particular, it seems that many of the disorders are associated with underdeveloped executive abilities, impaired social responsiveness, and underdeveloped abilities in language and communication. These are some of the most recent abilities to have evolved in humans and perhaps it is not surprising then that they are among the most fragile and most easily disrupted.

- In recent years, modern society has made great progress in no longer trying to conceal developmental disorders as a taboo subject. This growing willingness to acknowledge and engage with developmental disorders is associated with considerable improvements in approaches to education for children with special needs and also to the provision made by the health service to offer diagnosis and support. Legislation has been established in many developed countries, including the UK and the USA, to ensure that children with developmental disorders have adequate access to special education and that their needs are adequately covered by the health service. These changes have led to much improvement in the quality of life not only for the affected child but for his or her family too.

Essay Questions

1. Discuss the possibility that genes and environment work in combination in the progression of certain developmental disorders.
2. Compare and contrast the characteristics of three developmental disorders.

Further Reading

To find out more about cutting-edge research in various developmental disorders, try:

- Howlin, P., Charman, T. & Ghaziuddin, M. (Eds.) (2011). *The Sage handbook of developmental disorders: Science and practice*. London: Sage.

Chapter 7

Contents

Autism

7

Chapter Aims

- To describe autism, outline criteria for diagnosis and supply information on how common it is.
- To introduce the theory of mind hypothesis of autism.
- To introduce the theory that people with autism suffer inflexibility in thought process.
- To introduce the theory that people with autism have difficulty integrating information into a coherent whole.

INTRODUCTION

There are three distinctive and defining features of autism: (1) Impairment in social behavior and relatedness to others; (2) Impairment in verbal and nonverbal communication; (3) Narrowing of interests coupled with resistance to change. Wing and Gould (1979) identified these features as the triad of impairments that are the hallmark of autism. These are the features that guide a clinician when deciding whether or not a diagnosis of autism is warranted.

Autism is diagnosed according to the constellation of characteristically abnormal behaviors. In this respect, the identification of autism is different from other disorders in childhood such as Down's syndrome. The latter is diagnosed according to a chromosomal abnormality. Although Down's syndrome is associated with a certain psychological profile, including learning difficulties and an affectionate disposition, an individual who had normal intelligence and who was not especially affectionate could still receive a diagnosis of Down's syndrome. The distinctive chromosomal abnormality is sufficient for a positive diagnosis, no matter what the psychological profile. In contrast, autism is diagnosed exclusively according to psychological profile. But it does not mean that autism is purely psychological. There is probably a physiological basis to autism, which is likely to take the form of abnormality or damage in a certain part of the brain. At present, we do not know for sure where the abnormality is located or what form it takes.

Just as the physiological basis of autism remains a mystery, so the causes are not fully understood. One possibility is that there are multiple causes. What matters might be damage to a particular site in the brain, rather than how that damage came about. Just as paralysis could be caused by injury, such as a fractured skull, stroke, or genetic abnormality where part of the brain fails to

Key Term

Triad of impairments: Impairments in socialization, communication, and imagination, which are characteristic of autism.

develop normally, so autism could have multiple causes. There is an important difference, however. Whereas paralysis could occur later in life, that would not be true of autism. An individual who has autism will have had it from the beginning. It seems that the brain abnormality responsible for autism prevents development in the spheres of social behavior, communication, and openness to having a variety of interests. Once those developments have already occurred, they probably cannot be reversed by brain abnormalities that are acquired later in life.

Like Down's syndrome, but unlike certain disorders such as schizophrenia, there is no prospect to date of finding a cure for autism. This does not mean that people with autism remain equally debilitated throughout life. On the contrary, those with autism usually adapt to their condition to some degree, just as those with damage caused by stroke can develop new strategies to compensate for the old ones lost through damage. Neither is autism a progressive disorder, unlike multiple sclerosis or motor neurone disease, in which the individual deteriorates over time.

Autism used to be regarded as a rare disorder, affecting fewer than 1 per thousand of the population, but rates of diagnosis have increased and it now seems that the incidence of autism (at least in its broadest form) stands at around 1 per hundred of the population (Baird *et al.*, 2006). It is not entirely clear why rates of diagnosis are increasing, but a concomitant decrease in diagnosis of children with general learning disabilities suggests that clinicians are being more inclusive in diagnosing autism. Additionally, more children are being diagnosed who do not have accompanying learning disability. In previous years, suspected learning disability would have been the principal reason for clinical referral, whereas now, with growing awareness of autism, even children who do not have accompanying learning disability are likely to be referred if they present with severe social impairment.

Many more boys than girls tend to be diagnosed with autism and the ratio stands at 4:1. There is a broad spectrum of autism from mild to severe, where the mild forms include Asperger's syndrome. This is diagnosed in individuals who have characteristically autistic social impairment but who have no accompanying language delay.

Autism was first recognized as a disorder in its own right in the 1940s. It was identified independently by Leo Kanner working in the USA and Hans Asperger working in Austria. Both hit upon the name "autism" to mean social detachment or social nonintegration. The cases Kanner identified were rather severe, while Asperger identified individuals with both severe and mild forms of autism. Hence, those affected mildly tend to be diagnosed with Asperger's syndrome. Just because autism has been defined fairly recently, it does not imply that it is a new disorder, like AIDS. Autism has probably been around pretty much forever, and biographies of maladapted children such as the Wild Boy of Aveyron in the nineteenth century are evidence for the existence of autism well before the label existed (Frith, 2003). Earlier in the twentieth century, it seems that some with autism were diagnosed as having childhood schizophrenia. This label now seems wholly inappropriate when considering that core symptoms of schizophrenia, such as delusions, are thought not to occur prior to adolescence.

The poster published by the UK National Autistic Society for nonspecialists and parents (reproduced opposite) gives some idea of autism. It illustrates

Key Term

Asperger's syndrome: Having the features of autism but in the absence of language delay.

characteristic behaviors, and perhaps helps us to appreciate what autism is not. Autism is not an appropriate label for learning difficulties of a general nature. For example, it would be uncommon for a child with Down's syndrome to receive a diagnosis of autism. A child with Down's syndrome is very likely to have general learning difficulties but probably would not have the more specific kind of impairment that characterises autism. Autism, then, is a special kind of intellectual impairment.

Poster illustrating some of the ways in which autism is displayed. Copyright © 2012 The National Autistic Society. Reproduced with kind permission.

What are the signs of autism? Children with autism sometimes seem indifferent to others. Although they recognize people they know, they sometimes do not display more familiarity or affection toward them than to a complete stranger. Their indifference is also manifest as a lack of enthusiasm for playing with other children. They might join in with others if coaxed, but do not play as such. Generally, those with autism have a conspicuous impairment in social functioning and exhibit difficulties in verbal and nonverbal communication. The most severe form of disruption to verbal communication in autism is apparent in children who remain either permanently mute or have extremely delayed language and communicative development. Children who do communicate verbally show various peculiarities in their speech. For example, some repeat what they hear as a kind of echo or parroting. Perhaps linked with that, they also show reversal of personal pronouns, where they sometimes address others as "I" and refer to themselves as "you."

More able children who have developed linguistic competence characteristically show subtle forms of communicative impairment, such as talking endlessly and repetitively on a single narrow topic. Their interaction will tend not to be well adapted to the communicative needs of the person they are talking to. For example, there might be blatant signs that the person does not comprehend or is profoundly bored, but a person with autism typically would not notice these clues. Their verbal communication might also be characterized by discordant intonation, monotone, or an exaggerated sing-song manner.

A more subtle peculiarity of autism is a naive honesty and literalness. For example, if we had just washed the car thoroughly and then pronounced it "squeaky clean," a person with autism might be found subsequently with ear pressed against the car striving in vain to hear the squeaking. An individual with autism could be painfully honest in another respect, indeed to a point that could unwittingly upset another person. For example, someone with a salient cosmetic blemish might have it pointed out to them.

Children with autism show peculiarities in aspects of their nonverbal communication as well. Much of their communication is purely used as a means to satisfy some end and in consequence they can be inclined to communicate by physically leading or directing the other person. For example, instead of asking for the door to be opened, the child might tug at the sleeve or hand of the adult and lead it to the door handle, as if the adult's hand is a tool for opening the door. Another peculiarity of nonverbal communication is to be found in irregular eye contact. There is a myth that people with autism refuse to make eye contact but in fact it is the manner of the eye contact that is unusual. People form the impression that those with autism do not look at you but look right through you. Partly, this might arise from an autistic failure to react to the direction of another person's gaze. If you and I are holding a conversation whilst standing in a crowd of people and then someone catches my eye such that I redirect my gaze to one side, then you would probably be able to pinpoint precisely who it is I am looking at purely from tracing the line of my sight. People with autism are not so responsive to this cue (Baron-Cohen & Ring, 1994), which can lead you to suppose that they are not attuned to your attentional focus. In consequence, it might seem they are looking right through you, because they are unresponsive to subtle shifts in your direction of gaze. This might give the impression that they are not psychologically connected with you.

A further characteristic of autism is the narrowing of interests, which can bemuse those without the disorder because the topics very often do not seem to merit deep analysis. For example, people with autism might show a compulsive interest in different kinds of electricity pylon, or in bus routes, rail timetables, or aircraft registration codes. Sometimes this interest can culminate in an encyclopedic knowledge, to the amazement of others. There is another side to this obsessive focus, which is resistance to novel topics. As the National Autistic Society poster suggests, variety is not the spice of life in autism. Accompanying this narrowing of interests is an apparent lack of imagination. Autistic thought seems highly concrete, and the imaginative pretend play of normally developing children is conspicuous by its absence. If we give normally developing children a variety of toys, before long they assign pretend identities and incorporate them into some drama they create. Mundane wooden bricks become space ships, while coloring crayons become aliens that inhabit a distant planet. Apparently, this kind of fantasy play is absent in autism.

Sometimes, the special interests of people with autism can be astonishingly well developed. There are several celebrated cases of children with stunning artistic talents, as in Stephen Wiltshire whose architectural drawing of Tower Bridge was drawn from memory with fine precision after observing the subject matter for only a few minutes. Other people with autism have remarkable ability in calculating calendar dates, and will be able to state accurately what day of the week a particular date fell upon at any point in history. Some can memorize bus timetables to the finest detail, while others can make complex numerical calculations in their heads very quickly. Some are able to learn to read and play music with minimal tuition, while others learn extensively about a foreign language, such as German, just by reading an English–German dictionary.

THE THEORY OF MIND HYPOTHESIS

Alan Leslie (1987) made the astute observation that there could be an important connection between social impairment and the lack of pretence in autism. In a controversial and highly influential article, he proposed that the most basic understanding of other minds would be expressed as pretend play. At its most simple, his argument says that since other minds cannot be perceived directly, it must require a leap of the imagination to recognize the existence of the mind. Anyone who had the kind of imagination powerful enough to do that would probably express this in pretend play also. A child who shows no capacity for pretence therefore might not have the imagination needed to apprehend minds. Children with autism seem devoid of imaginative abilities so an implication is that perhaps they do not understand that minds exist.

Do individuals with autism have an impaired theory of mind?

Leslie's argument about the significance of the absence of pretence in autism is compelling, but it would be even more striking if there were independent evidence showing that children with autism are impaired in their understanding of the mind. In chapter 5 we looked at evidence concerning the development of an understanding that people's behavior is governed by their simple factual beliefs. If children with autism do not understand about the mind, then perhaps this would be evident, amongst other things, as a failure to acknowledge false belief. Baron-Cohen, Leslie, and Frith (1985) conducted a seminal study to obtain the relevant evidence. They adapted the unexpected

Key Term

Sally–Ann task:
A simplified version of the unexpected transfer test of false belief.

transfer test described in the previous chapter and gave it a new name: The Sally–Ann task, as shown in the figure below. This involved a scenario enacted with small dolls. Sally had a marble and she put it in the basket, then departed. In her absence, Ann moved the marble to the box. Finally, the narrator states that Sally is returning to get her marble and the observing participant with autism is asked to predict where she will look, the place she put the marble, or the place it is currently.

Eighty percent of the children with autism who participated in the study failed to take into account Sally's belief by judging that she would look where the marble was currently. This is a very striking result, but perhaps it reveals only that the participants were intellectually immature. Although they were mainly older children and teenagers, if their mental age was equivalent to that of a normally developing child aged 3 years, then the result is hardly surprising. Baron-Cohen *et al.* were acutely aware of this potential impediment standing in the way of clear interpretation, and thanks to this foresight they had assessed participants for intellectual ability prior to the study. Nevertheless, even those with a verbal mental age of 4 years or above had difficulty with the test of false belief. These participants had an intellectual profile that in normal development would have been sufficient to give a correct judgment of false belief.

Still, how can we be sure that children's errors resulted from their autism rather than their more general learning difficulties? If general learning difficulties led to errors in making judgments of false belief, then children with Down's syndrome, who have learning difficulties in the absence of autism, would also struggle with the task. Baron-Cohen *et al.* included a group of

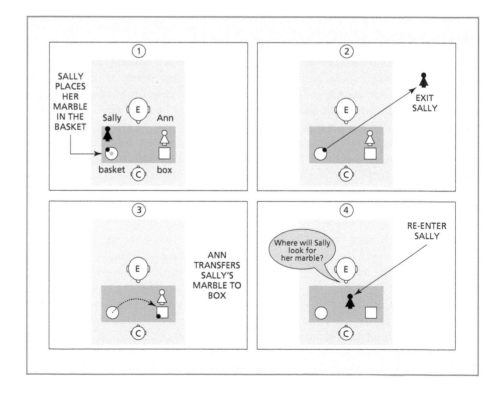

Sally–Ann test of false belief.

children with Down's syndrome, which matched the intellectual profile of those with autism. These participants were able to give a correct judgment of false belief without trouble. There was a statistical contrast between the groups in the sense that those with Down's syndrome performed significantly better than those with autism. Evidently, general learning difficulties and developmental delay do not prevent the child making a correct judgment of false belief.

Although a convincing argument can be made that autism entails a basic lack of insight into the mind, a further qualification needs to be stated about the method used by Baron-Cohen *et al*. De Gelder (1987) pointed out quite correctly that children with autism lack general imaginative abilities. Surely, anyone who lacked imagination would not even be able to follow the Sally–Ann task because it is based on make-believe. Indeed, why should we expect participants to take into account Sally's belief when she is after all just a doll without a mind? Leslie and Frith (1988) came to the rescue with a version of the unexpected transfer task that the participant could be involved in directly, with no need for make-believe. In this study, the researchers Alan and Uta interacted with the participant, during which Alan put a penny under one of two cups. He then left the scene and in his absence, Uta conspired with the participant to move the penny beneath the other cup. Alan was about to return when Uta asked the participant to predict where he would look for his penny. Those with autism showed the same failure to acknowledge false belief by judging that Alan would look in the place the coin was currently. In this task, the unexpected transfer element was built in to what seemed like a fairly normal interaction, yet this seemed not to help them at all. Further supporting evidence came from a study by Perner, Frith, Leslie, and Leekam (1989), who presented a deceptive box task to children with autism. Again, even many of those intellectually able participants with a verbal mental age above 4 years were unable to give a correct judgment that another person would say the tube contained Smarties™. Apparently, children with autism have difficulty acknowledging false belief that does not simply stem from problems they might experience when required to engage in make-believe.

In chapter 5, we saw that having an understanding of the mind equips children to carry out acts of deception, including lies. Sodian and Frith (1992) investigated the ability of children with autism to obstruct an adversary either by sabotage or by telling lies. Their task was to prevent a nasty burglar gaining access to the content of a treasure chest. Depending on the experimental condition, this could be achieved in one of two ways. Either they could lock the treasure chest (sabotage) or, if they were not issued with the key, they could tell the burglar a lie that the treasure chest was locked (deception). The participants with autism proved to be highly effective in sabotage, but not deception. They had no trouble locking the chest and withholding the key, but when asked directly by the burglar whether the chest was locked, they seemed helpless to do anything other than state honestly that the box was unlocked. Apparently, they could withhold the key but not withhold information to obstruct the burglar. It seems that the lack of insight into mind in autism might impair the rather dubious ability to be deceitful.

Critically assess the theory of mind hypothesis of autism.

CAN SOME CHILDREN WITH AUTISM ACKNOWLEDGE FALSE BELIEF?

A few of the children with autism in Baron-Cohen *et al.*'s study gave a correct judgment of false belief. If we define theory of mind as the ability to pass a test of false belief, then how can we reconcile the claim that autism entails lack of a theory of mind with the finding that some of those so diagnosed can pass a test of false belief? One possibility is that those who passed were wrongly diagnosed. But rediagnosis confirms that some children who pass false belief tests do indeed have autism. Another possibility is that perhaps those who passed did not really understand about false belief but somehow just made a lucky guess all the same when answering the test question. Actually, it seems this cannot explain all the instances of success, considering that some children with autism reliably give the correct judgment across a range of tests of false belief (Happe, 1994). A child who is just guessing might get lucky once or twice, but the "guessing explanation" begins to defy credulity once we see children reliably giving a correct judgment over and over again. Besides, there is a strong relation between the likelihood of success on a test of false belief and the child's verbal mental age (Happe, 1995). It would seem odd that those with higher verbal mental ages should have a monopoly on lucky guesses. Rather, it seems much more plausible that the greater intelligence of those who give a correct judgment is actually responsible for their success.

A further study designed explicitly to investigate the relation between verbal mental age and success in acknowledging false belief was conducted by Sparrevohn and Howie (1995). They recruited a sample of children with autism and formed two subgroups that were matched according to chronological age and nonverbal mental age. The two samples did differ, however, according to their verbal mental age. The researchers than presented a selection of tests of false belief and compared the performance between the two subgroups. Participants with higher verbal mental age were much more likely to succeed in acknowledging false belief compared with those of lower verbal mental age. The finding suggests that it is specifically the verbal aspect of intelligence that contributes to children's success in acknowledging false belief.

Why should verbal intelligence in particular be linked with children's success in acknowledging false belief? One possibility is that those who are verbally able are thus equipped to communicate in fairly sophisticated language with other people. Perhaps this opens opportunities to gain insight into other minds denied to those who are either mute or very immature in their oral communication abilities. Being verbally proficient allows children to gain access to a social world that would perhaps be inaccessible to any person who lacked a fairly well developed faculty of language. Communication might allow an opportunity to learn about other minds, an opportunity that comes rather belatedly to individuals with autism who suffer developmental delays in language and communication.

In summary, some children with autism are genuinely able to pass tests of false belief, and this ability is related with verbal mental age. Since verbal mental age increases with chronological age and experience in autism, presumably being able to pass a test of false belief is an attainable developmental milestone, as in normal development. Although development in children with autism might be slow, perhaps they get there in the end. Does this imply that once children with autism achieve a certain level of verbal sophistication, they then have the kind of insights into the mind that you and I possess? If the answer is "no," then how could anyone claim that being able to acknowledge false belief forms the essence of an understanding of the mind?

On one hand, it does seem that children with autism who succeed in passing a range of tests of false belief are more socially able than those who fail such tests. Frith, Happe, and Siddons (1994) conducted a survey in which they presented a questionnaire to people involved in the education and general care of children with autism. The questionnaire included items about social responsiveness and how well the children related to other people. Those who gained the highest score tended to be the same who reliably passed tests of false belief. The picture is somewhat complicated, though. The children judged to be relatively socially able and who passed tests of false belief were not rid of their autism. Although their autism was relatively mild, they were still unquestionably autistic according to the usual diagnostic criteria, and even if errors in diagnosis could explain some cases, it certainly could not explain all. In other words, although it might be possible that gaining insight into beliefs is related with a reduction in the severity of autism, children are not cured.

We now know, then, that difficulty acknowledging false belief is not universal in autism. But what about specificity? Is developmental delay in acknowledging false belief nevertheless specific to children with autism or is this also common in certain groups of children who do not have autism? Seemingly, children with sensory impairment also experience developmental delay in acknowledging false belief even in cases where a diagnosis of autism is not warranted. Minter, Hobson, and Bishop (1998) tested a sample of children with visual impairment with a mental age well above 4 years after developing a suitably modified test of false belief. In this case, participants made a judgment on what another person would think a teapot contained. The participants themselves knew that the teapot only contained warm sand and they also knew that the other person had limited sensory access in only being able to feel the exterior of the teapot. Participants with visual impairment had considerable difficulty acknowledging that the other person would wrongly think the pot contained tea.

Woolfe, Want, and Siegal (2002) discovered a similar developmental delay in some (but not all) children with hearing impairment who had a mental age well above 4 years. They devised a pictorial version of a test of false belief in which participants were asked to judge what a fisherman thought was on the end of his line. The participants had privileged access and could actually see an old boot on the end of the line! Participants who were not natural signers (in other words, who had not learned to sign from the age at which children normally learn language) had great difficulty acknowledging false belief while those who were natural signers performed similarly to children without hearing impairment. The two groups of children with hearing impairment had a similar level of ability in signing at the time of testing, so this cannot explain the difference between the two groups. Woolfe *et al.* suggested that children who were not natural signers were severely disadvantaged during the early years of life when children normally begin to learn about the mind via communication. They added that being denied access to other minds during the early years led to a long-lasting (though presumably not permanent) delay in understating the

Key Terms

Universal:
A characteristic is universal to a disorder if all individuals diagnosed have the characteristic in question.

Specificity:
A characteristic is specific to a disorder providing that individuals with a different disorder don't have the same characteristic.

mind, a delay that was apparent even after children had attained a good level of proficiency in language and communication.

Being able to understand other minds undoubtedly rests upon abilities in language and communication. This is evidently a good explanation for Woolfe *et al.*'s findings and it probably explains Minter *et al.*'s findings. The visually impaired children who participated in Minter *et al.*'s research had difficulty communicating that was brought about by their visual impairment. It was impossible for the children to secure joint visual attention with another person on a thing or event. Consequently, shared topics of conversation, which are typically about things or events, tended to be rather strained, resulting in reduction in quantity as well as quality of conversations. Perhaps the ensuing impoverished level of conversation presented fewer opportunities to learn about the mind, compared with children who do not have sensory impairment.

Difficulty acknowledging false belief is not universal among individuals with autism and now we learn that neither is the difficulty specific to autism. Some groups of children with sensory impairment also have difficulty acknowledging false belief even though they have a mental age above 4 years and even though they do not warrant a diagnosis of autism. Importantly, it seems that a developmental delay in acknowledging false belief might be related with tardy development in language and communication. Indeed, this raises the possibility that delayed communication in autism gives rise to difficulties understanding the mind.

INFLEXIBILITY IN THOUGHT

Which aspects of functioning in autism are beyond the scope of the theory of mind hypothesis?

The theory of mind hypothesis of autism has understandably generated a massive amount of interest. The hypothesis seemed to promise a great deal in the quest to understand and explain this perplexing disorder. And yet one of the most conspicuous and indeed defining features of autism falls outside the scope of the theory of mind hypothesis—namely, mental inflexibility. Ozonoff, Pennington, and Rogers (1991) were among the pioneers in systematically investigating mental inflexibility in individuals with autism. They presented something known as the Wisconsin Card Sort Test, which is as follows. The experimenter is armed with a large pile of cards of different color and with different symbols on each. The participant's task is to sort these into piles according to a principle known to the experimenter but that the experimenter does not convey explicitly. Rather, the participant has to identify this principle purely from feedback. Suppose the cards are to be sorted into two piles and the participant makes the guess that it is the color that counts. Accordingly, she puts the first card, which is colored red, into one pile. The experimenter says this is right. Reassured by the positive feedback, the participant puts the next card, which is green, into the other pile, and the experimenter says this is right also. Chance would have it that the participant had hit upon the correct principle in this case, which was rapidly confirmed by the positive feedback. If the participant had hit upon the wrong principle by sorting according to the symbols, with squares in one pile and triangles in the other, then this would be rapidly disconfirmed by negative feedback and the participant would soon hit upon the right principle by trial and error.

But what happens if the experimenter changes the principle halfway through the sorting? Clinically normal people quickly get over the confusion and allow themselves to be guided by the feedback to figure out the new principle. Some who have fallen victim to a certain kind of brain damage show a distinctive difficulty with this task, though. Whilst they are able to use the feedback to identify the experimenter's principle in the first instance, they then seem to fixate on that principle even at the cost of repeated errors when the experimenter changes the principle halfway through. These people are known to have specific injuries to the frontal part of their brain. People with injuries to other parts of the brain might have other problems, like difficulty comprehending language, but they do not show the same inflexibility in the card sort.

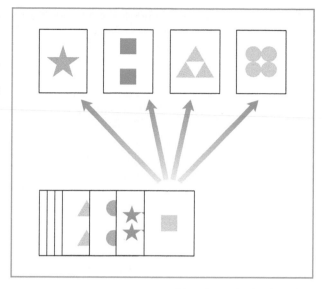

The Wisconsin Card Sorting Test—the participant's objective is to sort the cards according to an unspoken rule; by shape, color, or number. The experimenter can change the rules throughout. This test establishes the participant's ability to display flexibility in the face of changing feedback.

On noting the characteristic rigidity of autistic thought, Ozonoff *et al.* were struck by the possibility that autistic people would show exactly the same difficulty in the card sort task as people without autism but who had acquired damage to the frontal part of their brain. Ozonoff *et al.* recruited a sample of individuals with autism that ranged widely in age and intellectual ability, though they were mainly high functioning. Obviously, a person with autism who is severely intellectually impaired would not even be able to follow the basic instructions of the task. Apart from presenting the card sort, Ozonoff *et al.* also presented tests of false belief. The findings of the study clearly showed that while some participants with autism passed the tests of false belief, all lacked flexibility in thought when it came to the card sort task. It thus seems that inflexibility of thought might be a more reliable indicator of autism than failure to acknowledge beliefs. Accordingly, inflexibility of thought might be the more fundamental deficit in autism.

In a way, this revelation brings us full circle. Leslie (1987) deserves the credit for making a link between the fluidity needed to engage in pretend play and the imagination needed to apprehend the existence of other people's minds. Leslie actually dwelt upon whether or not people with autism had sufficient imagination to acknowledge the existence of the mind. A small change in the emphasis of what he was saying would allow compatibility between the findings reported by Ozonoff *et al.* and the claim that an essential feature of autism is the failure to understand about minds. Instead of debating whether or not people with autism have sufficient imagination to formulate a concept of the mind, perhaps we should be asking whether they have sufficient flexibility in their imagination to give correct judgments of false belief.

The issue becomes clearer when we consider a study conducted by Russell, Mauthner, Sharpe, and Tidswell (1991), which is relevant to the difficulty in carrying out acts of deception in autism, but which also highlights inflexibility in thought. They devised something called the windows task. The procedure formed two distinct stages. In the first, participants had to point to one of two boxes. The experimenter lifted whichever one they pointed at. Sometimes there would be nothing underneath while sometimes there would be a chocolate reward. When there was chocolate, the experimenter snatched it and took satisfaction in eating it while the frustrated child looked on. When there was nothing underneath, the child was then allowed to look under the remaining box whereupon he would find chocolate. This experience presented opportunity for the child to learn certain principles of the game, which were: (1) There was chocolate to be gained on every trial, but it was only under one of the boxes; (2) The experimenter always searched underneath whichever box the child pointed at and only under that box; (3) If the experimenter's search resulted in his finding chocolate, he always kept it for himself; if his search did not lead him to the chocolate, the child was then free to look under the remaining box and get the chocolate.

Children had practice at the task during the preliminary stage until they became thoroughly familiar with it. In the second stage, a small yet very important modification was introduced. Windows were cut into one side of each box but not the other. Child and experimenter sat at opposite sides of the boxes, such that the child could see into them but the experimenter could not. Hence, the child but not the experimenter could actually see which of the boxes contained chocolate. Otherwise, the game was as before. The situation, then, was that participants should have been able to gather that they needed to point to the visibly empty box if they wanted to win the chocolate reward. Actually, though, the participants with autism repeatedly thwarted themselves by pointing to the box with the chocolate. Trial after trial, the hapless children behaved in a way that led the experimenter to win the chocolate.

Russell *et al.* presented the same task to clinically normal children aged 3 and 4 years. The younger members of the sample, those mainly aged 3, behaved in a way that resembled the much older participants with autism. Namely, they seemed helpless to do anything other than point to the box that contained the chocolate. The older children, mainly those who had already celebrated their fourth birthday, behaved quite differently. They either immediately pointed to the visibly empty box on the first of the trials in the second phase, or they did so after only one or two trials.

The reason this finding is so enlightening is as follows. Superficially, the task seems to be about deception. To gain the chocolate reward, children need to make a deceptive gesture to the visibly empty box. That gesture would be sufficient, apparently, to cause the experimenter to hold a false belief. A person who had no concept of belief would thus not grasp the significance of pointing to the empty place. However, this procedure was not really about understanding deception at all. Rather, participants had to resist being drawn to the captivating spectacle of the chocolate visibly present in one of the boxes. It did not matter whether they understood the existence of the experimenter's mind. All they had to do to get the chocolate was point to the empty box.

It is probable that when participants with autism saw the chocolate they pointed to it impulsively as if saying "gimme." Their pointing was probably not intended as an act of communication but was just an expression of desire, which of course the experimenter was able to interpret to the participant's cost. Impulsivity of this kind is the other side of not having much imagination or flexibility of thought. Being flexible means going beyond immediate impulses. One who is unable to be flexible would instead be impulsive.

On the face of things, then, the windows task seems to be about deceptive pointing, but deeper consideration suggests that it is actually about flexibility of thought and inhibiting impulsive pointing. This characterization led Russell *et al.* to suggest that the difficulty children with autism show in tests of false belief stems from failed inhibition and inflexibility in thought; a lack of understanding of the mind would be secondary to inflexibility. In a traditional unexpected transfer test of false belief, to be coded as giving a correct judgment, children must inhibit pointing to the place where John's chocolate is actually located. And in the deceptive box task, they must resist blurting out what they have discovered as the true content (pencils) when asked what they used to think was inside the tube (Smarties™). The difficulty they show with these is perhaps not so much revealing a lack of insight into the mind but rather merely betrays their well-known failure to inhibit.

Is the difficulty experienced by individuals with autism in understanding other people's minds a by-product of inflexibility in thought, lack of imagination, and failure to inhibit?

WEAK CENTRAL COHERENCE

Frith (2003) made a similar suggestion concerning the character of autistic thought. She proposed that people without autism cannot help but integrate information to form a coherent whole. Examples are in the way we make sense of visual information to perceive a coherent scene. Our eyes are bombarded with information that must be processed if we are to perceive a world of interconnected objects. We do not perceive the side of a house to be a different object from the front. Rather, we perceive these as parts that contribute to the whole that are not normally separable.

Frith suggested that autistic thought is quite different. She proposes that while people with autism can perceive the world of solid objects in three dimensions, they do not automatically and inevitably integrate all the information into a coherent whole. Although one implication is that their thought is fragmented, another is that they should be at an advantage in certain analytical tasks that require mental dissection of information. In that case they should fare well in objectively observing a scene. In looking at a lawn, we "know" that the grass is green. This knowledge could prevent our perceiving the blueness of the shadows and could cause us not to acknowledge the hue of light reflected onto the lawn from an adjacent object. It is as if we have some kind of color constancy in operation that makes us see the grass as green even when parts are actually blue or yellow. This would happen if we are imposing meaning on the visual input—that it is a lawn and that lawns are green.

For people with autism, things might be a little different. Perhaps they are not destined to impose meaning on the input and in consequence are not blinded to the hues or shapes that combine to create the impression of the whole. We might say that they are less susceptible to capture by meaning, as Frith puts it, compared with those who do not have autism. In one sense, this would of course be an impairment, because they would not find it as easy as people without autism to impose sense on things. On the other hand, however, it would be an advantage in certain tasks. It might be that people with autism are able to analyze a visual scene more objectively and thus produce a realistic and

Key Term

Capture by meaning:
A tendency to overlook fine detail brought about by attention to the global meaning of a stimulus or event.

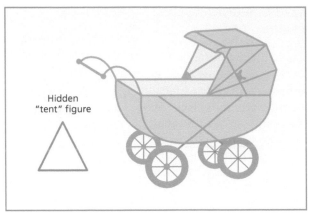

Hidden
"tent" figure

Embedded figures task.

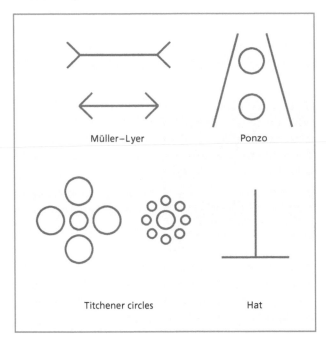

Müller–Lyer   Ponzo

Titchener circles   Hat

Individuals with autism might be less susceptible to these illusions compared with those who do not have autism. In the Müller-Lyer, the horizontal lines are of identical length. In the Ponzo and the Titchener, the pairs of inner circles are of identical diameter. In the Hat, the vertical is identical in length to the horizontal.

accurate drawing, so long as they have some basic skill in draughtsmanship. This could explain the remarkable skills of autistic artists like Stephen Wiltshire.

A task with the potential to reveal the absence of capture by meaning is known as the embedded figures test, shown in the figure on the left. The participant is asked to find the abstract target shape within the larger, more complex figure, and performance is measured in terms of how long it takes to succeed. The participant's task is to identify the smaller figure within the larger one by tracing its outline therein. Shah and Frith (1983) presented this task to a group of high functioning people with autism. Remarkably, they identified the embedded figure more swiftly than would be expected from knowing the general details of their intellectual profile. Indeed, they reliably solved the problem more rapidly than people with similar intellectual profile but without autism.

Happe (1996) suggested that weak central coherence might also protect individuals with autism from being seduced by visual illusions of the kind shown in the figure to the left. Take the Müller-Lyer as an example. The parallel horizontal lines are actually identical in length but the arrowheads create the illusion that the line with the outward pointing heads is shorter than the one with the inward pointing heads. We would not fall for this illusion if we did not integrate the arrowheads with the lines to be judged. Seemingly, this integration is something we do automatically, even though the arrowheads are actually extraneous to the task. People with autism might be different. If they do not routinely and automatically integrate pieces of information, then perhaps they would not be susceptible to the illusion and accordingly would judge correctly that the two horizontal lines are the same length.

Happe presented these illusions to people with autism and simply asked them if the relevant comparison lines were the same length/size or different. In nearly all cases, the children with autism suggested that the lines or circles were the same, though some did show susceptibility to the Müller-Lyer by judging that they were different. In contrast, children of similar intellectual profile but without autism apparently were susceptible to the illusions, given that they were highly inclined to judge that the comparison lines were different.

Ironically, the success of individuals with autism could actually betray a peculiarity of thought and perception that supposedly forms the essence of their autism. Although social functioning might seem effortless, in fact it requires a massive integration of all sorts of information to allow the appropriate sensitivity, discretion, and diplomacy. Likewise, to interpret what is said in communication, it is not sufficient to attend only to the literal meaning of the utterance. This has to be processed in conjunction with the context and has to be integrated with our knowledge of "where the speaker is coming from." Without that integration, communication would be very difficult indeed.

Despite the intuitive appeal of Frith's hypothesis, the evidence in support of weak central coherence has been patchy. A clever study illustrating the point was conducted by Pring and Hermelin (1993), who asked autistic participants with special artistic abilities to match a target image with one of a pair of other objects (see the figure below). One of the pair was similar to the target in structure while the other was related with the target in some deeper sense but not in structure. For example, the participants were asked whether an image of a wine glass went best with a tulip or with an image of a bottle of wine. There is no right or wrong answer, but the authors suspected that the individuals with autism might be especially attentive to structure, and not concerned with, and therefore not distracted by, deeper meanings. If so, they would match the wine glass with the tulip rather than the wine bottle. The authors expected to find more structural matching in those with autism compared with those who had similar intellectual profile but without autism. It stands to reason that if individuals with autism are not captured by meaning, as suggested by the theory of weak central coherence, then they would be confined to making a visual comparison with focus on the similarity of structure between pairs of stimuli. Contrary to expectation, however, the participants with autism judged no differently from those without, and in particular, they tended to match according to deeper meaning. For example, they were inclined to match the wine glass with the wine bottle. There was no evidence to suggest that they did not integrate the images with their knowledge concerning functional relations between the objects.

Another study suggesting the same was conducted by Ropar and Mitchell (2001a), who compiled a set of images that either did or did not have a specific associated color. For example, the typical color of a banana is yellow, while a car has no specific associated color given that cars have many different color schemes. These two objects would both be presented colored blue. For each image, participants were then asked to point to a patch of color to indicate which goes best with the object. One color was blue and the other was yellow. If participants coded the image of the blue banana superficially, and did not integrate what they were seeing with the knowledge of what bananas are like, then presumably they would point to the blue patch to make a visual match. This is what would happen if the participants had weak central coherence.

The results were not as predicted by the weak central coherence hypothesis, however. The participants with autism frequently selected the yellow patch of color to go with the blue banana, and they did this to the same extent as those with similar intellectual profile but without autism. Their choice of the

Participants with autism paired the wine glass with the wine bottle rather than the tulip, showing that they were attending to deeper associations rather than superficial visual similarity.

Critically assess the theory of weak central coherence.

yellow patch was confined to the banana stimulus. When shown a blue car, participants, with and without autism, appropriately chose the blue patch to make a visual match. In other words, it seems the participants were sensitive to the prototypical color of the object when choosing a color to go with the presented image. This would obviously require a level of integration that we would not have expected from Frith's hypothesis of weak central coherence.

Ropar and Mitchell (2001b) conducted a further investigation into susceptibility to illusions in autism. The main difference between this and Happe's study was in the way susceptibility was measured. Whereas Happe had simply asked participants to judge if the comparison lines, like those in the visual illusions figures, were the same or different in length or size, Ropar and Mitchell asked participants to *adjust* the length or size. Participants saw the illusion on a computer screen and were asked to adjust one of the comparison lines or circles so that it was identical to the other. For example, in the Müller-Lyer illusion participants could make the adjustable line longer or shorter by pressing the relevant arrow keys. An individual who was susceptible to the illusion would make the top line (if that was the adjustable one) shorter than it ought to have been. Under a control condition, participants made similar adjustments, except that the arrowheads were absent.

The participants with autism performed no differently from individuals with similar intellectual profile but without autism and indeed no differently from normally developing children of various ages. When presented with illusions, they made systematic errors that revealed their susceptibility. When presented with ordinary lines, they made accurate matches. A particular value of the procedure was that it measured the strength of the illusion effect, according to how far the participants adjusted the line. For that reason, it was highly sensitive in detecting any differences between populations, but in fact there was none. Why did Ropar and Mitchell fail to replicate Happe's result? A likely explanation is that participants did not understand what the experimenter meant by "same" or "different" in Happe's study. Also, Ropar and Mitchell's task was a little more concrete in the sense that participants had to make a physical adjustment to make the lines the same, and this might have been a little more understandable to them.

Nevertheless, individuals with autism seem to be less fooled by some illusions of perspective, such as the Shepard illusion (see the figure on page 152 in chapter 9) than those who do not have autism (Ropar & Mitchell, 2002; Mitchell, Mottron, Soulieres, & Ropar, 2010), and they seemed to be more accurate in drawing 3-D objects from an oblique perspective (Sheppard, Ropar, & Mitchell, 2009). Collectively, this evidence suggests that individuals with autism might be rather more effective than those without autism in visually analyzing the properties of 3-D images. It seems that people without autism have a shape-constancy mechanism that makes them see a rectangle as a rectangle even when viewed from an oblique perspective. A consequence is that when typically developing people are asked to draw what they see, they tend wrongly to draw a rectangle. People with autism, in contrast, seem to be able to set aside what they know the object is (a rectangle) and instead seem to attend to the shape projected onto their eye. In consequence, their shape-constancy process seems not quite as strong as in people without autism.

Summary

- Children with autism have social and communicative impairments, and they show inflexibility in their thought. They are developmentally delayed in understanding other minds, which almost certainly contributes to their social impairment. The delay in their understanding is more severe than would be predicted from their general intellectual impairment. Individuals with autism also suffer from a failure to inhibit. This might account for some or all of their difficulty in understanding other minds. It also helps to explain their difficulties in communication and resistance to change in routines. Interestingly, though, individuals with autism display heightened perceptual abilities, at least in some respects. In truth, though, we are still some way off a full understanding of this perplexing disorder of development.

Essay Questions

1. Critically evaluate the theory of mind hypothesis of autism.
2. Compare and contrast the various cognitive theories of autism.

Further Reading

An excellent book on this topic is highly readable and informative:

- Frith, U. (2003). *Autism: Explaining the enigma*. Oxford: Basil Blackwell.

Contents

Numerical development

What do young children understand about the world of numbers?

8

Chapter Aims

- To introduce evidence for numerical abilities in infants.
- To explore different explanations for these early abilities.
- To explain numerical development in children.

INTRODUCTION

Our cognitive arsenal would be incomplete if we did not have an understanding of numbers. Numbers are all around us—from prices in shops to numbers on credit cards and simple and complex mathematics. We have seen earlier in this book (chapter 3) that Piaget proposed that children have no sense of numbers and numerical relations until they are about 7 years old. Piaget demonstrated this in his conservation of numbers experiment, in which children had no sense that a row of buttons that is longer than another does not therefore contain a greater number of buttons. This notion that mathematics and numbers are difficult concepts to understand, which children only master in an advanced stage of development, seems to mesh nicely with the trepidation many adults feel when confronted with math. Many adults find mathematics difficult and it seems to make intuitive sense that it is only through an arduous learning process, supported by formal instruction, that we can master this abstract skill. This view would suggest that numerical understanding has its basis not in nature but in nurture. In the early 1990s, however, researchers conducted experiments that showed at least tentatively that children who are only a few months old seem to understand addition and subtraction. This, in contrast to

Key Term

Habituation paradigms:
Infants are shown a stimulus until they are bored and look away, when a test stimulus is shown. A display of renewed interest shows that infants perceive this as a different stimulus.

Piaget's claims, would suggest that we are born with some understanding of numbers, that is, we have some kind of innate numerical sense.

In this chapter we will investigate the highly creative experiments that researchers have used to test infants' understanding of numbers and numerical relations, and try to offer an explanation for why numbers seem to be child's play on the one hand—so easy that even babies who are a few months old can tackle them—and yet present so many of us with great difficulty when we are older and should be cognitively much more advanced and have received formal instruction in mathematics (nurture).

WHAT DO INFANTS KNOW ABOUT NUMBERS?

What is the evidence for infants' understanding of numbers?

Throughout this book we have investigated the notion that part of development is underpinned by our biological endowment (nature) and part is driven by a process of learning (nurture). If we are born with a sense of numbers then we should see some evidence that very young children, who have received no formal instruction in mathematics (or even in counting or language) have a grasp of some relational knowledge of numbers. Some of the earliest evidence that young children can compare numbers, thus demonstrating a fundamental ability to represent numerical relations, comes from Cooper (1984) and Starkey and Cooper (1980). Both studies used habituation paradigms with children who were younger than 1 year old. The idea of habituation is similar to preferential looking. Infants are repeatedly presented with a set of stimuli, until they have habituated to the stimuli, or in other words, until they are bored and no longer show any interest in them. Then the test stimulus is presented: if the infant shows renewed interest then they perceive it to be a new stimulus, but if they show no renewed interest, they perceive it to be the same as the preceding stimuli. It is possible in this way to investigate infants' understanding of numerical relations: changing the number representations on the stimuli between habituation and test will only elicit renewed interest if infants are sensitive to a change in this numerical dimension. If they are not, then they will perceive them as the same stimuli.

Starkey and Cooper (1980) presented infants with arrays containing two dots on a rectangular visual display. The dots were presented next to one another, so that they appeared adjacent on the display, and spaced out, so that they occupied the corners of the display, until the infant habituated to the display. This change in the visual aspect of the stimuli is important, because we need to make sure that infants are not just sensitive to a change in the visual appearance of the display, but in the numerical aspect of the presentation (see the figure on the left).

Stimuli used at habituation and test by Starkey and Cooper (1980). The number of squares is different in the test display, but the position of the stimuli is not new: all three positions have been occupied by squares during habituation.

In another condition, infants were presented with three dots at habituation, and this changed to two dots at test. The critical question is whether infants perceive this change in number as a new stimulus. Amazingly, infants who were just 5 to 6 months old looked longer at a display that changed the number of dots, indicating clearly that they were sensitive to a change in the fine numerical display from 3 to 2 or 2 to 3, and demonstrating that they can compare numbers.

If infants are able to compare quantities, such that they know that 2 is different from 3 and so on, then the natural question that follows is whether they are also capable of representing relational knowledge about numbers. At its most simple, relational knowledge allows us to understand that something can be *less than* or *greater than* something else. This is not just advantageous when working out which of two helpings of dessert one should choose, but also forms an integral underpinning of our understanding of number systems.

Robert Cooper (1984) investigated whether infants have a basic understanding of these relations in another habituation study. In this paradigm, infants habituated to pairs of arrays of colored squares, which either depicted the relation of *greater than* (e.g. 4 squares versus 2 squares) or *less than* (e.g. 2 squares versus 4 squares). In the test presentations, infants then saw one of three different relations: the reversed relation (e.g. 2 squares versus 4 squares), a relation representing equal quantity (e.g. 4 and 4 squares) or a novel representation of the same relation as at habituation (e.g. 3 versus 1 square). An example of a trial is depicted in the figure below. The results revealed a development in the understanding of numerical relations: 10-month-old infants dishabituated to the *equal to* only, indicating that they understand the difference between equality and inequality. 14-month-olds also dishabituated to *less than*, indicating that they also understand relational reversals. Taken together, these results already reveal a quite astonishing level of infant competence with numerical understanding.

How does this mesh with cognitive development in older children? Recall that Piaget demonstrated in children who were below 7 years old a failure to understand that a row of buttons that had been spread out, so that it took up more physical space, did not represent a change in quantity of number. This forms yet another cornerstone of numerical understanding. We know that quantities remain the same, unless something else is taken away or something is added. In their failure to conserve number, children seemed to demonstrate a failure to grasp this fundamental property of quantity and numerosity.

Karen Wynn (1992) investigated in one of the most famous and influential studies in this area whether young infants may actually have an understanding of this property of quantity, specifically whether they understand addition and subtraction, and show evidence of a true understanding of numerical concepts. We have already briefly mentioned this study in chapter 3 when we discussed Piaget's idea of object permanence, but the main focus of the study was the investigation of early numerical ability and this is what we will describe here. Wynn used a violation-of-expectation paradigm to test infants' understanding. In this kind of procedure, an

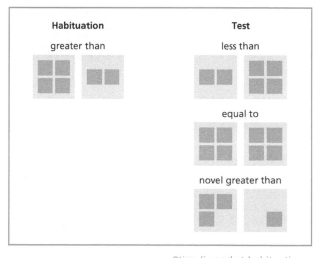

Stimuli used at habituation and test by Cooper (1984).

event occurs in a display area and then the area is occluded from the view of the infant. When the occlusion is removed a new event is visible, which is either expected or possible or unexpected because it is not possible or logical. Infants look longer at unexpected than expected events (they are surprised) only if their cognitive processes lead them to expect that something should or should not happen. In other words, it reveals that they have an understanding of whatever principle the second event violated.

Wynn (1992) wanted to test whether infants can calculate the results of simple arithmetic operations. The procedure is illustrated in the figure below. Infants view a sequence of events in which they first see an empty display area. Then a hand appears in the display area and places a Mickey Mouse doll, the hand retreats and a screen rotates up. In the addition condition, the hand appears again and places a second doll before retracting empty. The screen then drops and reveals the possible and logical outcome of two dolls in the display or the impossible event of one doll only. In the subtraction condition two Mickey Mouse dolls are initially placed and when the screen is in place the empty hand appears and then retracts with one of the dolls. The screen dropping then reveals the possible event of one doll only or the impossible event of two dolls remaining. Wynn measured the time infants looked at the possible outcomes compared to the impossible outcomes. If the infants have no

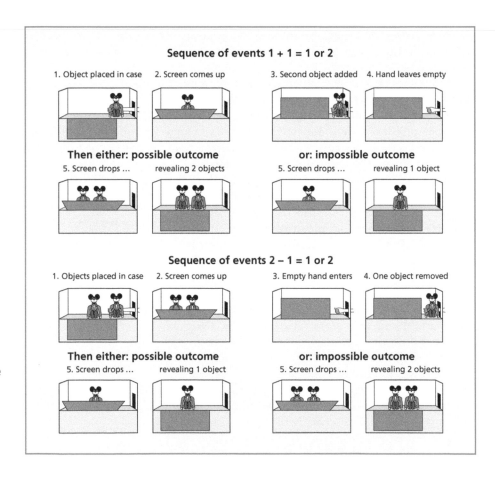

Experimental set-up in the addition and subtraction conditions by Wynn (1992). Copyright © 1992 by Nature Publishing Group. Reproduced with permission.

concept of numerical relations, then they should find either event as likely as the other, but if they have a concept of numerical relations then the revelation of one doll in the addition condition and two dolls in the subtraction condition should be surprising for infants, as it is for adults.

Can we be sure that infants solve the tasks by drawing on an understanding of numbers?

The results of this study are really quite astonishing. Wynn found that infants who were only 5 months old looked longer at the impossible events than at the possible events. This surprise suggests that 5-month-old infants can add and subtract small numbers: they can track and generate expectations about the results of simple additions (1 + 1 = 2) and subtractions (2 −1 = 1). And in a second experiment, infants revealed the longest looking time for (1 + 1) = 3, compared to (1 + 1 = 2) or (1 + 1 = 1). This led Wynn to speculate that infants have actually very precise expectations of the results of these additions.

It is truly astonishing to think that infants have such abilities with numbers. And before we accept this numerical ability as an explanation, we should investigate whether there are other, perhaps more plausible, explanations for Wynn's results that do not rely on attributing skills of arithmetic to preverbal infants.

The perhaps most convincing alternative explanation for Wynn's results was tested by Simon, Hespos, and Rochat (1995), who reasoned that in addition to violating principles of numerical relations, the impossible conditions also violated rules of the physical world. Specifically, objects magically appeared in the impossible subtraction condition and magically ceased to exist in the impossible addition condition. Simon *et al.* investigated the influence of impossible arithmetic and impossible physical events by replicating Wynn's study with two control conditions. In those control conditions the identity of the dolls was swapped—an impossible physical event, but the numerical outcome was correct. Simon *et al.* argued that if children displayed longer looking times for these impossible identity conditions it would suggest that the source of their surprise is the violation of general principles of the physical world, rather than more specific numerical principles. The results, however, supported Wynn's original interpretation. Infants seemed to pay no attention to the swap in identities, which did not lead to longer looking times, whereas the impossible arithmetic again elicited longer looking times. Taken together, these studies suggest that numerical ability emerges very early on in childhood.

HAS INFANTS' NUMBER UNDERSTANDING BEEN OVERESTIMATED?

The finding that infants from a few months of age discriminate between small sets of different numbers of objects seems very robust and was replicated in a number of carefully controlled experiments. But the question of whether this actually reveals infant competence with numbers led to a lively debate between researchers. If, for instance, infants' looking time is explained by some other superficial feature that allows them to distinguish between the two sets of stimuli than this would offer a more easily acceptable explanation rather than making reference to a very early competence with numbers. The stimuli used for the infant habituation studies therefore came under very close scrutiny to find whether an underlying common feature could explain performance. Most of these superficial features were, of course, controlled for by researchers, but

Why is it difficult to assess infants' numerical understanding?

as Melissa Clearfield and Kelly Mix (1999) point out, the physical feature of the stimuli sets that varies systematically with number is the contour size of the objects displayed. Take another look at the stimuli used by Starkey and Cooper (1980), which are displayed in the figure on page 130. Starkey and Cooper carefully controlled for the position of the two stimuli at habituation, but the area and contour length covered by their stimuli correlates with number. What Clearfield and Mix mean by contour length is quite simple: a square with sides that are 2 cm long has a contour length of 8 cm, giving the display of two a total contour length of 16 cm. Now, when you add the third square the contour length increases by 8 cm to make it 24 cm in total. If infants solve the task by assessing contour length then they solve the task not by reference to discrete numbers (2 versus 3) but by reference to some continuous variable that is related to a perceptual feature. What Clearfield and Mix argued is that we cannot be sure that infants respond to the change in numerosity and not contour length, unless they are systematically varied and teased apart in an experiment. In their experiment they therefore presented 7-month-old infants with two objects of a given contour length until they habituated to it. They were then presented at test with a display that changed either in number or in contour length. In the familiar number condition the test display showed two objects, but the objects were larger, such that the contour length was equivalent to having added or removed an object. In the different number condition the number of the objects changed (e.g. from two to four) but the contour length remained constant because the objects were proportionally smaller (see the figure below).

Clearfield and Mix compared looking times for these different test items and found that infants were only sensitive to a change in contour length: they looked longer at a change in contour length, even if the number was the same, but showed no difference in looking time when the number changed and the contour length remained the same. Clearfield and Mix conclude from this result that infants actually discriminate on the basis of basic perceptual variables, like contour length, and not on the basis of abstract number knowledge in this and in other studies we have looked at. Where does this leave Wynn's (1992) finding that infants can add and subtract? Clearfield and Mix (1999) cite evidence

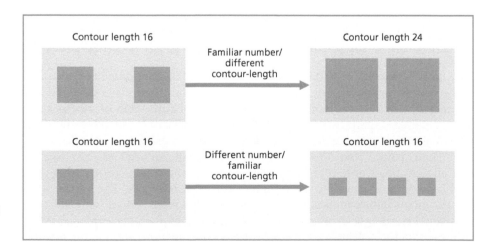

Stimuli used at habituation and test by Clearfield and Mix (1999).

from a study by Feigenson and Spelke (1998) that investigated a similar perceptual concept in Wynn's set-up. Feigenson and Spelke manipulated the size of the puppets behind the screen so that, for example, two small puppets were placed and when the screen dropped infants saw either one or two large puppets. As in Clearfield and Mix's study, in this set-up infants were sensitive to a change in mass and not in number. Mass, or the size of the puppets, is again a perceptual and continuous variable that does not rely on understanding of number.

Although Wynn's findings have been replicated successfully many times, there have been some challenges to the reliability of the results (Wakeley, Rivera, & Langer, 2000). These failures to replicate the results may say more about the challenges of working with very young infants than about the competence in the field (see Wynn, 2000, for an analysis). However, one of the failures of infants to discriminate seems to be systematically related to the size of the set that is compared. Antell and Keating (1983) presented infants who were merely 1 to 6 days old with displays testing their ability to discriminate between changes in dot numbers from 2 to 3 (and 3 to 2) and 4 to 6 (and 6 to 4) in a habituation study. Infants in the 2 to 3 (and 3 to 2) group dishabituated to the change in number, but infants in the group dealing with larger numbers 4 and 6 did not. This may suggest, again, that infants have no understanding of numbers as such, but solve the task by perceptual features; when these features become too complex in the larger displays, infants become unstuck.

Stimuli used at habituation and test by Xu and Spelke (2000).

Taken together these findings might suggest that the interpretation of infants' performance in these tasks has been incorrectly attributed to competence with numbers when they were perhaps indicative of infants' sensitivity to perceptual features (Mix, Huttenlocher, & Levine, 2002) or indicative of generic abilities to track objects that are not related to numbers (Simon, 1997). The debate on these issues is current and far from resolved, but we may be able to untangle this confusion by looking at related evidence for infant competence.

EVIDENCE FOR A FIRM UNDERSTANDING OF SOME NUMBERS IN INFANTS

Xu and Spelke (2000) set out to systematically investigate infants' competence with discriminating number sets in a very tightly controlled experiment.

As you can see in the figure above, the displays take account of object position and contour length, and present large number display sets. By holding constant all the factors that have been used as criticisms on earlier work, Xu and Spelke should be able to draw confident conclusions from any results they find. The purpose of the study was to test whether infants have the ability to represent approximate numerosities. 6-month-old infants were habituated to displays of 8 or 16 dots and then tested on 8 and 16 dot displays, which did not vary on continuous variables. The only difference between the displays was in the number of dots. Xu and Spelke found a significant difference in looking time between the displays, suggesting that infants at 6 months of age have a sense of numerosity, even if it is still somewhat rudimentary. Xu and Spelke also found that infants' discrimination is subject to ratio limits, that is, the size relation of one set of numbers compared to the other. At 6 months of age infants can discriminate number sets that are presented at a ratio of 1:2 (for example, 8 dots versus 16 dots), but only at 9 months old can they also discriminate ratios of 2:3 (for example 8 dots versus 12 dots). These ratio limitations are important and we will return to them later when we discuss the different ways in which numbers can be represented and understood in children and adults.

Converging evidence for infants' understanding of numerosity comes from a different domain (Wynn, 1996). Wynn took on the challenge that infants only respond to perceptual qualities of a display in making a discrimination between number sets. As adults we have a firm understanding that numbers generalize between different objects (two cats, two dogs, two chairs) and between different domains (two bell rings, two claps, two flashes). Wynn tested whether infants could enumerate items that were not objects located in space, but actions that are marked as countable items by the temporal quality of the action. This sounds complicated, but what it describes and what Wynn tested was children's enumeration of the number of times a puppet jumped in a display area. Six-month-old infants habituated to a puppet jumping a sequence of two jumps or three jumps and were then tested on two and three jumps. There was a significant difference in looking time at the sequence of jumps at test when it represented a new number. This suggests both that infants have a sense of number and that this enumeration system is quite general, as it carves up objects and actions and sequences into discrete events, much in the same way that adults do.

We are therefore presented with a complex picture of infant competence in the realm of numbers, but also systematic failure in some other specific tasks. How can we explain this pattern of ability?

BORN TO DO NUMBERS?

We now have a reasonable understanding that Piaget's assertion that children do not understand anything about numbers is incorrect. From 5 months of age children display an understanding of numerical quantities and relations. But whilst we can demonstrate that children have this understanding, it does not explain what drives and underpins this understanding. The prevailing theory of how young children achieve this feat is proposed in the numerical hypothesis.

THE NUMERICAL HYPOTHESIS: NUMBER SENSE FROM ANIMALS TO INFANTS

Preverbal cognitive abilities displayed by infants may well be shared by other animal species. Randy Gallistel and Rochel Gelman (1992) argued that

| Key Term |

Continuous and discrete variables: Variables that could take on any value in a range are continuous, whereas a discrete variable can only take on certain values such as whole numbers.

preverbal counting skills found in human infants are shared by even very distant relatives, evolutionarily speaking, like birds and rodents. Indeed, in many situations animals seem competent with basic numerical skills. Some of these reports of animals understanding numbers are based on anecdotes, and most do not stand up to rigorous experimental investigation.

What are the features of number sense?

One of the most famous examples of animal mathematical skills was displayed by the horse Hans, who at the beginning of the twentieth century delighted audiences in Germany with this ability to perform simple additions. Clever Hans would be presented with a problem, like 5 + 3 = ?, and present his answer by tapping his hoof on the ground the requisite number of times. It seems unbelievable that a horse should be capable of such mathematical feats, and we are right to be skeptical. As it turned out, Clever Hans' trainer gave subtle signs, that even he was not aware of, to Hans when he should stop tapping, and the build up of tension in the crowd was a further sign to Hans. This is a beautiful demonstration of how socially attuned animals often are, but it also highlights the need for rigorous experimental control when investigating amazing animal skills. Stanislas Dehaene (1997) points out the skill with numbers that animals display goes far beyond these showboating displays, and in tightly controlled experiments animals as diverse as rats, dolphins, salamanders, macaques, tamarin monkeys, and lions have shown the ability to tell apart stimuli that varied only in the dimension of numerosity (Dehaene, Molko, Cohen, & Wilson, 2004).

We can marvel at the number sense in animals, but how does it helps us to understand the development of mathematical understanding in humans? It actually helps because the system by which human infants and animals understand numbers may be one and the same.

In order to explain the ability that infants show with discriminating these sets of numbers, Dehaene (1997, and Gallistel & Gelman, 1992) proposed that humans, and animals, possess an innate number sense. This number sense is a specialized mental mechanism for processing numbers, and as a preverbal system, is accessible to human infants and animals alike and is still present in older children and adults. This number sense is an imprecise, approximate, and fuzzy system, perhaps by necessity, as it cannot be based on language or knowledge of precise number systems or even counting. So, how does it work? Dehaene (1997) describes a beautiful metaphor for the nonverbal number sense: the Accumulator (Meck & Church, 1983; Gallistel & Gelman, 1992). Imagine that you need to establish the number of sheep that enter a field, but you do not have the ability to count. Counting would give you an easy way of mapping exactly the right, precise, and discrete number representation on to the quantity of sheep in the field. If you did not have this wonderful ability to count, you could still keep track of the number if you had a number sense. The number sense might operate as in this illustration to establish how many sheep there are: Imagine a hollow vessel, like a tree trunk, and every time a sheep arrives in the field you pour a cup of water into this tree trunk. This would allow you to keep track of the quantity of sheep in the field because the water level in the trunk represents the number of sheep, and the higher the water level, the more sheep there are. Of course this representation is not exact, because you are trying to represent a discrete number of items (sheep) through a continuous variable (water level), or, in other words, you could count sheep accurately (1, 2, 3, 4, 5, 6) but the representation through water level is not discrete like that.

Illustrating how the Accumulator can keep track of quantities in the absence of numerical knowledge. Each time we encounter a sheep we fill a set quantity of water into a vessel. The level of water allows us to estimate the quantity of sheep in the field, even without any knowledge or reference to numbers.

And nor is it as accurate as number. Whilst the distinction between four and five sheep is quite clear when we can count them, the representation through the water level is not quite so finely tuned and accurate: even small fluctuations in filling the cup every time you add water to the vessel would lead to inaccuracies, particularly when trying to compare small differences in numbers like 4 and 5 or 5 and 6—that is, the system would not be very good when trying to discriminate between ratios that are very close to another. And as it turns out, animals are not very good at making these finely tuned distinctions. Rats can learn to press a lever about five times to get a reward, but they will not reliably press it five times on every trial, but sometimes four and sometimes six times. This is exactly what we would predict from such a fuzzy system.

You can of course still use your tree trunk to make comparisons of larger magnitudes, as long as you mark the water level. For example, when more sheep enter the field the next day you could add their number to the ones in the field, by filling the trunk up to the water level from day one and add again one cup of water for each additional sheep. You can now compare the number of sheep in the field today to yesterday: the comparison of magnitude can be made by comparing the new water level to yesterday's mark. If sheep are now leaving the field you can subtract their number: mark the latest water level, then pour out all the water. Now start adding a cup for each sheep that leaves. The difference between the new water level and the latest mark lets you make a comparison of magnitude.

CAN A NUMBER SENSE EXPLAIN INFANTS' UNDERSTANDING?

The number sense is a specialized mental mechanism that is dedicated to processing numbers. It does not rely on verbal ability and is therefore a mechanism that can explain counting abilities in infants and a variety of animals. The system cannot represent numbers precisely and this influences how easy it is to discriminate between numbers: the larger the ratio of difference between numbers the easier they are to discriminate.

Feigenson, Dehaene, and Spelke (2004) review evidence for this system of number sense, and specifically how this might explain the observed limits on infants' performance. The noisy and fuzzy representation of numbers characteristic of a number sense in infants and animals is actually also still found in adults. When adults are presented with two arrays of dots in such a way that they cannot count the number but have to give an estimate, they show the same principle of fuzzy representation as infants; that is, they can discriminate between the set of dots but only at certain ratios, when the numbers of dots differ by too small a ratio the system breaks down. When forced to rely on their number sense, adults and infants show the same ratio-dependent performance. Adults, of course, also have access to a much more precise way of keeping track of numbers in a system that we learn as children. And it is to this ability that we turn next.

COUNT ON ME

Having a number sense is a fundamental underlying principle, but if we asked anyone what numbers are, we would most likely get a reply that involves counting of discrete numbers in some way: 1, 2, 3, 4, 5, 6 … . All of these represent an idea of discrete quantity. Being able to count opens up whole new worlds and is a cornerstone of mathematical development, allowing us amongst other things to make very precise comparisons. By the time they are 3 years old, most children can count up to 10 visible objects correctly. But where does this ability come from? Do we have an innate counting ability? Or is counting a prime example of learning by imitation? Let us examine these extreme positions in turn.

Karen Fuson (cited in Dehaene, 1997) maintains that children start out counting in a parroting fashion without understanding the meaning of what they do. When children start out in this way they just repeat the numerical sequence they hear an adult say by repeating what is to them a meaningless string of sounds "onetwothreefourfive" as an uninterrupted chain. Only later do they learn to segment this chain into breakable parts such that it becomes "one two three four five." Through observing other people they progressively learn what counting is about and, specifically, that it is connected to quantities.

Rochel Gelman and Randy Gallistel (1978) take a radically different view. They suggest that children have innate principles of counting, that is, they do not have to be taught the main principles of counting. According to Gelman and Gallistel, this implicit understanding of counting is evident from the moment children learn number words. The reason they make errors in counting is related to problems with performance in a given task, but not with competence in counting itself. Gelman and Gallistel (1978) identified the following principles of counting:

1. One-on-one principle: each item should only be tagged with one unique number tag.
2. Stable-order principle: number words must be ordered in same sequence across trials.
3. Cardinal principle: the last number represents the cardinal of the whole set, that is, it determines the size of the set.
4. Abstraction: any objects can be counted.
5. Order irrelevance: the order in which items are counted (tagged with a number word) does not matter.

The first three principles determine how we should count, the fourth determines what can be counted, and the fifth distinguishes counting from labeling. What then is the evidence that children have an implicit understanding of counting?

Rochel Gelman and Elizabeth Meck (1983) tested whether children have knowledge of the five principles of counting. They hypothesized that children have competence in the skill of counting but that this competence is normally masked by making too many demands on children's performance in a task. If so, they reasoned, then competence should emerge in a task that makes low demands on performance but be absent in a task that makes high demands on performance. The task they used is one of error detection—here the child only has to monitor counting performance but does not also have to generate it.

Testing counting knowledge in an error spotting procedure (Gelman & Meck, 1983). In the pseudo-error condition, the puppet starts counting the set from the center object onwards, but continues the counting logically and does not violate any of the counting principles.

Three- and four-year-old children were asked to help teach a puppet to count by saying when the count sequence was correct and when it was not. In this way, the understanding of all the principles could be tested. Children displayed sensitivity to all five principles of counting: They judged that the puppet counted correctly on the correct and the pseudo-error trials (e.g. counting the items in the wrong order by not starting with the item on the left), but did not on the trials that violated a principle of counting (see the figure on the left).

It seems therefore that children are indeed sensitive to the principles of counting, as they demonstrated excellent understanding of when the rules of counting had been broken, but were not as successful in the comparison tasks in which they had to do the counting themselves. It seems that competence in counting is much greater than performance indicates. But is it possible that knowledge of the rules of counting also outstrips a true understanding of counting, that is, an understanding of why we count and what it actually means. According to Karen Wynn, children acquire the *how* of counting before the *why* and only understand counting when they are about 4 years old. The goal of counting is obvious to adults, we count to find out how many items are in a given set—the most important part is therefore the final, or cardinal, number as it represents the set size.

It is questionable whether children view counting in the same way: they seem to engage in counting as a kind of game. Evidence for this suspicion is described by Dehaene (1997). He suggests that a 3-year-old who has just counted all her toys in a basket would not know the answer to the question of how many toys she had. This failure to understand the connection between the act of counting and its goal (how many?) points to a failure in understanding. A sense of counting only develops later, possibly through an interplay of the number sense (having an idea of the quantity without having to count) and observation that a given number applies to the particular quantity in question. Dehaene suggests that after a number of observations children begin to learn that counting relates to quantity in a meaningful way.

PIAGET REVISITED

The idea that children do not understand counting, even though they are capable of the mechanisms of it, resonates perfectly with the Piagetian idea of number conservation, which we first encountered in chapter 3. In this experiment Piaget demonstrated that children do not understand the rules or the logic of counting, including one-to-one correspondence and cardinal number until they are 6 years old. Recall that Piaget presented children with a row of buttons that was spaced tightly together and a row of buttons that was of the same number but widely spaced so that it was longer in appearance. Children mistakenly report that this second line is longer than the first, ignoring the principles of counting. So how do these differences between competence reported by different experimenters emerge? At the simplest level we might say that the difference in ascribing competence emerges depending on how high we set the bar when we define competence. Piaget, as is often the case, set the bar for ascribing understanding very high, perhaps unreasonably so, whereas Gelman and Gallistel possibly set it too low. Whether we ascribe competence and understanding of numbers and counting to children depends to a large extent on how we define these concepts and the criteria by which they are measured.

Why do tests of children's counting abilities show such different results?

DOES COUNTING REPLACE NUMBER SENSE?

We have seen that infants start out with a number sense, an understanding of numbers that is fuzzy, not exact, but allows for approximation and comparison. We speculate that this system is innate and may also be present in other, nonverbal animals. When children grow older they learn to count and in time as language and reading develop, they learn that numerals exactly represent number. And at this point they also begin to receive formal mathematical instruction. What happens at this point in development? Does the exact symbolic system replace the fuzzy number sense? And do children therefore have to be instructed to perform additions, subtractions, and comparisons with the symbolic number system?

How might the number sense be useful in older children?

Camilla Gilmore, Shannon McCarthy, and Elizabeth Spelke (2007) conducted an ingenious study to find out whether children could draw on their number sense when asked to perform additions, subtractions, and comparisons in large number sets that were represented by numerals alone. Let's think about this for a moment to take in the difficulty of the task. Children who were 5 and 6 years old were asked to essentially answer questions like "Is 21 + 30 less than or greater than 34?" and is "64 – 13 less than or greater than 34?" It seems incredible to think that children at this age who have not received formal instructions on these problems would be able to answer such questions. And indeed, the teachers at the schools in which this research was carried out were extremely surprised to see that the children not only performed extremely well on these tasks but also very much enjoyed it! The experimental set-up is depicted in the figure overleaf. The pictures used as stimuli lower demand on short-term memory and other, irrelevant, task demands, but as you can see every effort was made not to give any clue to the quantity of what was being represented symbolically in the pictures themselves. Moreover, the comparison number (e.g. 34) is larger than the composite parts of the addition (21 and 30) so that a simple heuristic of comparing the numbers without performing the addition would yield an incorrect result.

Key Term

Cardinal number: The number that determines the size of a set.

(a) "Sarah has 21 candies" — "She gets 30 more" — "John has 34 candies. Who has more?"

(b) "Sarah has 64 candies" — "She gives 13 of them away" — "John has 34 candies. Who has more?"

(c) "Sarah has 51 candies" — "Paul has 64 cookies" — "John has 34 candies. Who has more candies Sarah or John?"

How did children perform such feats of arithmetic? Gilmore *et al.* (2007) argued that the children drew on their number sense to get to the correct answer. They were able to do this because the problem required an approximation, not an exact answer—conforming to the principle of the fuzzy number system. And the ratio of difference was different from 1 in such a way that the comparison was possible. Recall that comparisons at ratios of 1:2 or 2:3 are manageable for the number sense system but with ratios that approach 1 become impossible, both for children and adults. So in Gilmore *et al.*'s study we have evidence that the number sense does not get replaced by formal symbolic systems but instead underpins the performance of that symbolic system, giving children the ability to solve problems in arithmetic that far outstrip any instructions that they may have received. This is a beautiful illustration of the interplay between nature (number sense) and nurture (symbolic number representation) as a mechanism of learning and understanding concepts that we also discuss in relation to other core faculties, for example theory of mind (chapter 5), intelligence (chapter 11), language (chapter 12), and moral understanding (chapter 15).

TWO SYSTEMS FOR NUMBERS

We can see evidence abounding that our numerical understanding is underpinned by two systems, one innate system of number sense and one formal system of mathematics that is conveyed through formal instruction. Halberda, Mazzocco, and Feigenson (2008) found that individual differences in achievement in school mathematics at the age of 14 years old were associated with tests of mathematical ability reaching all the way back to nursery school and thus to a time prior to children receiving formal education. In other words, they uncovered the relation between the acuity of number sense driving the better achievement of learning formal mathematics throughout education.

Mundy and Gilmore (2009) also found that number sense is important for learning the formal aspects of mathematics. Underlying nonsymbolic representation as revealed by children's ability to map between a symbolic and nonsymbolic representation is related to how well they perform in mathematics at school. This relationship cannot be explained by any other relation, including IQ. Converging evidence for the importance of the nonsymbolic system comes from Gilmore, McCarthy, and Spelke (2010) who revealed a close relation between nonsymbolic numbers and success in mathematics in the first year of formal schooling.

Summary

- It is now easy to see how numbers can be both so incredibly difficult that they fill many adults with dread, and so simple that even infants and animals can master them. The difference is of course dependent on which number system we have to draw on. Numbers are easy when we can use our innate number sense to give an approximation of estimating magnitude or difference in quantities that differ in a ratio removed from 1. These core dedicated systems serve us well in many situations when we make rapid decisions about numbers and magnitude and present us with little or no problems. Numbers become very difficult when we try to go beyond the remit of this innate system and draw on the symbolic system that we have learned in years of formal instruction. How these systems interact and the precise mechanisms of each one of them, and even whether they are the correct way to describe understanding of number, are questions that current research is trying to address.

Essay Questions

1. Discuss the claim that preverbal children have an understanding of numerosity.
2. Why is it difficult to study the understanding of numbers in preverbal children?

Further Reading

- Dehaene, S. (1997). *The number sense: How the mind creates mathematics*. London: Penguin.

Chapter 9

Contents

Developing an ability to draw

9

Chapter Aims
• To introduce evidence suggesting that young children's drawings are characterized by intellectual realism.
• To explore the possibility that children regard drawing as a form of communication.
• To examine research that identifies lingering intellectual realism in adults.
• To explore how children express emotion in drawings.

INTRODUCTION

Drawings are one of the most primitive forms of human expression and communication. Thousands of years ago, our ancestors depicted scenes on the walls of caves. These communicate events in a way that enables the viewer to learn something about them without direct experience. This is one of the defining features of communication: to convey something in such a way that first-hand experience becomes unnecessary.

Then, in Egypt, between 5000 and 2000 years ago, people used sequences of small stylized drawings we now know as hieroglyphics. They are drawings of things, but ones that are so abstract it is necessary to know something about the convention of drawing that the Egyptians used in order to make an interpretation. The Egyptians also put the drawings in sequences, which adhere to rules of organization, thus qualifying as the first written language. Perhaps we could view this as pictorial art at its most lucid and communicative (providing we can read the inscriptions). The Egyptians also painted individual scenes, using less abstract images that were nonetheless highly stylized. In these, the minions are dwarfed by an enormous Pharaoh, whose status is reflected in the scale of depiction.

Key Term

Intellectual realism:
The phenomenon of children drawing what they know rather than what they see.

In more recent times, people still painted in a way that communicates a slightly different message. Under royal edict, painters depicted the glory of victorious armies and navies. Religiously inspired painters portrayed dramatic scenes from scriptures. Victorians had a passion for portrayals of an idealized rustic life. These works seem to communicate the beauty and simplicity of rural life, but conveniently overlook the squalor and tedium. The brilliant work of van Gogh communicates the three-dimensional solidity of things through gradations of color rather than gradations of light and dark. French impressionists communicated the fleeting quality of reality. Lucian Freud communicates something about the stark ugliness of the human figure in his life paintings. David Hockney, in his dual portraits, insightfully communicates about the psychological relationship between individuals. In all these examples, and in very different ways, painters do not just copy what is out there in nature, as a camera does, but instead they interpret and then communicate something about the world.

For thousands of years humans have communicated to each other through the medium of pictorial art. Perhaps there is a natural inclination to communicate through pictures and, if so, we should find that children's drawings communicate something essential to us about how they understand the world. Children naturally derive pleasure from drawing, just as they do from verbal communication. In our society, typical subject matter is pictures of people, houses, and cars. The figure below shows some examples. Some of children's earliest drawings are of the human form, and at their most primitive these characteristically resemble tadpole figures: a head with arms and legs attached but no torso (Goodnow, 1977). It is surprising that children spontaneously hit upon drawing tadpole figures even when this has not been modeled to them as an example.

INTELLECTUAL REALISM

One striking feature of children's drawings has been called intellectual realism, first described by Frenchman G.H. Luquet in the 1920s. If you ask a child under about 6 years to draw a car, you might find that she draws a fairly neat view from the side, but is nevertheless compelled to show features that she knows are there. For example, in the figure left, a 5-year-old girl, Tilly, knows that her family's car has a trunk and apparently felt compelled to add an appendage to the left of her drawing to represent this. Young children's drawings thus seem to be influenced by what they know, rather than what they can see, hence the term *intellectual realism*.

Piaget (Piaget & Inhelder, 1969) saw a link between intellectual realism in drawings, and children's tendency to choose their own view on the three mountains task. He argued that both arose from a failure to recognize the possibility of multiple perspectives. Although he did not say in so many words, Piaget seemed to take the view that intellectual realism in drawings arises from more general egocentrism.

Drawings by Tilly, aged 5 years.

Another way of looking at intellectual realism, however, is to view it as the product of a basic human desire to communicate through drawings, first seen in cavemen. The child knows that the car has four wheels. If she drew only two, therefore, the drawing would fail to adequately depict an important feature of the car. Indeed, perhaps the child feels that if the drawing only shows two wheels, then the vehicle could be mistaken for a motorbike, and would therefore be inadequate in communicating what the vehicle is.

Why do children tend to draw what they know rather than what they can see?

Looking at it this way, intellectual realism seems just the opposite of what Piaget claimed; a desire to communicate "what is there," rather than what can be seen at any one time, seems unlike an egocentric tendency. Consider the three mountains task in contrast. The egocentric child is said to be dominated by what he can see from his particular vantage point, and is unaware that the scene may look different when viewed from another side. Piaget argued that as the child's egocentrism fades, he comes to understand that appearances can be deceptive in relation to the underlying objective, enduring, and universal reality. In this respect, it seems odd to claim that intellectual realism arises from egocentrism. Egocentrism is defined as unawareness of whatever underlies the specific appearance from any particular viewpoint. It seems odd in two ways. First, it is odd that a young child who is supposed to be egocentric, might have concern about the way things really are. Second, it seems odd that a young child might be concerned to communicate something, as if to help another person to be better informed. Sensitivity to different levels of informedness is anything but egocentric.

Over the last three decades, researchers have put much effort into a systematic study of intellectual realism, particularly with regard to the possibility that it arises from the child's desire to communicate accurately the way things are. The basic phenomenon of intellectual realism was demonstrated experimentally by Freeman and Janikoun (1972), who asked children to draw a picture of a cup exactly as they saw it. The handle was out of view, whilst in view was the image of a flower on the side of the cup. Children below about age 7 omitted the flower and included the handle. Children above that age did the opposite, omitting the handle, but including the flower. This suggests that the young children were not concerned to include all information in the drawing, but only that relevant to its identity as a cup. A flower is irrelevant to identity: different cups have different patterns. The handle, in contrast, is highly relevant to whether or not an item of pottery is a cup. So far as the child is concerned, cups are things that have handles. Therefore, intellectual realism has a great deal to do with including the defining features of the kind of thing being drawn.

A study by Bremner and Moore (1984) confirmed that children's knowledge of the identity of the object was responsible for their tendency to add features to their drawing that were actually out of view. Like Freeman and Janikoun, they asked children aged between 5 and 7 years to draw a cup placed on the table in front of them. The cup had a handle that was not in view from where the child was sitting. Some children were first allowed to stand up and have a good look at the cup. They were able to see the handle round the back. The other children did not see the handle, and could therefore have mistaken it for a sugar bowl. Despite being asked to draw the cup exactly as they saw it, those who had seen the handle were very likely to include it in the drawing, thus

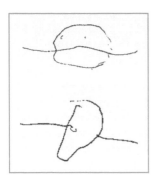

The top drawing was by a child who had seen a stick pushed all the way through the ball. The bottom drawing was by a child who saw that two sticks protruded from either side of the ball. The appearance of the ball and stick(s) was identical for both children.

What factors are responsible for intellectual realism in drawings?

displaying intellectual realism. In contrast, those who did not know about the handle were less likely to include it in the drawing.

Just as young children include the handle to identify the object as a cup, so they draw other hidden detail as though it were visible. Crook (1984) pushed a rod though a ball and asked children to draw it as they saw it. Five-year-olds typically started by drawing a circle, and then proceeded with an oblique line right across to represent the rod. The figure below shows an example. These drawings identified the thing as a ball with a rod penetrating from one side to the other. Under another condition, Crook poked a short rod into each of the two holes of the ball. This produced the same appearance, except children knew that it was not a single continuous rod extending all the way through. Five-year-olds were much more likely to draw two lines at either side of the circle, rather than a line right through. It seems that by not drawing a continuous line all the way through the ball, children were depicting the rod through the ball as discontinuous.

Intellectual realism also occurs when we ask children to draw two objects exactly as they appear, with one behind the other. If we ask children to draw two apples in such an arrangement, young ones characteristically draw them side by side, and separated by space. Light and Macintosh (1980) demonstrated that this tendency arises from an apparent desire in the children to depict the relationship between items. They asked 6- and 7-year-olds to draw a glass beaker with a small model house situated behind it. Often, children drew the two things side by side, showing that the two items were separated by space. Under another condition, the house was inside the beaker, yet from the child's viewpoint, it looked just as it did when it was behind the beaker. This time, children always drew the house within the outline of the beaker (see the figure on the next page). This strongly suggests that children were trying to capture the spatial relationship between the two items. Apparently, when the house was behind the beaker, children drew the two things side by side to show that they were separated.

Children's depiction of relationships between things was further demonstrated by Light and Humphreys (1981). They put a red and a green pig on a table, one following the other. Children aged 5 and 6 years were instructed to draw four pictures of the pigs, one from each side of the table. From two sides, one pig was partly hidden by the other, and from another two sides, they were both in full view, side by side. Interestingly, children always drew the pigs side by side, thereby depicting a space between the two pigs, irrespective of which side of the table they occupied when doing their drawing. Notably, children often captured the relationship accurately, with the green pig following the red one.

Children's portrayal of relationships between objects seems sufficiently powerful to override a desire to depict the correct identity of objects. This was cleverly demonstrated by Davis (1983). She put two cups in front of 4- to 7-year-old children, one with the handle in view and one with the handle out of view. Children were much more likely to correctly exclude the handle not in view when drawing the cups, compared with a condition in which they were asked to draw just one cup with the handle not in view. It seems that children excluded the handle of one cup when drawing the pair because this was the best way of depicting the relationship. Apparently, children effectively assigned higher priority to depicting this relationship than to depicting the cup as a cup by including its handle in the drawing.

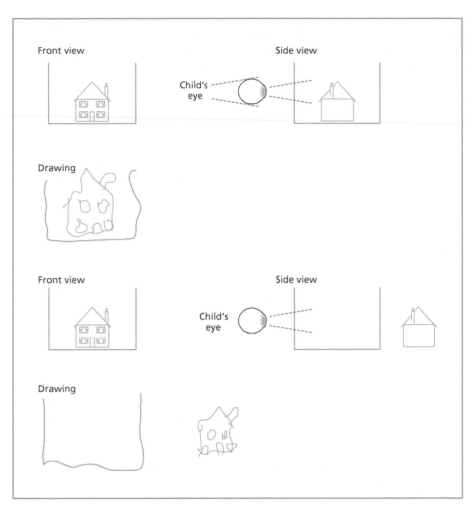

When the model house was inside the beaker, children drew it correctly, as shown in the top part of the figure. When the model house was behind the beaker, children tended to depict the house and beaker side by side.

Is intellectual realism one symptom of a broader inclination to draw the world as it is, or is it primarily a desire to communicate an accurate message to whoever might see the drawing? There is a subtle but important difference between these two possibilities. The desire to communicate implies a desire to present information in such a way that it enlightens the recipient of that information. In contrast, the desire to portray things as they are may or may not lead to a drawing that serves as a useful message. A study by Light and Simmons (1983) illustrates how this distinction can be examined empirically, as shown in the figure overleaf. The experimenter put a red and a blue ball side by side on the table in front of the child. The child sat at any one of the four sides of the table, and had to draw the balls in such a way that the next child, waiting outside, would be able to tell from the drawing where he had been sitting. The view from two sides of the table was of one ball behind the other. Would children with this view draw one ball behind the other? In other words, would the drawing serve as a useful message to another person? Alternatively, would the child persevere drawing the balls side by side, presumably based on a desire to show the balls as they really are, separated by space? In this case,

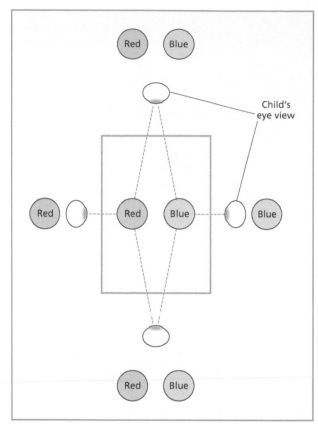

Red　Blue

Child's
eye view

Red　Red　Blue　Blue

Red　Blue

Looking down onto the table, we see the red and blue ball side by side. Children had to draw what they could see on the table from the four sides.

the drawing would not be a useful message that communicates the artist's vantage point.

The findings were clear: unlike older children, those aged 6 years drew the balls side by side. They continued to do this even after witnessing the consequences of their first attempt, when the next child went to the wrong side of the table after looking at the drawing. Despite seeing that the side-by-side drawing communicated the wrong location to the next child, 6-year-olds continued with similar inappropriate drawings on a subsequent attempt.

The case of intellectual realism seems to be one in which the child is dominated by what he knows is out there in the world, and appears to have little to do with a desire to communicate a message to help someone who might see the drawing. Perhaps the phenomenon of intellectual realism is a reflection of the child's striving to understand how the world is really, revealing that particular viewpoints are less important to the child. Although intellectual realism in drawings is a kind of error, perhaps we should look at it as a case of objectivity getting the better of subjectivity. In one respect, this is consistent with Piaget's view of human cognition. He asserted that the best adapted cognition is the one that is based on objectivity. In another respect, it calls into question Piaget's ideas about egocentrism. If intellectual realism represents striving for objectivity, then it cannot at the same time be a sign of egocentrism.

IS INTELLECTUAL REALISM CONFINED TO EARLY CHILDHOOD?

Intellectual realism is not confined to children aged 6 years and below, though it might be most potent at about that age. Reith and Dominin (1997) asked children aged 5–9 years to look at a couple of balls on the table, with the distant one partially obscured by the nearer ball. Sitting at the end of the table, the participants had to place shapes on a vertical pane of glass with the aim of blocking out the exact shapes of the two balls as they could see them. The pane of glass is known as a da Vinci window, and drawing or making shapes directly onto it is supposed to help the participant to depict the shapes in the scene exactly as they appear from the vantage point. The arrangement is shown in the figure opposite. Even some of the oldest children exhibited intellectual realism by placing two complete circles side by side to depict the scene, though the tendency was stronger in the younger ones. In fact, they should have placed a crescent against a circle to show that one ball was partially hiding the other.

Intellectual realism even prevails in a good many adult would-be artists. A common experience when entering art school is being told to draw what

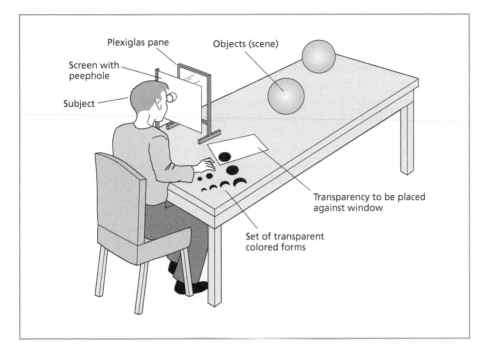

Plexiglas pane

Screen with peephole

Subject

Objects (scene)

Transparency to be placed against window

Set of transparent colored forms

Children aged 5–9 years had to depict the shapes they could see by placing matching forms onto the da Vinci window. They should have placed a circle next to a crescent but many placed two circles side by side.

you see, not what you know. The latter is a characteristic of the uninitiated. Intellectual realism in adulthood is of a different degree, but perhaps like children, there are vestiges in our drawings of what we know is out there at the expense of what we actually see. This topic was investigated systematically by Cohen and Bennett (1997). They asked participants to draw from a photo of a portrait and a photo of an industrial unit. As predicted, participants' drawings appeared rather stereotyped, as if the participants were influenced by what they thought a prototypical portrait or industrial plant might look like. The errors in drawings did not result from lack of control of the pencil, for drawings were very much better when participants traced, assuming that tracing and drawing require the same level of pencil control. Also, errors were not just a product of participants' poor decisions on how to translate a photo into a set of pencil lines. This became apparent when participants made errors even when the source material was not a photo but an accurate pencil drawing by another artist. In this case, the problem of how to depict the subject matter as a set of lines had already been solved for participants, and yet errors still prevailed in their drawings. Having ruled out various alternative explanations, Cohen and Bennett settled on the possibility that participants' misperceptions of the subject matter led to errors in drawings. In particular, they proposed that what participants knew of the class of objects being studied contaminated their perception of how this particular instance looked.

Direct evidence in support of Cohen and Bennett's conclusion arose from research conducted in Nottingham (Mitchell, Ropar, Ackroyd, & Rajendran, 2005). The aim was to investigate the link between misperception and drawing errors. Adult participants drew two different versions of the Shepard illusion (see the figure overleaf). The two parallelograms are identical in shape and size, even though the right-hand figure looks squarer. The illusion is present in both versions but strongest when legs are appended so that the parallelograms look like table tops. The greater illusion strength associated with the table version of the figure probably arises from the stronger 3-D cues in the stimuli. When participants draw a stimulus with weak 3-D cues, they ought to be fairly accurate, but when they draw a stimulus with strong 3-D cues they ought to make systematic errors. This is because when cues suggest the stimulus is being viewed from an oblique perspective, participants will nevertheless internally represent the object in the way it would look from an optimal vantage point. Put simply, while participants see a parallelogram, they will nevertheless represent it as a rectangle. And while they see foreshortened lines representing the width dimension, they will represent these as being longer, in accordance with the physical properties of the object being depicted. This is because the table version of the illusion conveys to the participant that there is a contrast between how the stimulus looks (e.g. a thin rectangle) and its "true" shape (e.g. a much squarer rectangle). In the parallelogram version of the illusion, there is no contrast between how the stimulus looks and its true shape. Hence, there is scope for intellectual realism to impact when drawing the table illusion but not when drawing the parallelogram illusion.

In support of these predictions, participants made systematic drawing errors of the table version of the illusion (making the right-hand figure squarer) but made accurate drawings of the parallelogram version. With the table but not the parallelogram illusion, participants could naturally work out what the table would look like when not viewed from an oblique perspective. Accordingly, it seems that participants' internal representation of the "real" shape of the table, in other words the properties of the table that are viewer independent, contaminated their drawing. In short, participants' knowledge of the stimulus interferes with their drawing of how the object looks from a particular vantage point. Remarkably, this is tantamount to intellectual realism, meaning that the phenomenon is pervasive and not just confined to childhood. Admittedly, intellectual realism is more conspicuous in childhood, but its effects do not fade altogether with increasing maturity.

Research into drawing the Shepard illusion raises a question about the kind of knowledge that impacts on drawings: knowledge about the 3-D properties of an object or knowledge of object features. Evidently, children's knowledge of defining object features influences drawings, for we have already seen that children tend to inappropriately include the handle of a cup and the four wheels of a car. Conversely, though, there are reasons for supposing that familiarity with an object would assist drawing in some ways. When drawing a truck, for example, the fact that you know that it has a cab, wheels, and a trailer or box might actually help you to plan the drawing and ensure that you don't omit any of the main features. Sheppard,

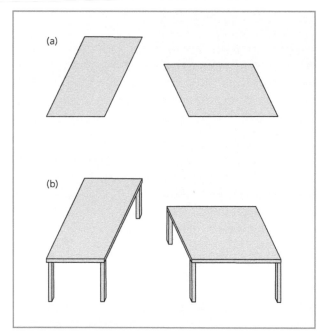

The Shepard illusion. The two rectangles side by side are physically identical in shape, even though the right-hand rectangle looks squarer.

Ropar, and Mitchell (2005) directly compared the effects of knowledge associated with 3-D properties and knowledge associated with general object features. They presented the stimuli shown in the figure right, which varied in either being meaningful (familiar features) or nonmeaningful (no familiar features) and also in either being 3-D (knowledge of 3-D properties could have impact) or 2-D (knowledge of 3-D properties could not have any impact). Interestingly, 7-year-old children made more errors when drawing 3-D than 2-D stimuli, irrespective of whether they were meaningful. Indeed, on average, children made slightly more accurate drawings of meaningful than nonmeaningful stimuli. It seems, then, that a major source of error in children's drawings is related with their difficulty depicting an object from a particular vantage point; their drawings instead are distorted toward viewer-independent properties of the object.

These four figures are composed of identical lines. The two left-hand figures are 3-D drawings and the two right-hand figures are 2-D drawings. The two top figures are drawings of recognizable objects and the two bottom drawings are of objects that are not recognizable.

SIZE OF DRAWING AS AN INDICATION OF SIGNIFICANCE OF THE TOPIC

For thousands of years artists have exaggerated the size of the principal subject in paintings. In ancient Egyptian art we find that Pharaohs take on giant proportions compared with their underlings. This characteristic is repeated in court paintings of the middle ages, where kings have huge scale. This is not just a perspective phenomenon; often, the principal subject is no nearer to the viewer than other characters. Only in relatively recent times of the Renaissance period has the fashion for exaggeration of the size of important people diminished.

Exaggeration of size is not confined to drawings of the human figure. Kings and children alike are often surprised and dismayed to find that their own country is relatively small when viewed in the context of neighboring nations. Like ancient kings, children are inclined to exaggerate the size of their own country, reflecting the importance it holds for them personally. This was demonstrated in a study by Axia, Bremner, Deluca, and Andreasen (1998). They asked children aged 8 and 10 years from different European countries to draw a picture of Europe. The resulting drawings seemed to reflect a kind of fish-eye lens effect, with regions nearest to the child's home depicted prominently in scale and detail. Other countries seemed to be scaled down as a function of their distance from where the child lived. Examples appear in the figure overleaf.

We would expect the size of children's drawing of a particular subject to vary as that subject acquired or lost importance. In an early study to investigate this, conducted by Solley and Haigh (1957), children were asked to draw a picture of Santa Claus both before and after Christmas. As Christmas approached, children's drawings of Santa became larger, but once Christmas had passed, their drawings became smaller. Presumably, as Christmas approached, Santa became more important to children, occupying their thoughts a greater

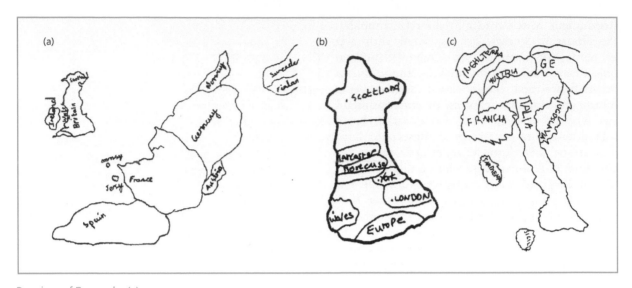

Drawings of Europe by (a) a Scottish 10-year-old, (b) an English 8-year-old, and (c) an Italian 10-year-old. From Axia *et al.* (1998).

When drawing a picture of a witch, children tend to make the drawing rather small. Why?

proportion of the time. This could well account for the increased size in their drawings. Another interpretation (Freeman, 1980) is that as Christmas approaches, children's greater exposure to images of Santa makes them aware of potential for more detail in their Santa drawings. As a consequence, perhaps they draw a larger outline in order to accommodate this extra detail. However, Fox (cited by Thomas & Silk, 1990) found that children still draw more important figures larger than less important ones, even when there is no extra detail in the more important figure. Therefore, it seems that, like our artistic ancestors, children may well have a tendency to portray important people as being relatively large.

Whether children view a person as pleasant or unpleasant also influences their size of figure drawing. Thomas, Chaigne, and Fox (1989) asked children to draw a picture of a person and they also asked them to draw a picture of a "nasty" person. Children reliably drew the "nasty" person smaller compared with when the experimenter gave no specifications about the person to be drawn. Further, Fox and Thomas (1989) found that children who said they were scared of witches drew smaller pictures of witches compared with those who said they were not scared. To account for these findings, Thomas and Silk (1990) suggest that children may draw small figures of threatening or unpleasant subjects as a kind of defensive reaction. If the subject of the drawing is unpleasant, then this might have less emotional impact on the child if she draws only a small figure: the smaller the figure, the less there is to threaten the child.

Both importance and how pleasant something is concern emotion, and the size of drawings of things or people with such properties could be classified as an emotional response to these things. Therefore, we can see that children may express their emotions and feelings about the world through their drawings. As such, children's drawings could be revealing about their emotional states, possibly even their psychological adjustment. This is certainly a view held by psychoanalysts, but it can be difficult to find a system of interpreting drawings that is unambiguous.

CHILDREN'S DRAWINGS IN CASES OF INCEST

In cases of suspected incest, the clinician given the task of assessing the child is faced with a difficult problem. We need to establish the details of the child's complaint so that we can decide whether action is essential to protect the child from the possibility of further abuse. The decision has to be considered very carefully, since apart from attempting to protect the child's future well-being, there could be drastic consequences for the future of the child's family, especially the alleged perpetrator of the abuse.

Asking children to make drawings has potential to help such a serious decision-making process. Medical examinations and lengthy interrogations could protract the child's trauma. Conversely, the trauma could be alleviated by an emotional release through the act of drawing. The resulting drawing itself could be informative about exactly what has happened. Furthermore, it may be easier, for younger children at least, to communicate through the medium of pictures rather than words, given that the child may find it difficult to formulate an account of the sequence of events accurately in narrative. This could be the case if the child simply does not have the requisite vocabulary for describing events that are beyond the sphere of normal childhood experiences, particularly if the child is not sufficiently verbally developed to give a detailed description of any event, let alone one that surrounded such profound trauma as incest.

To what extent are some of the characteristics of children's drawings explained as an attempt at communication?

Goodwin (1982) asked 19 children aged between 5 and 16, who were victims of abuse, to draw various pictures, which included a picture of the alleged perpetrator, and their family, doing something. These 19 cases were ones of difficult diagnosis, and so were referred for psychiatric consultation to aid the assessment. All were girls, and the alleged perpetrator was the father or stepfather.

Ten of the nineteen children were teenagers, and in seven cases, abuse was eventually adjudged to have taken place. Asking the adolescents to produce drawings proved to be useless. Either they refused to draw, or they produced factual drawings that were irrelevant so far as the alleged incest was concerned, irrespective of whether the father was ultimately convicted. In sharp contrast, drawings made by children aged between 5 and 12 years appeared to be highly informative.

This was particularly evident when children drew a picture of the alleged perpetrator. Although the children could demonstrate their artistic skill in various drawings, when it came to drawing the alleged perpetrator, they seemed to experience great difficulty, with frequent crossings out. Of the seven children who were finally adjudged to have been abused, six included an obvious penis in their drawing of the perpetrator. Of the two finally adjudged not to have been abused, neither included a penis in the drawing. Importantly, the inclusion of a penis was not in any way prompted by the clinician.

In at least three cases the drawings seemed to be informative about the situation in highly specific ways. In one of these the father had homosexual tendencies, which were contributing to his estrangement from the family. The child's drawing showed him in women's clothes, but with a penis prominently on display. In a second case, the father had administered severe beatings to the child during abuse sessions, and the child drew him with a large penis that had a baseball bat resting against it. In a third case, the father turned out to suffer from schizophrenia, and the child drew him with a penis in view and with various heads, which seemed to represent his "voices."

It is very unusual for a nonabused child to include a penis in a drawing of his or her father. We could not take such drawings as definitive evidence that there has been abuse, but it might be a useful complement to other sources of evidence from medical examination and interviewing the child and family. As the cases detailed above show, specific aspects of the drawings could prove to be informative about the nature of the child's trauma. This is useful in helping to understand the nature of the child's problem and in deciding how the perpetrator should be dealt with. For example, if the father was operating under the instruction of delusional voices rather than criminal intent, then he may be considered better dealt with through psychiatric rather than purely legal channels.

As Goodwin points out, drawing could have therapeutic value to child victims of abuse. Through a drawing, the child finds a medium of communication, and could gain comfort from the experience of being understood. This could well be the reason why abuse victims seem to get a sense of relief from doing drawings that are connected with the emotionally sensitive topic of the perpetrator. Also, drawing is a characteristic of childhood, just like pretence in play. Asking the child to draw may help her to identify herself as a child, and so distance herself from a premature venture into the adult domain of sexual activity.

It seems highly unlikely that incest could be confirmed purely or even largely on the basis of a child's drawings. Similarly, it is highly unlikely that an alleged perpetrator could be convicted on the basis of this kind of evidence. However, the drawings could help furnish some of the details of the child's trauma and perhaps serve a therapeutic purpose.

Summary

- Young children's drawings manifest intellectual realism, meaning that children seem compelled to draw not just what they see but also the defining features of objects, such as the handle on a cup. This could occur because children are at the mercy of unwanted intrusion from their knowledge, which interferes with their attempt to draw what they see. Alternatively, perhaps children deliberately include defining but hidden features as a way of using their drawing to communicate what the subject matter is. The evidence suggests that while drawings might reflect a tendency to communicate, intellectual realism is largely explained as an unwanted intrusion. Interestingly, intrusions from knowledge also impact on adult drawings to a small but reliable degree. This is most apparent in perspective drawing where participants systematically distort their drawing toward the "real" shape of the subject matter—that is, how the object looks when not viewed from an oblique perspective.
- Children are influenced by their emotional response to the subject matter when drawing. They tend to draw things that they like in large scale and things that they dislike in small scale. Additionally, there is some evidence to suggest that clues to maladaptive family relationships might be apparent in children's drawings.

Essay Questions

1. What is intellectual realism and how pervasive is it in young children's drawings?
2. Are children's drawings an attempt at communication? If so, in what sense?

Further Reading

- The following provides a well-written and authoritative account of this interesting subject:
- Jolley, R. P (2007). *Children and pictures: Drawing and understanding*. Oxford: Blackwell.

Chapter 10

Contents

Developing an ability to see the world

10

Chapter Aims

- To introduce and assess research that suggests many perceptual abilities are innate.
- To reflect on what kind of behavioral evidence suggests that babies interpret 2-D retinal images as 3-D space.
- To review studies suggesting that infants have an aptitude for perceiving socially-relevant stimuli.
- To review evidence suggesting that knowledge and experience impact upon perception.

INTRODUCTION

It seems astonishing that in our heads we have a rotatable light chamber that includes an automatically focusing lens and a light-sensitive surface at the back (called the retina)—see the figure overleaf. It is remarkable that this surface transduces the physical energy of light into a neural code that can be interpreted by the brain. Perhaps most amazing of all, though, is that the brain makes sense of this information, in such a way that we see things in the world. This "making sense of … " is what we call perception, which is very different from mere photography. If you take a photograph, then you are left with a recording of the physical trace of a pattern of light reflected off surfaces of objects. But this has no inherent meaning. It only becomes meaningful once it is interpreted, and the function of perception is to interpret patterns of reflected light (in the case of visual perception). By and large, we accurately interpret these patterns as solid, 3-D objects situated at varying distances from our vantage point.

In particular, we are not fooled into thinking that as we move away from an object, somehow the object shrinks with its diminishing projection on the

Cross section of an eye.

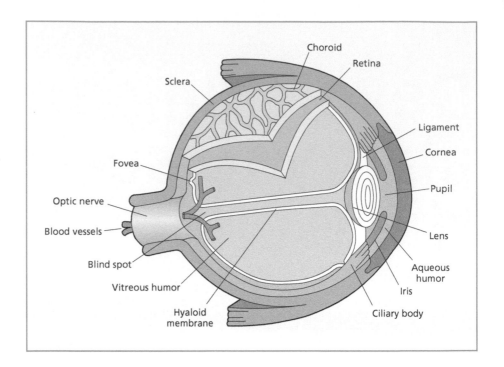

retina; rather, we somehow take our own movement into account in a way that allows us to appreciate that the object is really the same size and that its diminishing apparent size is explained by its being further away. This is a feature of perception that we call size constancy and it is vital in being able to perceive the world in 3-D. Simply, the apparent size of an object provides a clue to its distance. Other visual cues also tell us about distance: As we look down a train track, we see the lines apparently converge together; the granularity of a textured scene become finer in the distance than near to, as in a pebbled beach; more distant objects are partly or fully occluded by closer objects. Additionally, we gain information from parallax. Binocular parallax refers to the discrepancy in information received by each eye. When we focus on close objects, the parallax between the two eyes is great. Motion parallax refers to the apparent movement of one object relative to another as we move past them, where closer objects seem to shift more rapidly than distant objects. For example, when traveling by car, the street lamps seem to speed by whereas we seem to pass distant mountains rather slowly. In short, we have several different mechanisms for apprehending distance, and in doing so we thus understand that distant objects are not really small but only appear small. Hence, our perception includes a capacity for *size constancy*.

The brain impressively performs a phenomenal number of computations on the input from the eye, which enables us to see things stably located in space. Consider this example. We look at a chair from one viewpoint and then move to another. From the new perspective, the pattern of light falling on the retina is now quite different. Yet this experience does not throw us into terrible confusion about chairs going through a grotesque metamorphosis as we move around the room. We have no difficulty recognizing that the shape of the chair

Key Terms

Binocular parallax:
Discrepancy in information received by each eye that varies by degree according to how far away the object of focus happens to be.

Motion parallax:
Discrepancy in apparent movement as we shift vantage point of near and distant objects, depending on the relative distance of those objects.

remains constant (shape constancy), which shows that our brains are equipped to take our own movement into account.

In the course of travel from one point to the other, although images shift across the retina as we move, we do not experience this as an earthquake, with the environment suddenly becoming mercurial. The brain takes into account our body movement, and works out the implications for this in terms of the images moving across our retina. The brain works out whether the movement of the retinal image is just due to our own movement, or whether it is caused by movement of the object itself. We usually take this for granted, only to realize that such a process is taking place when the brain makes a mistake. Consider when we stop at a station next to another train that has a destination in the opposite direction. After a while, we move off leaving the stationary train behind, or at least we momentarily think that's what happened. Presently we find our brain has made an error, that we are still stationary, and that really it was the other train that moved away!

Do we have to learn to do these wonderful feats of perception, or are they something our genes equip us to do? If we do not need to learn to perceive, then is perception fully fledged from birth or does it become active with a kind of maturational unfolding? If the latter, does development progress through discrete stages or is there gradual change? One of the very first psychologists, William James, stated at the beginning of the twentieth century that the newborn's world is a "blooming, buzzing confusion." Apparently, James took the view that perceiving is not something we can do from the outset and furthermore he supposed that perception is the product of learning and experience. In other words, he thought that through experience with the world, we eventually come to make sense out of confusion. Specifically, James assumed that prior to perceptual learning, the visual sensations of the retina are an incoherent jumble. In recent years, psychologists have set out to investigate whether this is indeed the case, and their attempts are fascinating not just because of the discoveries they made, but for some of the ingenious methodology that has been devised as a means for coming up with answers.

To what extent are basic perceptual abilities innate?

Is the world that infants inhabit a "blooming, buzzing confusion"?

PERCEPTION OF THE WORLD AS 3-D

Are we born with the ability to perceive the world in 3-D? If we are, then there should be signs that babies perceive distance. One of the first studies was conducted by Gibson and Walk (1960). The now famous apparatus they constructed is known as the visual cliff. It was inspired by a visit to the Grand Canyon, when Eleanor Gibson feared that her baby would get dangerously close to the precipice. Was there a genuine risk, or would her baby show a healthy respect for the great height and keep well away from the edge? An experiment involving the Grand Canyon seems rather ungainly, not to mention unethical! Gibson and Walk set out to recreate a miniature, perfectly safe, precipice in their laboratory, and examine whether babies displayed fear when near the edge. If they did, this surely would be a sign that they perceived the drop, which would imply that they perceived that there was some distance (i.e. in the third dimension) between themselves and the surface located at the bottom of the precipice.

The visual cliff was essentially a very large box, the top of which was clear Perspex (see the figure overleaf). A black-and-white checkered pattern

Key Terms

Shape constancy:
A perceptual mechanism that enables us to appreciate that an object remains the same shape even though it looks different as we take up different vantage points.

Visual cliff:
Apparatus designed by Gibson and Walk that formed an apparent precipice for the purpose of testing perception of depth in babies.

Gibson and Walk's (1960) visual cliff.

was visible beneath the Perspex. The surface beneath one half, known as the shallow side, was pressed against the underside of the Perspex. The surface beneath the other half, known as the deep side, was a substantial way below the surface. A plank divided the deep and shallow sides, forming a kind of bridge across the apparatus. On the deep side of this bridge there appeared to be a nasty drop. On the shallow side, there was no such drop. Of course, this is the impression we adults have, but what about babies? Would they be reluctant to venture onto the deep side, suggesting that they could perceive depth? Gibson and Walk coaxed a baby onto the bridge, and asked the mother to call from the shallow side and then from the deep side. The youngest babies selected for participation were about 8 months, for the simple reason that younger babies were unable to crawl. Basically, the findings were that babies crawled to the mother across the shallow side, but refused to go onto the deep side. This neatly demonstrates that 8-month-olds perceive depth. Presumably, their reluctance to go onto the deep side suggested they were alert to the danger of the precipice. This could only result from the babies perceiving that the deep side was some distance down.

Did the infants perceive depth by binocular parallax—in other words, did the difference in information received by each retina provide a clue about the distance of the surface beneath the precipice? Interestingly, we can be absolutely sure that even if the babies tested by Gibson and Walk were capable of interpreting binocular parallax, this is not the only way they could perceive the deep side of the apparatus. The babies continued to be cautious about the deep side even when wearing an eye patch, making it possible only to see through the remaining uncovered eye. In this case, binocular parallax could not have provided a clue to depth.

Although we can rule out one clue to depth that the babies might have used, we cannot be certain how they actually perceived depth. Gibson and Walk put forward the plausible suggestion that the babies used motion parallax. Although the babies were not traveling from one place to another at any great speed, they still moved their heads; and as they did so, they would have experienced the edge of the plank shifting about considerably on the retina, while the pattern on the surface beneath the precipice would have shifted to a lesser extent. Can we conclude, then, that the ability to utilize information about motion parallax is with us from birth? Gibson and Walk's study suggests it is with us from an early age, but how can we be sure that the infants had not *learned* to use motion parallax during the first 8 months of life?

At least we might be able to argue against a special kind of learning and experience in perceiving depth. Gibson and Walk considered that if depth perception did depend on learning and experience, then it would probably be related with the baby's crawling. When babies are able to move about under their own volition, then they would almost certainly have collisions with other objects

Is the ability to perceive the world in 3-D a product of genetic inheritance?

if they were unable to perceive how far away those objects were. Consequently, perhaps when babies begin to learn the visual cues that precipitate a collision they effectively learn to interpret the cues that are informative of depth. This is the reason why Gibson and Walk recruited babies to their study who were only just beginning to crawl: They were sufficiently mobile to be able to take part in the study, but they had only very limited experience of moving under their own volition and therefore probably would not yet have had sufficient opportunity to learn about the cues of depth. At the very least, therefore, it seems babies can perceive depth even in the absence of the learning they could gain from the experience of moving under their own volition.

A subsequent study, though, suggested that being able to move under one's own volition might impact on perception in a subtle way (Campos, Bertenthal, & Kermoian, 1992). Babies aged around 7 months were divided into those who were just beginning to crawl and those who had not yet started to crawl. Even though both groups were the same age, they reacted differently when lowered over the deep side of the visual cliff. Those who had started to crawl exhibited a fear response, as marked by accelerated heart rate. Those who had not started to crawl responded with heart deceleration, which suggests they noticed the deep side but were not anxious. In a further study, 7-month-old infants who had not yet started to crawl were divided into two groups. One group was selected for experience navigating around in a wheeled walker and the other group had no such experience. Only those who experienced movement under their own volition subsequently showed a fear response when lowered on the deep side of the visual cliff. Evidently, moving under one's own volition is an important experience, at least in learning an appropriate fear response to a precipice.

A very imaginative experiment suggesting infants are capable of depth perception at a mere 3 months of age was conducted by Bower (1965). He placed a 30 cm cube one meter from the infants. The babies were offered a pacifier wired to a sensor that detected sucking. If they sucked when the cube was present, they were rewarded by an adult popping up and saying "peekaboo." The peekaboo experience excited the babies, and they continued sucking in search of the pleasurable experience. However, sucking only brought about a peekaboo when the cube was present and babies thus learned that it was useless sucking when the cube was absent.

Having done this, Bower then presented a variety of cubes of different sizes and distances, and noted which combination elicited most sucking. He found that a cube the same size as the original, but more distant and therefore giving rise to a much smaller retinal image, generated considerable sucking in the infants. Indeed, the sucking was at least as great as that elicited from a larger cube at greater distance that produced the same size of retinal image as the original. In contrast, a cube of different size from the original, situated at a distance that resulted in a different retinal size, elicited relatively little sucking from the babies.

In this experiment, the babies' sucking served as a sign of recognition of the original cube. Since babies sucked a great deal when the cube was moved into the distance, it suggests that the babies recognized this as being the original cube presented to them during the peekaboo game. It demonstrates that young babies have some understanding of depth, and seem to appreciate that an object that moves into the distance produces a smaller image in the eye. This shows that they know something about depth or distance at a younger age than demonstrated by Gibson and Walk. The earlier in development we can demonstrate ability, the more likely it is present from the outset, yet we still cannot rule out the possibility of early experience and learning accounting for these results.

Subsequent research established unequivocally that size constancy is indeed innate. We now know that newborns are genetically equipped with an understanding about the relationship between distance and the apparent size of objects. This was demonstrated in a ground-breaking study by Slater, Mattock, and Brown (1990), who tested 2-day-old babies. It is a well known fact that newborns prefer to look at novel things, and show less interest in familiar objects. Slater *et al.* began their study by repeatedly showing babies a cube bearing a distinctive pattern from a fixed distance. Over the course of this familiarization period we can suppose that the babies' interest in the cube would fade. Slater *et al.* then introduced a second cube similar to the first in all respects except for size, and over several trials the researchers varied the distances of the two cubes. If newborns have size constancy, they would prefer the new cube, irrespective of its distance and apparent size as projected onto the retina. In other words, they would prefer to look at the new cube even if its distance was such that the size of the image projected onto the retina was the same as that of the first cube during the familiarization trials, as illustrated in the figure below.

Strikingly, newborns did prefer to look more at the new cube than the old one, no matter how near or distant, and therefore no matter what the retinal size of each. In other words, babies recognized the new object as new, and the old object as old, despite apparent changes in size. This seems to demonstrate unequivocally that size constancy, and therefore an aspect of depth perception, is innate and functioning from the outset.

It is useful to think of the survival value a faculty would confer on a newborn. If it is considerable, then there is a possibility that the faculty in question would be innate. If it is low, then probably it is not innate. The perception of depth obviously has some kind of general survival value. For example, if the baby can perceive a precipice, then she is better equipped to avoid a nasty fall than if she were unable to perceive a great depth. Also, if the

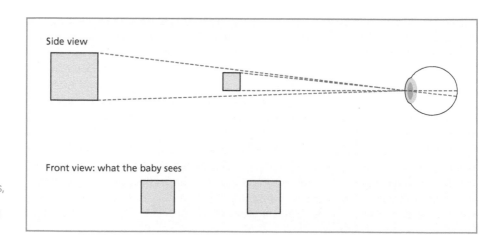

Although the two cubes projected identical images, babies attended more to the physically larger novel cube.

infant can perceive a source of food in space, then, providing she is mobile, she is unlikely to go hungry. In addition to these general considerations, there is a much more specific benefit to being able to perceive depth from the moment the infant is born. Objects fall or hurtle through space, and in some unfortunate cases, collide with the baby. There are everyday examples of such events, as when the mother is preparing to bottle-feed the baby, but then the bottle slips from her hand and drops onto the baby's face.

In view of this, perhaps from birth or at least a very early age, we might find that infants show some kind of defensive reaction to an object that is heading directly toward them. Such reaction, if it minimized harm, would be of great benefit to the infant's health and safety. Bower, Broughton, and Moore (1970) constructed an apparatus that made an object project toward the infant's face, but for obvious reasons stopped short just prior to collision. The reaction of infants as young as 2 weeks was typically defensive. Their eyes widened, they pulled their heads back, and raised their hands in front of their faces. This finding clearly suggests that the infants could perceive depth, and were equipped to take appropriate defensive action on perceiving an object on collision course. Still, could a 2-week-old infant have had sufficient opportunity to learn a defensive reaction to imminent collision? Maybe. However, the baby's behavior seems so universal and well defined, despite such little opportunity for learning, that it is most likely that perception of depth, and the accompanying defensive reaction when threatened with a rapidly approaching object, is largely a product of our genetic programming.

There are many different cues to depth that babies could have utilized in Bower et al.'s study. When an object rapidly approaches, the accompanying visual experience is that a minuscule retinal image quickly becomes very large. Consider an approaching train. At first, the train is just a dot in the distance, then, as it gets closer and closer, eventually the image of the train occupies the whole of one's visual space. In this case, the expansion of the image of the train tells us not that the train is getting larger, but that it is getting nearer. Was it the expansion of the image of the approaching object that provoked the defensive reaction in Bower et al.'s infants?

Ball and Tronick (1971) set out to investigate, testing infants under the age of 2 weeks. They supported babies in front of a screen, and projected a pattern onto the screen that could be expanded at the experimenters' discretion. Ball and Tronick found that a rapid expansion of the pattern produced a defensive reaction in the infants, similar to that reported by Bower et al. To adults, the expansion of the pattern created the illusion of an approaching object on a collision course. Another form of expanding pattern used in the study also created the illusion of an approaching object, but one that was not on a collision course. When presented to the babies, this pattern did not provoke a defensive reaction. The findings suggest that at least one aspect of our perception of depth is innate. At birth, the rapid expansion of an image has meaning for us: that a distant object is rapidly approaching.

Are we born with ability to understand something of the relationship between figure and ground? Distant objects are liable to be hidden, at least partly, by closer objects, and this gives a clue to depth. Interestingly, note, we interpret the closer object as *hiding* part of the more distant object. In other words, we assume quite naturally that the hidden part of the distant object still continues to exist even though it is invisible from our particular vantage point.

Key Term
Figure and ground: Objects in the foreground are interpreted as partly or fully occluding objects in the background.

More generally, are we born with an understanding that an occluded part of the background is continuous with the part of the background that we can see directly. If so, then we are born with an understanding of an important aspect of the relationship between figure and ground. Kellman and Spelke (1983) investigated this possibility in a preferential looking procedure.

Kellman and Spelke presented 3-month-old babies with the stimulus shown in the top part of the figure below. The figure shows an oblique white bar laid over a black bar. But the stimulus was not static; rather the white bar moved slightly back and forth, reinforcing the impression that it was not a part of the black bar but that it was in front of, and therefore occluding, part of the black bar. The movement of the white bar was restricted in such a way that during this first phase of the study, babies never actually saw the very middle of the black bar. Nevertheless, we would normally assume that aspects of the background that we can't see are continuous with aspects of the background that we can see; after all, that is implicit in perceiving figure and ground. So, is there a way of investigating whether 3-month-old babies made such an assumption?

Kellman and Spelke hit upon the idea of showing babies two different stimuli in the second phase of the study, and these appear in the bottom half of the figure below. They presented two black bars in the absence of the oblique white bars, where one was intact and continuous while the other had a break in the middle. Importantly, this break appeared at a location within the bar that the babies had never previously seen (because previously it had been obscured by the oblique white bar). In principle, the black bar that had been partly hidden by the white bar could have been continuous or it could have had a break. There was insufficient information available in Phase 1 of the procedure to be able to decide. Nevertheless, the 3-month-old babies apparently preferred the broken bar, for they spent much more time looking at it, suggesting in turn that it was novel to them: Remember, babies generally prefer to look at novel things. Putting it another way, the babies' preference not to look at the continuous bar suggested they were already familiar with it. Yet their only opportunity to become familiar was in Phase 1 of the study, effectively

During the training phase, babies were exposed to the stimulus shown in the top part of the figure. In the test phase, they were shown the two bars in the bottom half of the figure and they tended to look at the bar that did have a break in it.

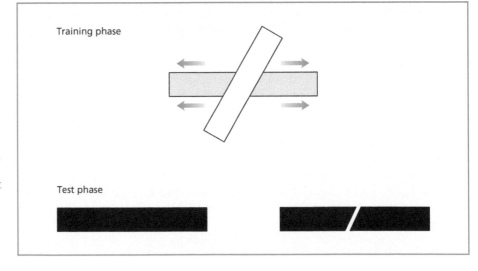

suggesting that they had perceived the partly hidden bar to be continuous. In other words, 3-month-old babies perceive figure–ground relations in a rather sophisticated way that contributes toward their perception of the world as 3-D.

A critic might argue that babies preferred to look at the broken bar in Phase 2 not because they interpreted it as novel but because they found the broken bar inherently more interesting. That is to say, although we know that babies prefer to look at novel objects, they are likely also to prefer more interesting objects and in this case the broken bar has more interest owing to its added complexity. Fortunately, Kellman and Spelke anticipated this criticism and took appropriate steps by including a control condition in which babies were shown the two stimuli at the bottom part of the figure above but in the absence of Phase 1. If babies preferred to look at the broken bar because it was more interesting, rather than because it was novel, they would still prefer to look at it even if they had not experienced Phase 1. In that case, both bars would be equally novel. The findings of the control condition suggested there was no systematic preference for looking at the broken bar. Having ruled out an alternative explanation for preferential looking in the main part of the study, we are left with the theoretically more interesting possibility that babies did indeed relate to the broken bar as if it were novel, which in turn is consistent with the possibility that they construed the two bars in Phase 1 as having a figure–ground relationship. This study gives remarkable insight into the perceptual proficiency of babies aged 3 months and we now know that the findings were not just a fluke: Slater *et al.* obtained the same results with newly born infants. Evidently, perceiving figure–ground relations is something we do from the outset.

Babies are born with a surprisingly effective perceptual memory, as demonstrated by Slater, Mattock, Brown, and Bremner (1991). They exposed 2-day-old babies to a pair of straight lines joined at an angle of 45 degrees, and presented this stimulus rotated through a variety of orientations. Subsequently, they presented the stimulus in the company of another pair of lines joined together in a similar way, but this time at the obtuse angle of 135 degrees (see the figure right). The babies spent much more time looking at the new pair of lines, irrespective of how either stimulus was oriented in space. This suggests that the babies could distinguish between the two stimuli according to whether they were familiar or novel, indicating that they could conceptualize line pairs as forming a single object no matter how it was positioned in space. In other words, the babies seem to have surprisingly good memory for the enduring properties of objects that maintain despite changes in orientation.

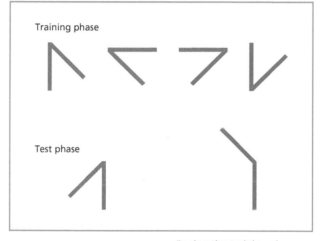

During the training phase, babies were acquainted with the stimulus in various orientations. In the test phase, they were presented with the same stimulus in a novel orientation and also a completely new stimulus. They preferred to look at the new stimulus.

PERCEPTION OF SOCIAL STIMULI

Is there is a link between innate perceptual abilities and early social behavior? Parents typically note that as they look into the cot of their 6-week-old, the

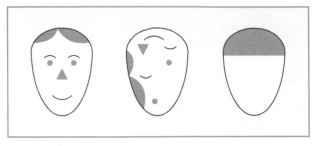

Babies preferred to look at the schematic face in preference to the other two figures.

baby smiles. This gives a great sense of joy to the parent, who is then encouraged by the experience to devote more and more attention to the baby. It is thus to the baby's benefit to look at the parent and smile; it is hardly surprising, then, to find that babies have a preference for looking at the human face. Fantz (1961) demonstrated as much when he presented the stimuli in the figure on the left. One-month-old babies preferred to look at the schematic design that resembles a face. Note that one of the figures has the same complexity and even contains all the same features. This did not attract babies' attention, perhaps because the features were not configured as a face. A study employing eye-tracking technology (Fogel & Melson, 1988) offers converging evidence in demonstrating that babies aged between 4 and 8 weeks tend to fixate on the eyes when looking at a photograph of a face.

Bower (1982) reports that even a crude mask will elicit a smile from a 6-week-old. Further research, to find out what aspect of the mask produced the baby's smile, revealed that it was just the two dots that formed the eyes. This is demonstrated by the fact that if we show the baby a card with two dots on it, separated proportionally to the eyes in an adult face, the baby will smile. The best interpretation of this finding is that the baby is adapted from birth to smile at dots! What possible value could such behavior have? Actually, the behavior could be of great benefit to the baby. The dots that the baby is most likely to be confronted with are those in the face of parents or caregivers: the eyes. If the baby smiles at eyes, then it is likely that she will be rewarded with attention and love from the adult, rewards that are important to the baby's survival and development.

When do babies begin to recognize their parents? To find out, Carpenter (1975) propped up babies in front of a screen that had a face-sized window in the middle. Various people appeared in the window, sometimes the baby's mother, and sometimes a female stranger. From about the age of 2 weeks babies looked at the mother's face much more than at a stranger's, demonstrating not only recognition but a preference for their mother. The finding seems especially striking when we consider that babies usually prefer to look at novel stimuli. Their preference for their mother was obviously sufficient to overrule that bias.

Having a preference to look at faces facilitates babies' capacity for imitation. Meltzoff and Moore (1983) observed a striking aptitude for imitation in babies as young as 3 months. The babies reliably poked out their tongues, opened their months, and puckered when an adult modeled these various behaviors. In one sense, it seems natural that babies should imitate an adult and yet it remains mysterious that a baby can know how to make the same facial expression that is modeled to them; after all, they had no opportunity to sit in front of a mirror and learn by trial and error which muscles are needed to pull the same face that the adult expressed. Meltzoff and Moore called this intriguing phenomenon inter-modal mapping in recognition that the babies needed to map between the modality of vision to the modality of motor control if they were successfully to imitate the adult.

Key Term

Inter-modal mapping: Mapping from one modality (e.g. information acquired through visual perception) to another (e.g. making a facial expression).

THE ROLE OF EXPERIENCE AND LEARNING IN PERCEPTUAL DEVELOPMENT

The first part of this chapter presented abundant and compelling evidence about innate facets of perception. Evidently, we are born with a capacity for interpreting the 2-D pattern of light projected onto the retina as a world of solid objects that vary in distance. Moreover, our perception is social from the outset, meaning that we are primed to visually attend and respond to socially relevant stimuli. Does all this mean there is nothing to learn where perception is concerned? According to Richard Gregory (1966), learning is involved in perception, even in perception of depth as cued by lines of perspective. He argued that our susceptibility to certain illusions, such as the Müller-Lyer (see the figure on the right) serves as testimony to perceptual learning. The parallel lines are physically the same length but the arrowheads induce an illusion that belies that fact. Why are we susceptible to the Müller-Lyer illusion? According to Gregory, the arrowheads, by their very shape, give perspective clues to depth. The outward-pointing heads make the vertical line appear to project toward us, as in the corner of a building. Because we perceive the line as being nearer, we wrongly compensate in a process of size constancy, which makes us think it is smaller than it really is. The opposite effect occurs for the inward-pointing arrowheads, which give cues akin to the interior corner of a room.

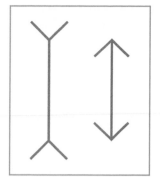

Müller-Lyer illusion. The two vertical lines are physically identical in length.

Gregory suggested that our susceptibility to the Müller-Lyer illusion results from exposure to straight edges and corners, which are abundant in the carpentered environment of the developed world. He predicted that in some cultures, where straight edges and corners are uncommon, people would not be susceptible to the Müller-Lyer illusion. Findings suggest that the people who belong to hunter-gatherer tribes, whose environments contain few straight lines or corners, may well be less susceptible to the Müller-Lyer illusion than people brought up in a Western culture. By implication, Gregory seemed to suppose that size constancy results from learning and experience, yet this is patently contradicted by studies by Bower and Slater *et al.*, described previously.

It is now clear that Gregory's explanation of the Müller-Lyer illusion is incorrect. As you see in the figure overleaf, the illusion still works even when balls rather than arrowheads appear at the end of the comparison lines (Robinson, 1972). It is impossible that these balls give misleading perspective cues that provoke a compensating perceptual distortion. It is unsatisfactory to have one explanation for one version of the Müller-Lyer and a different one for a different version. Since the "carpentered environment" hypothesis cannot predict illusory distortion with the version that has balls at the end of the lines, there are no grounds for regarding it as adequate with respect to the version that has arrowheads. Precisely how we should explain the effect of the illusion remains a moot point.

Nonetheless, there is other convincing evidence that suggests knowledge of the world does feature in perception, showing that some aspects of perception are influenced by learning and experience. The evidence to support this view comes from a study conducted Mitchell and Taylor (1999), inspired by Thouless's (1932) classic research. Thouless asked participants to stand at the end of a table and look at a dinner plate (see the figure overleaf). He asked them to draw the dinner plate exactly as it appeared, meaning in effect that they should draw an ellipse. Thouless found that participants tended to

Key Term

Carpentered environment: An environment containing straight lines and 90-degree angles, which is typical in industrialized cultures.

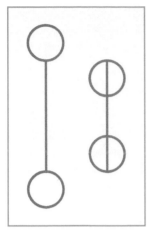

A variant of the Müller-Lyer that can't be explained by the "carpentered environment" hypothesis.

draw a more circular ellipse than they could actually see, as shown in the bottom figure overleaf. What caused the participants to exaggerate circularity? According to Thouless, the ambient perspective cues were responsible. When these were removed, participants no longer exaggerated. He demonstrated this in a study where participants looked into a darkened chamber in which a slanted disk was the only thing visible. All perspective cues were eliminated under this condition, and participants drew the shape accurately. However, in a replication (Taylor & Mitchell, 1997), in which participants reproduced the shape of a slanted disk using a computer, exaggeration of circularity was common, even when the disk was in a darkened chamber with all perspective cues removed. Participants' knowledge that the shape was a circle was sufficient for them to exaggerate circularity. Under a control condition, though, in which participants looked into the chamber and saw the ellipse without realizing that the shape was really a circle, their judgments of shape were accurate. This shows that participants did not have a general inclination to exaggerate circularity; rather, their exaggeration of circularity seemed to be linked specifically with their knowledge that the thing they were looking at was circular.

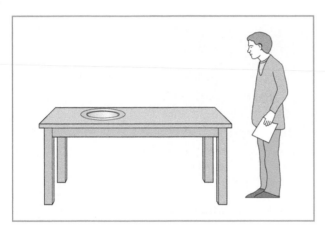

In Thouless's classic study, participants looked at a dinner plate on the table and had to draw it exactly as it looked from where they were standing.

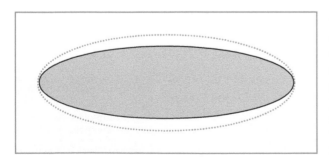

The inner, colored ellipse is the shape projected onto participant's retinas. The outer dotted line is the average shape they drew.

In a subsequent study, Mitchell and Taylor (1999) tested children aged between 3 and 7 years. Interestingly, the younger children exaggerated circularity even more than the older ones, but only when they knew that the ellipse they could see actually arose from a slanted circle. If they knew that the shape was a real ellipse, then they judged accurately. Hence, children's preconceptions about what they are looking at primes and guides their perception. How they see the world must therefore depend to an extent on what they have learned through prior experience: this would determine the character of their preconceptions. For this reason if for no other, experiences demonstrably influence perception, meaning that perception is more than just an innate mechanism.

It seems that learned knowledge does not impact upon everyone to the same extent in how they perceive the world. Ropar and Mitchell (2002) asked participants with autism to estimate the shape of a slanted circle either in the presence or absence of perspective cues. When perspective cues were present, participants with autism exaggerated circularity just like other participant groups. When perspective cues were eliminated, participants with autism exaggerated circularity to a much lesser extent. The participants understood that they were viewing a slanted circle, but this information apparently did not impact upon their perception. It seems that although perception is influenced by perspective cues in individuals with autism just as in participants without autism, those with autism are unique in their perception being less influenced by the knowledge that is separate from what we can glean from perspective cues.

In general, it seems likely that innate knowledge and knowledge that is learned through experience combine to facilitate perception. The possibility that there are two distinct forms of knowledge is supported by the finding that some individuals, namely those with autism, exhibit attenuation in the benefit they gain from but one form of knowledge.

Critically evaluate evidence that putatively shows how learning and experience feature in perceptual abilities.

Summary

- In one sense, the findings reported in this chapter serve as definitive evidence to the effect that William James was wrong. James suggested that the world of the newborn is a blooming, buzzing confusion. Thanks to some excellent research, we now know this is untrue, and that in fact young babies can perform an astonishing range of perceptual feats. The newborn is capable of figure–ground perception, and perception of depth by other means. The newborn appears to have the rudiments for perception of faces, and is drawn to focus on the region of the eyes. Young babies seem capable of size constancy, recognizing that an object is the same size, even though its retinal image changes with distance. They also seem to recognize an object as the same, despite changes in orientation. In sum, the baby is equipped with a considerable range of basic perceptual abilities, which confers potential to make sense of what she can see from the earliest age.
- However, it hardly need be said that perception is only possible in an environment that is waiting to be perceived. Features of this environment, and one's particular experiences of it, could have an important bearing on some aspects of perception. There can be no doubt that much of the detail that we are able to perceive is dependent on our knowledge base, and therefore on our learning. Being able to perceive as we do is influenced in a substantial way by both genetic and environmental factors working together.

Essay Questions

1. Is the ability to perceive the world in three dimensions innate?
2. To what degree does knowledge and experience play a role in the development of visual perception?

Further Reading

A very accessible and engaging book specializing on infants' perceptual abilities is:

- Kellman, P. J. & Arterberry, M. (1998). *The cradle of knowledge: Perceptual development in infancy.* Cambridge, MA: MIT Press.

chapter 11

Contents

The role of heredity and environment in intelligence

11

Chapter Aims

- To introduce the concept of intelligence.
- To introduce ways in which intelligence is measured.
- To assess the roles of nature and nurture in intelligence.
- To highlight some of the problems faced when testing intelligence.

INTRODUCTION

Intelligence really matters to people's lives; those that are deemed intelligent are perceived to be cut out for better jobs and more prosperous and fulfilling lives. The idea of intelligence as a measurable entity is only about a 100 years old, and yet it is firmly ingrained in our folk psychological perception of ourselves and others that we can be ranked in terms of our intelligence. One of the central questions that researchers have investigated is whether intelligence is inherited or whether it is a result of education and other environmental factors, in other words, it figures in the nature–nurture debate. Unlike some other topics, this debate reaches beyond the realms of academia and pure scientific interest because intelligence is assigned such high status in our society and, moreover, it has implications for educational and social policy. In this chapter we look at how intelligence is measured and reflect on the role of nature and nurture.

WHAT IS INHERITED?

Before we look specifically at intelligence, it is worthwhile establishing more generally whether there is some way of telling which part of the way we are, and the way we behave, is determined by the genes passed on to us from our parents. At a glance, this may seem a simple question to answer. All we have to do is watch newborn babies: They have had little or no time to learn and so presumably whatever they can do is determined genetically, and therefore is likely to be inherited from the mother, the father, or both. By observing newborns we could compile a long list of behaviors: crying, swallowing, blinking, defecating, sucking, yawning, sneezing, coughing, grasping, etc.

Although we can be confident that these behaviors are genetically determined, how can we be sure that behaviors which emerge later in development are learned—that is, develop as a consequence of exposure to the environment? What about walking? Are we genetically programmed to do this, or do we have to learn to walk? What about riding a bicycle, a skill that seems similar to walking on the face of things? These are both behaviors that emerge sometime after birth, yet only one of them is genetically programmed.

Babies begin to walk around the age of 12 months. There is little learning involved, and babies "know" before they begin to walk how to move their legs and balance. By suspending the newborn from its arms we can demonstrate that the young baby knows how to walk. It will make characteristic "walking" movements. This shows that the newborn has a latent knowledge, that is, knowledge of how to walk, which is put on hold until it is approximately 12 months of age.

In contrast, riding a bike is something we have to learn to do to a large extent. We can be completely confident about this fact for the simple reason that bikes are a relatively recent invention. Our ancestors, except for our very close ones, had no opportunity to ride bikes. Therefore, there has been no opportunity in the slow process of evolution for bike-riding genes to emerge in the population, perhaps until recently. As such, we can ride bikes only in so far as this skill falls within the scope of our general capability, but we are not genetically endowed with specific bike-riding knowledge.

Although we can make a clear distinction between walking and bike-riding in the extent to which genetic programming features in each of these behaviors, it also makes sense to suppose that general potential to do things, to acquire new skills, is partly under genetic influence. For example, we have a good sense of balance and good hand–eye coordination, and of course the actual shape of humans suits the design of a bike: It is difficult to imagine a snake riding a bike; but then bikes were invented by humans for humans.

The human/snake example is based on the rather gross case of genetically determined body shape, and how that affords learning certain skills. Still, there could be "hidden" genetic factors that influence our learning to ride a bike. Suppose two children of the same age begin learning to ride bikes. One has mastered the skill within 24 hours and the other is still struggling after a month. Bearing in mind Piaget's ideas, we might wonder whether the child who acquired the skill rapidly was able to make a parallel between bike-riding and some other skill or skills she possessed, and apply these to the bike-riding situation. For example, perhaps the child was already accomplished in riding a skateboard, and was able to apply her balancing knowledge to bike-riding with success. In other words, perhaps a process of assimilation accelerated acquisition of the bike-riding skill. Putting this aside, however, some people may have a general ability to pick things up quickly, whether or not assimilation is brought into play—a general ability that has a genetic basis.

A visit to any classroom can leave us in no doubt that some children simply learn to do things more rapidly than others. It might be because the fast learners have a serious attitude toward study, because they concentrate harder, because they do extra work out of school hours, which benefits the process of assimilation. None of these factors need have anything to do with a general genetic potential to understand things easily. Nevertheless, a prevalent belief in our society is that some children are simply more able than others, whatever their experiences. In other words, it is widely held that some children are endowed with more of this mysterious genetically determined general ability. Of such children, we may say, "She's bright…she's clever…she's intelligent." We may think of these children as being the ones who will do well at university, and perhaps have a successful career in a professional capacity. In contrast, we may think of the "less gifted" children as being the ones who leave school early and work in a lower-status job.

Perhaps we should take a moment here to ask whether this prevailing attitude is actually warranted. Are some people really genetically gifted with high intelligence? Perhaps the most difficult question of all: How do we go about investigating whether individual differences in intelligence are determined by our genes?

INTELLIGENCE: HEREDITY VERSUS ENVIRONMENT

How do we find a way of measuring intelligence? Educationists and psychologists use the IQ test. "IQ" stands for "intelligence quotient," which simply means "intelligence score." The first IQ tests were devised jointly by Alfred Binet and Theodore Simon at the beginning of the twentieth century in France. It was around this time that a massive expansion in education occurred and it quickly became apparent that some children did not seem to learn very well. The educational establishment was searching for a basis to categorize children in order to find out who would benefit from systematic tuition in a mainstream setting and who had special educational needs. The parallel in modern-day schools is streaming, though it is unlikely that IQ tests are involved in the process.

The rationale for the IQ test seems simple and sensible on the face of things: The educationists were not particularly interested in how good the children were to begin with in art, creative writing, math, etc., but how good they were likely to become after having the benefit of education. If they had potential to be excellent, then education served a useful purpose, whereas if they were unlikely to be any better than when they first started, then education would be a useless waste of time and resources. The educationists, to their great credit, recognized that simply interviewing the child, or presenting some "home-made" tests of ability, could be biased. Another potential pitfall with the interview is that some extravert children might appear confident and relaxed, perhaps giving the impression that they were intelligent, while some introverted children might be intimidated by the experience and appear mute and dull. Extraversion–introversion almost certainly is not related to intelligence and learning, but it might influence our ability to *perform* well, that is, it might have a bearing on how well we can express what we have learnt in some test situations. Clearly, when we want to assess learning and intelligence we need to avoid biasing tests so that some children would

Alfred Binet (1857–1911).

Key Term
IQ: The intelligence quotient is an index of an individual's intelligence score. It falls on a normal distribution with a mean of 100.

perform better, irrespective of whether they have *learnt* better. Also, it is difficult to audit the objectivity of interviews, so prejudice could unwittingly or even cynically creep into the procedure. There is always a concern that interviewers might be influenced by how much they like or dislike a particular child or even show nepotism. The trouble with home-made tests is that a given child may or may not "pass," depending upon the nature of the particular test. In brief, a standardized test was required. This is where Binet and Simon entered the scene.

They devised a test that presents a series of problems that supposedly rely minimally on practical knowledge or experience. The belief was that if practical knowledge and experience are of no help in solving the problems, then the child must call upon her "genetic general intelligence" for the solution. Here is an example of the kind of problem you might find in an IQ test:

Write the next number in the sequence: 2 6 18 54 162 ?

To solve the problem, you have to identify a simple formula that can account for the increased value of each subsequent figure, and then apply that in order to extrapolate to the next value in the sequence. In this case, the formula is "multiply each successive figure by 3" and the answer is of course 486.

A second belief was that speed is important, with the idea that intelligent people can do the same mental things faster than dull people. For this reason, the tests were timed. A third belief was that more of one's intelligence potential can be realized with increasing maturity, so in calculating IQ score, age of the child is taken into consideration. The idea was that if a boy had IQ 100 at age 7, then he might still have IQ 100 at 15, even though at the older age he managed to solve many more of the problems in the time available. The test designer achieves this in the following way: Let IQ 100 be the average score. Thus, if on average 7-year-olds solve 10 out of 30 problems in the allotted time, then we will say that any 7-year-old who gets 10 right has IQ 100. If on average 15-year-olds solve 20 out of 30 problems correctly, then we will say that any 15-year-old who gets 20 right has IQ 100. You can see from this that the number of problems an individual gets right is expected to increase with age, but IQ can remain constant. Consequently, if the number of problems solved correctly does not increase with age, then IQ would decrease. Also, you can see how mental age can be calculated. In the example given above, if the 15-year-old solves only 10 problems correctly, then we might say that he has a mental age of 7 years. In the early days, IQ score was linked to mental age and contrasted with chronological age in the following formula:

$$\frac{Mental\ age \times 100}{Chronological\ age} = IQ$$

If we select, say, 500 people from the population at random, and then gave them an IQ test, we would find that the pattern of the 500 scores conformed to a "normal distribution," as shown in the figure opposite. The average score would be 100. Sixty-seven percent of scores would be between 85 and 115, and ninety-six percent of scores would be between 70 and 130. In other words, most people have IQ 100, or somewhere near that figure. Only a small minority of people have extremely high or extremely low scores. This normal distribution fits many natural phenomena, such as height or weight. For example, most adult males are about 175 cm tall. Proportionately few are above 200 cm, and few are below 150 cm. Tallness is under substantial genetic influence, and, like many genetic characteristics, we can see how the pattern of heights in the population conforms to a normal distribution. To argue that intelligence is a genetic trait, like tallness, it is useful, but not conclusive, to show that IQ scores conform to such a distribution. As a result, devisers of intelligence tests have been at pains to make sure that the pattern of population IQ scores

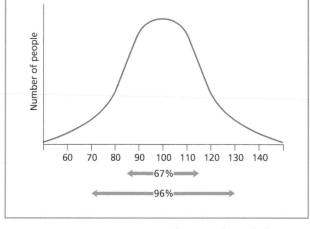

The normal population distribution of IQ scores forms a bell-shaped curve. Sixty-seven percent of the population have a score between 85 and 115; ninety-six percent have a score between 70 and 130.

is normally distributed. This has been achieved by adding or removing specific IQ problems, according to how they influence the population distribution of scores the test yields. IQ tests are widely used today, and their construction owes a great deal to Binet and Simon's original efforts.

One of the problems with this approach to the construction of intelligence tests is that there are no recognized principles to determine what items should or should not be included. In other words, test construction is atheoretical. There is no theory of intelligence to specify that one kind of item should be included while another should be left out. Rather, inclusion is determined pragmatically, according to the effect an item has on the shape of the distribution of scores it generates from a given population. In consequence, the devisers of intelligence tests are at a loss to define intelligence. They can only state the tautology that intelligence is what an intelligence test measures. You can immediately see the problems that arise from such a circular definition—and ideally, of course, we would want to know what it is we are measuring before we devise a test to do so. After all, if we don't know beforehand what we are trying to measure, then how will we know whether we have devised a test that is successful at doing so? The response often heard to this argument is that we know IQ tests are successful at measuring intelligence because they correlate with later scholastic success. This equation of intelligence as scholastic success seems rather unsatisfying, like the tautology in the earlier definition.

We all have an intuitive idea of what intelligence is, and who we think is intelligent and who is not. Providing a more scientific definition has proved a challenge for psychologists and educationists for the last century or so. We have already seen that devisers of IQ tests claim that intelligence is exactly what an intelligence tests measures. The trouble is that even if we have no theory on what intelligence is when we devise a test, we still have to make some assumptions. Imagine for example that you wanted to devise a measurement of how self-confident someone is. Without a clear definition of that concept you could still amass a number of questions which you and others think will tap into self-confidence. How would you validate the test? Your only option would be to give it to people who you think are very self-confident and those who are not very self-confident and see whether the test results confirm your observations. You could then add or remove items until your measure of

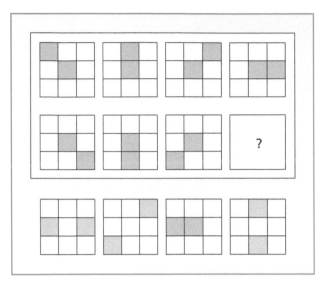

Raven's Progressive Matrices are widely used nonverbal intelligence tests. In each test item, the participant's aim is to select the missing part required to complete a pattern. In this example the third option is the correct one.

Key Terms

g:
General intelligence is the concept of intelligence as a single factor that influences all cognitive functioning.

Stanford–Binet test:
The modern version of the first IQ tests, testing verbal and nonverbal items.

Raven's Standard Progressive Matrices:
A nonverbal intelligence test requiring analogous reasoning on geometric shapes and patterns, which was designed to be culture-free.

Fluid intelligence:
A fundamental factor in intelligence that represents the ability to think and reason on your feet.

Crystalized intelligence:
A fundamental factor in intelligence that represents the accumulated knowledge of an individual.

self-confidence corresponds to your observations. This does not seem a very satisfying way of measuring self-confidence and even less so for intelligence. After all, your performance on IQ tests can directly influence what kind of job you are going to get. And we can also see easily, that even without being able to give a good theoretical definition of self-confidence we still needed to make assumptions of what kind of questions we thought would make sense in this context.

DESCRIBING AND TESTING THE CONCEPT OF INTELLIGENCE

Although there are difficulties with defining intelligence, there are nonetheless some assumptions of what intelligence is and how it should be measured. These are based on different descriptions of the concept of intelligence, which differ fundamentally in how many components they propose intelligence to be made up of.

According to the concept of generalized intelligence *g*, intelligence is a single construct that influences all cognitive functioning. If this were true then we should find that people who do well on one measure of cognitive ability would also do well on another, even if the measures are superficially dissimilar. There is good evidence that this kind of correlation exists between tests (Geary, 2005). Tests that seem well suited to tap into this single measure of intelligence are the Stanford–Binet test (a modern version of the Binet–Simon test) and the Raven's Standard Progressive Matrices.

The Raven's Matrices presents tasks that are meant to tap into a single underlying intelligence, and Spearman considered them to be the best measure of *g*. The test presents participants with a series of nonverbal, visual puzzles in which they have to form perceptual relations between elements in the series and, for example, identify the continuation of the series by analogous reasoning. The performance on this test should not benefit from levels of formal schooling, or be influenced by cultural differences. We will discuss these claims more critically in connection with environmental influences on IQ later in this chapter.

In spite of the evidence for *g*, it is not an unchallenged concept. Cattell (1987) proposed that intelligence is not a single concept, but is instead composed of fluid intelligence and crystalized intelligence. Fluid intelligence describes the cognitive functioning component, that is, the ability to deal with novel problems and concepts, think on your feet, process information, and adapt your chosen strategy to deal with any given situation. This component of intelligence is not influenced by formal schooling, but may be thought of as an innate endowment. Crystalized intelligence, on the other hand, does benefit from schooling and learning, as it directly represents all the stored factual information an individual has. How are the components of fluid and crystalized intelligence related? In some ways we might argue that the factual information you have does not influence your ability to reason about novel problems. If you had learned all the member states of the European Union, this knowledge would not increase your general reasoning ability, or, *fluid* intelligence, but it might help you to reason about situations related to European politics. In addition, we would intuitively expect that people whose fluid intelligence is superior will find it easier to acquire knowledge and facts and adopt strategies that allow them to do so at a faster rate. What kind of evidence would support a claim for these two components of intelligence? If there are two components to intelligence we would expect a strong relationship between different tests of fluid intelligence and different tests of crystalized intelligence respectively, but for the relationship between tests of fluid and crystalized intelligence compared to one another to be much weaker. And we would expect different developmental trajectories: Crystalized intelligence should increase throughout an individual's life-span, but fluid intelligence should not. Several studies have found good supporting evidence for both these conditions (Geary, 2005; Horn, Donaldson, & Engstrom, 1981).

The Wechsler Intelligence Scale for Children (WISC) and Wechsler Adult Scale for Intelligence (WASI) are possibly the most widely used intelligence tests. The WISC has two sections—a verbal section and a performance section—and may thus directly tap into both crystalized and fluid intelligence. In the verbal section the child's language skills and general knowledge of the world are tested (crystalized intelligence), with tasks that test knowledge of information, comprehension of similarities, competence with arithmetic and vocabulary, comprehension of concepts, and memory for digit spans.

The performance section tests spatial and perceptual abilities (fluid intelligence) and includes tasks that require identifying a missing part to complete a picture, arranging several pictures so that they tell a coherent story, coding different geometric objects in accordance with a prescribed scheme quickly and accurately, recreating a printed geometrical block design with patterned wooden cubes, assembling parts of objects meaningfully, and drawing a path through a maze. These verbal and performance sections are scored separately before they are combined to give a final overall intelligence score.

PROBLEMS WITH TESTING INTELLIGENCE

As we have seen in previous sections there is a lack of a clear definition of intelligence and the models proposing a different number of components to intelligence are all supported by good evidence. This leaves a situation that is inconclusive and that has not been resolved to date. The lack of a satisfying and agreed upon definition of intelligence and therefore a lack of agreement of what the tests actually measure is a problem, but it is not the only one. Fundamentally, it is surely wrong to assume automatically that IQ tests probe a general *genetically determined* intelligence. Although certain children may not have experienced the particular problems presented in the test, it is still possible that some would be at an advantage if they had the benefit of experiences of a more general nature they could call upon in solving the problems. For example, if one is well practiced in manipulating numbers and using formulae, then presumably one would have a head start in solving the kind of problem presented earlier (working out the next number in the sequence: 2 6 18 54 162...).

Key Terms

WISC:
The Wechsler Intelligence Scale for children is one of the most widely used IQ tests, split into a verbal and a performance component, which are combined to give a full-scale IQ.

WASI:
The Wechsler Adult Scale of Intelligence is the adult version of the WISC and contains the same components.

In other words, the process of assimilation will be brought into play to help solve the problem, showing that experience could aid performance on the IQ test. A second point, which is related, is that as one's experiences become more enriched and varied, so perhaps this would be reflected in higher IQ. If this turned out to be true, then it is patently wrong to think that IQ could serve as a useful tool for predicting how a child is going to progress through education, because this would depend on the potentially beneficial yet unpredictable effect of future experiences. Hence, IQ might not be quite so static, contrary to what some seem to have supposed (e.g. Jensen, 1980) and we can disengage from a gloomy picture of the world where a large part of the population is held back because of their low IQ.

HERITABILITY OF INTELLIGENCE

What is the value of studies that investigate the IQs of identical twins reared apart?

Putting aside the absence of a definition or theory of intelligence for the moment, we can investigate the heritability of IQ by testing identical twins, known as monozygotic twins (MZ). They develop from the union of a single sperm with a single egg. Shortly after conception, the fertilized egg splits to form two separate individuals who are genetically identical. These individuals are different from fraternal twins, known as dizygotic twins (DZ). In this case, the mother has two eggs, both of which are fertilized by different sperms. Genetically, these twins are just like ordinary brothers and sisters, sharing 50% genetic constitution, and they are only special in that they share the mother's womb. Because identical twins have the same genetic constitution, any differences in IQ can be attributed to experiences—environmental factors. If IQs were identical, this could either be because genetic constitution is identical, or it could be because the twins have had the same experiences. Therefore, the really big question surrounds the difference in IQ of identical twins who are brought up in different families.

On the other side of the coin we can consider pairs of previously unrelated children adopted into the same family. Obviously these children have human genes, but with respect to the overall variability in the human gene pool, they have nothing in common. Nonetheless, they share a very similar environment, which could have an important influence on IQ. For example, a house rule could be that all children in the family have to do homework for an hour each day after school. It is possible that such a regimen could almost guarantee a reasonable educational performance, which in turn could benefit IQ. Note, however, that we can never say that any two people have an identical environment, or identical experiences. The best we can do is say that members of the same family are likely to have similar experiences. If it emerged that children in their teens who had been adopted into a family from birth had completely different IQs from each other, it would not necessarily show that experiences are irrelevant to IQ.

We depend on a statistical tool for comparing the similarity between IQ scores, called the correlation coefficient. This is a test calculated on pairs of scores, which yields a figure that indicates the relatedness of the pairs. The correlation score can range from −1 to +1, where +1 indicates a perfect relationship between pairs of scores. This is what we would find if each twin had the same IQ as his identical twin brother. In other words, if we knew

Key Terms

Monozygotic twins:
Identical twins who share 100% of genetic material because they develop from a single egg and sperm.

Dizygotic twins:
Fraternal twins who share 50% of genetic material because they develop from separate eggs.

one twin's IQ, then we could be confident that his brother would have exactly the same IQ, and this would be reflected as a correlation score of +1. We would find a correlation of 0 if IQs of twin pairs were unrelated, and we would find a correlation of −1 if there was a negative relationship. This could result if it was always the case that when one twin had a high IQ, his brother had a low IQ. In practice, correlations usually appear as a decimal, falling somewhere between the extremes of −1 and +1.

Monozygotic twins have the same genetic constitution, so differences in IQ can be attributed to environmental factors.

Knowing the correlation of IQ for identical twins helps to specify the heritability of IQ, within certain margins of statistical error. Given that genetic constitution is constant across identical twins, and in so far as twins did not share the same experiences, presumably the degree to which pairs of scores are similar reflects the shared genetic profile. What about the actual figures? Identical twins reared apart from an early age are rare, but during the course of this century, many researchers have found samples of such children. In an analysis of data combined from all these studies, Plomin and DeFries (1980) found that the correlation between pairs of IQ scores from identical twins reared apart is .72 (see the table below). A correlation of this order was supported in a further study (Bouchard, Lykken, McGue, Segal, & Tellegen, 1990). Bouchard *et al.* tested 56 pairs of identical twins from all over the world separated within the first 2 years, who typically were not reunited until adulthood. In plain language, a member of an identical twin pair identified as bright by the IQ test was very likely to have a co-twin who was also identified as bright according to the same test, even if that co-twin had been brought up in a different family. Similarly, a member of an identical twin pair identified as dull was likely to have a co-twin also identified as such, again, even if they were brought up in different families. This suggests that genetic profile is a very important factor in determining an individual's IQ.

Correlations based on the IQ scores from pairs of individuals (data summarized from Plomin & DeFries, 1980)

Kind of pairing	Number of pairs	Correlation
Identical twins reared together	4,672	.86
Identical twins reared apart	65	.72
Fraternal twins reared together	5,546	.60
Nontwin siblings reared together	26,473	.47
Nontwin siblings reared apart	203	.24
Genetically unrelated sibling pairs (adopted children)	369	.34

The table above shows that the correlation for fraternal twins reared together is .60. As mentioned, these individuals have a 50% shared genetic constitution. Remarkably, the correlation for identical twins reared apart is higher than that for fraternal twins reared together. Studies investigating the

IQ of biologically unrelated individuals who had been adopted into the same family at an early age, find a correlation of .34. This seems to suggest that the environment certainly contributes something, but that this contribution looks somewhat modest. Nonetheless, common sense says that as twin pairs get older, the prediction of one twin's IQ from the other would becomes less precise, because the IQ score would reflect a larger proportion of particular experiences over the life-time. Paradoxically, however, the opposite seems to be the case. McClearn *et al.* (1997) reviewed studies suggesting that the heritability factor (which is derived from the correlation value) shows as 20% in infancy, 40% in childhood, 50% in adolescence, and 60% in adulthood. McClearn *et al.* went on to test a sample of octogenarians, which included 110 identical twins. The heritability figure derived from these individuals showed as 50%. These striking figures raise two questions: Why does the heritability figure increase during childhood? Why doesn't the heritability figure decrease over the course of adulthood? The answer to the first question might be found in the administration of the test itself. Younger children might suffer more general confusion than older ones over what they are supposed to do in the test, and this could introduce statistical error that masks the true heritability value.

Discuss changes in intelligence over time, both within the individual and within society.

The answer to the second question is perhaps more interesting. One's cognitive abilities are not necessarily stable over the life-span. Certainly old age is a time when cognitive functioning can change substantially, particularly in an individual who acquires a disorder like Alzheimer's disease. Such a disorder would cause a serious deterioration in IQ. It seems there is genetic susceptibility to disorders of old age, in which case both members of an identical twin pair might have a similar profile in terms of the effects of aging. If a pair of twins both suffered Alzheimer's then both would have suppressed IQ; if both were free of this disorder, then both might have a relatively high IQ. Looking at the implications more generally, it might well be that our IQ is influenced by our life experiences. However, our genetic profile might play an important part in determining what form these experiences take.

The difficulty with quantifying the relative influence of genetics and the environment and thus addressing the questions of why the influence of heritability increases during the life-span is that such an investigation would require an enormously large sample size. Recently, this challenge has been taken on by a team of researchers who combined data from 11,000 pairs of twins from four countries (Haworth *et al.*, 2010; also Davis, Haworth, & Plomin, 2009). We already know from previous studies that the relationship between genes and environment is not that as people grow older the accumulation of life experiences would account for more individual differences than the genetic endowment present at birth, as common sense would suggest. In this large-scale investigation we find again that the influence of genetics *increases* as people get older: from 41% at 9 years old to 66% in young adulthood at 17 years old. The same pattern holds in older individuals, from young adulthood to late middle age (Lyons *et al.*, 2009). How then is it possible for genetics to exert this increasing influence? Haworth *et al.* (2010) speculate that the effect is driven by an interaction between the genotype of the person and the environment they live in, such that we are not passively living in the world, but are actively creating, seeking out, and forming experiences that further accentuate any differences based on genotype. The role of the environment is therefore very important, both in terms of what we create for children growing up, but also in terms of the opportunities we give children to create their own environment for learning and development.

How compelling is the evidence that suggests intelligence is largely inherited?

EVALUATING THE TWIN STUDIES

In view of the correlations and heritability figures cited above, it is clear that performance on IQ tests is considerably influenced by genetic constitution. The point is no longer in dispute. However, many still feel that advocates of the heredity position are inclined to overstate the scale of the genetic contribution. In connection with this, it is interesting to find a difference in correlation values between ordinary siblings and fraternal twins (see the table in the previous section). The correlation for the fraternal twins is higher than for ordinary siblings despite the fact that their shared genetic constitution is no greater. It might be that because twins are born at pretty much the same time, they are particularly likely to have experiences in common.

Devlin, Daniels, and Roeder (1997) point out that the similarity of experience actually begins in the womb. They note that maternal smoking and poor diet can adversely affect birth weight and general health of babies; on the other hand, a good maternal diet and general good maternal health is associated with good health in the baby. Getting off to a healthy start in life could benefit intellectual development more generally. In contrast, a sickly child would probably have fewer stimulating experiences and could well gain less from those experiences compared with a healthy child. It might always be a struggle thereafter for an unhealthy child to make up the lost ground. Adults might assume the child could not cope with intellectual challenges, and would not think it appropriate to stretch the child.

The suggestion made by Devlin *et al.* helps to interpret the high correlation between the IQ scores of identical twins. Twins reared apart have often been thought not to have experiences in common. In consequence, many assume that the shared genetic constitution is the only way to explain the high correlation. However, given that identical twins shared the same environment in the womb, this could have made a substantial contribution to the correlation. In brief, all identical twins have some experiences in common, even if they have been reared apart from birth, given that they shared the same womb at the same time.

On the other side of the coin, we can be confident that any *difference* we find in IQ of identical twins is due to environmental influence (and general statistical error in the testing): It cannot be due to differences in genetic constitution because that does not vary across identical twins. Looking at the correlation between IQs of identical twins reared in different families is not particularly meaningful without knowing in what way the families were different. It may be that in many cases the families were very similar, so it might not be accurate to say that co-twins were reared in a different environment. In fact, many twin pairs classified as "reared apart" had been adopted into different households belonging to the same extended family. For example, one member of a twin pair may have been adopted by an aunt in a neighboring street. In this case, although the twins do not live in the same house, presumably they have a very similar life style and education. Even when twins were adopted into unrelated families, in many cases the class status and education were comparable. What we need to know, then, is whether IQ is different in co-twins who are reared in radically different environments. If so, this would show that particular experiences do have an important impact on IQ.

In a classic study, Robert Woodworth (1941) investigated 19 pairs of identical twins, some of whom were reared in similar environments, and some of whom were reared in completely different ones. He found that when separated identical twins were reared in similar environments, IQs were very nearly the same. For twins reared in different environments, another picture emerged. In the case of one twin pair, the difference in IQ was 24 points—a very substantial figure indeed. The twin with the higher IQ was reared in a prosperous family, went to college, and then became a schoolteacher. The twin with the lower IQ was reared by a poor family, and attended school only for 2 years. Since that study, several subsequent researchers have found the same. Namely, identical twins reared apart who enjoy a similar life style have very similar IQs. Those who have completely different life styles have big discrepancies between their IQ scores.

What do these findings tell us? They tell us that environmental factors can have a large influence on IQ. They also tell us that there is an important genetic factor involved in IQ, given that identical twins reared apart but in similar environments have very similar IQs. To appreciate the importance of the genetic contribution, this fact has to be considered in relation to the modest correlation between the IQs of unrelated children adopted into the same family. In many of these cases, similarity of environment has been insufficient to bring about similar IQ scores. What we see in the case of high correlations between identical twins reared in similar environments, whether or not they are in the very same family, is shared genetic constitution and similarity in environment combining together to contribute to IQ.

So how much intelligence, reflected in IQ, is transmitted to us through our genes? Nobody really knows the answer. Indeed, some see it as a silly question for the simple reason that intelligence must be a product of heredity and environment in combination. IQ is impossible without both acting together. Interestingly, Bouchard *et al.* (1990) suggest that part of the link between genetic profile and IQ might have an indirect character. For example, the genetic contribution to temperament, inquisitiveness, and aggression could have a knock-on effect where IQ is concerned. A child whose genetically determined temperament is not well suited to the social dynamics of the school situation may experience discomfort that prevents him getting on with learning and developing academically. As a consequence of this individual's unpleasant experience in school, he may perform badly on the IQ test and other scholarly measures. In this case, the poor performance would be due to the individual's unfortunate experiences, but had his temperament been different, he could have flourished in an academic setting. If he had an identical twin brother, who had the same genetic basis of

If this child's temperament is not suited to the social dynamics of his school, and in turn his education suffers, then, according to Bouchard *et al.* (1990), his genetic constitution may indirectly exert a negative influence on his performance in an IQ test.

temperament, he would probably perform badly on an IQ test also. In sum, Bouchard *et al.* argue that nature (genetic constitution) could exert its influence via nurture (experiences).

Another reason why identical twins (who are reared together) are likely to share experiences is because they may be treated as being the same person by others who find it difficult to discriminate between them. In contrast, fraternal twins are no more alike than ordinary brothers and sisters. It is unlikely that members of fraternal twin pairs would be treated as the same individual. We can see, then, that not only do identical twins have a more similar genetic profile than fraternal pairs, they are more likely to have the same kinds of experiences.

Haworth *et al.*'s (2010) and Lyons *et al.*'s (2009) large-scale investigations showed very clearly the interplay between the genotype of an individual and the environmental influences on cognitive ability, with a particular focus on the role the individual plays as an active creator of these environments in which they can flourish. The best way forward is therefore to look at environmental influences on IQ. There is nothing we can do about an individual's genetic constitution, but there is an awful lot we can do to change the environment and to let individuals be active participants in enriching their own environment. In other words, what kind of experiences might benefit or damage an individual's IQ?

ENVIRONMENTAL FACTORS AND IQ

The question is straightforward: Does an enriched environment give rise to higher IQ? The question is a simple one, but things can become tricky when we try to define "enriched" in relation to the environment. Let us begin with a basic issue. Common sense says that the environment should be such that children are well provided for in terms of diet and nutrition. Bearing this idea in mind, perhaps it comes as no surprise that schoolteachers often feel their children underperform in academic activities due to an intake of too much "junk food" and not enough decent, wholesome food. Is this feeling completely unfounded, or is there hard evidence to support it?

In what ways can the environment affect intelligence?

One schoolteacher, Gwilym Roberts, teamed up with David Benton (Benton & Roberts, 1988) to find out. They gave an 8-month course of tablets to 30 Welsh 12-year-olds. The tablets contained a wide range of vitamins and minerals. Another 30 similar children received an inert tablet that was indistinguishable from the vitamin, both in appearance and flavor. Children were ignorant as to whether the tablets they were taking were vitamins or the inert substance, as were the helpers who handed them out. Subsequently, all 60 children attempted an IQ test and the results were startling: The IQ of those who received vitamin supplementation increased by approximately nine points on average, whereas the IQ of those taking the inert tablet hardly changed (see the figure on the right).

Giving children vitamins, rather than an inert placebo, seemed to dramatically increase their IQ (Benton & Roberts, 1988).

When the provocative findings of this study were published, the news swept across the nation, and stocks of vitamins in pharmacies were rapidly depleted! Since then, however, the finding has been called into question.

Benton and Buts' (1990) study on the dietary habits of Belgian children suggested that additional vitamins will not improve performance in an IQ test, if that child's diet is already adequate in terms of vitamin content.

Crombie, Todman, McNeill, and Florey (1990) tried to replicate the Benton and Roberts (1988) study with a group of Scottish schoolchildren, but found no improvement in IQ following a course of vitamin supplementation. However, another investigation achieved a successful replication with a group of 15-year-olds in the USA (Schoenthaler, Amos, Doraz, Kelly, & Wakefield, 1991).

Benton (1991) explains discrepancies in the results of studies as follows. He proposes that so long as the child's diet is adequate in terms of vitamin content, additional vitamins would be redundant, and therefore of no benefit to performance in an IQ test. In contrast, if the child's diet is vitamin deficient, this could prevent her brain operating to its full potential, just as a car running on low-grade fuel lacks high performance. To investigate this possibility, Benton and Buts (1990) supplemented the diets of several groups of children in Belgium. In this study, the researchers monitored the daily nutrition of the children over and above what they received through the vitamin tablets. The findings were exactly as Benton predicted, in that the unfortunate children who had an impoverished diet benefited considerably from vitamin supplementation, as reflected in higher IQ score. In contrast, those who already had a good healthy diet showed no improvement in IQ following vitamin supplementation. Apparently, the good diet of these children enabled them to function at full potential, so in their case vitamin supplementation was redundant.

The lesson to be learned, it seems, is that a healthy diet is not only to the advantage of physical development, but also to mental functioning. Vitamin supplementation can improve mental functioning in some cases, but if the child already eats enough healthy food, this will be unnecessary. So it is clear that an environment which provides adequate nourishment is one that is conducive to good mental performance. There are probably no wonder drugs or magical vitamins that can increase the potential of mental functioning, but an inadequate diet could be a distinct disadvantage. Precisely what form this disadvantage takes is not so clear. A commonly held view is that certain additives to processed foods, like coloring and preservatives, can be associated with hyperactivity in some children. This is bound to impair performance on an IQ test. It might be that any adverse effects of additive compounds are more potent in the absence of an adequate concentration of vitamins. Alternatively, it might be that vitamins exert a more direct effect on the function of the brain. Some vitamins play a key role in the synthesis and metabolism of the chemical messengers that feature in communication between brain cells. A person starved of vitamins might thus be restricted in their mental functioning.

THE SOCIAL ENVIRONMENT

What about the social and psychological environment—to what extent can this affect IQ? The first step is to identify factors we think would facilitate cognitive development. Such an undertaking was carried out by Elardo, Bradley, and

Caldwell (1975). They compiled a list of items that in their judgment contribute to an enriched environment, including:

- When speaking to the child, the mother's voice conveys positive feeling.
- Mother structures child's play periods.
- Mother reads stories at least three times weekly.
- Family provides learning equipment appropriate to age of child.
- Child gets out of house at least four times a week.
- Mother shouts at child relatively infrequently.
- Mother spontaneously vocalizes to child relatively frequently.

Elardo *et al.* visited 77 children from lower-class homes, when the children were aged 6 months, and again when they were 24 months. The investigators had compiled a checklist to establish whether the family environment conformed to their definition of "enriched." Having done this, the investigators visited the children twice more, once when they were aged 3, and again when they were 4½. This time, the visit was to administer IQ tests.

After completing the checklist, Elardo *et al.* correlated the score assigned to the family with the IQ of the child. The correlations ranged from .44 (family visit at 6 months, IQ tested at 4½ years) to .70 (family visit at 24 months, IQ tested at 3 years). In all cases, the correlations were substantial, showing a strong relationship between family environment and the IQ of the child.

These figures give the strong impression that an ideal social environment can yield higher IQ. However, this conclusion could be too simple. It is possible that the children who had high IQ also had "intelligent" genes, passed on to them by intelligent parents. It might be these genes that caused the high IQ, and the effect of the environment could have been illusory. This could have come about if more intelligent parents, because they are more intelligent, arrange the environment in a way that happens to conform with Elardo *et al.*'s vision of what is ideal. For example, the more intelligent parents could be the ones who structure the child's play periods, read stories to the child, and so on. Yet it might be the intelligent genes transmitted from parent to child that are responsible for the high IQ, and not the way the intelligent parent arranges the environment. It would be especially useful to know whether the findings reported by Elardo *et al.* could be repeated in children who are adopted into a biologically unrelated family. Such a study was conducted by Plomin, Loehlin, and DeFries (1985), who found reassuringly much the same as did Elardo *et al.* The correlation between family environment and IQ was not as high, but nevertheless a relationship between the two was clearly evident. Accordingly, it seems appropriate to conclude that family environment can have an important bearing on IQ. Again, it is not so clear precisely how certain kinds of family exert a beneficial effect. The simplest explanation is that the child is able to profit from the intellectually stimulating experiences that are offered. Another important factor might be the emotional climate of the family. An environment that is "good natured" may encourage the child to feel at ease in such a way that she is able to benefit from intellectually stimulating experiences. It is likely that the intellectual and emotional characteristics of the home combine to nurture intelligence.

Another important feature of the family environment is the number of children in the home. Zajonc (1983) reports that the average IQ of children with several siblings tends to be lower than that of children with just one sibling or none at all. Indeed, he found that IQ correlates negatively with the number of siblings to form a linear trend. Moreover, within families the average IQ of the first born tends to be higher than that of the second born, which in turn is higher than that of the third born, and so on down the birth-order list. These effects are small, but nevertheless we can be confident they are present. Note that this is a trend derived from averages, so there could be many exceptions in individual families. Zajonc explains the pattern with his "confluence theory." His basic premise is that parents' attention to children is emotionally and intellectually stimulating, which is therefore bound to help intellectual growth. Since there is only so much time in the day, the parent's input is necessarily finite. If this finite input is divided between lots of children, then each individual stands to benefit less than a singleton who individually received a greater proportion of the parent's attention.

If Zajonc is correct, his research has serious implications for the teacher–pupil ratio in the classroom. If the intellectually beneficial effect of the adult's input is diluted when the group of children in her care is large, then this would be a further reason for suggesting that steps should be taken to reduce the ratio. However, there are reasons for being cautious about Zajonc's confluence theory. Families with many children tend to be less well-off than families with few children. The parents tend to be in relatively low-paid jobs or perhaps unemployed. This is compounded by the fact that it is expensive to rear children, so the more children, the greater the financial burden. The negative correlation between number of siblings and IQ might have more to do with the dilution of financial resources than dilution of parental input. Zajonc was aware of this impediment to clear interpretation, which is why he was keen to show that birth-order is also relevant to IQ. Apparently, he supposed that the parent's social status and income would not decrease with each successive child. This view might be incorrect, though. As mentioned, limited financial resources have to be stretched further with more children. Also, it might be that both parents are able to continue working with one or two children, but presumably that would become rather difficult with more children. This in itself would engender a reduction in income.

The influence of the environment can also be seen in that children seem to be getting more intelligent! We saw earlier that devisers of IQ tests take great pains to ensure that the results conform to a normal distribution, or bell curve. In order to achieve that, IQ tests are periodically recalibrated to conform to a bell curve and to have 100 as the mid-point on this curve. However, Flynn (1984, 1987, 1999) pointed out that without this readjustment we would see an average increase of IQ test performance of about three points per decade.

This apparent increase in IQ is termed the Flynn effect and can be seen the world over. The data sets Flynn analyzed and presented are vast, but all show a similar trend. Some of the largest increases were seen in the Netherlands where performance on the Raven's Progressive Matrices showed an increase of 21 points between 1952 and 1981, in France the gain was 25 points between 1949 and 1974, and in the USA the Stanford–Binet test results for 1932 and 1971 revealed an increase of 10 IQ points. These results would not pose a problem if they could only be found for items that test general knowledge, because we would expect each generation to benefit from the culturally accumulated

Key Term

Flynn effect:
The increase in IQ scores from one generation to the other, which averages about 3 points per generation and cannot be explained by an increase in intelligence in the population.

knowledge of the generation before them. Any one of us would probably do better than Newton on a test of general knowledge, without indicating that we're geniuses and Newton was not. The striking finding is that the gain is observed in tests, such as the Raven's Matrices, that are meant to be free from the influence of culture and learning. Flynn took this as an indication that IQ tests do not actually measure intelligence, but something that correlates weakly with intelligence. This weak relationship, Flynn argues, does not allow us to make particularly meaningful comparisons across generations and should make us very cautious when comparing between cultures and races.

We can visualize the striking workings of the Flynn effect when we look at how children would do on an old IQ test, which has not been recalibrated, and imagine how children from the beginning of the last century would fare on a modern-day test. Howard (2001) describes such a scenario by looking at changes in average performance on the Stanford–Binet test, a standard IQ test. In 1932, a child would be considered to have average intelligence if their IQ was 100 and to have "very superior intelligence" if their IQ was over 130; only about 3% of children achieved this highest classification. However, if the 1932 test was taken by children in 2007, the mid-point of the bell curve would be around an IQ of about 120 and 25% would be described as having very superior intelligence, that is, one in every four children would be described as having a superior intellect! This improvement in test performance cannot have come about because of changes due to biological evolution, because there is simply not enough time for these changes to have taken place. The effect, if not biological, must then be attributed to the environment and here the most likely candidates for bringing about these changes are an improvement in the education system, better nutrition, and perhaps also a more supportive parenting style. We can speculate on these factors, but it has to be acknowledged that the Flynn effect is real although not entirely understood.

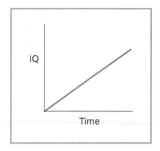

The Flynn effect is the year-on-year rise of IQ test scores, an effect seen in most parts of the world, although at greatly varying rates.

IQ, ELITISM, AND RACISM

Some individuals with a political axe to grind have latched upon differences in IQ between social groups as a basis for arguing that various social ills have a genetic origin. Perhaps the most controversial account is presented by Herrnstein and Murray (1994). They demonstrated a small but reliable correlation between low IQ and things such as crime, poverty, and marital disharmony. Their conclusion is that people of low intelligence tend to do stupid things like indulge in crime, lose their job, recklessly spend money, and fail to show care and respect to members of their family. They suggest that since IQ has a genetic basis, it is pointless to introduce changes to the environment. In other words, they take the fatalistic view that one's destiny is at the mercy of the genetic credentials dealt by nature, and programs of social welfare are unable to change that fact. This view is questionable, as we are still no closer to finding the actual genes that determine intelligence. As the search for the "intelligence gene" continues it becomes increasingly obvious that it is rather unlikely to be a single gene that is responsible for intelligence, but rather that there is a more complex interplay between facets of genes and the environment that correlate with a person's intelligence. The current thinking is that these genetic factors involved in intelligence are more like the factors involved in

Streetwise skills such as the commercial, bargaining, and economic abilities these children possess are not measured by conventional intelligence tests.

a person's overall height: they are unlikely to be solely genetically determined, but still malleable by the environment in which they are expressed (Johnson, 2010).

Another obvious objection to a very determinist view of intelligence would be to say that IQ tests are culturally unfair. Perhaps the form of an IQ test tends to be alien to members of socially disadvantaged groups, in which case an individual's IQ score might not reflect their true ability. Herrnstein and Murray refute this suggestion, however. It is possible to make predictions of an individual's kind of employment and earning from IQ. It is also possible to predict how many years they spend in education and indeed their educational performance. The reliability of these predictions remains the same whichever social class the individual belongs to. For example, just as low IQ predicts low income, low status employment, or unemployment in somebody of working class, so it predicts the same in someone from a middle-class background. If individuals from a lower class were underestimated by IQ, then we might expect their employment and salary to be higher than predicted by their IQ, but on average this is not so.

However, there are many ways in which Herrnstein and Murray's argument is specious, that is, it seems superficially sound and convincing but falls apart under scrutiny. For a start, it might be that the very same cultural unfairness that led unprivileged people not to succeed in education or to prosper also prevented the individual gaining a high score on an IQ test. The underlying point here is that even those who are most vociferous over the heritability of IQ concede that there is a substantial environmental contribution. Hence, we cannot be sure whether the various social ills that correlate with low IQ actually correlate with the genetic component of IQ or the environmental component. Herrnstein and Murray assumed it was the genetic component that counted, but there is nothing in their data or argument that makes the assumption plausible. On the contrary, it seems much more likely on the face of things that alienation from society for social and environmental reasons would give rise both to the social ills mentioned and to underperformance on IQ tests. Had society been different, it is conceivable that those who are currently socially alienated would have prospered, would thus have no reason to engage in crime, would have not suffered the kind of embitterment that damages personal relationships, and in consequence would have enjoyed the high self-esteem that allows good scholastic performance and success in IQ tests.

There is now mounting evidence to suggest that the conclusions Herrnstein and Murray drew from the data are wrong, and we should consider some of these here. In America, black children scored about 10–15 points below the average of white children (Lynn, 1996). It is important to remember though that this is only one part of the information: We could also consider that many black children score higher than white children and many white children score lower than black children. The distribution of scores overlaps and by looking only at the mean score the impression of a large difference can be created.

Moreover, in a changing, more tolerant and just society, opportunities for education and success are open to more people. And in recent years the gap in average IQ between black and white children has begun to narrow (Ogbu & Stern, 2001), although this view of a narrowing gap is not uncontested (Rushton & Jensen, 2010). However, if this trend continues we may see that in future an improvement in the learning environment will eradicate a difference that was falsely attributed to genetics. And we may even see that with the development of better tests all children will have a better chance to put in a good performance in the test situation giving a truer and better reflection of their learning. After all, the poorly defined concept of intelligence has produced a number of tests, but many of the comparisons between ethnic groups are based on tests that have been strongly criticized (e.g. Sternberg, Grigorenko, & Kidd, 2005). Nisbett (2003), who wrote on a number of cultural factors that shape differences in cognition between members of different cultures, also highlights that people from Eastern and Western cultures have different ways of defining intelligence; intelligence tests in use today are biased toward a Westerner's style of thinking and reasoning. Many attempts have been made to construct tests that are fair and not biased, but so far this has not been entirely successful.

Summary

- There are several theories on the factors involved in intelligence, ranging from conceptualizing it as the single factor g, which touches on all other cognitive functioning, to the proposal that there are at least two factors, fluid (think on your feet) and crystalized (stored knowledge) intelligence. However, these conceptualizations are atheoretical and we remain without a proper definition of intelligence. This has not prevented researchers from developing IQ tests. These tests are often loosely related to a particular conceptualization of intelligence, for example the WISC tests components that may tap into fluid and crystalized intelligence, respectively, whereas the Raven's Progressive Matrices are designed to minimize the influence of culture and learning and aim to tap into a single underlying ability measure, or g. Without a theoretical definition of intelligence, however, it is difficult to say with certainty whether these tests actually measure IQ or something that correlates with, but may not be, intelligence. This is particularly apparent when considering the instability of IQ test measures over generations, as described by the Flynn effect. IQ tests remain a useful tool, particularly in educational settings, in which they are a good predictor of an individual's future academic attainment.
- Having reviewed the evidence on the question of heritability of intelligence, we can be left in no doubt that environmental factors have an important influence on IQ. Also, there can be no doubt that the genetic material transmitted to us from our parents makes a contribution. Genetic and environmental factors combine in determining IQ: both are essential, and IQ is impossible one without the other. To illustrate how the two factors might combine, a child who has learning difficulties, due to genetic error, may never

be able to attain a high IQ, no matter how stimulating the environment. Of course this does not mean that the child's IQ could not be improved. On the contrary, no doubt appropriate educational programs could prove to be very beneficial to IQ. The crucial point is that perhaps the child with learning difficulties may never attain a *high* IQ. In contrast to all this, the child who has potential for very high IQ may never reach this potential if he lives in a severely impoverished environment. We find a similar interaction between height and nutrition: Two people might have the same genetic expression for tall body height, but differences in their nutrition and health might mean that they will attain a different actual body height. If people have a genetic expression that is related to shorter body stature then no amount of nutritious food is going to allow them to grow taller. This is perhaps why with improving diets and healthcare successive generations of people have become taller. And maybe also why they have become smarter (the Flynn effect)!

- Debates about how much of IQ is due to genes and how much to the environment ultimately seem rather futile for the simple reason that it is difficult to envisage how we could ever arrive at a definitive answer. Perhaps the more useful approach is to accept that both are important, but given that we cannot or would not want to do anything about the genetic side of things, we should channel our energy into investigating what might be the most intellectually beneficial environment.

Essay Question

1. Is nature or nurture a greater influence on a person's intelligence?
2. What is the value of twin studies in investigating intelligence?

Further Reading

The book we recommend gives a very clear and accessible account of the logic and evidence that can be marshaled to argue about the mutual contributions of heredity and environment to intelligence:

- Plomin, R., DeFries, J. C., McClearn, G. E. & McGuffin, P. (2008). *Behavioral genetics* (5th edn.). New York: Worth Publishers.

Chapter 12

Contents

Language development

INTRODUCTION

Language has been described as the jewel in the crown of cognition (Pinker, 1994). Indeed, our ability to use language is often cited as something that sets us apart from other animals. However, on a fundamental level language is something we use to communicate, and there are many other living things that communicate with each other. For example, bees convey the location of rich sources of pollen to other inhabitants of their hive with an elaborate "dance." Is this dance something we should call language? Human language is similar to bee dancing in that both are tools of communication, but in other respects they are very different. Bee dancing is not a language, and it is better to reserve the term for the system of communication used by humans. The reason for this will become clear when we take a look at what language is and how children learn it.

None of us can remember much about our first attempts to acquire a mother tongue. However, many of us do have the experience of trying to learn a second language, and that gives insight into the complexity of the process. It is sometimes said that the easiest way to acquire a second language is to pick up an extensive vocabulary. That may be a big help, but there is much more to language than simply knowing lots of words. Inside our heads, whether or not we realize it, there is a store of rules that governs the way in which we combine words, particularly with regard to the categories of words we choose to use in order to speak in sentences. Consider the two simple statements:

The dog chased the cat.
The cat chased the dog.

Key Terms

Grammar:
A set of rules governing language.

Syntax:
A set of rules that governs how words can be combined into phrases and sentences.

The words used in both are identical, yet each statement has a completely different meaning. To an alien visiting earth for the first time, it would not be obvious why one arrangement of a specific set of words had one meaning, while another means something else. This simple example shows that sentence meaning amounts to more than the sum of the component words. Meaning also depends on word order, which is governed by what we call grammar and syntax, a set of rules stored in our brain.

There is nothing inevitable about the particular rules we happen to use. It might have been that "The dog chased the cat" referred to a scene in which it was the dog being pursued by the cat. In learning a second language, we find that some orderings of words turn out to be right, and others turn out to be wrong. It is not always obvious to begin with which is the correct ordering; to know that, we have to get to grips with the rules of grammar.

Bees, like humans, have rules of communication stored inside their brains. The rules are used to govern the way in which a communicating bee dances, and are used by the observing bees to interpret the dance in terms of navigation to a source of food. Invariably, a *round* dance indicates that the source of food is close by, whereas the *waggle* dance (waggling the bottom from side to side) indicates that food is further away. In the case of bees, then, the rules of communication are on the surface, and can be transcribed from the movements in the dance. We might therefore say that the dance is little more than an expression of the rules of communication. In contrast, human language involves both rules and words that are to be manipulated by those rules. Like bees, we use rules of language, but unlike bees we use these in conjunction with a vocabulary of words to produce an infinite variety of sentences. This allows us to say virtually anything about anything. That is not true of bees, who have no equivalent to "words." Their more rigid system allows them only to communicate the whereabouts of food in a set number of ways: Is it close by or further away? In an experiment to test the flexibility of the bee communication system a source of food was placed high above the hive (see the figure below). The scout bees found the hive, but on their return could

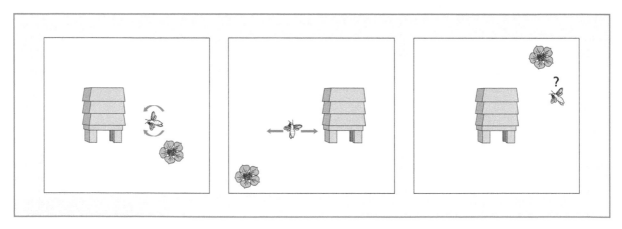

Bees can communicate the location of rich sources of food to other bees. To indicate that food is close by, a bee will fly around in a circle; to indicate that food is further away it will waggle its bottom, with the speed of waggling indicating about how far away the food is. When a source of food was placed high above a hive, the scout bee had no way of communicating the location "up" and the other bees could not find the food (von Frisch, 1954).

not communicate its location (von Frisch, 1954). This puts into stark contrast the possibilities afforded by the bee and human communication systems: The flexibility provided by the combination of grammatical rules and vocabulary affords a communication system that is the most powerful on earth because of its infinite generativity, that is, it allows us to produce and understand an infinite number of utterances made up from a finite number of words.

Most 5-year-olds are highly competent users of language. If babies and young children can acquire language so easily, then we might conclude that perhaps the rules of language are simple. A quick look at a heavy tome setting out the fundamental rules of grammar in the English language quickly tells us that this could not be further from the truth. To illustrate the point, once again consider the case of learning a foreign language. In most cases, this involves not just considerable exposure to the language, and practice in using it, but also tuition, perhaps to degree level to gain what we might call a high level of competence. Even then, there is a big difference in the fluency of the person speaking a second language and one speaking his mother tongue. In educational circles learning a second language is considered intellectually demanding, just like learning high-level algebra. Bearing in mind this comparison, it seems remarkable that a child below the age of 5 picks up language apparently with no effort on her part, and in the absence of formal tuition. Indeed, it would be difficult to prevent the child from acquiring language. Yet the idea of a young child learning complex algebra is unimaginable!

Another example provides further testimony to the difficulty involved in getting to grips with a language other than one's mother tongue. This is the case of hieroglyphics. Hieroglyphics are the systems of writing involving stylized drawings found on tombs in Ancient Egypt, developed between 5000 and 2000 years ago. These vaguely resemble the symbols found in travel brochures indicating the amenities of hotels and such places. Linguists spent decades trying to decipher hieroglyphics to understand how the language works and thus learn about the culture that generated them. Despite the considerable attention of highly trained experts, some hieroglyphics remain uninterpreted, demonstrating how elusive unfamiliar codes and grammar can be.

For these reasons, children's acquisition of language presents an intriguing puzzle. The newborn lacks the scholarly intellect of the professional linguist or the university student studying a second language—she knows next to nothing about the world. It is bordering on miraculous that young children rapidly master their mother tongue, apparently with the greatest of ease, and with minimum effort.

Perhaps young children do not need to acquire language at all; perhaps the rules for language are written into our genes, just as they are with bees. Of course it cannot be the case that specific features of English, French, Chinese, etc., are written into the child's genes. If an English newborn were adopted into a Chinese family, there is

Hieroglyphs from the preliterate artistic traditions of Egypt.

no doubt that the child would acquire Chinese, equally well as a native Chinese child. This shows that in some sense language acquisition is dependent upon experience and the environment. The question of how much of our language acquisition depends on learning from those around us and how much of it we might be born with is one of the fundamental questions in psycholinguistics. To help unlock this mystery, let us begin by examining the way in which language development proceeds.

THE COMPONENTS OF LANGUAGE

In order to understand language and produce it, children have to be competent with all its components. We have already mentioned most of these components in the preceding paragraphs, and describe them here in the order in which they occur developmentally. Words in any language are made up from distinct sounds. The smallest unit of sound is called a phoneme. Words are made up of combinations of phonemes, which also allow for the distinction between different words, for example cake and lake. One or more phonemes combined can make a word and thus create a morpheme. A morpheme is the smallest unit of meaning, or the semantics, of language. Phonemes make up morphemes, which are the basic building blocks of language. However, if you combined words in a nonsystematic or random way, it would be almost impossible to convey meaning. Syntax specifies the way in which words can be combined. It encompasses the grammatical rules of language, for example, the position of the noun, object, and verbs in a sentence. In addition to rules of grammar, there are pragmatic rules of language, which dictate how language is used in communication, for example, "Do you mind switching off your cell phone?" is not really a question, but a command because it is a request to complete the action. Understanding it as a command rather than a question requires going beyond the syntax and taking into account the conversational rules of this particular culture. How then does children's understanding of all these components develop?

A DESCRIPTION OF LANGUAGE DEVELOPMENT

During the first month following birth, the baby uses its voice for little other than crying. Between about 1 and 8 months, the baby develops an increasing repertoire of vocalizations, including laughing and cooing. Until 8 months, the baby largely makes vowel sounds, and a developing variety of pitch is noticeable during this period. Then, at about 8 months, the baby's vocalizations go through a sudden and radical transformation. One day the baby will begin babbling, and will continue doing so periodically from that moment on. The babbling is actually a combination of vowels with consonants, and sounds remarkably like speech, but without meaning. The baby is thus beginning to master the phonemes of the language around them.

There comes a point, perhaps 2 months after the first babbling, when the parents feel that some of the vocalizing is the baby's first genuine words. Unlike the onset of babbling, it is hard to decide when it is appropriate to say that a

Key Terms

Phoneme:
The smallest unit of sound making up language.

Morpheme:
Is made up of one or more phonemes and is the smallest unit of meaning in language.

Pragmatic rules of language:
A set of rules that dictates how language is used to communicate; an understanding of pragmatics is often essential to understand what the speaker means.

babbling sound is actually a word. To qualify as a word, the baby has to make a sound, or sequence of sounds, reliably used in relation to a thing. The first words are typically names of things, used to point something out or to catch the adult's attention, for example, "Mamma."

The expansion of vocabulary is slow to begin with. The baby may use one or two words at 12 months, and by 18 months it is likely that she only has a repertoire of 10 words. After this, she will undergo a rapid increase in vocabulary, saying a few new words for the first time every day (Goldfield & Reznick, 1990). Then, by 24 months, the baby is likely to have a vocabulary of around 300 words. In most cases, these early words are nouns—the names of objects around them. Following this, vocabulary expansion is of astronomical proportions, giving the average 6-year-old a repertoire of 14,000 words, although some children do not conform closely to this pattern. That does not necessarily mean there is anything amiss.

It is one thing for babies to use single words, or morphemes, to refer to objects around them. It is quite another thing for the child to use words in combination that engender the kind of meaning you might find in a sentence. Yet babies succeed in conveying sentence-like meaning by combining gesture with single words. For example, the baby might say "rattle," while grasping out in the general direction of the rattle. As parents we cannot help but interpret this as "pass me the rattle." These single-word gesture combinations, which embody sentence-like meaning, are known as holophrases. Holophrases are characteristic of the baby in the second year of life. After this, the baby begins to use combinations of two, and then three and four words, making communication of the intended meaning not so highly dependent on gesture.

When the young child begins to use words in combination, we find that she has a very characteristic pattern of speech. For example, she might say "Big doggie drink water," to mean "The big dog is drinking water." This style of early language is known as telegraphic speech, for obvious reasons. Telegraphic speech is highly ungrammatical in some respects. Many grammatical words are absent, such as "the" and "is." Also, words are not adapted to form grammatically correct sentences. For example, the child says "drink" instead of "drinks." However, in other respects, the young child does adhere to grammar, particularly with respect to word order. It is highly unlikely that the child will use a word order of the kind "Drink water big doggie." This shows that although young children have a lot to learn about the way in which words must be modified, according to grammatical tense and so on, they already possess the rudiments of syntax in its grammar of word ordering.

By the age of 3 years, the child's speech is less telegraphic. The child begins to acquire some of the finer points of grammar, reflected in the use of grammatical words. She also begins to alter words in order to indicate past tense. For example, whereas the younger child may have said "Walk Mummy shop," the older child may form the correct sentence, "I walked with Mummy to the shop." Unlike the younger child, the older one has learned that a different form of the verb *to walk* is used to form the past tense.

Beyond this point, however, the child's grammar seems to take a curious backward turn. It is common to find a 5-year-old who a year previously had said "ran" now saying "runned." This phenomenon is known as "overregularization," where the child treats all verbs as regular, adding -ed to the end in order to form

Key Terms
Holophrase: Using a single word, often in combination with a gesture, to express a more complex idea.
Telegraphic speech: An early style of language, resembling the efficient use of language in telegrams, in which children use few words to get their point across.

the past tense. It seems that although the younger child had learned the past forms of verbs individually, the older child has discovered the -ed rule of verbs and has applied that rule to form the past tense right across the board. The trouble is that some verbs are irregular, with the consequence that the child says "runned" instead of "ran." We have to wait a couple more years to find the child once again using irregular verbs correctly. Although overregularization is a type of error, it also suggests that the child is acquiring the principles or rules of grammar.

It takes many years for children to acquire most of the subtleties of grammar. The acquisition process can extend well into the school years. For example, it seems that not until age 8 or 9 do children have a good comprehension of passive sentences, such as "John was hit by Mary." Prior to this age, children hearing this sentence often have difficulty identifying whether it was John or Mary who did the hitting. Despite the continuing development of grammar at this older age, there can be no doubt that the biggest leaps in acquisition of grammar occur before the child is 5 years old. In a recent study, for example, Noble, Rowland, and Pine (2011) showed that from the age of 2 years old children have an understanding of rules of grammar. In a clever experiment they presented children with cartoon pictures of a duck and a rabbit, where one picture showed the duck acting on the rabbit (e.g. the duck lifts the rabbit's leg) and the other showed the duck and the rabbit acting independently. Children heard sentences with made-up words whilst they looked at these pictures, for example, *The duck is glorping the rabbit*. Now, *glorping* of course, is not a real word, but the sentence follows certain grammatical rules, which we can easily appreciate when we substitute *glorp* for a real word like *push*. In the sentence *The duck is pushing the rabbit* we know immediately that the duck is acting in some way on the rabbit. By using a made-up word like *glorp* the researchers could investigate whether young children use the rules of grammar to help them with learning words. And, indeed, this is what they found. Two-year-old children pointed at the correct picture when played the sentence with the made-up word, demonstrating that they could use the rules of grammar to learn the meaning of novel words. Even though 2-year-olds hardly put more than two words together in sentences and do not express this knowledge of grammar in the language they produce, they can use grammar to learn meaning.

VOCABULARY DEVELOPMENT

How does the baby form a link between words and objects? For example, how does the baby come to know that the word *dog* is a suitable label for the smelly, hairy quadruped that has assumed the status of "family pet"? According to the behaviorist B.F. Skinner, there is not much mystery once we understand his theory of rewards and punishment as reinforcement in learning. Skinner's (1957) view of language development is just one aspect of his general account of learning. It is based on the simple principle that rewarded behavior is more likely to be produced in the future, whereas unrewarded behavior, or behavior followed by punishment, is less likely to be produced in the future. In ordinary parlance, "reward" usually means money, candy, or some other goody. Skinner means something much more general than this. He means anything that happens to be gratifying to the individual.

Most of Skinner's research into learning was done with pigeons and rats, and there can be little doubt that very nearly every action these animals make is

Key Term
Reinforcement: Any stimulus that, when following behavior, increases the probability that the organism will emit the same behavior in the future.

understandable in terms of reward and punishment: Behavior that has pleasant consequences is likely to be repeated in the future, whereas behavior that has unpleasant consequences is likely to be extinguished. Circus performers have impressed audiences for centuries with their enchanting control over animals, a control that arises from the careful administration of reward and punishment. Skinner himself has frequently demonstrated astonishing feats of control over animal behavior. He trained pigeons to play the piano and to play table tennis. He assumed that the principles of reward and punishment are among the universal principles of behavior, and therefore could account for such things as human language development.

According to Skinner's theory of reinforcement, the parent's excited reaction to the child's attempt at speech shapes the infant's language development.

Skinner's view is not that parents know all about the principles of reward and punishment, and apply these to train the child to speak; rather, the parent's excited reaction to the child's attempt at speech is both fortuitous and rewarding to the child, so that the parent unwittingly trains the child in the skill of language. Skinner's idea is that in effect, language development owes a great deal to serendipity.

Let us consider Skinner's view of language acquisition in more detail. When the baby makes a sound that is similar to a word, the proud parent exhibits joy, which is rewarding to the baby. The baby makes a similar sound shortly after, with the same reaction from the parent. Eventually, however, the word-like sound from the baby no longer excites the parent quite so much, and so her reaction fades. Then the baby happens to make another sound that is not just babble, but actually resembles a known word, such as doggie. Again the parent becomes excited, with rewarding consequences for the baby. However, the sound the baby makes begins to lose its impact on the parent. When the baby makes that sound in the presence of a dog, then the parent's excitement is rekindled. When the baby says "doggie" in the absence of the dog, it provokes less of a reaction in the parent, so the baby learns to say "doggie" only in the presence of a dog. At this point, the parent may proudly announce to friends and relations that her child knows the word *dog*.

In this way, the adult's rewarding reaction to the baby's babbling has the effect of shaping that babbling into speech. According to Skinner, that is all there is to language development. In that case, could animals learn to speak? Alas, according to Skinner, only humans have the appropriate vocal physiology to talk. In other words, animals would be perfectly capable of talking if only they had the same throat and mouth as us.

Skinner's account of vocabulary development cannot withstand scrutiny (see the figure overleaf). Parrots have a suitable vocal physiology for articulating words, but their vocabulary is limited, devoid of meaning, and apparently arises largely by way of imitation and not from the consequences of reward and punishment. Moreover, deliberate attempts to teach sign language to chimpanzees explicitly based on Skinnerian principles have achieved very limited success. Apes are capable of acquiring a small vocabulary but in the absence of evidence of genuine understanding of the meaning of words. Apart from anything else, it seems obvious that imitation plays a large part in human

Skinner suggested that verbal behavior was the same as any other behavior. A stimulus (a light or a picture) is followed by a response (a lever press or an exclamation) and reinforced (food or a smiling host). However, Chomsky pointed out that the possibility for verbal responses is almost limitless (e.g. "beautiful," or "it clashes with the wallpaper"), but the rat's response range is not ("press lever" or "not press lever"). Moreover, the light is a specific stimulus, but we do not know whether people will comment on the picture or something else. Therefore, stimulus, response, and behavior are not equivalent between rat behavior and language and different principles must apply.

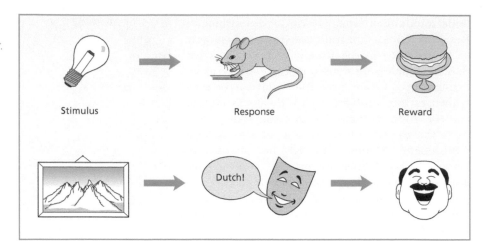

vocabulary development. With respect to the capacity for imitation, what does the human infant possess that the parrot lacks, apart from a large brain?

Innovative research by Baldwin and Moses (1994) gives part of the answer. Human infants, unlike parrots, are distinguished by the fact that they use nouns to refer to things. But how do they form an association between a word and the correct thing? For example, how does the infant learn to call a dog *dog* and a cat *cat*. On the face of it, you might suppose that the infant hears the word *dog* uttered in the presence of the dog and forges the association accordingly. In practice, infants are frequently captivated by their favorite toy or some novel object, when the adult appears on the scene and names a *different* object. For example, while the baby is fixated on the cat, the mother might mention "dog" in connection with the walk she is planning. What is to stop the infant calling the cat *dog* following this experience? In practice, infants seldom mislabel objects and it is intriguing that their acquisition and use of nouns appears so unerring.

Baldwin's research uncovered the answer to this intriguing mystery. She found that when the mother uttered a word or sentence, the infant will typically cease looking at whatever had occupied his attention and direct his gaze instead toward his mother. Normally, the mother would be looking at the thing she was naming. From about 18 months of age, infants are equipped to trace the mother's gaze and pinpoint the object of her attention. Learning fundamentally depends on attention in children and adults alike (Smith, Colunga, & Yoshida, 2010) and the importance of this process is highlighted in a further study by Baldwin. She introduced a novel toy to infants and then asked mothers, who were sitting nearby, to use a nonsense word, like *wug*, while looking at a different novel object. Subsequently, infants were asked to point to the *wug*. There were two objects in front of them—the novel object they had been playing with and the novel object the mother had been looking at when she uttered "wug." The infants reliably pointed to the object the mother had looked at in preference to the one they had been playing with. Hence, toward the end of infancy, children are able and disposed to secure a state of joint attention with others. This ability supports their early vocabulary development such that infants associate the uttered word with the object of the mother's attention rather than the object of their own attention. This explains how infants pick up vocabulary so rapidly and why they seldom

Key Term

Joint attention: The process of intentionally sharing the experience of observing an object or event through the use of pointing gestures or following gaze.

mislabel objects. Presumably, the capacity for joint attention is not shared with parrots. There is some evidence to suggest that chimpanzees are capable of joint attention (Povinelli & Eddy, 1996) and this might even allow them to understand human language in some contexts (Savage-Rumbaugh *et al.*, 1993), but there is no evidence as yet to suggest that chimpanzees are capable of producing language.

Children's understanding of the meaning of words is not fixed but changes with development. In particular, it seems that although children might correctly understand words to refer to broad classes of objects, they sometimes err on the side of being overinclusive. Nouns usually refer to a class of objects. Take the word *fish* as an example. This could be used for cod, trout, pike, carp, and so on. What is the essence of *fish*, if you like, the rule that permits us to use this word in relation to certain creatures? Perhaps it would be: "a creature that can swim and spends most of its time in water." This definition will not do, since it would mean that dolphins are fish, whereas in fact they are mammals. They breathe air and do not lay eggs. Obviously, the definition of *fish* has to be more specific. Perhaps we could add to the definition "creature with scales, lays eggs, has gills." However, this then presents a problem of under-inclusiveness. Loaches are fish, yet they do not have scales. Also, guppies are fish, yet they are live-bearers that give birth to baby fish rather than eggs. This example shows that when we use words correctly, we exhibit some understanding of the category of things included by that word, and by implication, the category of things excluded.

What we find in the case of children aged about 2 years is that they seem to err on the side of overinclusiveness in their use of nouns. This phenomenon is known as overextension. For example, in playing a ball game with the child, we may find that the child picks up the word *ball*, and uses it correctly in the context of the game. We may find subsequently, though, that the child wrongly uses "ball" to refer to the moon, eggs, round cakes, and a miscellany of other rounded or spherical objects. Similarly, it is common for toddlers to overextend by calling all men "Daddy"! We could argue that overextension is illuminating about cognitive development more generally in that it suggests young children understand their environment in terms of broad classes of things, and only later come to distinguish between subclasses. For example, maybe the young child is inclined to pick up the word *ball* in relation to any round or spherical object because she thinks of her environment in terms of broad categories such as "round," "square," "living," "big," and so on. This kind of cognition may then be reflected in the child's use of nouns, particularly in the error of overextension.

However, another side of the coin is that since young children clearly have a strong urge to communicate, coupled with limited vocabulary, perhaps they use the best words at their disposal, which gives rise to the impression that they overextend word categories. So, for example, the young child may be well aware that although the moon is like a ball in that it is circular, it is quite different in important ways: It is not

From about 18 months of age, infants can trace the mother's gaze and pinpoint the object of her attention.

possible to play "piggy in the middle" with the moon, or to put it away in a toy cupboard. The child could recognize this, yet call the moon "ball" for no other reason than that she does not know the word "moon." In that case, the phenomenon of overextension would not be revealing about a tendency to lump together things in broad categories, but instead just a symptom of trying to make the best communicative use of a limited vocabulary. Therefore, all we can say is that at this moment in time we do not know the cognitive developmental implications of the phenomenon of overextension.

In addition to overextension, children also show the opposite phenomenon of underextension related to the meaning and use of words. It describes children's early tendency to use words in a narrower context than they are commonly used, for example, a child might think that "dog" refers only to their family pet, but not to dogs in general. How do we reconcile the effects of overextension and underextension?

Both overextension and underextension might reflect a fundamental aspect of the function of language, which is, of course, that it allows us to communicate. In order to communicate, children therefore have to learn that words label groups or categories of objects with common properties, such as pet, furniture, people, plants, birds, etc. Now some of the members of these categories are more typical of the category as a whole compared to others. This is known as the typicality effect, which denotes situations when a typical category member shows some advantage over atypical category members; for example, people might be faster to confirm that a dog is a pet than that a Vietnamese pot-bellied pig is a pet. Children's development of word learning also shows this typicality effect. In early development children's word learning is influenced by how category typical the object is; for example, they might readily label a sparrow, but not an ostrich, as a bird, and only extend this context later on in development to also include the less typical category members (Meints, Plunkett, & Harris, 1999). Typicality effects were also found in a range of grammatical categories, for example, prepositions like "on" or "under" (Meints, Plunkett, Harris, & Dimmock, 2002), and in verb learning (Meints, Plunkett, & Harris, 2008).

THEORIES OF LANGUAGE ACQUISITION

Are we born with a language acquisition device?

How, then, do children acquire language—not just vocabulary, but also all the rules of language, that is, grammar? Forty years ago a debate developed between B. F. Skinner and Noam Chomsky, the two main protagonists at the time. Skinner naturally took an extreme environmentalist position, while Chomsky held the opposite stance. Skinner's (1957) account had prevailed for some time in a period when the behaviorist account of psychological phenomena was dominant, whereupon Chomsky (1959) wrote an exposition that shattered Skinner's stronghold and contributed to the start of the *cognitive revolution*. As mentioned before, Skinner maintained that language is unwittingly shaped by parents and other adults according to the principles of his theory of behavior. We have already seen that this does not give an adequate explanation of vocabulary development, but could it nonetheless explain how children acquire the *rules* of language? The really big question therefore is, does parental reward enable children to acquire grammar? In a nutshell, the answer is "no." Brown and Hanlon (1970) observed parental approval (reward) and disapproval (punishment) following child speech and found negligible reaction to bad grammar. When children said such things as "feets" and "they sings," parents did not disapprove, just as parents did not approve when their children used correct grammar. In contrast, when children made factual errors in their speech, such as calling the moon a ball, then the parents offered a correction. Contrary to a Skinnerian account, parents reacted to the meaning of what their children said, and overlooked the good or bad grammar their children used to express that meaning. Because children's grammar continues to develop regardless, it becomes very hard to believe that the rewarding and punishing effects of parental reaction have much to do with their children's development in this respect.

Chomsky comments that if Skinner's account were true, we would expect children to grow up speaking ungrammatically, but telling the truth by saying things that are factually accurate. What we actually find is the opposite! A second blow to Skinner's account comes from a study by Nelson (1985). She identified some parents who rewarded their children's good pronunciation and punished bad pronunciation, and found that these children had smaller vocabularies, compared with those who did not have such corrective or directive parents. It suggests that parental reward and punishment concerning certain aspects of language development could have indirect detrimental effects on other aspects of language acquisition, namely vocabulary development.

Skinner's account is an extreme environmental one, in that it seeks to explain language development just by specifying things in the environment (parental reward and punishment). Skinner's particular focus on reward and punishment appears to be unsatisfactory, but perhaps language development can be explained with reference to other environmental features. The most obvious feature in the environment likely to affect language development is the language of other people, particularly the parents. Given that the aural environment is suffused with speech, why not suppose that the child simply imitates her parents, and acquires language via that process? In this way, the child's language is just a mirror of whatever happens to prevail in her linguistic environment.

There can be no doubt that the child's imitation is an important factor in her language development. After all, children do speak the same language as their parents. Moreover, they have the same accent, and many of the verbal mannerisms. Children can often be heard parroting words or sentences they hear, apparently for no other reason than the sheer pleasure of repetition. Also, children who have a tendency to imitate others seem to acquire language more rapidly than those less likely to imitate (Bates, Bretherton, Beeghly-Smith, & McNew, 1982). The imitation in question is of a general nature (actions and gestures), but it leads us to wonder whether the imitation of others' language accelerated the child's language development. There are other interpretations of the link between imitation and accelerated language development. One is that those who imitate more are also more alert and attentive, and tend to develop any new skill more rapidly. In other words, instead of imitation causing rapid language development, both could be symptoms of a lively intellect.

Although imitation obviously does feature in language development, Noam Chomsky (e.g. 1975) made a very severe criticism of environmental accounts: The child hears relatively few utterances; these are often grammatically imperfect; yet it is only a short period of time between the birth of the child, and the child using grammar. Apart from anything else, language acquisition is universal amongst typically developing children, so it seems that no matter what the environment, language will be acquired. Indeed, it is difficult to imagine how we could prevent language development. This led Chomsky to conclude that language, or at least the important parts of language, have a big innate component.

CHOMSKY'S THEORY OF INNATE LANGUAGE DEVELOPMENT

Chomsky needed to explain how it could be that even though different people speak different languages, depending on the culture in which they grew up, language is nevertheless largely innate. To solve this problem, he suggested that there are two levels to language, the surface structure and the deep structure. The surface structure is the specific grammatical features of individual languages. The deep structure is the innate language, stored inside our brains, passed on to us through our genes. This has a universal grammar, possessed by all humans. The universal grammar works on the level of grammatical subject and object. Chomsky claimed that subject and object relations in all human languages are the same.

Babies are equipped with a "language acquisition device" (LAD), which identifies the specific features of the grammar of a language, and translates these into the innate deep structure. According to Chomsky, the idea of an innate deep structure, based on grammatical subject and object, casts a whole new light on the mystery of babies being able to master such a complex ability as language. The reason babies find it so easy to acquire language, according to this view, is that the rudiments already exist inside their brains.

Chomsky further suggests that there is an innate grammatical mechanism that can translate one grammatical form into another. For example, we can change a sentence from active voice to passive:

"John hit Roger."—"Roger was hit by John."

Key Terms

Surface structure:
The specific grammatical features of a specific language.

Deep structure:
An innate grammatical structuring of language that is both universal among humans and is unique to humans as a species.

Universal grammar:
A set of formal structural rules common to all languages.

LAD:
The language acquisition device is an innate device for acquiring language.

Chomsky suggests that these relations between subject (John) and object (Roger) are stored in the deep structure, and can be translated into various surface structure forms by a mechanism called "transformational grammar." Chomsky's theory is philosophical rather than psychological. In other words, Chomsky is not engaged in a program of research studying children acquiring language, but instead reasons about how language acquisition is likely to take place from the perspective of an understanding of the form of language. It is difficult to envisage how anyone could collect evidence which can show that grammar has an innate component, but Goldin-Meadow and Mylander (1990) have sought to do just that. They studied a group of children aged approximately 3 years who were born deaf, and received no language tuition of any kind—whether oral or gestural. These researchers wanted to know whether the children displayed any rudiments of language in the gestural system they developed spontaneously.

We can say with some confidence that the very fact that the children were so willing to attempt gestures shows that they were born with an inclination to communicate. However, as we have already discussed, mere communication does not necessarily count as language. What we look for is evidence of grammar. Was there any grammatical pattern to the gestures used by the children that could be viewed as evidence for an innate LAD?

Anyone not acquainted with sign language may view this as a peculiar question, but it is not. Many people with hearing impairment who do not speak use a formal gestural code to communicate. This code combines gestural units as "words" according to rules of grammar to form "sentences," and for this reason we can say that such languages deserve that label just like spoken languages. What about Goldin-Meadow and Mylander's children? Did their gesture combinations conform to any word-order rule? It was certainly the case that the children used gestures to name things, and therefore, their gestures qualified as words. Also, they used gestures in combination, and these did appear in certain orders rather than others.

A commonsense explanation is that perhaps the children's parents provided the initiative, by generating gestures for their children to imitate in the first place, and perhaps they produced gestures in certain combinations. However, Goldin-Meadow and Mylander rule this out, and report that it was the children themselves who pioneered the gestures and the gesture combinations, with the parents following suit. Goldin-Meadow and Mylander conclude that their findings show that children are born with an appetite for communication, and that they know via their genes that communication is formed from patterns of units of meaning.

Goldin-Meadow and Mylander's study provides evidence in support of Chomsky's view that language has an innate basis. Despite this, it falls short of demonstrating that we have an innate deep structure based on subject-verb-object relations, or demonstrating that we are genetically equipped with a language acquisition device. Language is something that develops over a period of time, and learning must be involved since the child speaks the particular tongue of her parents. Is it the case, as Chomsky claims, that the learning involved is controlled by genetic factors?

The account Chomsky presents is frequently very technical, and often esoteric. That said, it is not necessary to grasp all the details of his idea about innate features of language development in order to assess whether such strong emphasis on innate factors is warranted. In claiming that language acquisition is largely determined by innate factors, Chomsky implies that the environment does not have much of a role to play. Putting it that way, perhaps it is useful to take a second look at what goes on in the environment. We might find

Sign language is a form of code that combines gestural units as "words" according to rules of grammar to form "sentences." It contains phonology, morphology, semantics, syntax, and pragmatics just like spoken languages. Shown here is American Sign Language (ASL).

Is the nature–nurture debate informed by research into language development?

that there is little in the environment that could benefit language acquisition, which is what we would expect from the point of view of Chomsky's theory. Alternatively, perhaps we will find that there are ways in which the environment could be valuable for the process of language acquisition. If so, that might be sufficient to persuade us that it is the environment that is most important, rather than innate factors.

A SECOND LOOK AT THE ENVIRONMENT

Connectionism

Chomsky argued that the language babies are exposed to is often degenerate, in other words, grammatically poor. In doing so he tries to convince us that language acquisition is guided by some kind of rule that exists in the baby's mind from birth. Children's ability to form the past tense by adding -ed to verbs (e.g. walk-ed) seems on the face of things to arise from the application of a rule. Obviously, there is no specific human gene for forming the past tense with an -ed rule, since different languages around the world have different patterns of past-tense formation. However, nativists sometimes claim there is a higher order and more abstract rule for forming the past tense and handling other aspects of grammar, which guides the individual in assimilating the particular application of the past tense in her mother tongue. They argue that the linguistic environment is too impoverished to allow a young child to be able to abstract the principles of grammar without assistance from innate rules of language.

What do computer simulations of language development tell us?

Even though the argument might seem persuasive, we now know it is wrong. Connectionism simulations of language acquisition demonstrate that computer models abstract a generalization of such things as the -ed rule in the absence of any guiding principle. This was demonstrated in a classic study by Rumelhart and McClelland (1986). They utilized a computer connectionist learning network and fed verb stems (e.g. *walk*) into it as the input. The target output was the correct formation of the past tense (e.g. *walked*). The computer's output was then corrected, which fed back into the network as an output weighting. Initially, the computer produced no output because it did not have the benefit of any information on what counted as a correct response. After a few trials, however, it started to produce the past tense appropriately, thanks to the feedback. The majority of the verbs fed into the system were regular, but a few were irregular, such as *hit*. The aim was to reflect the ratio of regular to irregular verbs in natural language.

In the early stages, the computer formed the past tense accurately for the relatively small number of verbs presented, whether regular or irregular. However, as more verbs were added, revealing errors began to arise. Interestingly, the system tended to add -ed to novel irregular verbs, and there was apparently a small amount of resistance to forming the appropriate irregular past tense of these. This occurred because the system had become biased to add -ed to verbs, as reflected by the fact that the great majority of verbs in its vocabulary had such a form in the past tense. In effect, the system had abstracted a generalization concerning -ed, which was occasionally manifest as overgeneralization. As the system gained even more practice, along with the accompanying feedback, it eventually formed the past tense correctly, and reliably so, for its entire vocabulary.

> **Key Term**
>
> **Connectionism:**
> The idea that cognitive processes can be explained as a result of the interplay between several simple interconnected units.
>
> **Overgeneralization:**
> At one stage in language development children apply the rule for forming the past tense inappropriately to irregular words.

The striking feature of the learning phase of this connectionist system is that it resembled the pattern we see in children's development. Plunkett and Marchman (1993) performed a computer simulation that was more authentic in terms of the content and expansion of vocabulary, and then compared the behavior of the system with archived records of children's language development. Their study confirmed that the character of development, especially with respect to overregularization, was strikingly similar in human and machine. In both computer and child, there was an initial phase in which a small number of verbs were handled correctly, whether regular or irregular. Presumably, they are acquired individually by means of rote learning. As the vocabulary expands, systemic errors arise in the form of overregularization. We know that this happens in the computer as an abstraction of a generalization. Surely, there is no reason to search for a different kind of explanation in children. Hence, there is no reason to suppose that overregularization in children is a sign of genetically endowed rules of language.

Despite the virtues of the connectionist approach, it is limited by the fact that it concentrates on the form rather than the meaning of the language. The two come into conflict when we encounter a verb like *ring*, which is ambiguous in its meaning: to ring a bell; to place a ring on her finger. In one meaning, the past is irregular, as in "I rang the bell," whereas in another it is regular, "I ringed her finger." Ultimately, grammar does not make much sense and is therefore not very useful without a grasp of meaning. Children learn the form of language incidentally to interpreting and communicating meaning. It thus seems appropriate to consider the wider meaningful context in which language is acquired.

"Infant-directed talk" and social constructivism

When talking to babies and young children, adults usually speak shorter and simpler sentences. These typically have simpler grammar, and are more likely to be grammatically correct, compared with speech to other adults. Adult talk to babies and young children is generally slower, with longer pauses at the end of each sentence. The talk is nearly always about concrete things that are present, and therefore visible to the child. Also, the pattern of adult speech seems to be well tailored to the child's linguistic level. As the child speaks longer and more complex sentences, so the adult talks to the child in a more mature manner. It seems that the adult usually pitches her speech at a slightly more advanced level than the child's and is thus intuitively attuned to the child's better comprehension than production of language. This distinctive style of adult speech to children was known as "motherese," not because it is used exclusively by mothers, but because mothers are usually caregivers of babies and young children, and therefore the ones who use this style most. In order to reflect this meaning better, motherese is now known as infant-directed talk. Children from a very young age are highly attuned to this infant-directed talk. When 5-month-old infants were presented with an adult who used adult-directed speech or infant-directed speech, they showed a subsequent preference for the person who had used infant-directed speech, even though the person was no longer talking at the time (Schachner & Hannon, 2011). Presumably the manner of infant-directed speech gives a good indication to the infant that they have encountered

Key Term

Infant-directed talk:
A special style of speech used when talking to infants.

Motherese, or infant-directed talk, is nearly always about concrete objects that are within the child's line of vision.

Compare and contrast behaviorist and social constructivist theories of language development.

a social partner who is attuned to their needs and it is beneficial for them to pay attention to and form a bond with that person in preference to a person who seems less attuned to their needs. Infant-directed speech thus also has an important social function, as infants not only prefer to listen to infant-directed speech (Cooper & Aslin, 1990) but also make social judgments about the people who engage in this mode of speaking.

Without studying what goes on in homes, Chomsky presumed that babies are subjected to "degenerate" language. However, the researchers who have visited homes and observed parental speech found something rather different. Indeed, infant-directed talk seems to be an ideal form of speech for introducing the baby to language. This raises the possibility that the steps taken by parents regarding the linguistic environment of the home, whether or not they know it, might be instrumental in the child's language development. So although Skinner's account about reward and punishment is obviously not tenable, other features of the environment could be crucial for language acquisition.

In an excellent book, Jerome Bruner (1983) has detailed a theoretical framework that suggests how the home environment might contribute not just to language development, but to culture acquisition. Bruner views language development as a part of the overall culture transmission from parents to children. He calls this a "language acquisition support system" (LASS) to contrast with Chomsky's "language acquisition device" (LAD).

Bruner proposes that we should think of the psychological environment in the home as a supportive edifice of "scaffolding." The scaffolding supports the child initially, and is then removed piece by piece as the child develops and becomes more able to stand alone. As the child gets a cognitive grasp of the environment, particularly the prevailing language, the parent withdraws the scaffolding that has been supporting the child's intellect, thereby allowing him to become more cognitively independent. An example in infant-directed talk is that parents gradually speak in longer and more complex sentences to their child as the child's language develops and becomes more sophisticated. As the child develops, parents begin to withdraw the linguistic support they provide.

Bruner also lays emphasis on the fact that the child must be strongly motivated to acquire the rules of grammar, since that provides the key to communication, and therefore provides a means to fulfill his desires. If the child wishes to eat, play, use the potty, and so on, it is much easier to communicate these things if he can express his meaning in a way that can be understood by parents. The most efficient way to do that is by using grammar.

In this respect, Bruner's analysis helps us to view language development in a completely different light. The impression we get from Chomsky's view of language development is detached from the environment. This is nothing like what really goes on in language acquisition. Language is acquired in an environment in which the child's well-being is greatly aided by having a channel of communication—namely, language. Against this background of support from the social environment, in which there is a powerful incentive for being able to communicate, we also need to acknowledge the child's role in actively striving to master language. At the very least, we should assume that children are capable of abstracting generalizations, such as how to form the past tense. If a relatively dumb computer running a connectionist simulation can abstract a generalization, it is a fair bet that a child can do the same or better. After all, the child is attuned to meaning in addition to form and has the benefit of a supportive environment.

Usage-based language theory and pragmatic cues

According to Tomasello and Brooks (1999), we should further view the child as playing an active role in understanding these generalizations as the rules or principles of language. They argue that children effectively construct the rules of language in a way that is supported by the characteristics of the social environment. Hence, the characteristics of language acquisition will be relative to the particular culture to which the child belongs, and cross-cultural studies offer supporting evidence along these lines. Tomasello (2003) claims that children learn the rules of language from using language, in what is called a usage-based language theory. In this sense children can learn the rules of language by generalizing more abstract rules from the words they are exposed to (Frank & Tenenbaum, 2011).

Tomasello claims that we do not need to invoke a dual process of language learning, but that language is a sociocognitive skill like many others and is learned in the same way. Tomasello particularly stresses the role of theory of mind in language development and in a series of ingenious experiments demonstrated how sensitive children are to the intentions and emotions of the speaker and pragmatic rules of communication. Pragmatic cues and understanding the communicative intent feature strongly in children's learning of new object labels, verb labels, and helping them to decide what exactly a new label describes. Tomasello and Barton (1994) presented children with a finding game, in which the experimenter announced her intent to *find the toma*. The experimenter then looked in a series of buckets, all of which contained novel objects. Sometimes she would find *the toma* in the first bucket, the success of the search indicated by her smiling and terminating the search, but other times she would look in a series of buckets and scowl and frown at the discovered items until she was successful. Children as young as 18–24 months old learn that the object label refers to the object greeted by a smile and that leads to a termination of the search, regardless of how many buckets the experimenter searched in unsuccessfully. This clearly indicates that children are sensitive to the social-pragmatic cues contained in the announced intention to finding an object and in the emotional reaction to discovering wanted and unwanted objects. Children even learn the label correctly when the object is absent after being labeled and a distractor is smiled at (Akhtar & Tomasello, 1996) and when four novel objects are present at the same time and the referent of the label has to be inferred purely based on the speaker's excitement (Akhtar, Carpenter, & Tomasello, 1996). When learning the labels for novel objects children are sensitive to the intentions and emotions of the speaker and 18- to 24-month-old children can learn the communicative intentions of the speaker.

Key Term
Usage-based language theory: The idea that there is no specific cognitive module for language learning, but that children learn both vocabulary and rules of language through using it in trying to communicate with others.

Learning verbs may be even harder than learning the names for objects, because the referent is transient and it is not always obvious which part of an action the label refers to. Tomasello and Barton demonstrated that children are distinguishing between intentional acts and accidental acts when applying a label to an action. In their study an experimenter announced that she was going to *dax* a Mickey Mouse doll and then performed one action on the doll that was accidental (accompanied by an exclamation of *Whoops!*) and an intentional act (*There!*). Twenty-four-month-old children learn that *dax* refers to the intentional act, regardless of which one was carried out first. This demonstrates that children are sensitive to the intentionality of the speaker when learning action words and objects.

We know from classic research by Brown (1973) that children are sensitive to the linguistic context in which words are used, when they decide whether a novel word refers to an action, object, or adjective. In a clever experiment Tomasello and Akhtar (1995) demonstrated that children also use pragmatic cues when they decide whether the speaker used a novel label to describe an action or an object. Children were introduced to a curved pipe, down which objects could be thrown. In one of the experimental conditions, the adults took one novel object and threw it down the pipe, then another, and then announced "*Now modi!*" In this context, 24-month-old children thought that *modi* referred to the third object thrown down the pipe. In the second condition, the experimenter took a novel object and performed one action on it, then another, and then announced "*Now modi!*" throwing the object down the pipe. In this context, children thought that *modi* referred to the act of throwing an object down the pipe. Children seemed to associate whatever was novel in the communicative situation with the label being used, which seems to show that children's understanding of adults' intentions is flexible and deep.

Based on the evidence presented here and in a host of other studies, Tomasello claims that a set of general cognitive skills coupled with children's desire to communicate with others drives language development. In Tomasello's view, no innate language-specific mechanisms are needed to account for language development, which is instead explained in the same way as other facets of development that take place in a social environment. Children learn the formal properties of language in the process of learning to communicate with people. This theory has many merits, particularly in stressing that language learning probably does not have *specific* innate mechanisms. However, like the early environmental accounts it still has some difficulty showing how a child, even if paying very close attention to the language used around her, could learn all the rules of language so unerringly.

Summary

- Although children may be born with very primitive knowledge that communication takes place via patterned units of meaning, as yet no one has shown that most aspects of language acquisition are dependent upon a specific innate process or mechanism. Indeed, it may never be possible to show this, and it may always remain that we have to juggle with ideas to help determine the contributions of heredity and environment.

- By looking at infant-directed talk, and coupling what we know about that with theories of social constructivism and social cognition, it is plausible to suppose that grammar acquisition is much the same as other aspects of culture acquisition. In other words, there is no need to think that there might be an innate language acquisition device. In that case, why did Chomsky's theory ever seem so appealing? Perhaps it arose from a peculiarity in the development of the two disciplines of linguistics and psychology. Prior to Chomsky, the dominant account of learning was Skinner's theory about reward and punishment. Because that could not explain language acquisition adequately, it gave Chomsky's theory a niche to provide an explanation on innate grounds; perhaps Chomsky's strength lay largely in Skinner's weakness. The debate between an innate and learning account of language is by no means over, and Skinner's ideas of language learning are reflected in the associative word learning theory which posits that children learn words through associating sounds with salient aspects of the perceptual environment (Smith, 2000; see Tomasello, 2003, for a discussion of associative theory).
- Chomsky's writings certainly started a lively debate and he is one of the 10 most cited sources in the arts and humanities (alongside the Bible, for example). However, now that we have a better environmental and constructivist account, perhaps there is no longer reason to think that innate factors feature quite so prominently in language acquisition. A view with which Chomsky seems to partly agree now, as he states in a more recent paper that the innate component of language is limited to our ability to build recursive structures, that is, our ability to put sentences into sentences (Hauser, Chomsky, & Fitch, 2002).

Essay Questions

1. Assess the claim that language is innate.
2. What is the role of sociocognitive skills in language development?

Further Reading

An excellent account of the nativist position can be found in the following text, which is notable for its clear and amusing prose:

- Aitchison, J. (1998). *The articulate mammal* (4th edn.). London: Unwin Hyman.

A very enjoyable, well-written account of language acquisition can be found in:

- Bruner, J. S. (1983). *Child's talk: Learning to use language*. Oxford, UK: Oxford University Press.

A more recent book on language development, which takes into account many of the other sociocognitive skills children develop, is:

- Tomasello, M. (2003). *Constructing a language: A usage-based theory of language acquisition*. Cambridge, MA: Harvard University Press.

Chapter 13

Contents

Developing an ability to communicate

13

Chapter Aims

- To explore the extent to which young children adapt their utterances to their listener's informational requirements.
- To explore the extent to which young children are attuned to a speaker's intention.
- To examine when children begin to understand that what a person says give a clue to what they believe about the world.
- To examine when children begin to understand that some utterances are open to several different interpretations.

INTRODUCTION

Without much reflection, we may think that language and communication amount to the same thing. Not so! There are many ways of communicating without using verbal language, as in conveying meaning with gestures. For example, we put a thumb up to signify approval, or wave as a farewell. These gestures do not form part of language because, unlike formal sign language, they do not have any rules of grammar to govern the organization of units of meaning. To put it simply, you could not string together these informal gestures to make a sentence.

Nevertheless, it is possible to convey meaning very effectively with informal gestures. A thumb or raised eyebrow could leave the recipient with no doubt what you wish to communicate! It is possible to convey even more information efficiently with verbal language, but it does not necessarily follow that one who is skilled at using the rules of grammar to form sentences, and has an extensive vocabulary, will automatically be skilled at communicating the appropriate meaning to a listener.

Consider people with autism, who typically have great difficulty communicating. In cases of profound autism, there may be little or no communication at all. In less severe cases, a person with autism could have considerable mastery over language, yet remain impaired at conveying meaning in speech. According to Frith (2003), failures of communication in people with autism are rife because such individuals find it very difficult to infer others' intentions, due to an impaired theory of mind. In that case, can we expect to find that typically developing young children will also have great difficulty communicating prior to their theory of mind being well developed? This would follow if verbal communication owes as much to having some kind of insight into people's intentions as it does to knowing how to string together words in a grammatical way.

This ability, to make inferences about others' intentions, is important both in speaking and in listening. Anyone who has had a telephone conversation with a 5-year-old will appreciate the point. The young child often seems to presume that he and his listener inhabit a shared visual environment. The child might say, "I got this for my birthday. It opens there and things come out, and go along and there's a light here ...." If we could only see the toy, no doubt it would become clear what opens, what things come out, and so on. The trouble is, the young child seems to talk as though we can see what he can see. Again, this appears to be a symptom of young children failing to take account of the minds of their listeners.

EGOCENTRIC SPEECH

Is it fair to say that young children have egocentric speech?

Jean Piaget characteristically viewed opaque aspects of young children's speech as a symptom of egocentrism. Piaget defined egocentrism as "failure to take into account views of the world other than one's own." The case of the young child speaking on the phone offers a good example, with the child apparently failing to take account of the fact that the listener cannot see what he can see.

Piaget identified three kinds of egocentric speech, as follows:

- Repetition. Young children sometimes repeat sentences or phrases immediately after hearing them, where the child's voice acts as an echo. There is no apparent reason why the child repeats the utterance, and it seems to be a case of repetition for its own sake. The meaning of the utterance seems to be irrelevant, and indeed often is unimportant as far as the child is concerned.
- Individual monologue. Piaget noticed that young children sometimes made a running commentary on a task they were engrossed with, as if thinking aloud. In fact, this is an experience familiar to all of us: sometimes adults talk aloud when tackling a challenging problem. Piaget's point seemed to be that this phenomenon was particularly common in young children.
- Collective monologue. Piaget suggests that the child may (but may not) intend to communicate information to others in the group, but the egocentric nature of his speech prevents anyone else being able to grasp the meaning. Piaget depicts a group of children all talking, but none understanding what

| Key Term |

Egocentric speech: Speaking in a way that does not respect the informational needs of a listener.

anybody else says. It is not possible to grasp the meaning because the child does not elaborate sufficiently to allow that, in much the same way that the child speaking on the telephone fails in the example given above. Piaget claimed that approximately 30 to 40% of 5-year-olds' speech falls into the category of collective monologue.

Since Piaget's writings, a considerable amount of research has been undertaken to make a systematic examination of young children's communication abilities. This research set out to investigate whether it really is appropriate to suppose, as Piaget did, that when young children speak they take no account of the communicative requirements of their listeners. Krauss and Glucksberg (1969) paved the way by developing a game that requires a great deal of explicit communication. It involves two players, one of whom takes the role of speaker, while the other acts as listener (see the figure below). The two players sit at opposite sides of a table, which is divided in the middle by a wooden screen. Although the two players are sitting opposite, they cannot see each other because of the screen. The speaker is supplied with a dispenser, which issues six blocks, one at a time. Each block bears an abstract design. The listener, meanwhile, has an identical set of six blocks, not in a dispenser, spread out before her (see the figure below). The aim of the game is for the speaker to describe each block as it comes from the dispenser in such a way that the listener can select a matching one from her set.

Children aged between 5 and 10 years participated in the experiment. They easily understood the instructions, and were perfectly happy to play the game. At first all children in the role of speaker, irrespective of age, had difficulty describing the designs in a way that allowed their listener to choose the matching block from her set. On successive attempts, a substantial difference in the abilities of

The communication game devised by Krauss and Glucksberg (1969).

Children had to describe an abstract design in sufficient detail to allow their partner to select the correct one from a matching set.

children above and below the age of about 6 years emerged. Older children were very successful with practice, frequently giving descriptions that enabled listeners to choose the correct block. In contrast, the young children continued with idiosyncratic descriptions, which meant little to their listeners. For example, on looking at one design, a 5-year-old said, "Daddy's shirt." On seeing the next, the child said, "Another of Daddy's shirts." Although this child could imagine some kind of resemblance between the designs and her father's shirts, the descriptions were completely useless as an aid to the listener's selection. Krauss and Glucksberg's findings lend support to Piaget's suggestion that young children are poor at communication because they are insensitive to the communicative needs of their listeners.

YOUNG CHILDREN'S SENSITIVITY TO THEIR LISTENER

Subsequently, many researchers sought to investigate whether young children are sometimes sensitive to their listeners' informational requirements, and tailor their speech appropriately. This research generated a substantial number of findings, suggesting that young children do indeed modify their speech according to the needs of the listener, giving the impression that their communication was not plagued with egocentrism. A few examples follow.

Shatz and Gelman (1973) allowed 4-year-olds to play with a novel toy, and asked them to explain how it worked either to an adult, or to a 2-year-old. The 4-year-olds communicated in a very different way when addressing the 2-year-old. They used shorter and simpler sentences. Also, they took more care to make sure the 2-year-old was looking at the appropriate part of the toy when they were giving the explanation. Rather similar results were reported by Guralnick and Paul-Brown (1977). They observed children aged 4 years who attended a school with a mixed intake of normal achievers and children with learning difficulties. When the children addressed those with learning difficulties, they used simpler sentence structures and a limited vocabulary, compared with when addressing normally achieving peers.

In a slightly different kind of study, Maratsos (1974) asked children aged 3 years to communicate to the experimenter which of a set of toys they had chosen. Under one condition, the experimenter had his eyes closed and could not see, whereas under another, there was no impediment to the experimenter's view. Children gave more explicit descriptions when the experimenter could not see. Menig-Peterson (1975) devised a more elaborate procedure by staging an accident, witnessed by 3- and 4-year-old children. An adult who was serving drinks of orange juice to the children clumsily spilt one of the cups and made a mess. The experimenter then involved the children in a clean-up operation. The following week, an adult interviewed each of the children, and asked about the accident. This adult was either the one who had spilt the drink, and therefore had witnessed it first hand, or a person who had been absent. Menig-Peterson noticed that these young children provided detailed descriptions for the adult who had not witnessed the accident. In contrast, they were not nearly so explicit when relating the event to the adult who had been present at the scene.

Far from being insensitive to the requirements of their listeners, these findings show that young children are capable of modifying their speech adeptly. When speaking to younger or intellectually impaired children, 4-year-olds seemed to recognize that care was needed to speak in a simple way, otherwise their listener would not understand. Also, they seemed to realize that more detailed information was in order when relating an event to someone who knew nothing about it. These findings seem to fly in the face of the claim that young children are egocentric in their communication.

Shatz and Gelman (1973) discovered that 4-year-olds took more care to ensure that the 2-year-old was looking at the appropriate part of the toy when they were giving the explanation of a novel toy than they did when explaining the same toy to an adult.

STRENGTHS AND WEAKNESSES IN YOUNG CHILDREN'S COMMUNICATION

At this point we seem to have reached a contradiction. On the one hand, Piaget's observations, coupled with the findings of Krauss and Glucksberg, suggest that young children are ineffective in communication, as though they fail to adapt their language to the requirements of the listener. On the other hand, subsequent findings suggested that young children can modify their speech appropriately. How can we reconcile these two conflicting sets of findings?

A study by Sonnenschein (1986) seems to provide an answer. The children she tested formed two age groups, 6-year-olds and 9-year-olds. She showed the children a set of 10 drawings of toys, which included a spinning-top, a wagon train, and a sledge, and asked them to describe one of them so that another child would know which she meant. The "other child" was either the speaker child's best friend, or an unfamiliar child. Sonnenschein assumed that people tend to communicate in more explicit detail when speaking to an unfamiliar person, rather than when speaking to a close friend. She wanted to know if this kind of sensitivity to the listener would be evident in children's descriptions of the pictures.

In one respect, Sonnenschein's findings were consistent with those from the earlier studies carried out by Shatz and Gelman (1973) and Menig-Peterson (1975): Children in both age groups gave more information when the listener was an unfamiliar person rather than their best friend. In another respect, the findings were consistent with those of Piaget and of Krauss and Glucksberg: There was an important difference in the quality of the information provided by the two age groups. The information given by 9-year-olds was specific to the picture they were thinking about and none other, whereas the information given by 6-year-olds very often could have referred to any of the pictures. For example, 6-year-olds said "it's something you play with," "you can get it from the shop." This information could have applied to any of the items in the pictures. In contrast, 9-year-olds said "it's got wheels," "it's red," thus providing specific information, which enabled the listener to single out the particular card she was thinking about.

From these findings, the following preliminary conclusion seems apppropriate. Young children appear to understand that they should alter their

Do young children grasp the distinction between what is said and what is meant?

speech to satisfy the specific needs of different listeners. Sometimes this leads to effective communication, as in the case of a 4-year-old speaking to a 2-year-old. However, it seems that up to the age of about 6 years, children might find it difficult to understand the relationship between the information in the message and the understanding of the listener. In particular, they seem not to grasp that in order to help the listener comprehend, the information in the message has to be specific to the item they are thinking about, and only to that item.

We might enquire, then, about the age when children begin to understand about the communicative value of different messages. Mitchell, Munno, and Russell (1991) presented scenarios to children in which a speaker protagonist had given an inaccurate description to a listener. In one scene, for example, a customer (the listener) was in a supermarket looking for the manager. She asked a shop assistant (the speaker) who the manager was, and the shop assistant commented (the message) that he was the man standing over there holding the pen. Children had been told earlier that in fact it was a pencil the manager was holding. In this case, the description was inaccurate (pen instead of pencil) but only mildly so, and we can suppose that the listener would know who the manager was after hearing the description. Under two other conditions, the description was grossly discrepant (man holding a sack of potatoes) or perfectly accurate.

Five-year-olds frequently judged that the listener knew who the manager was after hearing a mildly discrepant description, and curiously they judged likewise after hearing a grossly discrepant one. Nine-year-olds, in contrast, judged that the listener knew who the manager was less frequently when the description was grossly discrepant. In one respect, this finding is consistent with Sonnenschein's (1986) research, that young children lack understanding of the relationship between the communicative value of the utterance and the listener's understanding. However, another finding suggested that Sonnenschein's view of things may require modification. Although 5-year-olds frequently judged that the listener knew something following a discrepant message, they judged that the listener knew even more frequently when the message was perfectly accurate. This shows that although they do not presume that a discrepant message would necessarily pose an impediment to listener comprehension, they recognize that a perfectly correct message would be more satisfactory. Therefore, they seem to have some grasp of the relationship between the communicative value of the utterance and the listener's understanding.

DO YOUNG CHILDREN TREAT UTTERANCES AS CLUES TO MEANING?

Elizabeth Robinson (e.g. Robinson & Whittaker, 1987) suggests that young children fail to recognize the clue-like qualities of verbal messages. The speaker wishes to communicate something to a listener, and she uses verbal messages to provide the listener with clues about it. Because the message is merely a clue it may or may not furnish the listener with adequate understanding and, according to Robinson, young children have difficulty understanding this.

Key Term
Communicative value: The effectiveness of a message in informing a listener.

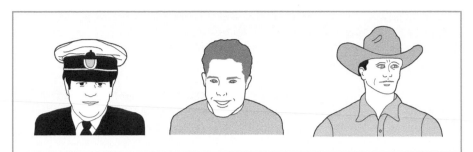

Young children's failure to understand the clue-like characteristics of utterances is manifest in several ways. First, children below approximately 6 years judge ambiguous messages to be good and informative. Robinson showed children three men (see the figure above), two of whom were wearing hats, and explained that she was thinking about one of the men who was wearing a hat. Children then had to judge whether she had told them enough to select the correct man. Those below around 6 years selected one of the men wearing hats, and judged that she had told enough (i.e. that her message was good). Those above this age typically said they did not know which man she meant, and that she had not told enough because she did not say which of the two men wearing hats she was thinking about.

You might feel that the young children judged Robinson's ambiguous message to be adequate merely because they thought it would be bad manners to call into question an adult's ability to communicate effectively. This alternative explanation can be rejected, however, since young children judged ambiguous messages to be adequate even when they were inadvertently generated by the child herself, by a puppet, or by a peer.

To cast more light on matters, Robinson proceeded to engage children in a communication game, similar to the one devised by Krauss and Glucksberg. The two players had identical sets of play people, and the experimenter and child took turns at describing one of the play people so that the listener could choose the identical one in his or her own set. As in Krauss and Glucksberg's game, the players had to rely on verbal communication because a screen prevented each player seeing which play person the other had chosen. Occasionally, on removal of the screen, it turned out that the two players had selected different play people because the message had been ambiguous. Sometimes it was the experimenter who gave an ambiguous message (on purpose, though the child did not know that), and sometimes it was the child. Robinson asked the children whose fault it was that they had chosen different play people. Children below around 6 years wrongly judged that it was the listener's fault on the grounds that she had chosen the wrong one. Children above that age correctly judged it was the speaker's fault for being imprecise in her description. It never made any difference whether the speaker was the adult experimenter or the child. Again, this finding seems to show that young children do not understand how an ambiguous message can lead to communication failure. The finding is consistent with the idea that young children have difficulty viewing utterances merely as clues to meaning.

Key Term
Ambiguous message: An utterance that fails to specify a single item uniquely.

Why do young children fail to detect ambiguity in utterances?

Nevertheless, young children do understand that utterances have to be relevant to the thing they purport to communicate about. If the experimenter says she has selected the man, when in fact she has selected the horse, young children will judge that the message is inadequate. Their difficulty lies in assessing when a relevant message is sufficiently precise to allow selection of the correct item with 100% certainty. Perhaps judgments that ambiguous messages are adequate are part of a more general tendency in young children to overestimate their own comprehension or knowledge of things.

CHILDREN OVERESTIMATE THEIR ABILITY TO INTERPRET CORRECTLY

In subsequent research Robinson (Mitchell & Robinson, 1990, 1992; Robinson & Mitchell, 1990) investigated the features of children's overestimation of their own knowledge. Children saw a set of five pictures of unfamiliar cartoon characters (such as the ones below), and were then asked to pick out "Murkor," an invented and unfamiliar name. Those aged around 6 years and below needed no further encouragement to choose one of the pictures. After that, children judged whether they knew that their chosen picture was Murkor. These young children were much more likely than older ones to say that they did know.

This finding came as no surprise to teachers, who had many experiences of their young children saying that they knew something when in fact they did not. The next task was to find out why they said they knew. Presumably, we adults would say "don't know" on the grounds that we had no prior experience of Murkor, and therefore could not know which one he was. Apparently, young children based their judgment on a different criterion. When asked in the absence of pictures if they knew who Murkor was, young children usually acknowledged their ignorance. Hence, children realized that they had no prior experience of Murkor, but judged nevertheless that they could pick out Murkor from a set of pictures. Children seemed to think that so long as they could choose a picture, this was a sign that they knew who Murkor was.

In the case of ambiguous utterances, being able to choose an item may exert a similar influence on young children's judgments. Providing the message

Many children aged 6 years judged that they knew which of these pictures was "Murkor," despite the fact that they had never seen any of the characters before and "Murkor" was an invented name!

is relevant to items in the set, they will find that they can make a choice, and derive confidence from the very act of choosing. In consequence, they may feel that the utterance is interpretable, and that they have chosen correctly. In contrast, we adults might feel that it is necessary to scrutinize the message for unfamiliar words, like "Murkor," or for ambiguities, and feel uncertain about our comprehension if we detect any problems. Putting it another way, we adults treat the message as a clue to correct meaning, and in so doing we make a distinction between what the speaker means and what she says.

If we did not distinguish what the speaker means from what she says, it would be an impediment to successful communication: Instead of analyzing the message, children may feel that they understand just because they can do something, such as select an item from a set. This possibility has prompted researchers to investigate more directly whether young children draw the say–mean distinction. Beal and Flavell (1984) attempted just this with a task in which children tried to detect problems with messages which were either ambiguous or unambiguous. Six- and 7-year-olds listened to a tape recording of a nursery-age child, called Sheri. Child listeners were told that Sheri frequently made mistakes, and did not say things clearly, and that the children's job was to spot when they could not understand exactly what Sheri meant. The children looked at a selection of paintings, supposedly done by Sheri. Sheri's tape-recorded voice then gave a "clue" to inform the child which of the pictures she (Sheri) had selected. She said, "I've picked the one made with paint." This was ambiguous, because all the pictures were made with paint. Many of the children tested were old enough to recognize that Sheri had not said enough, and that they could not tell which picture she meant.

In another similar attempt at the game, though, the experimenter pointed to the picture Sheri had chosen, as the tape recorder played her message. This time, children heard an ambiguous message, but knew Sheri's intended meaning thanks to the experimenter's help. Under this condition, children often said that Sheri had told them enough to identify the picture she meant. Beal and Flavell suggested that when children knew Sheri's intended meaning, they fixated on this, and as a result were unable to analyze Sheri's message for problems. This is a sign that they found it difficult to differentiate between the words of the utterance and the meaning intended by the speaker.

Mitchell and Russell (1989, 1991) suggested young children sometimes can make the say–mean distinction, but find it very difficult to determine when there is a difference between what is said and what is meant. Children listened to stories about a girl called Mary who asked John to fetch her reading book. She gave a description of the book, including a comment that it had a picture of a dog on the cover. Children then learned either that Mary had a really good memory for things, or that she had a really bad memory for things. In the story, John subsequently went to look for the book, and found one that fitted Mary's description in every detail, except that it had a picture of a cat on the front. Children then judged whether this close approximation to the description was the book Mary intended. Even 5-year-olds judged just as much as older children that this book with the cat on the cover was the one that Mary intended. They seemed to understand that what Mary had said (book with dog on the cover) was not what she intended (book with cat on the cover), and as such it seems they were making the say–mean distinction.

> **Key Term**
>
> **Say–mean distinction:** Understanding that what people mean might differ in subtle ways from what they actually say.

However, in another respect, these young children differed greatly from older ones. When the story indicated that Mary had a very good memory for things, 9-year-olds usually judged that the book John found with a cat on the cover was not the one Mary intended. When the story indicated that Mary had a bad memory, they judged that it was indeed the one Mary intended. The older children seemed to understand that if Mary's memory is bad, then she is likely to get the details of the reading book wrong, and so the one John found with the cat on the cover is really the one she intended. Five-year-olds, in contrast, were not influenced by information about Mary's memory. So although they often seemed to understand that what Mary meant was not what she said, they appeared not to understand the connection between Mary having a bad memory and Mary giving wrong details about the reading book. In other words, they seemed unclear on precisely when there was a difference between what Mary had said and what she meant. This study demonstrates that young children have considerable difficulty understanding the implications of bad memory in relation to the accuracy of the speaker's description, but suggests that they are aware in some sense of the communicative intent of the speaker over and above the meaning of her message.

ARE YOUNG CHILDREN TOO LITERAL?

Using a different procedure, Robinson and Mitchell (1992) demonstrated that even 3-year-olds are capable of nonliteral interpretations. They acted out a scene with two play people, one representing a girl called Jane, and the other representing her Mom, which is schematized in the figure on the left. The story was set in Jane's living room. Mom was tidying away a couple of bags of material. She put one bag into the cupboard, and the other bag of different material into the drawer. Mom then went into another room. In Mom's absence, Jane got the bags out and played with them. The trouble was that she got them mixed up and swapped them around. So, she put the bag that used to be in the cupboard into the drawer and she put the bag that used to be in the drawer into the cupboard. Later, Mom was doing some sewing when she discovered that she needed a little more material to finish the job. In fact, no material was in view, and children had to engage in make-believe. The researchers stressed to children that it was very important Mom got the right kind of material.

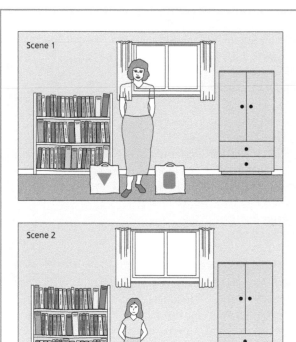

In Scene 1, Mom puts one bag in the cupboard and the other in the drawer. In Scene 2, Jane swaps the bags around in Mom's absence.

She called through to Jane, and asked her to get the bag in the drawer. Observing children were then asked which bag Mom really wanted, the one in the drawer or the one in the cupboard. We know that Mom really wanted the bag in the cupboard because the bag she thought was in the drawer is now in the cupboard. The 3-year-olds exhibited an astonishing amount of insight into the scenario, and a good many judged correctly that Mom really wanted the bag in the cupboard.

Perhaps the children did not follow the story at all, and sometimes said "cupboard" simply because they had not listened to Mom's request properly. In other words, they may have given the right answer for the wrong reason. Fortunately, this explanation was ruled out by having another condition in which after playing with the bags, Jane put them back in the places Mom had left them originally. Under this condition, children had no difficulty judging correctly that Mom really wanted the bag in the drawer, as she had said. Therefore, the confusion explanation will not do, because it would have predicted that sometimes children judge "cupboard" even when Jane returned the bags to the place where Mom had left them.

This study demonstrates unequivocally that even some 3-year-olds grasp the distinction between meaning conveyed by a message and the intention of the speaker over and above that. Consequently, they are not destined to make a literal interpretation. We can say without hesitation that although young children experience difficulty with some aspects of communication, as documented in the studies reported above, these are not due to a complete inability to distinguish utterance meaning from intended meaning.

To what extent do young children understand the intended meaning that lies behind the literal meaning?

Note that only *some* young children can resist making literal interpretations; what of those who reliably point to the place that Mom mentioned—the drawer? What lies behind the error they make? There are two ways to account for their error. Either, they are actually overly literal, with the consequence that they do not distinguish between what is said and what is intended. Alternatively, perhaps they do not process the utterance adequately and act impulsively on a superficial understanding of what was said. After all, children are bound to grasp that their task is to point to a particular location (the drawer or the cupboard). They play these kinds of games with considerable enthusiasm and in consequence might act a little too hastily as soon as they hear a location mentioned ("drawer"). This impulsiveness might mask an underlying potential to interpret nonliterally (by pointing to the cupboard). Basically, the question boils down to, "Are the children who make errors impulsive or overly literal?"

To answer this question, Mitchell, Robinson, and Thompson (1999) included a vital control condition: Mom's request changed to, "Please get me the bag *I put* in the drawer." Her request was identical in the standard condition, except that it excluded the phrase *I put*. If children's errors of interpretation arose from impulsivity, they would point to the drawer whether or not the request included *I put*. This is because they would impulsively point to the location that was mentioned. If their errors arose from a tendency to be too literal, they would point to the drawer when the request did not include *I put*, but would point to the cupboard when it did include *I put*. It is literally true that the bag Mom put in the drawer is now in the cupboard. Children could thus correctly point to the cupboard without having to distinguish what was said from what was intended.

The results of the study formed an interesting pattern. Excluding those who consistently gave correct judgments, the children aged 3 years tended to point to the drawer (the location mentioned in the request), whether or not the request included the phrase *I put*. In contrast, children aged 4 and 5 years interpreted differently according to the inclusion of *I put*. When included, they correctly pointed to the cupboard, but when excluded, they wrongly pointed to the drawer. Children aged 6 years tended correctly to point to the cupboard irrespective of the inclusion of *I put*. These results suggest that children aged around 4 or 5 years who point to the drawer when *I put* is excluded specifically find it difficult to distinguish between what is said and what is intended. Apparently, their error of interpretation cannot be explained as failure to process utterance meaning that arises from impulsivity. Their correct interpretation of a request that includes *I put* demonstrates an impressive ability to process utterance meaning and to resist acting impulsively. Approximately half of those aged around 4 and 5 years seemed to have specific difficulty venturing beyond literal meaning.

EVALUATING UTTERANCES AND DETECTING AMBIGUITY

Perhaps the difficulty some young children have with nonliteral meaning is part of a broader nonreflective tendency that accounts for their failure to judge that ambiguous messages are inadequate. Mitchell and Robinson (1994) investigated this possibility in a direct comparison between children's ability to evaluate ambiguous and discrepant utterances. In an ambiguous scenario, Mom asked for the bag in the drawer when in fact there were two drawers containing bags of material. They were asked if Mom did a good job of saying exactly which bag she wanted. In a discrepant scenario, Jane swapped the bags around between the drawer and the cupboard in Mom's absence and then Mom asked for the bag in the drawer. Children were asked if Mom said the right thing for the bag she wanted.

Children aged around 5 years were much more likely to give a correct evaluation of a discrepant message than an ambiguous message. They were much more likely to say that Mom said the wrong thing for the bag she wanted than they were to say that she did a bad job when her utterance was ambiguous. It seems that children aged about 5 years are capable of evaluating some utterances. Hence, they are capable of reflecting on the quality of utterances as shown by the fact that they were effective in judging that Mom said the wrong thing for the bag wanted. It seems that ambiguity in particular presents a special kind of problem for them. Why?

There is no impediment to making an interpretation (whether correct or incorrect) of an ambiguous utterance. When Mom says that she wants the bag in the drawer, there is an even chance that the bag the child chooses is the correct one. Being able to choose one of the bags (which could well be the correct one) seems sufficient for children to judge that the utterance is adequate. They seem to treat a possible interpretation as the correct interpretation. The basis of children's error is perhaps similar to that which was responsible for their judgment that they knew which of five unfamiliar cartoon characters was Murkor, as mentioned previously (Mitchell & Robinson, 1990). Being able to make a judgment that could be correct seems sufficient for the children to think that it is correct. This seems to lead them to think that an ambiguous utterance is adequate, and accordingly to give a positive evaluation.

IS EGOCENTRISM RESPONSIBLE FOR CHILDREN'S COMMUNICATION DIFFICULTIES?

The research reported here shows that children require much more besides grammar and vocabulary if they are to enjoy a meeting of minds with other people. What they also grasp during the early school years are the basic skills of communication, part of which involves conceptualizing utterances as clues to meaning. This understanding underpins the child's formation of good messages, or in Piaget's terminology, nonegocentric speech. It also allows the child to analyze messages she hears in order to assess whether she can be confident in her comprehension of what the speaker intended.

It seems appropriate to think there is a link between communication and theory of mind. Good communication requires an understanding of the way verbal messages affect the contents of the listener's mind (Mitchell *et al.*, 1991). Also, accurate judgments about one's own comprehension involve a good awareness of one's own mind. Piaget maintained that young children's poor communication is a symptom of egocentrism. There is some similarity between the claim that young children are egocentric and the claim that they lack a mature theory of mind. Therefore, is it appropriate to say that young children's poor communication amounts to egocentrism?

Probably not, because the term *egocentric speech* carries the connotation that poor communication abilities in young children are just one manifestation of a broader state of egocentrism. In other words, the implication is not that poor communication is due to a lack of certain experiences specific to communication, but rather that, irrespective of the child's experiences, his speech will be egocentric if he is in the stage of egocentrism. Was Piaget right in this respect?

Other work by Robinson (Robinson & Robinson, 1981) suggests Piaget was wrong. Robinson assessed children's ability to detect the problem with ambiguous messages, and then observed the children communicating with their mothers at home. Mothers usually know what their children mean, no matter how poor the communication. This is evident from the fact that even though the child's teacher and classmates may not understand what he says, the mother nearly always does. Despite this, in some households, Robinson found that mothers refused to hazard a guess at what their children meant when the communication was poor. These mothers told their children that they had not spoken clearly enough, and that it was impossible to understand what they meant. Robinson discovered that children who had this kind of mother were much better at communicating in an informative manner, and also were better at judging ambiguous messages to be inadequate. This strongly suggests that it is children's specific communication experience that is responsible for their poor communication abilities, rather than a general stage of egocentrism, contrary to Piaget's claim.

Summary

- Some findings suggest young children lack skill or understanding, whereas others suggest the opposite. Let us see if we can offer clarification. For a start, we can say with confidence that it is inappropriate to attribute young children's communication problems to egocentrism. The idea of a stage of egocentrism has now been discredited. Furthermore, Robinson's findings suggest poor child communication is related with home experience rather than with a general cognitive stage.
- Nevertheless, young children are poor at communicating compared with older ones. Even though they adapt their speech to the requirements of the listener, this could be due to a general strategy they have learned to deploy, rather than to a good understanding of the relationship between the communicative value of the message and listener comprehension. Sonnenschein's (1986) research suggests as much. But young children are not completely lacking understanding of the relationship between message adequacy and listener comprehension. The study by Mitchell et al. (1991) suggests that while 5-year-olds are lacking in some respects, at least they seem to understand that a speaker's intention can be somewhat different from the literal meaning of the message. Indeed, we now know that even some 3-year-olds understand speaker intent over and above the meaning conveyed by the words of the message (Robinson & Mitchell, 1992). Children still continue beyond this age to develop their understanding about the relationship between what is said and what is meant, given the findings of Beal and Flavell (1984) and Robinson and Mitchell (1992). These studies suggest that children can understand that utterances are but clues to meaning from a young age.
- So although it may look as though there is contradiction in the findings on the face of things, in fact there is not. The apparent contradiction vanishes once we accept that development is not an all or nothing phenomenon, and that instead it takes place gradually: 3-year-olds grasp the rudiments of the say–mean distinction, but it takes a few more years before they acquire more elaborate understanding. This more elaborate understanding is evident when children begin to appreciate that some utterances are open to different interpretations.

Essay Questions

1. Is young children's speech egocentric?
2. If a child is competent in language, does it follow that they will also be competent in communication? Why/why not?

Further Reading

A special focus on early language and communication development from the point of view of a speech and language therapist makes a fascinating read:

- Buckley, B. (2003) *Children's communication skills: From birth to five.* London: Routledge.

Chapter 14

Contents

Parenting and the development of love and attachment

14

Chapter Aims

- To introduce research on different styles of parenting.
- To describe procedures for investigating the quality of attachment between carer and baby.
- To examine evidence on whether it is possible to form multiple bonds of attachment.
- To examine claims that prolonged separation in infancy is a major cause of delinquency.
- To examine the relationship between the quality of attachment and cycles of abuse.

INTRODUCTION

Different people approach parenting in different ways. Some overindulge their children, some exercise discipline perhaps too severely, some use insufficient discipline, some do not give enough attention to their children, and some assign too much responsibility to their children. Parents interact with their children in a variety of different ways and a widely held opinion says that many of the ills of society can be blamed on *bad* parenting. A popular conception promoted by some of the Media is that irresponsible parenting explains why children play truancy, why they develop antisocial behavior, and why they are thoroughly self-centered. It is not for the discipline of Psychology to judge what is good or bad parenting, though it is appropriate to seek a systematic description of parenting and to consider what effects these different styles have on children and their cognitive, psycho-social, and emotional well-being.

Parenting is natural to humans. If our ancestors had not had sufficient parental skills to rear children then of course we would not be here today. In Darwinian terms, being a good parent has tremendous selective advantage. Children who have good parents are likely to thrive and to grow up to have children themselves. They are in turn the beneficiaries of a healthy genetic inheritance that is selected for good parenting, which combines with the good example shown to them by their own parents. The starting position must be, then, that humans are essentially good parents. Nevertheless, there is a big difference between what you need to do to ensure survival of your children and what you could do in an ideal world that gives your child an experience that is optimal for their mental and physical growth. Sadly, the world is not ideal and usually compromises have to be made. For example, many parents have to juggle child rearing with work and looking after the house, and they might not always feel that they have dedicated as much time and energy to child rearing as they would have liked. Even so, different parents use the time available to spend with their children in markedly different ways, and it is worth inquiring about the consequences of the different approaches to parenting. Especially as it is the style of parenting, rather than factors such as social class, that is most importantly associated with subjective feelings of well-being and self-esteem and measurable health and risky behavior even as far as the teenage period of development (Chan & Koo, 2011).

The style of different parents varies by a matter of degree. Nevertheless, it is possible to identify three broad approaches to parenting that are all associated with positive and negative outcome: the authoritarian, the permissive, and the authoritative/democratic (Baumrind, 1967, 1997). Each of these is defined in turn.

Authoritarian parenting

This style of parent exerts power and coercion through the authority of status. The parent's manner toward the child is not of one person to another, but is based on power and coercion. The parent is high status and the child is low status; the parent dictates and the child is required to follow unquestioningly. The parent demands respect rather than tries to earn respect. He or she would characteristically exert harsh punishment at the suggestion of insubordination. The parent might deliver punishment not so much in the interest of the child's learning and development but in the interest of making the parent feel better.

Authoritarian parents exert power and coercion through the authority of status.

Children reared in an authoritarian family are unlikely to show much initiative or independence and display excessive anxiety in unfamiliar situations, coupled with low confidence and low self-esteem. Children in authoritarian households also tend to have underdeveloped morality, which is likely to be focused externally rather than internally. The child is likely to act or not act according to anticipated reward and punishment from a figure in authority. For example, the child might steal another's sweets so long as they think they will not be found out. The child is not likely to act in a way based on principles concerned with what is right and wrong.

Permissive parenting

A permissive parent leaves their child pretty much to take care of themselves. The parent will seldom or never exert direction or control. The parent might accept their role to satisfy basic needs and occasionally play with the child. To a very large extent, though, the child is left to fend for themselves and to entertain themselves. They can go to bed when they want, can eat or not eat what they want and when they want, they can play with whom they like and when they like, they can watch whatever TV programs they want, whenever they want, irrespective of content and rating. It is most unlikely that the parent would place any premium on the child developing self-discipline, good manners, or courtesy. The parents do not express any expectations with respect to the child's achievement. The parents would yield to the child's demands and countenance unpleasant behavior, such as tantrums. In turn, the child is likely to hold the parent in low esteem, is likely to hold the parent in contempt, and is likely to manipulate the parent where possible.

The child of permissive parents characteristically shows low self-control, is impulsive, and has a short temper. The child shows a careless attitude and has little respect for adults. The child does not adhere to rules and does not show sensitivity toward other people. The child shows little capacity to work systematically and strategically to fulfill a long-term goal. Instead, he or she seeks instant gratification.

Authoritative/democratic parenting

This kind of parent implicitly through example, or explicitly through discussion, communicates principles that underlie appropriate behavior. The parent is not satisfied only to demand "good" behavior but is also compelled to convey the principles that justify why the behavior is good. For example, you must not step out into the street without looking and listening because you might get run over; you must not take Sarah's sweets because they have been given to her as a present for her to enjoy; you must not watch this program because it contains frightening pictures that might give you bad dreams. The hallmark of the authoritative parent is the willingness to explain and reason with the child. The child is treated as an individual capable of understanding. The parent will show a consistent response to the child and not yield to a tantrum or other similarly obnoxious behavior.

Authoritative/democratic parents implicitly through example, or explicitly through discussion, communicate principles that underlie appropriate behavior.

If the child exhibited unwanted behavior, the parent expresses disapproval and might implement punishment that is just sufficient to curb the behavior without being overly harsh. The parent shows enthusiasm and encouragement for the child's interests, and delight in the child's success in attaining achievements. The parent shows respect for the child's opinion and engages in discussion as appropriate. The parent sets aside the time and space for the child to tackle homework and helps to structure leisure activities. This could involve helping the child to join sports or hobby clubs or simply helping to make arrangements to visit friends or invite friends round. The parent might also get involved in the child's activities directly, by joining the same club or by arranging visits to theme parks or soccer matches. Importantly, the authoritative/democratic style of parent behaves consistently.

One of the most important aspects of development relates to socialization and especially the child's ability to empathize with other people (see chapter 5). Parental style plays an important role in this process, as demonstrated by two landmark studies. Dunn *et al.* (1991) observed a relation between the quality of parents' conversation with their toddlers when aged 33 months, and the children's ability to understand other people's mental states 6 months later. Some parents observed at 33 months had a talent for explaining things to their children, especially other people's behavior. For example, they explained why their grandmother refused to give a sweet shortly before dinner, why their daddy refused to read a scary story just before bed, and why their teacher asks children to put on a coat at playtime. Children with parents who explained things were among the first in their peer group to pass a test of false belief, which is a widely used measure of understanding other people's minds. The children's success indicated developmental advancement in understanding other people's minds, which is likely to be a consequence of their parents' style of communication.

Undoubtedly, the parents observed by Dunn *et al.* who made efforts to explain things to their children generally exhibited an authoritative/democratic style of parenting. However, Dunn *et al.* were not content to rely on broad generalizations; rather, they sought a more detailed examination of the relation between parental communication and the benefits to the child's interpersonal development. The study tells us that certain aspects of authoritative/democratic parenting have a beneficial effect on children's understanding of other minds.

The other landmark study was conducted by Meins *et al.* (2002, 2003). Rather than directly observing parents' behavior, they obtained an indirect measure of parenting by investigating how parents conceptualized their child. In the study, parents were asked to describe their child, without any special instructions on what kind of description was required. Parents fell broadly into two categories, those who were mind-minded and those who were not. Mind-minded parents were identified when they described the psychological characteristics of their child. A parent who said their child thinks about how to relate to other people, or that their child tends to forget what the parent says, is one who understands their child as a thinking entity and thus is defined as being mind-minded. In contrast, a parent who solely describes the physical characteristics of their child, how tall the child is, the color of her hair, and so on, would not be defined as mind-minded.

Meins *et al.* discovered that children with parents who were mind-minded tended to pass tests of false belief at an earlier age than children of parents

Key Term
Mind-minded: A parent who is attuned to her child on a psychological level and not just in terms of physical needs.

who were not mind-minded. Hence, parental mind-mindedness seemed to give children a head start in understanding the social psychological world. It is fair to assume that parents who are mind-minded tended to interact with children differently from parents who were not mind-minded. Indeed, it would not be surprising if mind-minded parents tended to be the kind of people who were good at explaining things to their children, like those parents observed by Dunn *et al*. This follows in that if parents related to their children as thinking beings, then the parents would appreciate that their child's thinking can be assisted by hearing explanations of things.

Interestingly, it seems that parental mind-mindedness is linked with the quality of attachment between parent and child (Meins, Fernyhough, Russell, & Clark-Carter, 1998). How can we explain this? Later, we shall look at attachment between child and parent and find that attachment is measurable from the first half of infancy. Because attachment takes place so early in development, it seems unlikely that the parent's style of communication with the infant plays a causal role in promoting attachment. Rather, it seems more likely that the underlying factor responsible for attachment is also responsible for parental style. Specifically, it seems that some parents are oriented from the outset to think of their child as a psychological entity, which expresses itself in the mother's behavior with at least two positive benefits. One is that the parent behaves in such a way and thinks of her child in such a way as to promote attachment. The other is that it impacts upon the mother's style of interaction such that she displays an authoritative/democratic style that in turn encourages the child to be psychologically attuned. This parenting style has a measurable outcome on teenager's behavior. Chan and Koo (2011) identified authoritative parenting as the style of interaction that is most strongly associated with positive youth outcomes, such as feelings of subjective well-being, lower odds of smoking and getting into fights, and lower odds of having friends who use drugs. Parenting styles and attachment are thus important for the individual and for those around them. Having said that, it is wrong to think of attachment as an all or nothing thing, as explained later.

LOVE

The origins of love can be found in infancy. It is very difficult to identify precisely what love is. We can describe physiological changes people experience when in the presence of someone with whom they are infatuated. We can try to describe emotional feelings of security we enjoy when in the company of a loved family member. However, it is difficult to say what forms the glue of attachment between human beings that we call love.

Throughout life we occasionally meet people who are incapable of love. These people seem devoid of any moral scruples, are ruthless, and act only for their own gain. They seem to love nobody other than, perhaps, themselves. It is likely that there are fewer such people in the world than we imagine. When somebody takes action that is counter to our interests, because we are offended and affronted it is tempting to think the perpetrator is a person who acts only in their own interest. Yet we might find that this individual has the capacity to be highly altruistic in other contexts. Thus, we have a tendency to overgeneralize about people's personality traits after witnessing isolated acts. A common example is that of resenting admonition from someone who holds an office of high status, and then rationalizing the affair by assuming that the boss is a nasty individual who is incapable of sympathy regarding our difficult plight. These instances apart, it appears there are people who behave in a ruthless way irrespective of context, with no regard for loyalties, who apparently betray "friends" without a second thought. Indeed, such people may have no conception of loyalty, and friendships could only be one-sided. Anyone who betrays the trust of another individual without any bad feeling of conscience cannot be said to have genuine friendship bonds.

These loveless people were labeled by Bowlby as affectionless psychopaths. Thanks to Hollywood, the term "psychopath" conjures images of a murderer who experiences delusions and hallucinations about dead people telling him to carry out heinous deeds. The truth is that affectionless psychopaths do not experience hallucinations unless they have the misfortune to have a psychotic disorder also. The juveniles labeled as affectionless psychopaths by Bowlby might now be diagnosed as suffering from *Reactive Attachment Disorder* (RAD), which describes disturbed and developmentally inappropriate ways of relating socially in most contexts as a consequence of failing to form early attachments. The terminology describes a disorder that shares some characteristics with Bowlby's definition of affectionless psychopathy but is less evocative and more grounded.

What are the developmental consequences of maternal deprivation?

According to John Bowlby (1965), affectionless psychopathy can arise from either a failure to form a bond with the mother during infancy, or it could arise if a bond has been formed, but then is broken in the event of mother and child being separated. Bowlby was careful to stress that the mother need not be the biological mother, and in fact could be anyone who played the role of mother. The individual need not even be a woman. Bowlby claimed that "maternal" deprivation gives rise to affectionless psychopathy, which could reveal itself in delinquent behavior in later years, due to the individual's lack of moral concern for others. This is a contentious claim that has prompted vigorous debate. Later, we shall look in some detail at Bowlby's claim about maternal deprivation, and its consequences for disordered personality. First, let us look at how bonds form between caregiver and baby in normal development.

ATTACHMENT

One of the major figures in this area is Mary Ainsworth (e.g. 1973), and much of what follows is based on her research. A bond of attachment normally develops in the baby around the age of 9 months with the primary caregiver. Prior to that age, the infant does have a preference for the caregiver, but is not attached in the strict sense. The relationship between child and parent is nonetheless very important in this early stage after birth. The prenatal period can be very stressful for mother and child and this prenatal stress has adverse affects on later development. These potential negative consequences of prenatal stress are moderated by a positive relationship immediately after birth, for example, by reducing stress-induced anxiety in the child (Bergman, Sarkar, Glover, & O'Connor, 2008). At 2 to 3 months, the baby will smile and "coo" at the mother, more so than at other people. Indeed, the baby will prefer to be with the caregiver, even if fed all his life by another individual who otherwise does

Key Term
Affectionless psychopath: A person who is unable to form an emotional bond with other people.

not provide as much attention as the caregiver. Also at this age, the baby may seem equally attached to a secondary caregiver who gives lots of attention, but who spends a relatively small amount of time with the baby, for example the father.

If it is not feeding that is the primary factor responsible for this preference, then what is? It is most likely that physical bodily contact is an important ingredient, as in picking up, carrying, and cuddling the baby. This suggestion comes from a study by Anisfeld, Casper, Nozyce, and Cunningham (1990), who noted the extent to which mothers made bodily contact with their babies. Babies who had been picked up and carried a great deal very early in infancy were much more securely attached to their mothers at 13 months of age. The authors of the study concluded that early bodily contact between mother and baby promotes the development of a bond of love between them.

Although the baby shows preference for the caregiver from early infancy, a substantial change takes place at about 9 months, as demonstrated by the onset of separation anxiety. A task known as the "strange situation" was designed to reveal separation anxiety: The mother takes the baby into an unfamiliar room, where he is allowed to play with toys. Then a stranger enters, and shortly afterwards the mother leaves the room. A short time later, the mother calls from outside the room and then returns, whereupon the stranger leaves. Then the mother leaves a second time and after a while the stranger returns and greets the infant. A short time after this, the mother calls from outside the room and then returns a final time. This sequence of events usually provokes a response from the baby, a response that should be revealing about the baby's sense of security and the comfort he gets from his mother. In sum, his response should be revealing about the quality of his attachment.

A typical response from a child aged more than 9 months is as follows: When the mother gets up to leave the room, we see the baby walking, if he is able, or perhaps crawling after her. When she goes through the door, the baby cries, and generally appears distressed. In the mother's absence, the baby is likely to remain immobilized, and perhaps continue crying. On the mother's return, he will appear relieved, and might initiate cuddling. The baby's reactions to the mother's departure are more pronounced when he finds himself left alone with a stranger, compared with when left in an empty room. Thus, the baby experiences "stranger anxiety."

An aspect of attachment in 10- to 12-month-olds is social referencing. When the baby is confronted with a stranger or a new toy, he is likely to turn to the parent apparently in order to read her emotional expression to find out whether the person or thing is safe. If the parent's expression shows fear, then the baby is likely to stay close to her. If the expression is happy, the baby is likely to venture near to the person or thing. This reference to the facial expression is specific to the main caregivers, and babies do not seek information or reassurance from other people's faces in this situation (Zarbatany & Lamb, 1985). Although many infants spend more time with their mother than their father, typically the father's facial expression will have just as much influence over the baby's behavior (Hirshberg, 1990; Hirshberg & Svejda, 1990). These findings suggest that 10- to 12-month-old babies use the parents as a safe base from which to explore the world. The attachment

Key Terms

Separation anxiety:
A state of anxiety experienced by a baby when her mother leaves the room.

Strange situation:
A task designed to reveal both separation anxiety and the quality of attachment between mother and baby.

Social referencing:
Babies periodically look at their mother's face for signs of encouragement or anxiety, especially when they are in a novel situation.

figure (i.e. the mother) also becomes a source of comfort when the baby is stressed or distressed.

On the face of things, the relatively late onset of separation anxiety seems rather curious. We have already seen in the chapter on perceptual development that babies as young as 6 weeks recognize their mother, given that they spend more time looking at their mother's face than looking at an unfamiliar woman's face. Also, as reported earlier in this chapter, babies of 2–3 months smile and "coo" more at their mother than at other people. What is responsible, then, for the sudden change at about 9–10 months?

The chapter on Piaget's theory (chapter 4) reports that babies have an underdeveloped concept of object permanence; in other words, they do not distinguish between themselves and the rest of existence. As far as the young baby is concerned, once an object is out of sight, quite literally, it is out of mind: The baby has no conception of the existence of things that cannot be perceived directly. Although this claim is somewhat controversial, it has been put forward to explain the sudden onset of separation anxiety at about 9–10 months of age.

Piaget claimed that the concept of object permanence is not completely acquired until about 18–24 months of age. However, he also suggested that object concept undergoes changes prior to this, and an important period is between about 8 and 12 months of age, which, interestingly, coincides neatly with the onset of separation anxiety. Piaget's test involved putting two cloths (A and B) side by side, and placing a rattle under one of them (A). A typical 8-month-old will have no difficulty whisking away the cloth and grabbing the rattle. This is repeated three times, with the baby successfully retrieving the rattle on each occasion. Then, on the fourth hiding, in full view of the baby as usual, we put the rattle under cloth B. The baby will search under A, and then lose interest in the game having failed to find the rattle there. In contrast, a typical 12-month-old will search directly at B and recover the rattle.

The 8-month-old's failure to retrieve the rattle from B could signal lack of awareness of the existence of objects once they have gone out of sight. Piaget suggested that perception is subordinate to action, meaning that after three hiding trials, the baby had come to represent the object in terms of her own reaching action. In short, the baby supposedly understands the external world with reference to an aspect of self (her own reaching) and is thus profoundly egocentric. Not being able to understand the world as distinct from self could explain why young babies do not exhibit separation anxiety. They might not be able to conceive that the mother has moved to a different place, perhaps even quite some distance from the baby. In contrast, an older baby will be capable of this, and will become anxious at the mother's absence in consequence.

Lester (1974) conducted an intriguing study to examine the relationship between the concept of object permanence and separation anxiety. Babies aged either 8 or 12 months were allowed to play in an unfamiliar room in the company of their mother. Then the mother left. More of the older babies froze on the mother's departure, losing interest in the toys, which can be taken as a sign of separation anxiety. However, independent of age, there was a very close relationship between passing Piaget's object permanence test and manifest separation anxiety.

This important finding tells us that separation anxiety, and perhaps by implication the first genuine bond of attachment, arises when the baby comes to recognize that other people are separate from him. It seems that the baby develops a strong emotional attachment to the caregiver when on realizing she (the caretaker) is an autonomous individual who continues to exist in another part of the world even when out of sight. In other words, bonds of love are formed when the baby recognizes other people as people.

TYPES OF ATTACHMENT

Attachment bonds, once developed, take various forms, and researchers have found it useful to place these into broad categories.

- *Secure attachment* occurs in approximately 50–67% of baby–caregiver relationships in developed countries. Babies venture to explore the room and especially the toys while looking back periodically to check that their mother is present and happy. When their mother leaves the room, they are likely to be distressed and will welcome her return and be comforted by her. After a short while, the baby will resume exploring the room and play with the toys. In effect, the baby seems to treat the mother as a safe base from which to venture into an unfamiliar environment.

- *Insecure/resistant attachment* is detected in about 10% of caregiver–baby relationships. Compared with the securely attached baby, the insecurely/resistant attached tends to be clingy from the beginning of the strange situation, which curbs exploration and play. When the mother leaves, the baby tends to become very upset. When she returns, the baby approaches her for comfort but, paradoxically, tends to resist her when that comfort is offered.

- *Insecure/avoidant attachment* is detected in around 15% of baby–caregiver relationships. Babies falling into this category tend to be aloof and turn away from their mother when she is in the room. When she returns after a short absence, they typically fail to greet her.

- *Disorganized/disoriented attachment* is present in about 15% of caregiver–baby relationships. These babies behave in a contradictory way, for example approaching their mother apparently for comfort, yet wearing an anxious expression or looking away. These babies may seem calm for a while but then suddenly become severely distressed, or freeze, or seem dazed or disoriented. These babies seem to want comfort from their mother while also feeling wary of her.

Ainsworth's studies show how strongly and adaptively a securely attached baby bonds with his caregiver, and the distress he experiences when separated only for a short period of time. Just knowing this might be enough to persuade us that a prolonged separation from the caregiver

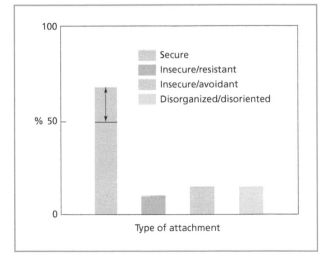

Types of attachment in baby–caregiver relationships.

could be severely damaging to the baby's mental health. Bowlby (1965) suggests that prolonged separation from the caregiver, or the lack of opportunity to form a bond of attachment to any single individual, will cause a personality disorder that might manifest later in life as affectionless psychopathy, or at the very least as delinquency. Two of Bowlby's concerns focused on the lack of opportunity for children to form a bond of attachment when reared in an orphanage, and the disturbance to a bond, for example if the baby had to be separated from his mother for a stay in hospital. Bowlby points out that when deprived of maternal care, the baby's development is nearly always retarded, physically, intellectually, and socially. Additionally, symptoms of physical and mental illness may appear. In particular, Bowlby tells us that separated babies display the following characteristics:

- failure to respond to a "coo"
- poor appetite, no matter how desirable the food
- failure to gain weight, irrespective of how nourishing the food is
- sleeping badly
- low IQ.

THE SOCIOBIOLOGY OF ATTACHMENT

Bowlby argues that a readiness to form of a bond of attachment is programmed into the baby for sound biological reasons. Babies who stay close to an adult are likely to benefit from an umbrella of protection against an environment that can be very harsh both in climate and predators. Therefore, in a natural environment, babies who had a trait to attach themselves to a caregiver stood a good chance of reaching maturity, and passing their genes to the next generation, genes for the attachment trait. In that case, failure to form a bond in infancy, or the disruption of a bond, would be counter to the baby's natural tendency, with dire social, psychological, and physical consequences. Another way in which it makes biological sense for the baby to attach to a caregiver is that the caregiver is likely to feel encouraged by the baby in a way that leads the caregiver to exert even greater effort toward the baby.

The sociobiology of human attachment is illuminated by studies of attachment in animals. Nobel Prize winning Konrad Lorenz demonstrated a primitive form of attachment in geese. He observed that shortly after hatching, the goslings followed the mother wherever she went. This has obvious implications for survival, so he wondered whether this tendency was innate. But the goslings could not have a perfect image of their mother programmed into their brains from birth, so Lorenz wondered instead if they are programmed to attach themselves to the first conspicuous moving thing they see. This would almost certainly be the mother.

To find out, Lorenz isolated some eggs and used an incubator to hatch them in his own presence. The resulting goslings attached themselves to Lorenz, and duly followed him around. The goslings ignored their biological mother, and any other goose for that matter. If, however, goslings were deprived of an opportunity to attach themselves to anything during the first 30 hours after hatching, then they never formed an attachment bond, even when presented with the opportunity to do so. These goslings grew

Konrad Lorenz with his goslings.

up to be socially isolated from other geese, and seemed incompetent at mating.

Taking a lesson from sociobiology, Bowlby supposed that the attachment between mother and child might be of a similar kind to that between gosling and mother goose. In both cases, attachment has the same biological survival value. Bowlby believed that if the baby is prevented from forming an attachment bond, or if a bond is disrupted, then the individual would suffer problems relating to social attachment in later years, and would show a lack of empathy with others.

In geese, attachment occurs up to 30 hours after hatching. Bowlby believed the timescale for humans might be different, and viewed the period between 6 and 9 months as crucial. This is roughly the period when the baby first shows signs of separation anxiety. He observed that babies separated around this age undergo radical changes in behavior. In the initial period of separation, the baby is likely to scream, shout, and run or crawl about wildly, and get no comfort from the attention of a sympathetic adult. Following this comes a period of despair, when the baby becomes immobilized by lethargy of depression. If the baby sees tokens associated with his mother during this period, he might become enraged. Bowlby suggested that he is disturbed by reminders of earlier more secure days. If the mother should return after a protracted separation of several months, the baby might seem uninterested in her presence, and subsequently be unable to form an attachment with anybody.

Bowlby believed that the period between about 6 months and 4 years is the most important regarding the baby's emotional adjustment. Beyond the age of 4, the child seems to accept the mother's temporary departure, perhaps for a few days or even weeks, without experiencing excessive trauma. By this age, the child can accept substitute attachment figures, such as the grandparents. If a baby is separated for 3 months or more, or has no opportunity to form any attachment, Bowlby suspected that there could be permanent emotional damage. To investigate, Bowlby

What is the best theoretical framework for understanding attachment: psychodynamic, cognitive, or sociobiological?

conducted a study on 44 people convicted of stealing, to find out whether their antisocial behavior could be traced back to maternal deprivation. He compared the thieves with 44 emotionally disturbed people who did not commit antisocial acts. Of the thieves, 14 were diagnosed as having affectionless characters, and 17 had suffered complete and prolonged separation of 6 months or more during their first year of life. Nearly all the affectionless characters turned out to have a history of maternal deprivation. In contrast, the emotionally disturbed people who had not committed antisocial acts were fortunate enough to have had intact relationships with their caregivers during early development.

This, coupled with a variety of case studies, led Bowlby to conclude that maternal deprivation has the following detrimental consequences for later personality. The individual has only superficial relationships with no capacity to make friends. He is psychologically inaccessible to others, and displays little emotional response or concern. He frequently engages in pointless deceit, evasion, and stealing, and has an inability to feel guilt.

There can be little doubt that the prolonged separation from a caregiver during infancy is profoundly damaging to physical and mental development, and that the damage could well be permanent. However, two details of Bowlby's claim have generated controversy. In particular, Bowlby stressed that, to ensure mental well-being, the baby must form an attachment with only one person, usually though not necessarily the mother. Second, he suggested that a consequence of maternal deprivation is likely to be the development of a delinquent personality.

SINGLE VERSUS MULTIPLE ATTACHMENTS

As regards attachment to a single person, this idea has implications for parental practices, particularly the concept of the working mother. In modern society, many more mothers go out to work compared with a few decades ago. Could this give rise to partial deprivation, as Bowlby called it, resulting in damage to the child's emotional adjustment? If so, perhaps we should recommend one of the parents stays at home. Obviously we would not want to jeopardize the baby's health, but such a recommendation could have serious consequences for the family's well-being. First, the family budget may pressure both parents to work. Second, the psychological adjustment of the parent who stays at home could be jeopardized because he or she is denied the fulfillment that work sometimes affords. In sum, we need to know whether parents can be confident in the knowledge that when they leave their baby with somebody, perhaps another family member, the baby's emotional development will not be compromised.

If we establish that babies are capable of forming multiple bonds, bonds with two or more people, this would show that separation from the mother, at least for relatively short periods, need not have detrimental consequences—providing the baby is in the company of someone with whom he shares a bond of affection.

Several studies have employed the strange situation to investigate whether babies display separation anxiety in relation to different caregivers. One study (Fox, 1977) explored separation anxiety in children reared in an Israeli kibbutz. The kibbutz system is based on an ideal of equitable rights, avoidance of materialism, and avoidance of possessiveness. Although babies sleep in the

Key Term

Partial deprivation: Insufficient contact between mother and baby that brings about negative consequences for the baby's emotional development.

same quarters as their parents, they are cared for by groups of adults dedicated to babycare, thus freeing the parents of the restrictions of parenthood. Interestingly, and contrary to Bowlby's expectations, these babies displayed separation anxiety when left alone by their parents and by their daytime caregiver, showing that they had formed multiple bonds. Meanwhile, Schaffer and Emerson (1964) discovered multiple bonds even in conventional families. Surprisingly, the more bonds the baby formed, the greater the strength of the bond with the main caregiver. This was not always the mother, and in a minority of cases, the strongest bond was with the father.

Leiderman and Leiderman (1974) investigated whether multiple bonding was associated with adverse effects, which is what Bowlby would have predicted. They studied childrearing practices in east African farming communities, and identified some homes that had a single mother figure, and others that had multiple caregivers, with none more prominent than others in the role. Babies with multiple caregivers did seem a little less emotionally secure compared with those who had a single prominent caregiver, as demonstrated by greater stranger anxiety. However, this can be weighed against the finding that babies with multiple caregivers seemed more cognitively advanced than those with a single prominent caregiver.

As babies are capable of forming multiple bonds, this supports the view that separation from the mother, whilst she is at work for example, need not have detrimental consequences, so long as the child shares a bond with other caregivers.

It might even be possible to form affection bonds simultaneously with each of several other children in a peer group. Freud and Dann (1951) studied six children who had lived in pre-Second World War Germany, and were separated from their families prior to 1 year of age. Eventually, they were taken into Freud and Dann's institution in England, between age 3 and 4 years. The children appeared to be highly attached to each other, but cared little for anyone or anything else. When one of the children was separated from the group, he became very distressed, even for short periods. He constantly asked for the other children, and, meanwhile, the rest of the children seemed worried. These children had no adult to attach themselves to, but in consolation seemed able to profit from the love of each other. Their care for each other was quite unlike the normal sibling relationship.

Is having multiple bonds a good thing or a bad thing?

Together, these studies show several things. First, Bowlby's claim that babies must form a bond with a single person is not only unfounded, but appears wrong. Second, those with multiple attachments may be different from babies with just a single bond in some respects, but this difference does not necessarily amount to disadvantage. As a result, leaving the baby with someone who shares a warm relationship with him need not compromise emotional well-being. But what about the direct consequences of mothers going out to work? The idea of working mothers still causes heated debate and the best way we can contribute to this debate is not through preconceived opinion, but through assessing the evidence. Georgia Verropoulou and Heather Joshi (2009) investigated the effects of maternal employment on children's behavioral and cognitive development. In line with the importance given to early attachment and bonding, Verropoulou and Joshi focused on children who were up to 5 years old when their mothers were working and investigated math and reading scores as well as anxious and aggressive behavior.

Kagan *et al.*'s (1978) study found that, compared with similar babies reared at home, the daycare infants displayed no ill effects from their experience.

What advice would you give to a mother with a young baby who is contemplating taking a full-time job?

Children included in this investigation were born in Britain in the 1970s and the authors could therefore assess the interesting question of whether maternal employment in the first 5 years of life might have "sleeper effects." In other words, does maternal employment disadvantage (or advantage) children when they are adults, even though they may seem perfectly unaffected earlier in development. Verropoulou and Joshi's analysis revealed that maternal employment in the early years of a child's life has no influence on their later math ability or anxious or aggressive behavior. There was an isolated effect of a minor disadvantage in reading ability, but this was only true for children whose mothers were less well educated and who worked in the first year of the child's life. This isolated effect stands against the lack of any effect in the other areas investigated and should be interpreted within that context. It is also unclear whether this minor effect is due to child rearing and maternity leave arrangements in the 1970s that may have changed in more modern times. As a matter of fact, a more recent investigation in the US found a small *advantage* on similar behavioral and cognitive measures for children whose mothers worked in the first 3 years of their lives (Jaffee, Van Hulle, & Rodgers, 2011). As such, investigating the available data we find that maternal employment is not the cause of children's problems in life.

Perhaps Bowlby's main concern was that *institutions* might be damaging to the baby's emotional development. The potential for multiple bonding shows that in principle this need not be the case. To find out whether in practice institutionalized care is detrimental, Kagan, Kearsley, and Zelazo (1978) studied children between the age of 3½ months and 29 months of age who attended a daycare center. Compared with similar babies reared at home, the daycare infants displayed no ill effects from their daycare experience. It has to be said that the daycare center had an excellent reputation for the competence and compassion of its staff, and it is conceivable that had the care not been of such a high standard, the children could have suffered. However, presumably children of incompetent parents suffer in a similar way also. In sum, the potential for multiple attachments need not result in damage to the baby's mental health even if the baby is cared for by someone other than the primary caregiver. This is true at least in the sense of separation from the mother on a daily basis. Given this, Bowlby's concern about partial deprivation seems unfounded.

DELINQUENCY

The other contentious point concerned Bowlby's emphasis on a strong link between maternal deprivation and later delinquency. Although many of the thieves Bowlby studied had experienced separation from their mother for a prolonged period during their first year, we cannot necessarily conclude that individuals who are unfortunate enough to have experienced separation in infancy will develop delinquent tendencies; only some of those individuals might become delinquents. Findings obtained by Goldfarb (1943) serve to illustrate the point. He studied babies separated from their mothers before the age of 9 months. Some of the babies went directly into a foster home, where presumably there was opportunity for a bond of attachment to form with the foster parents.

The remaining babies were sent to an institution for 3 years, before being found a place in a foster home. The institution benefited from the highest standards of physical hygiene, but was lacking in its provision for emotional bonds to develop between staff and babies. Indeed, babies had little opportunity to form a bond with anyone, given that they individually inhabited single cubicles. This was done in the interest of preventing the spread of any diseases, but unwittingly was against the interest of social attachment. The babies only had contact for short periods each day, when nurses dressed or fed them.

The study was longitudinal, meaning that the children were observed periodically during development. Compared with those who went directly into a foster home, the children in the institution, who were completely deprived of any social bonds, fared worse on assessments of intelligence and the ability to make friends. Evidently, early deprivation of attachment bonds had the predictable damaging effect. However, only one of the children who had been institutionalized truanted, stole, and committed other antisocial acts. Although separation can have a devastating effect on the child's emotional development, contrary to Bowlby's claim it seems far from inevitable that the child will become delinquent. A recent re-examination of Bowlby's cases offers a different explanation for the occurrence of juvenile delinquency in the sample. Follan and Minnis (2010) suggest that on closer inspection of the cases the prolonged separation may not be the causing factor in delinquency, but rather that the children experienced some form of maltreatment.

A study by Rutter (1972) yielded similar findings. In a broad survey of teenagers, Rutter found that many who had suffered prolonged separation from their mother during infancy seemed well adjusted. Those who were maladjusted had experienced a particular kind of family break-up, namely due to divorce or psychiatric illness in the family. Such experiences in themselves could be disturbing to the young child, over and above the separation. Therefore, perhaps the particular circumstance of separation is a factor in emotional damage. Obviously separation is traumatic for a young child, but perhaps there is scope for emotional repair when normal family life resumes in many cases. In contrast, Rutter found that teenagers who had no opportunity to form an attachment bond during infancy typically were disturbed. He suggested that we should make a distinction between individuals who experience separation and those who never form a bond in the first place. Perhaps only the latter group of people suffer from the syndrome described by Bowlby.

Altogether, it seems Bowlby correctly recognized the importance of affection bond formation during infancy, and what can go wrong with later development if a baby is deprived of love. However, he overlooked the importance of multiple bonding in normal development, and perhaps overestimated the adverse effects of separation. Having said that, for obvious reasons it is preferable if separation does not occur. But if separation does occur, the child's emotional adjustment forever after need not necessarily be doomed.

INTERNAL WORKING MODEL

Bowlby postulated that from our relationships with others we abstract an "internal working model," which is an internal representation of ourselves, the people we have a relationship with, and the characteristics of that relationship. He proposed that (1) the internal working model is not amenable to conscious scrutiny and (2) that the template for a lifelong internal working model develops from our first relationships. In other words, the quality of our attachment to the primary caregiver during infancy sets the tone and character for the relationships that we experience thereafter. Moreover, the quality of the earliest attachment impacts indirectly on our ability to function in the social realm. Children who are securely attached tend to hold a positive conception of themselves, a positive conception of their caregiver, and a positive conception of the relationship. These children also tend to be popular among peers, which is probably because their positive self-esteem enables them to relate to others in a way that conveys good adjustment. This, in turn, promotes good relationships with other people, which sustains a positive working model. Consequently, the individual is likely to relate well to their own children, allowing a positive working model to pass from generation to generation.

The other side of the coin, unfortunately, is that infants who are insecurely attached are in danger of developing an internal working model of maladaptive relationships and have low self-esteem, with the knock-on effect that they tend to be unpopular among peers. This helps to explain the cycle of abuse phenomenon. It is a dreadful irony that parents who abuse their children tend to have been victims of abuse when they themselves were children. Abused children do not inevitably grow up to be abusers; but those who are abusers do tend to have been abused themselves. This is explained by the internal working model. Abused children develop an aberrant internal working model, one that represents perhaps an exploitative and even sadistic relationship. This maladaptive working model is then responsible for the individual developing abusive tendencies if/when they become a parent. This nasty trait thus has opportunity to pass from generation to generation.

What is the link between an individual's quality of attachment early in life and their ability as a parent?

The cycle of abuse is by no means inevitable. It can be broken if the internal working model evolves thanks to experiencing well-adjusted relationships later in development. It is unfortunate in this case, though, that the quality of the earliest relationship sets a pattern for later relationships. It is not a completely intractable pattern, but it is perhaps resistant to modification.

In recognition of the possibility that we have an internal working model from childhood that influences the character of our relationships as adults, researchers have sought to get a handle on this. It is a tricky task if we accept Bowlby's suggestion that the internal working model cannot be accessed consciously. Main, Kaplan, and Cassidy (1985) developed the adult attachment interview for the purpose, which is a semi-structured interview about the participant's relationship with their primary caregiver. Main *et al.* were not as concerned about the content of participants' responses as with the tone and manner of their responses. From this information they identified broadly different types of response.

According to Bowlby, infants who are insecurely attached may develop an internal working model of maladaptive relationships. This could result in low self-esteem and unpopularity among peers.

• *Autonomous* individuals described their relationship objectively, commenting on positive and negative aspects in an appropriately measured way. Their descriptions were coherent and complete. According to Main and colleagues, these individuals had benefited from being securely attached to their mother during childhood. In contrast, individuals not securely attached presented in one of the following three different ways.

- *Dismissing* participants seemed to have a poor memory for their childhood and especially for the relationship with their mother. They tended to describe their childhood according to an ideal or a stereotype of what childhood might have been like in some mythical golden age; they were dismissive of negative experiences during childhood and steered away from emotional territory.
- *Preoccupied* individuals were rather incoherent in their recollections, as if overloaded with memories that were hard to reflect on and organize into an orderly manner.
- *Unresolved* participants seemed to be living with enduring trauma from their childhood, perhaps associated with the loss of their primary caregiver. These individuals struggled to put their childhood behind them and move on.

Summary

- Babies can form multiple bonds, and prolonged separation from a primary caregiver, although far from desirable, need not have dire consequences for the child's emotional development if he can develop bonds with other carers. Moreover, people who are separated from a primary caregiver need not be at risk of developing delinquency. Nevertheless, the earliest relationships set an enduring but not necessarily intractable pattern for the rest of one's life. The chief factors associated with these relationships are parental style and the quality of attachment. The pattern set by early attachment influences the character of subsequent relationships and the concept of the internal working model is illuminating in this respect. It is especially useful in understanding the cycle of abuse.

Essay Questions

1. Is too little discipline in parenting bad for the development of a child?
2. Evaluate the evidence for a link between attachment and delinquency.

Further Reading

This book provides a comprehensive account of Bowlby's findings and arguments:

- Bowlby, J. (1965). *Child care and the growth of love* (2nd edn.). Harmondsworth, UK: Penguin.

A view that contrasts with Bowlby's, suggesting that interruption of the relationship between mother and baby need not result in permanent emotional damage, is presented in this text:

- Rutter, M. (1972). *Maternal deprivation reassessed*. Harmondsworth, UK: Penguin.

Chapter 15

Contents

Moral development

Chapter Aims

- To introduce Piaget's research into children's judgments about moral dilemmas.
- To introduce Kohlberg's theory of developmental stages in moral reasoning.
- To explore the developmental roots of empathy and prosocial behavior.
- To explore the extent to which moral behavior is the product of social convention and emotional response, rather than principled reasoning.
- To investigate foundations of moral understanding in infant's social judgments.

INTRODUCTION

Our sense of morality is one of the things that defines our humanity. Societies the world over share many moral codes, for example that killing and incest are wrong; many other moral codes depend much more on culture. Whether you agree or disagree that we live in a moral world probably depends a lot on how you define morals. Let us ignore for the moment those moral codes and laws that are set down by religious and other authorities and take a look at our everyday behavior. Have you ever paid more for coffee or chocolate in order to buy something that is from an ethical source? How do you feel about child labor used in products you buy? Do you think it wrong to discriminate against people because of their race or gender? Most of us have a strong sense that discrimination and exploitation are wrong: We have a *sense* that it is wrong and this is evidence for a sense of morality that pervades many aspects of our lives, without us even being aware of it. We sometimes act in a prosocial or altruistic way, meaning that we do something that is not motivated by what is best for ourselves, but by what is good for others. Examples are giving up some of your time to do voluntary work, donating money to charity, or buying ethically sourced goods. Sometimes people act in a highly moral or highly immoral way on a much larger scale and these acts evoke very strong emotions. The most extreme case of altruism must be when individuals act knowing that by doing so they will sacrifice their lives to preserve that of others. There are many moving examples of such acts. One such case arose from the long-lasting conflict in Northern Ireland. Somebody threw a hand grenade into an open-top bus in Belfast. In a barely comprehensible act of bravery, one of the passengers smothered the device by lying on top of it. In doing so, he sacrificed his own life, but preserved those of the other passengers. Humans really are curious creatures. Callous deeds and terrifying destructiveness defy the imagination, yet humans are also capable of extreme acts of self-sacrifice and altruism.

In this chapter we are going to look at the development of prosocial or altruistic behavior, which in many cases results from the development of a moral conscience. And we are going to examine whether all moral reasoning and behavior is a result of rational thought processes.

PIAGET'S MORAL REALIST AND MORAL SUBJECTIVIST

Moral conscience and behavior is not the province of people in just one culture, but is something that we find the world over. If everybody learns to distinguish moral from immoral acts and feels a sense that they should act in a moral way, then we need to identify a powerful mechanism that can explain such universal learning. One way of explaining this learning would be to suppose that altruistic and prosocial behavior is learned from parents, peers, and television programs, an idea that we are going to pick up again in the next chapter. But here, we shall focus on belief structures, empathy, and sympathy to help us understand the development of moral consciousness.

Beliefs and attitudes govern behavior in humans. We might therefore think that if an individual believes it is correct that self-interest should be sacrificed for the well-being of others, then the individual is likely to engage in altruistic behavior. This could range from making donations to charity to laying down one's life for the sake of others. Thus, to understand altruistic behavior, it is useful to understand the thought processes underlying that behavior.

The developmental psychology of Jean Piaget has much to say about the acquisition of the thought processes needed for moral consciousness. As you recall from chapter 3, Piaget supposed that under approximately 6 years children are egocentric. In other words, the child finds it difficult or impossible to empathize, to imagine someone else's point of view. If the child has no capacity to *empathize*, to feel the joy or pain of others, then it follows that she is unlikely to *sympathize*, that is, not just feel how they feel but experience concern at their emotional state or condition. Piaget argued that young children's cognitive limitation imposes a constraint on their capacity for concern about others, which is likely to be reflected in a lack of altruistic behavior. The assumption here is that once the child can empathize, altruism will automatically follow, and there is no need to go to great lengths to account for this. Looking at it the other way round, a lack of altruism could be the result of delayed or impaired cognitive development. Piaget proposed that the games children play teach them a lot about morals and rules; these can be rules that should always be followed and rules that might be interpreted differently, depending on the situation children find themselves in.

Piaget devised a test directly related to moral issues to find out about the child's moral reasoning and judgment. He did this by telling stories involving moral puzzles. In these, a protagonist caused some damage, either with good or bad intent. In order to understand the moral issue at stake, the child had to focus on the intent of the protagonist. Of course, as Piaget repeatedly claimed, this is something that does not come easily to young children, who, so Piaget supposed, have difficulty considering others' viewpoints.

Children listened to pairs of stories presented together. One was about a little boy who wanted to help his father by filling the father's inkwell. In doing so, he clumsily but accidentally spilled the ink over the tablecloth, making a very large and unsightly stain. Another story was about a little boy who wanted to play with his father's inkwell just for fun, even though he was forbidden to do so. While playing, a spot of ink fell on the tablecloth and made a small mark (see the figure below).

Children listening to the stories were then asked which of the story protagonists was naughtier. Younger subjects, those about 6 or 7 years, often judge that the naughtier protagonist is the one who made the large stain, simply because the stain he made was big. Older children, in contrast, judged that the child who made the large stain was not naughty because he had good intent. What we find, then, is that younger children overlook good intent, and focus instead on the scale of damage caused when making moral judgments.

Piaget suggested that we should view the older child as a moral subjectivist, in that she considers subjective factors, such as the good or wicked intent of the protagonist, in judging whether or not he was naughty. Piaget calls the younger child a moral realist, since she neglects intent and simply focuses on the extent of damage. For these children, moral judgments are based on criteria relating to events in the real world, rather than on psychological factors.

Although younger children are prone to moral realism, and this is likely to have something to do with egocentrism, the age of transition to moral subjectivism is less tidy compared with other Piagetian phenomena, such as conservation. This is probably because adults sometimes punish children according to extent of damage, rather than intent behind the action, which is likely to hinder their grasp of the importance of intent in the moral evaluation of behavior. This idea gets support from a study by Leon (1984), who discovered that children of parents who punish according to the extent of damage are more likely to be moral realists than children whose parents punish according to naughty intent underlying the act. So it seems that even when children have

Key Terms
Moral subjectivist: A person who judges moral acts according to the intention behind the act rather than according to the physical consequences of the act.
Moral realist: A person who judges moral acts according to the physical consequences of the act rather than according to the intention behind the act.

Piaget's test of moral reasoning: The child who had good intentions creates a large mess, but the child who was just naughty only creates a little mess. Children have to decide who was naughtier.

Critically evaluate Piaget's theory of moral development.

the cognitive capacity to take into consideration the intent of others, it may take a while to bring this reasoning to bear on moral dilemmas, depending on how justice is handled at home.

EVALUATION OF PIAGET'S THEORY

Piaget's pioneering work has been the subject of methodological criticism. An obvious problem is that Piaget's stories place substantial demands on memory, which could be too great for the fledgling cognition of young children. A point made by Parsons, Ruble, Klosson, Feldman, and Rholes (1976) is that information about good or bad intent of the story protagonist appears early in the story, whereas information about the extent of damage caused by the action appears at the end of the story.

Piaget reports the phenomenon as children's focus on extent of damage as opposed to intent, but Parsons *et al.*'s comment raises the possibility that, due to memory limitations, perhaps the young children recalled only the most recently presented information, which happened to be the extent of damage caused, and focused on this when making their judgments. If this were true then children might appear to have an immature morality, when all the test really demonstrates is that their memory is still quite weak. This alternative explanation of Piaget's findings was investigated by Wimmer, Wachter, and Perner (1982). They prepared a story conforming to Piaget's formula, though it was different in detail. The story was about a person painting a fence. In one version of the story this person was depicted as a boy who was lazy and put in very little effort. Although he was lazy, this boy actually painted quite a lot of the fence, because he was a big boy equipped with a large paintbrush. In another version of the story, the protagonist was a boy who put in huge effort, but because he was small and equipped with only a small brush, he did not cover a great area of the fence. After listening to the story, children had to reward the protagonist by giving cookies. All the key information was accompanied by pictures, which remained in view once the experimenter had introduced them, and thus were available to prop up the weak memory of the younger participants. So, when the experimenter explained that the little boy tried very hard, and was hard-working, accompanying this was a picture of the protagonist being diligent and energetic. In contrast, when the experimenter explained that the big boy was lazy, an accompanying picture portrayed this protagonist as tardy (see the figure on the left).

A big, lazy boy with a large paintbrush paints a lot more of the fence than a little, diligent boy with a small paintbrush. Wimmer *et al.* (1982) asked children which boy deserves the greater reward.

This experiment can test directly whether Piaget's or Parsons *et al.*'s predictions are correct. Piaget would predict that younger children judge the boy who covered more of the fence to be the good boy, and reward him with more cookies accordingly. His prediction would be based on the idea that young children are moral realists, focusing on the outcome of the deed, rather than on effort. Parsons *et al.* thought that children simply had a problem memorizing the key information from the stories, which does not allow them to make morally mature judgments. With the memory demand severely reduced they should now be able to demonstrate their true moral reasoning ability.

The results supported Piaget's earlier findings, in that children aged 4 and 6 years tended to allocate reward to protagonists according to outcome, in this case concerning how much fence was painted. In contrast, children aged 8 years were much more likely to take into consideration how much effort the protagonist had put into the job. This time, the outcome bias exhibited by younger children could not be attributed to memory failure, since all the relevant information concerning effort remained in view up to the moment when children allocated reward. So it would seem Piaget was correct to view young children as moral realists.

A number of other criticisms have been leveled at Piaget's account. Nicholls (1978) suggested that young children's peculiar outcome-based moral judgments could be more to do with failure to understand cause–effect relationships rather than to do with failure to give sufficient weight to good or naughty intent. In Piaget's stories there is no obvious cause–effect relationship between the intent of the protagonist and the extent of damage that resulted, because neither the good nor the naughty boy intended to spill ink, rather it was just that one boy accidentally caused some damage while engaged in a forbidden activity. Consequently, we cannot say that the naughty boy's bad intent was responsible for the ink stain. However, Wimmer *et al.*'s experiment serves to answer this criticism, too. In their story the effort the protagonist expended presumably was related to outcome, except that one protagonist had a large paintbrush. Despite this, it might still be the case that the young subjects did not understand that all things being equal, greater effort results in a larger area of the fence being painted. If so, young children's apparent moral realism would be due to lack of understanding how effort features in outcome, rather than due to ignoring intention (in this case expressed as effort) as an important factor in making moral judgments.

To check for this possibility Wimmer *et al.* asked children to estimate how much fence would be painted by a protagonist who put lots of effort into the job, and how much would be covered by one who put in only little effort. Even many of the 4-year-olds seemed to understand that all things being equal, more effort results in more of the fence being covered, and therefore these children clearly did understand the relationship between effort and outcome. Most important, despite understanding the cause–effect relationship, younger children allocated reward according to outcome rather than effort. So although Nicholls' criticism of Piaget could have turned out to be valid, in fact Wimmer *et al.* show that young children have a good understanding of the cause–effect relationship, yet still function as moral realists.

The central ideas of Piaget's account of moral reasoning have been supported by experimental evidence. However, it seems Piaget did underestimate young children's inclination to take the intentions of a wrong-doer into account. In experiments that made the intentions more salient (e.g. Yuill & Perner, 1988), even younger children take intentions into account when judging how naughty someone else is. Despite some of the shortcomings of Piaget's theory and its rather simplified account of moral reasoning, it has been very influential.

KOHLBERG'S STAGES OF MORAL REASONING

Kohlberg was heavily influenced by Piagetian theory when he devised his more elaborate account of moral reasoning. For many centuries, an individual's virtue has often been judged according to how well that individual observes and adheres to laws and rules dictated by a higher authority. In the case of Christian societies, in times gone by the highest authority was the word of God, as stated in the Bible. Thus, a "good person" was one who followed the laws of the Bible very closely. In our more secular society many of the laws of the Bible have been replaced by civil and criminal laws and those who do not observe these laws are likely to be considered bad people, as in the case of the drunk driver, thief, or murderer.

However, there might also be cases when the morally correct thing to do is *not* to follow the law. Consider the apartheid laws that used to exist in South Africa as a case in point. Most people recognize the shameful character of these laws, but things are not always so clear-cut. A moral dilemma arises from these cases of controversial laws. We generally accept that the correct thing is to follow the laws of the government, particularly if we accept the constitution of that government. Yet we may feel sometimes that the law is wrong, and decide to act according to another moral code, thus placing ourselves in a difficult situation. In this sense, it may take courage to act contrary to the law, as expressed by the novelist E. M. Forster, who said, "If I had to choose between betraying my country and betraying my friend, I hope I should have the guts to betray my country."

Lawrence Kohlberg (e.g. 1981) advanced a stage theory of thought processes related to externally instituted rules. The theory proposes three levels of moral development, each subdivided into two stages, thus making six in all. The three levels coincide with three of the main stages in Piaget's theory of cognitive development:

- Level 1, preconventional morality, coincides with Piaget's stage of preoperational intelligence.
- Level 2, conventional morality, coincides with Piaget's stage of concrete operations.
- Level 3, postconventional morality, coincides with Piaget's stage of formal operations.

To demonstrate stage-like changes in moral thinking, Kohlberg, like Piaget, composed stories depicting moral dilemmas. Here is the most famous of them:

A woman was near her death from a special kind of cancer. There was one drug that the doctors thought might save her. It was a form of radium that a druggist in the town had recently discovered. The drug was expensive to make, but the druggist was charging 10 times what the drug cost him to make. He paid $200 for the radium, and

Key Term

Moral dilemma:
A dilemma arising from conflict between two moral codes, for example acting in accordance with the law and acting in accordance with one's conscience.

charged $2000 for a small dose. The sick woman's husband, Heinz, went to everyone he knew to borrow the money, but he could only get together about $1000, which is half what it cost. He told the druggist his wife was dying, and asked him to sell it cheaper or let him pay later. But the druggist said, "No, I discovered the drug and I'm going to make money from it." So Heinz got desperate and broke into the man's store to steal the drug for his wife.

One of the moral dilemmas presented by Kohlberg: A man has to decide whether to steal the life-saving medicine for his dying wife.

Following the story, Kohlberg asked a series of questions to assess the moral reasoning of the participant. He was not so much interested in whether participants gave the right or wrong answers. After all, who is to say what is right or wrong regarding these moral dilemmas? Kohlberg was mainly concerned with the kind of moral reasoning people engage in when tackling the dilemma, by asking them a series of questions like these: Should Heinz have done that? Was it actually wrong or right? Why? Is it a husband's duty to steal the drug for his wife if he can get it no other way? Would a good husband do it? Did the druggist have the right to charge that much when there was no law actually setting a limit to the price? Why?

These questions were designed to probe awareness of the conflict, that on the one hand stealing is bad but that on the other hand every effort should be made to preserve life. In particular, Kohlberg sought to establish whether participants attached most importance to rules instituted by society, or to a personal sense of the difference between right and wrong, even if this went against societal rules.

Kohlberg conducted a longitudinal study in which he assessed the moral reasoning of boys at various ages and identified the following stages:

- *Level 1, Stage 1*: During this stage the child might abstain from stealing purely because she fears she would be shouted at. Actions are judged according to the physical consequences they have, and the intent behind the action plays no part in moral evaluation. In other words, young children are moral realists, as described by Piaget. Accordingly, the child conducts herself according to anticipation of reward or punishment, and the intrinsic moral correctness of the act is not recognized.
- *Level 1, Stage 2*: At this stage, the child understands correct behavior to be that which satisfies her needs. During this stage, children appear to use their friendship as a form of barter: for example, "If you give me some of your sweets, I'll be your best friend." In this stage, then, the child is purely geared up to approving or disapproving of others' behavior according to whether that behavior is to their own advantage.

Key Term

Longitudinal study: A study conducted over a long period of time (months or even years) with the same participants in an attempt to document changes that occur during development.

- *Level 2, Stage 3*: The transition to the new level is marked by growing awareness of others' points of view and intentions, and an inclination to conform to institutionalized order. The child's morality seems to revolve around seeking approval from figures who wield power and represent authority. No assessment of moral worth of an act for children in this stage extends beyond the reaction of the authority figure. As such, the child is highly conformist, and the concept of the "good boy" or "nice girl" features prominently.

- *Level 2, Stage 4*: In this stage, the child seeks to uphold and justify social norms, and identifies with individuals or groups who hold senior positions in the maintenance of social order. The child perceives the rules as fixed and sacrosanct, and judges moral behavior according to the extent to which any individual adheres to these. So in relation to the story about Heinz, children in this stage would judge that Heinz was bad because he stole, given that there is a law against stealing. They are unwilling to accept that Heinz's act was good in the sense that he might have saved life, simply because there is no law to say that a person should go to great lengths to save another person's life. Such an act is not recognized as morally good simply because there is no law pertaining to it.

- *Level 3, Stage 5*: The individual no longer views rules and laws as fixed, and the product of an inevitable order of the universe. Instead, the individual has come to appreciate that rules are relative, and merely constructed by certain groups. The laws are viewed as phenomena that can be understood by examining the history of any particular group, with the corollary that if the historical background had been different, then the laws would be different too. The individual is now able to adopt a legalistic mentality, with the attitude that if a law seems wrong or unjust, then that law ought to be changed. However, the individual may ultimately feel that morally correct behavior is behavior that falls within the predefined bounds of the law. So the individual may recognize that laws are unjust, yet nonetheless uphold the idea that laws are morally binding, and that it would be immoral for any individual to violate democratically agreed rules.

- *Level 3, Stage 6*: This is the highest stage of moral development according to Kohlberg. The individual may adhere to externally imposed rules much of the time, but now her behavior may also be governed by her own moral principles, independently of rules imposed from an external source. The individual functioning at Kohlberg's Stage 6 has the capability to perceive higher moral principles, those which transcend any specific laws. These relate to justice, equality of human rights, and respect for the dignity of other people.

According to Kohlberg, we gravitate toward Stage 6, but not everyone gets to the top of the hierarchy. Indeed, Kohlberg acknowledges that perhaps only a minority of the population progress all the way to the highest stage. So nobody can move down a stage, but on the other hand it is possible that a given individual might fail to move up into a higher stage. Another central point Kohlberg makes is that it is impossible for any of the stages to be skipped during the course of an individual's moral development.

Critically evaluate Kohlberg's theory of moral development.

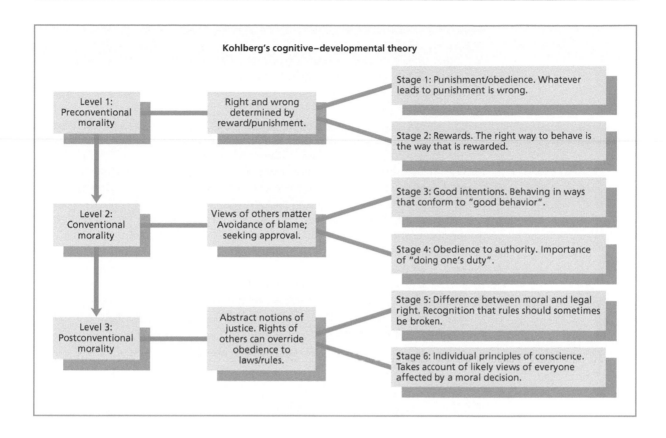

EVALUATION OF KOHLBERG'S STAGE THEORY

Many studies have been conducted to test the accuracy of Kohlberg's description of moral development. In a review, Rest (1983) concludes that moral development does proceed in the way Kohlberg suggests, and that the sequence of stages maintains across a variety of cultures investigated throughout the world. There is, however, some concern that the definition of the stages is culturally biased toward Western society. In Western society the rights, freedom, and independence of the individual are highly valued. This is not the case to the same extent in more interdependent, community-focused cultures where the individual is perhaps not perceived to be as important as the group as a whole. In such a society, the higher levels of moral reasoning, as defined by Kohlberg, might then clash with the core values of the society an individual lives in. If we found that individuals from this more community-oriented society did not attain the highest level of moral reasoning, we might take this as a sign that their moral reasoning is underdeveloped. However, this conclusion might well be fallacious when we consider the important implications that different cultural values have. It might well be safer to assume that Kohlberg's stages describe the moral reasoning development of children in Western societies, and that whilst some core moral values are shared between people of all cultures, there also exist differences that do not so easily translate. In that sense Kohlberg's stage model has contributed much to the thinking about moral development, but

Compare and contrast Piaget's and Kohlberg's theories of moral development.

does not present a universal account of development (Gibbs, Basinger, Grime, & Snarey, 2007).

The American author and adventurer Ernest Hemingway defined moral behavior, perhaps rather flippantly, like this: "Moral is what you feel good after and immoral is what you feel bad after." If Kohlberg's idea of stages in moral development is right then children who have passed from Level 1, Stage 2 to Level 3, Stage 5 should feel the same as Hemingway about moral and immoral acts. One study in particular has generated an intriguing finding exactly as Kohlberg would have predicted (Nunner-Winkler & Sodian, 1988). Children aged 4–8 years listened to a story in which a protagonist stole some sweets she wanted. Child listeners were then invited to judge whether the protagonist thief felt good or bad about what she had done. Nearly all the 8-year-olds tested judged that the protagonist felt bad, and recognized that she would feel guilty about succumbing to her temptation to steal. In contrast, many children of 6 years and below judged that the protagonist felt good, reasoning that she had got what she wanted. In the older children, then, we see reasoning according to violation of a well-known rule that people should not steal. In contrast, in younger children, we see reasoning according to the "feel good" principle. This finding is perfectly consistent with the kind of shift Kohlberg suggested occurs during moral development.

PROSOCIAL BEHAVIOR

Kohlberg was concerned with the ability to reason about moral behavior in a situation where there was no right or wrong answer. Thankfully, this is not the kind of situation we are most regularly faced with. Often the decision we have to make is just between doing something that is good for us and doing something that would help someone else: in other words, prosocial behavior. The tendency toward prosocial behavior, empathy, and sympathy might start earlier than the results from moral some reasoning tasks suggest, because an ability to recognize the importance of intention or effort is not all there is to moral development, although Eggum *et al.* (2011) show that there is a clear link in children's prosocial behavior with theory of mind. Nonetheless, empathy starts much earlier in life. According to Martin Hoffman's (1970) influential work, the foundations of moral conscience are laid down in the first year of life. Hoffman points out that young infants find crying and laughing contagious: They cry when others cry, and laugh when others laugh. According to Hoffman, this forms a basis for empathy, and empathic concern is a major driving force in prosocial behavior and morality.

In the first year of an infant's life a change takes place when the youngster develops an awareness of the independent existence of people. Now the infant knows that when another child is crying that other child is in a state of distress even if he, the beholder, feels fine. In other words, the infant has developed the capacity for empathy. Hoffman (2000, 2002) argues that children can take the perspective of another person on a basic level, for example in understanding that another is feeling distressed. This kind of empathy might emerge as early as 8 months old (Roth-Hanania, Davidov, & Zahn-Waxler, 2011), but at this stage it is still self-focused, because the sound of another's distress causes a similar emotion of distress in the infant, they experience empathic distress. It

Key Term

"Feel good" principle: A kind of morality that says an act is justifiable if it yielded positive benefits for the person carrying out the act.

is only in the second year of life that we see a shift from this empathic concern to an other-oriented empathic concern, or what we might call sympathy. There is a difference, however, between having sympathy for someone's plight and being able to help alleviate that plight. In anecdotal observation we often see that young children are a little egocentric when it comes to ways of alleviating another's distress. This may be demonstrated by them offering something to someone who is upset that they themselves would like to have in the same situation. An example might be a boy seeing his friend upset and crying and offering him his own security blanket, rather than the upset boy's. This would demonstrate a capacity for empathy and sympathy, feeling the distress of someone and acting to alleviate it, but still betray some egocentrism, because the best thing to do might be to give the upset person their own security blanket.

Young children are sensitive to violations of moral codes and other norms from a very early age. Helwig and Turiel (2002) presented young children with stories that concerned violations of moral principles and social conventions. A moral violation concerned a school where the teachers allowed pupils to hit each other, and a social convention violation was about a school in which pupils ran around naked on hot days. In both cases these were sanctioned by the authority in charge and we would expect from Kohlberg's account that such young children would be inclined to obey authority. However, children as young as 3 years thought that it was wrong to hit people and refused to behave in this way, but they were content to run around naked, if that was in keeping with the rules of the school.

This is a surprising finding with respect to both Piaget's and Kohlberg's theories because it suggests that even very young children seem attuned to a moral principle that leads them to say effectively that sometimes there is more to morality than just following rules. Whereas a social convention is seen as something that is relative to time and place, a moral principle is seen as something that transcends boundaries of context. It is notable that from a very early age children make such a subtle yet profound distinction. Children at the age of about 3 years old will also intervene when they see someone engage in moral transgressions against someone else; for example, when a puppet destroys another child's artwork they try to intervene and will tell on the perpetrator (Vaish, Missana, & Tomasello, 2011).

Discuss the evidence relating to children's developing understanding of social conventions and moral principles.

The same might be true for the notion of fairness that is deeply ingrained in our culture. If you and I contributed equally to the success of a task and did half the work each, then we should reasonably expect that any reward for our efforts is also split down the middle. Whenever this is not the case, we tend to feel rather aggrieved and unhappy. The same is true for children from about the age of 3 years old. When two children help the experimenter tidy away toys and get a reward of stickers for their efforts, they are unhappy when this reward is unevenly allocated, for example one child gets two stickers and the other four. Whilst this is particularly true for the disadvantaged child, the emotional response in all children appears to be motivated by an aversion to inequality of distribution (LoBue, Nishida, Chiong, DeLoache, & Haidt, 2011).

By the age of about 10, Hoffman suggests that children come to understand not only the plight of individuals, but that of groups of people. This understanding undergoes further development into the teens and

| Key Term

Social conventions: A code of behavior that is based on convention rather than principle.

What is the relation between moral reasoning and prosocial behavior?

adulthood, as the individual forms a coherent set of attitudes and behavior according to moral or political movements. For example, the individual may come to feel that it is immoral to pollute the environment with human waste, and begin by altering his own behavior in accordance with that view, and may then come to take an active part in environmentalist rallies and protests to persuade others to adopt the same attitudes and behaviors. So as the individual approaches adulthood, behavior of moral relevance can be strongly governed by attitudes and beliefs concerning the correct way to live one's life. These moral values need not be imposed upon the individual, as in the case of religious teaching, but rather they could be constructed by the individual.

We can now bring the story full circle. We began this chapter with comments on human altruism, and proposed that moral reasoning is likely to play an important part. One point made was that once a child is proficient in attending to and assessing others' plights, she is better equipped to sympathize compared with the early stage when empathy is not so easy. That point seems to be a valid one, but Eisenberg (1986) has proposed ideas that complement Kohlberg's, specifically in relation to moral development and altruistic behavior.

Eisenberg presented a story to children about a child going to a friend's birthday party, whereupon he comes across another child who has fallen and hurt himself (see the figure below). The moral dilemma is: Does the child on the way to the birthday party stop and give assistance, thus jeopardizing his opportunity to have a piece of birthday cake, or does he proceed to the party without helping someone in need? The findings are consistent with what we might have predicted from Kohlberg's theory. Namely, children who we might suppose were in Kohlberg's Level 1 apparently operate on a hedonistic principle of judging that the story protagonist should proceed to the party in order not to miss out on the cake. In contrast, older children, who we might suppose were in Level 2, seem to operate on a principle concerned with the needs of others. These children put the needs of others before themselves in some circumstances, given that they judge that the story protagonist should stop and give assistance even if it means missing the birthday cake.

Eisenberg's study neatly demonstrates the link between moral reasoning and prosocial behavior. What we see is a general shift at approximately 5 years of age from holding the concerns of themselves as foremost to entertaining ideas about the well-being of others.

Eisenberg (1986) tested children's prosocial behavior with scenarios like this one. Should this child help the injured child and miss out on the birthday party treats?

How do children realize what is the right thing to do in this situation? And is there anything that parents or teachers can do to influence how children will act in this situation? A study conducted by Yarrow, Scott, and Waxler (1973) addressed the matter. In their study, 3- to 4-year-olds were assigned to a caregiver who modeled altruistic behavior in various ways. She displayed a warm, nurturant attitude, offering help, sympathizing, and protecting. The adult also modeled altruism in play sessions, when she offered assistance to disadvantaged characters in scenes involving the children's toys. Finally, the adult modeled altruism in a real-life situation by showing sympathy to a visitor who bumped her head. The observing children witnessed their caregiver display concern and offer medication.

Some weeks later, children went to visit the home of a mother with her young baby. The mother had difficulty managing the situation, and dropped some of her sewing on the floor, and her baby dropped some of his toys. The investigators wanted to know whether the visiting children would come to the aid of the mother and baby. The findings were very clear. Those children who had witnessed their own caregiver behaving in a consistently altruistic manner spontaneously offered help to the mother and baby. Things were different in the case of children whose caregiver had only been partially altruistic. For example some children had a caregiver who had been warm and nurturant toward them and to toy characters in the pretend play situation, but not to the visitor who bumped her head. These children were not so willing to offer help to the mother and baby in difficulty.

Yarrow *et al.* successfully demonstrated that under the right conditions, young children adopt a nurturant and altruistic attitude displayed by an adult model. The adopted behavior is not confined to direct imitation of the model. Had that been the case, children might have been sympathetic to a person who bumped her head, but not to the mother and baby in need because they had never seen prosocial behavior modeled in that particular situation. It turned out this was not the case, and it seemed the children had acquired a generally altruistic mode of functioning.

The possibility that young children can learn to be altruistic does not necessarily imply that their altruistic behavior is merely mechanistic. On the contrary, Eisenberg *et al.* (1990) report that 4-year-olds observing another child in distress are affected on a physiological level, as indicated by increased heart rate. When the observing child has opportunity to provide assistance, thus reducing the difficulties of the distressed child, heart rate slows down. This finding suggests that observing suffering in others, and helping to relieve that suffering, have a physical and emotional effect on young children.

Looking at these studies into the more general framework of moral development, we can say the following. The work of Piaget and Hoffman collectively tells us that as children develop, their improved cognitive faculties make them better equipped to think about the intentions underlying the behavior of others, and so they are better able to focus on this rather than just on the consequences of the behavior of the other person. It might be the case, therefore, that young children are poor at making moral judgments because they are lacking ability to empathize. However, although a lack of empathy may adversely influence moral judgments and moral thought, it need not adversely affect sympathetic and altruistic behavior. Young children are highly receptive to behavior modeled by adults. Yarrow *et al.* demonstrated that when children are exposed to a consistently altruistic model, they will adopt a general prosocial pattern of behavior.

THE CRADLE OF MORALITY

Early research on morality focused particularly on the aspect of moral reasoning. This is quite a cognitive component of morality and we would perhaps not expect it to emerge very early in development. Hoffman's (e.g. 2002) work though has shown that even infants in the first 12 months of life show empathy, even if it is still self-focused. More recent research on morals and prosocial behavior has focused particularly on the faculties that perhaps form the foundations of morality with the aim of uncovering when they emerge in a person's life. One of the defining aspects of morality is perhaps prosocial behavior and one of the cornerstones of that is helping others. Earlier in the chapter we mentioned anecdotal observations of infants being somewhat egocentric when helping others in distress, for example handing an adult their (the child's) security blanket to alleviate upset, when something else altogether might be required. Even though this might reveal some aspect of being self-focused it is nevertheless helping behavior, and from the age of about 18 months old children engage in this type of empathic helping; that is, they try to alleviate a negative emotional state in the adult experimenter (Svetlova, Nichols, & Brownell, 2010).

Another form of helping behavior emerges even earlier in life. In a series of ingenious experiments, Warneken and Tomasello (2006) showed that infants as young as 12 months old will help an adult complete an action, specifically when help is needed. Felix Warneken, who carried out the testing with the young children, contrived a number of situations in which he required help to complete an action; for example, observed by the child he would start hanging an item of washing on the line, but then drop one of the clothes pegs. He made to reach for the clothes peg on the floor but could not grasp it as it was out of reach, and this prompted even the youngest children to move over to the clothes peg on the floor, pick it up, and hand it to Felix. This is quite an astonishing feat, because it not only requires the infant to want to engage in helping behavior, but also means that they have to work out the intention of the actor, the goal state of the action, and what is required to achieve this state. A critic might argue that the infant's behavior might have been motivated by myriad other things, or perhaps just by a game-like understanding that we pick things up when they have been dropped. Warneken and Tomasello's design can answer such objections. First, they presented infants with a number of scenarios, some familiar (like hanging washing) and others not familiar (dropping a spoon in a box) and the helping behavior emerged in a number of scenarios, so was therefore unlikely to be based on learned behavior. Second, all of the scenarios had a related control condition in which the action of the experimenter indicated that no help was required. For example, in the clothes hanging control condition the experimenter willfully threw one of the clothes pegs across the room. If infants picked it up in this situation, then we might conclude that their behavior is somewhat mechanical and not attuned to the intentions of the actor. However, in these control conditions infants were significantly less likely to engage in the helping behavior. Their helping seems to be attuned to the needs of the person in the given situation.

Children from a very early age thus seem attuned to prosocial behavior, which enables them to act as "good people" in a social world. Importantly, we need another skill to successfully navigate the social world: We need the ability to spot nice people whom we want to associate with and distinguish them from nasty people whom we want to avoid. One way to distinguish nice from nasty is to evaluate people's actions and the intentions behind these actions. Amazingly it seems that infants can make these evaluations before they have acquired any verbal, and thus verbal reasoning, ability. Hamlin, Wynn, and Bloom (2007) presented 6-month-old infants with a play scenario in which a character, a Red Ball, was trying to get up a steep hill, but had some difficulty making it to the top. Enter the nice character, the Blue Square, who helpfully pushed the Red Ball up the hill, whereas the nasty character, the Yellow Triangle, would push the Red Ball down the hill and thwart its efforts to reach the top. After being shown these scenarios, infants were presented with the toys, who acted as nice or nasty characters in these scenarios, and reliably the infants would choose the nice character when asked which one they wanted to play with (the nice and nasty roles were counterbalanced between the characters). Infants thus make a preference judgment about whom they want to play with that depends on having observed the action of those characters. Like we might do as adults, they choose to associate with those they perceive as nice in preference to those they perceive as nasty. This experiment might reveal the very early foundation of judging others' social behavior as right or wrong in relation to others. In a follow-up study, this preference for helper over hinderer was even shown in 3-month-old babies (Hamlin, Wynn, & Bloom, 2010).

Infants both display prosocial behavior (Warneken & Tomasello, 2006) and show a preference for others who engage in positive social rather than negative social behavior (Hamlin *et al.*, 2007, 2010), but is there a relationship between these two aspects of social behavior and evaluation? In other words, we need to know whether children help those who engage in positive and prosocial behavior more than those who in engage in negative and harmful behavior. The answer to this question is provided by a study in which 3-year-old children watched the experimenter harm or help another adult. Children were subsequently more likely to help the person who had been helpful rather than harmful (Vaish, Carpenter, & Tomasello, 2010). The results of Vaish *et al.*'s (2010) second experiment are particularly interesting with regard to Piaget's early work on moral judgments. Recall that in the story about the boy and the inkwell, young children thought that the boy who produced the bigger ink stain was naughtier, irrespective of the fact that his intention had been to help, whereas the boy who produced the smaller ink stain had set out to be naughty. In Vaish *et al.*'s (2010) second experiment, children watched as an adult intended but failed to harm another compared to one who was accidentally harmful. In line with Piaget's finding we would expect that children would help the adult who did no actual harm, in spite of their intentions, but not the one who did harm, although their intentions were good. The findings, however, go against Piaget. Children helped the unintentionally harmful adult, but not the one who intended but failed to harm. In evaluating the social behavior of adults, the children took the intentions and not just the actual damage into account.

The picture that emerges overall is that children from a young age engage in social evaluations that guide their own prosocial behavior.

MORAL EMOTIONS

All of the early accounts of moral development that we have looked at strongly stress the *reasoning* aspect of moral understanding and moral behavior. This is problematic for at least two reasons: First, prosocial behavior, empathic concern, and social evaluations, which are all fundamental aspects of morality, emerge in preverbal infants. It would thus be difficult to see them as subject to reasoned thought. And, second, of course, the focus on reasoning carries the assumption that morals are rational and therefore amenable to reason. When we are confronted with a moral dilemma and have to make a moral judgment, do we reason about it dispassionately and come to a conclusion, like a judge in the courtroom? Most of the moral codes in Western society are based on the idea that to harm others is immoral. Piaget and Kohlberg's moral reasoning accounts stress the welfare of the individual, who should not be harmed. It follows that if no one is harmed in an act, we should not see this act as a moral violation. The social psychologist Jonathan Haidt (2001; Haidt, Koller, & Dias, 1993) tested this by presenting children and adults with short stories like this:

> *A family's dog was killed by a car in front of their house. They had heard that dog meat was delicious, so they cut up the dog's body and cooked it and ate it for dinner.*

Most adults and children thought that this was the wrong thing to do and felt very strongly about it. But, why would people feel that way? No one was intentionally harmed in this act—the death of the dog was an accident—and the family did not suffer any adverse consequences. And yet, after going through all the reasons for why this behavior is wrong and discovering that none stand up to scrutiny we might end up saying, "I can't give you a reason why, but it just *feels* wrong."

Haidt (2001) and Haidt *et al.* (1993) suggested that not all moral judgments are rational. Does it feel wrong to think that someone might eat their pet after it has died naturally?

Experiments like these have compelled Haidt to claim that many of our moral judgments and decisions are not the end product of a reasoning process. Instead, we are faced with a situation (eating your pet) that we have a strong emotional reaction to and feel that there was a moral violation. Now if we or somebody else questioned our judgment we would have to engage in moral reasoning. However, this reasoning comes *after* a decision has already been made. Instead of being a judge in the courtroom, evaluating evidence dispassionately, we may be more like lawyers, defending a stance we have already taken, even in the face of other available evidence. Perhaps when we revisit some of the stories that Kohlberg presented we can get an idea of how our reasoning worked. When you hear the story about Heinz and his sick wife, do you feel sorry for them and angry at the greedy druggist? And if so, will that not influence your reasoning about the situation? On the other hand, it is possible that you have an emotional reaction, but then try to put emotion to one side and reason through the situation. But does this apply to all the moral decisions that children and adults make?

Haidt and Joseph (2007) argue that morality is based on five foundations, which have evolved as adaptations to challenges early in our evolutionary history. These principles are harm and care (protect and care for kin), fairness and reciprocity (get benefits out of interactions with nonkin), ingroup loyalty (get benefits from cooperating with group), authority and respect (negotiate hierarchy), and purity and sanctity (avoid microbes and parasites). Part of the strength of this account is that it places emphasis on emotion and intuition which sits well with the developmental evidence that a moral sense emerges so early in babies. Pizarro and Bloom (2003) agree with Haidt's (e.g. Haidt, 2003) account to a point. They acknowledge that emotion has a large part to play in our moral decisions and behavior, but they also claim that conscious deliberation can happen even before we make a moral judgment. The intricate analysis of Haidt's account (e.g. Suhler & Churchland, 2011) and whether it stands up to scrutiny in its philosophical and empirical foundations is beyond the scope of this book. However, we should bear in mind that some of our moral reasoning and behavior is based on an affective response that we have, but some is more likely the result of conscious deliberation.

Bloom (2010) offers an elegant argument for the role of conscious deliberation, arguing that we cannot understand how our morals, both as individuals and as humankind, change just by considering emotional and nonrational processes. Even in the last 40 years attitudes of people in the Western world toward race, sexuality, and women's rights have changed dramatically, and we have very different intuitions about child labor, slavery, and homosexual rights from people 100 or so years ago. Bloom (2010) argues that the driving force of this change often is human contact, which widens our social circle and thus our moral circle, but makes a passionate plea to also include the processes of persuasion and deliberation in changing our attitudes and stance and perhaps make us receptive to the notion of widening our social and moral circles. Such profound influences may be found in literature, with Bloom citing the example of the book *Uncle Tom's Cabin*, which he sees as an instrumental part in helping to end slavery in the US. Moral emotion, moral intuitions, contact with others, and conscious deliberation all need to be incorporated into a comprehensive framework of human morality. At the time of writing no such single framework exists, but much exciting work is being carried out to identify the pieces needed to create it.

Summary

- We have discovered that children's developing reasoning about moral issues and justice appears to have an important bearing on their general moral development. In terms of judgments about punishment and reward, this is reflected in a developmental shift from judgments based on outcome, such as extent of damage caused by action, to judgments based on intention or effort underlying the action. In terms of judgments about correct behavior, this is reflected in a developmental shift away from hedonistic criteria, exclusively pertaining to what feels good to the child, to concern about adhering to rules, and ultimately to concern about deeper moral principles over and above particular rules. We make many moral decisions very quickly, whether they are judgments or guides for our behavior, perhaps too quickly to suggest that they are the end-product of a deliberate reasoning process that happened at that time.

- One could get the impression from this chapter that children (and adults!) are all little angels who know exactly what is right and wrong and act accordingly. Perhaps this state of affairs is partly created by asking questions about hypothetical moral dilemmas that we are not particularly involved in, rather than forcing a sharp look at our everyday behavior and the decisions we have to make in a variety of situations. We said at the beginning of the chapter that we live in a moral world, and we think this is largely true.

Essay Questions

1. Do morality and prosocial behavior entirely depend on the development of rational reasoning skills?
2. Evaluate Kohlberg's stage theory of moral development.

Further Reading

One of the most engaging chapters on morality is found in this excellent book:

- Bloom, P. (2005). *Descartes' baby: How the science of child development explains what makes us human*. London: Arrow Books.

Contents

chapter 16

Development of antisocial behavior

16

Chapter Aims

- To compare and contrast the Freudian account of aggression with social learning theory.
- To examine the relationship between viewing violent TV programs and being aggressive toward peers.
- To examine the role of various factors in aggression, including punishment, frustration, computer games, and gender.
- To examine factors that might help to reduce aggression.

INTRODUCTION

Humans can be highly destructive creatures, and apparently have an appetite for violence and aggression. To some extent, what we are going to examine in this chapter reflects a starkly contrasting side of the human character compared to the content of the previous chapter. There we looked at the development of prosocial behavior and examined whether we live in a world that is populated by moral people. However, this is not the whole story and here we are going to look at the development of antisocial behavior and aggression.

Poignant examples for human aggression and violence can be found just as easily as examples of extremely good and moral behavior. In the history of humankind there was probably always a war fought somewhere in the world. And by human standards perhaps conflict is to be expected, as wars seem to be characteristic of civilization. Any brief history of "civilization" amounts to little more than a list of death, looting, and pillage on a massive scale, perhaps reaching pinnacles with several recent attempts at genocide, the erasing of a whole people. Perhaps then we could view human aggression as a consequence of pathological bureaucracies or the psychotic and despotic tendencies of certain tyrannical leaders. This seems to be true to some extent but there is certainly more to the story than this. Consider mob violence at football matches, in which supporters of opposing teams meet in hand-to-hand clashes. There is no authority figure instituted by society commanding these hooligans to pick fights. On the contrary, they are explicitly told to refrain from such delinquent behavior. An attraction toward violence is not just a phenomenon of collective behavior, though. We only need to consider the popularity of boxing and resistance to measures that would make the sport safer for the fighters.

We could go on presenting evidence for an apparently unquenchable thirst for aggression. But amidst this apparent appetite for destruction we can still see that people in the majority of societies do not view aggression and violence positively and there seems to be a prevailing longing for peace. If children develop moral reasoning and emotions so easily and early, how do we explain the development of aggression and violent behavior?

WHAT IS AGGRESSION?

It is not difficult to conjure up an image of aggression or aggressive behavior that can express itself in many different forms in a variety of situations. All of these aggressive behaviors seem to be aimed at harming others, but there are differences in the intent or in the expression of aggression. When aggression is motivated by the aim to achieve a specific goal, it is called instrumental aggression, because the aggression is used as an instrument to get something else. An instance of instrumental aggression might be when two children play together and one has a toy that the other wants. Hitting the child to get the toy would be an instance of instrumental aggression. As children get older the hitting may be replaced by an act of verbal aggression, for instance saying something nasty, but this verbal aggression would still be instrumental. This type of aggression can also be relational, that is, aimed at harming the peer or other social relationships of the target, perhaps by excluding them from a group activity like playing. As children get older aggression often is not instrumental but *hostile*. Hostile aggression does not have a specific goal but may just be aimed at harming another person, sometimes as a reaction to perceived threat toward self-esteem. Violence is an extreme form of aggression (assault or murder) and of course not all aggression is as extreme as violence. However, all violence is an act of aggression.

The main goal of the aggression in this picture is to obtain a "reward" by stealing the bag, rather than to hurt someone. This is an example of instrumental aggression.

ARE CHILDREN BORN GOOD OR BAD?

As developmental psychologists, we need to question how violent people come to acquire that trait. Various thinkers over the centuries have taken different stances. The philosopher Rousseau argued that humans in their natural state are peaceful, nonaggressive creatures, and that aggression is a by-product of a social pathology inherent in our society. In particular, Rousseau believed that society can make us mean, selfish, and hostile to our peers.

Sigmund Freud, in one of the earliest psychological accounts of human aggression, took the opposite view (Bushman, Baumeister, & Stack, 1999). He suggested that we are born with a death instinct, Thanatos, which lies behind all violence and destruction. Freud supposed that Thanatos was not only responsible for aggression on an individual level, but also for that at a societal or intersocietal level, as in international conflicts. In other words, Freud believed that the death instinct of individuals instills a violent undercurrent in society.

In contrast to Rousseau, Freud considered that society may serve to harness or at least neutralize much of natural human aggression. Freud took the view that, in a natural state, humans are much more outwardly aggressive than in their civilized state. This is a theme that seems to have been adopted by Nobel prize-winning novelist, William Golding. In his story, *Lord of the Flies* (1954), Golding depicts young boys who are stranded on a desert island. Initially, the boys are friendly and cooperative, but this altruism turns out to be a legacy of the civilized norms of the boys' culture, which is rather superficial and soon wears away. After a short while the boys segregate into two opposing factions and rain death, destruction, and terror on each other.

Are humans naturally aggressive or does the environment (e.g. society) lead some people to develop into aggressive individuals?

CATHARSIS, OR LEARNING TO BE VIOLENT

Freud put forward ideas on how society might help dissipate our aggressive impulses. He took the view that, although violent tendencies cannot be curbed, they can be channeled into a harmless activity. For example, engaging in vigorous sport will provide a socially acceptable outlet for aggressive impulses. Freud's view was not that violence should be suppressed but that it should be expressed in a way that can do no harm. Freud also suggested that violent impulses could be vented vicariously in a process he called "catharsis." An implication is that watching a violent sport such as boxing could have the therapeutic effect of reducing aggressive impulses in the viewer, given that the viewer's violent instincts are expressed vicariously by the fighter who beats the daylights out of his opponent. In general then, it seems Freud took the view that exposure to violence is a good thing. Were Freud alive now, he would no doubt have advised parents to allow their children to watch violent television programs or play violent computer games. He would have believed that viewing programs like this would be conducive to good psychological adjustment and nonviolent behavior in children.

According to Freudian theory, watching violent TV programs could have a cathartic effect. Discuss.

However, we have seen in the previous chapter that children learn part of their prosocial behavior from watching others engage in altruistic acts. Perhaps then we should consider that the same might apply for antisocial behavior? And if so, Freud's imaginary recommendation to watch as much violence as possible would have catastrophic consequences. This is the view that we encounter in the social learning approach to child development. Basically, this school of psychology holds that a great deal of the child's behavior is based on imitation, particularly when there is some incentive.

Social learning theory seems to make a good deal of common sense. If children witness aggressive behavior, then that behavior will become legitimized to the child by the very fact that there is now a precedent. Without seeing the act of aggression, perhaps the child would not have thought of behaving in that way, and even if he had, perhaps he would have dismissed it immediately from his mind for the simple reason that quite literally it is not the done thing. In this view, witnessing a behavior that is either positively reinforced (approval) or negatively reinforced (no punishment) would combine to "teach" a child to engage in similar behavior.

Let us consider an example of some common vandalism. Suppose a house in the child's neighborhood becomes derelict, and he witnesses other children throwing stones and smashing the windows. He might feel encouraged to do likewise, having seen that the others did not get reprimanded and that it seems a daring and fun thing to do. Common sense says that surely the boy who sees this kind of vandalism is much more likely to smash windows in the derelict house than a boy in a similar situation who was not exposed to a model of destructive behavior. We might also add that if the scenario had been different, and the vandals were immediately punished for smashing the windows, the observing boy would not follow suit in throwing stones. The boy would learn from the models that in this case vandalism didn't go unpunished, though the observing boy may have made a mental note of the delinquent behavior as an exciting thing to do in some future situation, providing the risk of punishment is minimal.

AGGRESSIVE BEHAVIOR CAN BE LEARNED

Support for this commonsense view comes from social learning theorists Bandura, Ross, and Ross (e.g. 1961, 1963), who presented children with situations in which they observed an adult acting violently and aggressively, or nonviolently, and either receive praise or punishment for their actions. Although these studies were conducted about 50 years ago, they were truly ground-breaking at the time and continue to exert great influence on current thinking in psychology and it is still worthwhile to look at this work in some detail. In one of their studies, 3- to 5-year-old children observed through a special viewing window the antics of an adult in an adjacent room, which was well stocked with toys. One of the toys was a giant "bobo" doll. This is the kind of doll that always bounces back into its upright position when knocked over, due to its special shape and strategically located weights. The adult behaved in an exceedingly aggressive manner toward the doll, punching it, kicking it, hitting it with a hammer, shouting at it, and so on. Eventually she ceased this onslaught and left the scene.

Following this the children were shepherded into the room with the bobo doll. What would the children do? Freud's catharsis theory would predict that watching the violence would have rid the children of all aggressive impulses and they would now play peacefully with the attractive toys available in the room. But what actually happened provided no evidence for the catharsis theory and plenty for the social learning theory: The children went straight to the bobo doll and continued where the adult had left off. They assaulted it with a hammer, punched it and kicked it, and used aggressive language such as "punch him, kick him, bash him" (see the figure opposite). The children's behavior was not an exact copy of the adult's, but rather seemed to be an adoption of her general pugnacious manner. In this study we see that children's inclination to follow the example of the violent adult outweighed any desire they may have had to play with the attractive toys also present in the room.

In this first condition, then, the adult's behavior went unpunished. In the next two conditions there was a much stronger reaction to the adults' behavior, either praise or punishment. When the adult was rewarded and praised for her acts of aggression by other adults, children became violent when they gained access to the bobo doll just as they had done when no consequences followed the adult's hostility. The results were even more interesting when the adult was punished and severely reprimanded. If the adult's acts were followed by punishment, children did not abuse the doll. However, the behavior sequences and the attitude displayed by the adult apparently had been noted by the children, since they exhibited a repertoire of violent acts, originally committed by the adult, when later on they were praised for aggression. It therefore seems that children had learned the aggressive behavior patterns and may only have abstained from performing the learnt behavior to stave off punishment. Seemingly, the behavior patterns had been assimilated by the children and lay dormant, waiting to be triggered by a suitable opportunity for their expression.

Two issues arise from the classic work of Bandura and his associates. The first concerns the screening of television violence in children's programs. In these TV programs, children witness actors behaving violently toward one another, ranging from cartoon violence (an anvil falling on Wile E. Coyote's head) to adults behaving violently toward other adults or children, for example in a Harry Potter film. Freud's view might have been that, by watching this program, children's aggressive impulses would be dissipated harmlessly, but Bandura *et al.*'s findings suggest just the opposite: Exposure to violence instigates violence in the children and therefore violence breeds more violence. But just because children will mimic an adult they are exposed to in a real-life

Discuss the ethics of studies that have investigated the causes of aggression in children.

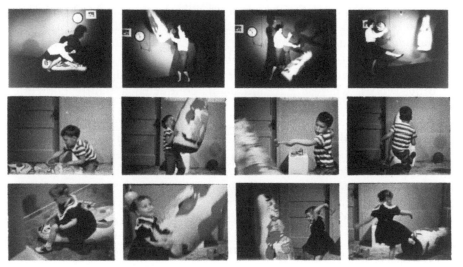

A child watches an adult shout and hit a bobo doll aggressively with fists and a hammer. The child will then copy these observed actions, rather than just play with the toys peacefully.

act of aggressive violence, it does not necessarily follow that they will imitate actors in television programs. Perhaps children have enough sense to recognize that what goes on in dramatizations has little to do with what goes on in the real world and therefore should not be imitated.

The second issue is that although children were willing to imitate an adult abusing a doll, we do not know from Bandura *et al.*'s findings whether they would imitate if it meant being nasty to real people. In other words, it could be that imitation where aggression is concerned is limited to inanimate objects. After all, we have seen in the last chapter that even very young children think it is always wrong to hurt someone, even when an adult says so, but that it is ok to break social conventions when told to do so by an authority figure. Perhaps then we could speculate that hitting a doll does not equate in the children's mind to violence and is not a general expression of their likelihood to engage in aggressive behavior toward others. Moreover, these are single incidents, which might not generalize to behavior in general. But if they did, this would be a serious concern in view of the violence contained in children's TV programs.

DOES WATCHING VIOLENT TV MAKE CHILDREN VIOLENT?

Does watching violent TV programs as a child lead the individual to grow up into an aggressive adult?

Children, on average, watch a lot of TV. In the US, children from the age of 2 years old might be watching TV for more than 32 hours a week, which is more than a whole day a week (published in the LA Times, 2009). Given how much children are exposed to TV watching, it seems pressingly important to find out whether this might have any detrimental effect on their social behavior. This is not a new issue: as TV sets began to enter more and more households, academic research began to try to address the question of whether watching violent TV makes children more aggressive, and, as with Bandura's work, some of these early studies continue to influence much of our thinking on the subject.

One of the most important research programs in the field is a longitudinal study conducted by Leonard Eron (Eron, 1982, 1987). Eron's study began in the early 1960s, when the subjects were about 8 years old, and continued into the 1980s when they were in their 30s. This study was unlike Bandura *et al.*'s in one respect: Bandura *et al.* studied children under the rather artificial conditions of a laboratory investigation, whereas Eron was more concerned with how children behave in their daily surroundings. In other words, whereas Bandura *et al.* conducted a tightly controlled experiment, Eron sacrificed this level of control for a more naturalistic setting.

Eron asked children how much television they watched and which programs they liked best, how similar to real life they thought these programs were, and how much they liked certain characters. Meanwhile, Eron commissioned a panel of independent raters to judge the level of violence in a variety of children's programs, and the level of violence displayed by specific characters in them. To find out which of the children were aggressive, Eron asked them to rate each other. For example, he asked, "Who is it that is always pushing and shoving?" He also got children to rate their own aggression as follows: "Steven often gets angry and punches other kids. Are you just like Steven, a little bit like him, or not at all like him?"

Eron was thus able to construct a profile for each child based on:

- their television viewing habits, including amount of violence watched and attitudes toward the violence (whether or not the child thought it was a reflection of real life); and
- their violent temperament, as rated by themselves and by their classmates.

His next step was to examine the relationship between these two variables.

The findings were highly revealing, and precisely as predicted from social learning theory. There was a very strong relationship between watching violent television programs and aggressive behavior in the children. Those who stated that their favorite programs were ones notorious for violence were the very same children judged by their classmates to be the most violent in the class, and who judged themselves to be violent. Those with the biggest reputation for violence were the children who judged violent programs to be lifelike, and judged that they liked the most violent characters in those programs.

The second phase of the study took place when the participants were 19 years old. Those rated highly aggressive at age 8 were usually rated by peers as aggressive at age 19. Interestingly, the violence on television watched at age 19 was not related with violent behavior of the subject as rated by peers. Remarkably, however, the violence watched on television at age 8 was strongly related with violent behavior at 19. It seems that the violent disposition acquired at age 8 became a legacy that perpetuated violent tendencies. Yet this violent disposition acquired at the early age did not necessarily promote the continued watching of violent television programs.

The third phase of the study took place when participants were aged 30. It remained that individuals who had watched violent television at age 8, and who were rated as most aggressive by their peers during childhood, continued to be aggressive at age 30. This time, however, the researchers had more than just self-ratings and judgments by peers as evidence for aggression. First, compared with participants who had not watched violent programs as children, these aggressive individuals had more convictions for drink-driving offences, and had committed various other traffic violations such as speeding. Second, their marriage partners were more likely to complain of being bullied and beaten by their aggressive spouse. Third, these aggressive individuals were more likely, by their own admission, to inflict severe beatings on their children. Finally, most surprising of all, and at the same time persuasive of the detrimental consequences of watching television violence in childhood, was the following: The more violent programs an individual watched at age 8, the more criminal convictions they had at age 30. Eron argued that this is very strong evidence indeed for a direct relationship between viewing television violence as a child and antisocial behavior as an adult.

It seems astonishing that television viewing patterns at age 8 should have such profound and enduring consequences. Eron suggests that there may be a sensitive period between 8 and 12 years, and that personality formation is highly susceptible to experiences at that time. In common parlance, we might say that the child is at an impressionable age. If the child is exposed to copious

Key Term

Sensitive period:
A period in development when learning of a certain kind readily takes place.

Children imitate things they see on TV, including violent behaviors. There is a link between watching violent TV programs and engaging in violent behavior, even years after watching these programs.

violence on television at this age, it may lay the foundations for an enduring disposition for violence.

Now we can return to the issues identified earlier arising from Bandura *et al.*'s research. It does seem to be the case that children imitate adult models on television, particularly when children perceive the events in the program to be akin to what goes on in real life. Second, imitated violence is not limited to that directed against inanimate objects. Unlike the children in Bandura *et al.*'s study, those observed by Eron were frequently violent against their classmates.

NATURALISTIC AND CONTROLLED STUDIES OF THE LINK BETWEEN TV AND AGGRESSION

Perhaps we are being a little premature in supposing that watching violent programs causes children to be aggressive. In Bandura *et al.*'s study children from a university playgroup were randomly assigned to one of the experimental conditions, so we can assume that there were children with varying degrees of aggressive inclinations in all the groups. The situation is different in Eron's study because it is more naturalistic. This conveys several advantages: It allows us to observe what happens in a normal situation over a long time. But on the downside it creates a chicken-and-egg problem, in that we cannot be sure which came first, watching violent television or having a violent disposition. It might have been that children who were born violent preferred to watch violent television programs. In this case, we would find a strong relationship between watching violence and behaving violently, but it would not be the case that the violent television caused the violent behavior. Rather, the cause–effect relationship would be the other way round.

Naturalistic studies like Eron's are best suited to describing what happens in development, and any inferences about causes of certain patterns of development have to be tentative. To make stronger statements about cause and effect, we need to intervene and manipulate hypothesized causes to find out if they do indeed have the expected effect. Eron carried out one such intervention investigation with a group of 10-year-old children who were renowned amongst classmates for their violent tendencies. Eron began with the idea that these aggressive children came to be aggressive by watching violent television and believing that the events depicted were just like real life. To combat this, he set about persuading the children that the events in violent programs were unrealistic. He attempted this by exposing children to the techniques used by the film makers to achieve realistic special effects. He then got the children to write a paragraph on why television violence is unrealistic and why watching too much television is bad. Eron read the paragraphs, made comments, and then asked each child to rewrite their paragraph in the light of the feedback provided by the comments. Having done this, children read out their paragraph and were videoed doing so. Finally, they watched themselves when the tape was played back to them.

A group of equally violent children went through a very similar procedure, except for one crucial difference. Instead of writing about the lack of realism of television violence, they wrote about what they did last summer. The findings revealed that those alerted to the lack of realism in television violence showed a marked reduction in their aggressive behavior over the ensuing 4 months. Also, the relationship between viewing television violence and violent behavior in these children disappeared. In other words, even if these previously violent children continued to watch violent television programs, they now remained nonviolent in their behavior. In contrast, children who were not alerted to the lack of realism of violent television programs showed no change and were still violent. Although insight into the lack of realism helped reduce aggression in children in general, a few remained violent. Interestingly, these children continued to rate violent programs as portraying the kind of things that go on in real life, despite the tutoring they received to help them think otherwise. So the important factor appears to be whether or not the child can accept that television violence is unrealistic. It is also important to note that the quality of realism in itself does not necessarily attenuate the influence of exposure to TV violence. This is particularly noticeable in cartoons, which often display violence in a humorous and unrealistic way, in which the suffering of the victim mainly does not feature. When adults are shown such cartoons that are typically aimed at children they often do not consider them to contain any violence at all! The effects of exposure to such unrealistic violence are often demonstrated when children are observed in field studies, but are seldom shown in controlled experiments (see Kirsh, 2006, for a review). Given that some effects can be observed in naturalistic settings, even this portrayal of unrealistic violence merits further investigation in terms of the potential influence it may have on development.

Nonetheless, Eron's intervention study neatly demonstrates that coming to terms with the lack of realism in television violence can curb subsequent aggressive behavior in children. However, it does not show directly that exposure to violence on television promotes aggression, even if the findings are highly suggestive. Rather, the findings only show that certain tutoring can reduce violence. For evidence showing directly that exposure to violent television promotes aggression, we turn to the findings of other researchers.

EXPOSURE TO VIOLENT TV PROMOTES AGGRESSION

A number of studies have demonstrated a link between watching violent TV programs and aggressive behavior. Stein and Friedrich (1972) arranged for 4-year-old children to watch selected programs for a 4 week period. Some children watched violent programs, such as *Batman*, and some watched nonviolent programs. Meanwhile, teams of observers watched the children in their play sessions. These observers were not informed about which child had been assigned to which television regimen, so any personal views they may have held about the effects of television violence could not have biased the results. The findings were exactly as predicted, in that children who watched the violent programs became more aggressive over the period of observation.

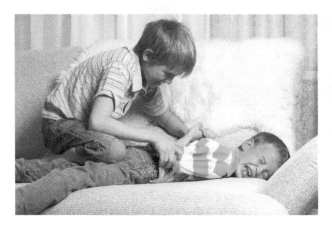

Liebert and Baron's (1972) study found that children who had watched the violent program were more aggressive in their play compared with those who had watched the nonviolent program.

Another study obtained essentially the same result. Liebert and Baron (1972) showed an episode of *The Untouchables*, a violent cops and robbers program, to 5- to 9-year-old children. Another group of children watched a film of a sporting event, which was judged to be equally action-packed, but lacking violence. Subsequently, the children were allowed to play. Predictably, those who had watched the violent program were more aggressive in their play compared with those who had watched the nonviolent program. The same effect has also been observed with older children. Parke, Berkowitz, Leyens, West, and Sebastian (1977) studied boys in a detention center for juvenile offenders. Some watched a series of violent films over a period of a week, while others watched nonviolent films. As usual, those who watched the violent films were more aggressive, both in physical assaults against peers and in verbal hostility.

These studies conclusively show that exposure to violent television promotes aggression in children, but watching violence can also have a more insidious effect. Even if children watching violence do not become aggressive themselves, the exposure to violence could desensitize them toward aggression, and make them perceive violence as a legitimate and quite normal activity, perhaps numbing feelings of empathy or sympathy. This was demonstrated in a study conducted by Thomas, Horton, Lippincott, and Drabman (1977). Children aged 9 years watched either a violent police drama or an action-packed sporting event. After the film, children from both conditions witnessed a violent exchange between some younger children, which involved verbal abuse, punching, and kicking. The scene had been staged by the experimenters, taking care to make sure nobody really got hurt. While the nursery children squabbled, the experimenter observed the onlooking older children who had just been watching the films. The findings revealed that those who had watched the violent program reacted less emotionally (failing to squirm or make anxious comments) than those who had watched the nonviolent program. Apparently, those who watched the violent program had become hardened to aggression, reducing the emotional impact further violence had on them.

All these studies examine specifically the influence of television violence on children's aggressive behavior, so it might seem that if we kept violence out of TV programs we could easily solve problems associated with this influence on aggressive behavior. A recent investigation reveals though that the problems caused by exposure to television may be more general. Manganello and Taylor (2009) analyzed data from over 3000 families in the US to investigate possible influences on childhood aggression, including corporal punishment, maternal depression, parenting stress, and living in a disorderly neighborhood, and, central to our interest, a measure of how much TV children watched directly and how much they were exposed to TV in the house. This last measure is simply reflecting how many hours the TV is on during the day, irrespective of whether anyone appears to be watching it or not. Manganello and Taylor found that 3-year old children who were more exposed to TV (whether directly or indirectly) showed the most risk for exhibiting aggressive behavior. Of course we do not know from these numbers which programs were showing and therefore we do not know whether any violence was portrayed, but this makes the effect exposure to TV has on behavior perhaps more alarming. How can this effect be explained? We might speculate that in households in which the TV is on for the longest duration there is also the least time for child-focused activity that might have a beneficial effect on children's development. The lack of these beneficial effects is then expressed in the data as an increase in behavioral problems. Moreover, whilst we do not know what programs were showing on the household TVs that children were indirectly exposed to, we might speculate that the programs were probably not suitable for children, and may well have contained graphically violent elements.

In sum, the evidence is overwhelmingly in support of the idea that watching television and watching television violence can promote violent behavior in children. Moreover, Eron's findings suggest that the aggressive tendencies impressed on children through viewing television violence can be very long lasting, and may nurture an aggressive personality. All the studies we have reported so far were carried out in America, and it would be perfectly reasonable to question whether the findings are specific to the American culture. For example, perhaps American children are exposed to more violent television programs than children in other countries. However, studies conducted along the same lines as Eron's have replicated his results in countries as diverse as Finland, Poland, Australia, Holland, and Israel—alas, the findings are not purely an American phenomenon. Huesmann, Moise-Titus, Podolski, and Eron (2003) also analyzed whether the long-term effects could be explained through the social class of the children's parents, their parenting style, or the children's intelligence. However, even if we take into account all these potential factors that may be associated with violent behavior, we still find a clear relationship between the amount of violent TV watched as a child and the propensity for violence later in life.

Let us take stock of the findings reported so far, in relation to their theoretical implications. Freud suggested that we have an innate inclination to be aggressive, arising from the hypothesized instinctual drive, Thanatos. Freud held the view that aggressive impulses can be vented, and thus reduced vicariously, by observing violence. From this account we predict that watching violent television programs would reduce aggression in children. The findings actually show this is not the case, but rather that the opposite maintains: Watching violent programs promotes violence in children. This finding is consistent with the idea that aggressive behavior arises from the child's experiences, and that aggression is not instinctive after all.

OTHER INFLUENCES ON AGGRESSION

Violence on television is unlikely to be the only experience that can promote aggression in children. Aggression and violence are not new phenomena even though violent crime may seem to be on the increase in society. Our species has indulged in bloody battles and brutality over the millennia, and clearly all this cannot be attributed to the relatively new phenomenon of television violence. What factors might be responsible for such aggression? Presumably, aspects of parental practice are important. As we have seen in relation to

In what ways can we investigate causal factors that might be involved in the development of aggression?

altruistic behavior, there is a strong influence of the parents' altruistic behavior on children's subsequent prosocial behavior. Let us examine whether the same holds true for antisocial behavior. Views on childrearing practices change over time, but it is still fairly common to hear that perhaps violence is on the increase because parents do not keep their children under sufficiently strict control. For example, a popular view in relation to antisocial behavior seems to be that if the offenders received a sound thrashing occasionally then their unruly behavior would be brought under control, and they would become more civilized. However, the available evidence suggests this "commonsense" view is wrong. Indeed, it seems not only that corporal punishment fails to curb aggression in children, but on the contrary, it may promote it. Once again, some of the first data come from Leonard Eron's studies. In addition to finding a relationship between television viewing habits and aggression, Eron also found that children subjected to corporal punishment in the home were the ones who were more aggressive at school, as judged by classmates.

Eron argues that physical punishment causes aggression in children for the following reason. By lashing out at the child, the parent may provide a model of what is the appropriate response when frustrated. So although the parent could be punishing the child with the aim of curbing the child's aggression, the parent may unwittingly provide the child with a model of aggressive behavior in the face of frustration. As a result, when the child experiences frustration in other situations, he may react in the way he assumes is appropriate, by committing an act of violence.

Apart from this, punishment only indicates what the child should not do. But punitive measures executed like this do not show the child how she should behave when in that situation again because there is little indication of the alternative appropriate behavior. Thus, one aggressive response of the child that is followed by punishment could simply be replaced by another aggressive response that has not yet been punished.

Eron's argument that physical punishment causes aggression, that aggression begets aggression, is a highly plausible one, but the relationship between corporal punishment and aggression toward peers can be interpreted in other ways. It might be that aggressive children are born aggressive, and that their parents feel they have to resort to corporal punishment as a severe attempt to control the aggression. We will never be able to find out for sure, since we are unable to carry out an intervention study on this topic for reasons of ethics. It would be unethical to subject a child to corporal punishment for the purpose of finding out whether aggression increases as a consequence. If we have to rely on argument to help determine the cause–effect relationship then it has to be said that Eron's argument is highly plausible. And more recent empirical studies support this view. It is difficult to establish a cause–effect relationship between corporal punishment and aggression because there are often a multitude of factors that vary between children who are subjected to such punishment and those who are not (Morris & Gibson, 2011). Having said that, taking into account some of these differences we find that children who are exposed to the least physical punishment in earlier childhood show the lowest levels of antisocial behavior in adolescence (Lansford et al., 2009).

Physical punishment seems therefore to breed physical violence, aggression, and antisocial behavior. But these are not the only types of aggression. At the start of the chapter we also introduced the idea of relational aggression, a more subtle form of aggressive behavior that is aimed at destroying or purposefully manipulating relationships, feelings of acceptance, and social inclusion. We see this type of aggression when somebody is given the "silent treatment" by a group of people, social exclusion, spreading of malicious rumors, and so forth. Kuppens, Grietens, Onghena, and Michiels (2009) investigated the effects of parental control on children showing this type of relational aggression. They found that the more parents engaged in controlling children's emotional and psychological development (e.g. invalidating feeling, love withdrawal, guilt induction) the more children showed subsequent relational aggression. It therefore appears that parenting styles have a wide-spread influence on children's subsequent social or antisocial behavior and the strictest parenting may not always lead to the best outcomes.

FRUSTRATION AS A CAUSE OF AGGRESSION

Another factor we might suppose is involved in aggression is frustration. Perhaps aggression inevitably follows frustration, and therefore if we could reduce frustration we would witness a decrease in aggression in the world at large. In this case, "frustration" refers to instances when the individual builds up an expectancy about receiving some reward, or some enjoyable experience, but then the expectation is thwarted. Such a suggestion is sometimes put forward to account for acts of vandalism committed by less privileged members of society.

Television commercials and advertisements in newspapers and magazines often encourage us to hope for, and sometimes perhaps to expect, a more salubrious lifestyle that in fact is out of financial reach. Those poorer members of society who are repeatedly frustrated in their quest to attain societally defined expectations may ultimately resort to acts of aggressive vandalism as a natural response to the situation. Is there any evidence to support this view?

The pioneering study was carried out by Barker, Dembo, and Lewin (1941). They led a group of young children to believe they would be able to play with some attractive toys, but then they were prevented from doing so by the experimenter, and were only allowed to look at the toys through a transparent screen. After a frustrating wait, the experimenter grudgingly allowed the children access to the toys, and observed their behavior. The children behaved very violently, throwing the toys at the wall and generally abusing them. Another group of children who had immediate access to the toys played with them peacefully. We might have expected that children who had to wait would have had greater respect for the toys, valuing them more highly after being deprived of them for a sustained period. That was not the case, and it seems instead the children's frustration at having to wait caused them to behave violently.

Evidently, aggression in response to frustration does seem to occur. However, it is not an inevitable consequence. Mallick and McCandless (1966) investigated factors influencing whether frustration leads to aggression. In their study, children aged 8 years were thwarted from attaining a cash prize due to

Barker, Dembo, and Lewin's (1941) study found that the children's frustration at having to wait to play with the toys caused them to behave violently once they were permitted access.

the awkward behavior of a peer upon whom they were relying. Under one condition, children were told that the person responsible for the failure was sleepy and upset, whereas under another condition no explanation was offered. The findings were that when children had been given a good reason for the behavior of the child who frustrated them, they directed little aggression toward him. In contrast, if no explanation was given, children were much more aggressive to the person who had been an obstacle to their goal. This shows that although aggression is likely to be targeted at a source of frustration, this need not be the case; aggression is not an inevitable consequence of frustration.

We have seen then that frustration may lead to aggression, but not in all circumstances. In the previous chapter and earlier in this chapter we discovered that children learn both prosocial and antisocial behavior from role models. The important influence of this kind of prior learning on dealing with frustration was demonstrated powerfully in a study by Davitz (1952). Children aged around 8 years played in small groups. Members of some of these groups were rewarded for aggressive and competitive behavior; others were rewarded for cooperative and constructive behavior. All children were then subjected to a severely frustrating experience. They were led to believe that they would be able to watch an entertaining movie and that they would be issued with chocolates. The chocolates were handed out and the movie commenced. Half-way through, just as the movie was getting to an exciting point, the experimenter switched it off and claimed back all the chocolates from the children. Finally, they were given opportunity to play. Predictably, those who had been rewarded for aggressive and competitive behavior expressed a great deal of aggression in their play session following this frustrating experience. In sharp contrast, those who had been rewarded for constructive behavior were far less aggressive in the play situation, and instead engaged in some constructive play activities.

Once again, the findings show that aggression is not an inevitable consequence of frustration, and that, in particular, prior learning experience can help curb aggression in the face of frustration.

ATTENTION SEEKING AND REJECTION

Another common view of aggression in children is that it forms part of a more general corpus of naughty behavior expressed by the child in order to get attention from adults. Perhaps children prefer to be infamous rather than anonymous. The implication is that if children do not get sufficient adult attention, if they are ignored by their caregivers, they will engage in behavior that the adult simply cannot ignore. Such behavior might be hurting other children or smashing toys, in short, a range of aggressive behaviors.

Brown and Elliot (1965) conducted a study pertinent to this issue. Teachers in a particular nursery agreed to ignore their 3- to 4-year-old children when they expressed aggression, but to provide plenty of attention when children were engaged in peaceful and constructive behavior. After a few weeks of the study, aggressive behavior diminished substantially in the nursery, suggesting that once aggression failed as an attention-getter, its expression no longer served any purpose for the children. The findings support the idea that aggression could emerge as part of a complex of attention-seeking behavior. It seems then that when aggression is expressed as an attention-getter, it is an indication that the caregiver has been remiss in giving attention to the child when she is engaged in peaceful and constructive activities. However, when the child receives positive attention and experiences, we see once again that this can reduce her aggression, and that the child can learn to behave nonviolently.

Psychological rejection seems to be strongly associated with aggressive behavior in children. Eron (1982) questioned parents about their attitude toward their child, particularly whether they were satisfied with the child's table manners, whether they thought their child was too forgetful, or whether they thought their child was a poor reader for her age. Children whose parents had expressed dissatisfaction about them in response to these questions were the same who were viewed by their classmates as being aggressive. In this case, Eron took disapproval of the child by parents as a sign of parental rejection.

A study by Dodge, Coie, Pettit, and Price (1990) also identified a relationship between aggression and rejection, but this time the rejection was by the child's classmates. In this study, children who tended to be rejected by their classmates, those who had few friends, were the same who exhibited most aggression in play sessions. Once again we are faced with a chicken-and-egg problem. We cannot be sure whether children became aggressive because they were upset at being rejected, or whether they became rejected by parents and peers only after they had acquired a catalog of aggressive incidents to their name. Whatever the cause–effect relationship, it is hardly surprising that social outcasts tend to be aggressive. Our everyday observations tell us that this is so.

GENDER, CLASS, AND VIOLENCE

A popular view is that girls are less likely to be aggressive than boys. Some of the studies on child aggression have recruited male participants only, as in the research of Parke *et al.* (1977) looking at the relationship between television viewing and violence in boys detained in a center for juvenile delinquents. We cannot be completely sure that the findings would have been the same had girls been the participants in the study. However, from studies in which girls have been recruited, there is no reason to suppose that factors influencing aggressive behavior are any different for boys and girls. Huesmann, *et al.* (2003) found that the link between TV violence and aggression was present in both boys and girls. In sum, girls seem to be just as susceptible to factors that influence aggression as boys. That is not to say females are equally aggressive as males: Differing crime statistics associated with the two sexes suggest otherwise. However, the same processes apply for girls as they do for boys as regards aggressive behavior. And, moreover, recent crime statistics show an increase in female violence and arrests for delinquent behavior.

Key Terms
Attention-seeking behavior: Misbehavior that attracts a punitive response from an authority figure.
Psychological rejection: Being shunned and ignored by peers and other individuals.

EXPOSURE TO MEDIA VIOLENCE AND AGGRESSION

Most of the studies we have discussed so far were conducted in an age where children's TV was limited to particular times of scheduling, for example a Saturday morning. Since then we have seen an explosion in the availability of TV and other media, particularly with computer games, the Internet, and perhaps also an increase in the explicitly violent content of song lyrics in popular music.

Violent computer games and song lyrics often get discussed at times of tragedy, for instance after the Columbine High School shootings. In 1999 two teenage high school students killed 12 of their fellow students and a teacher before killing themselves. Their intention had been to kill many more, but, luckily, the explosive charges they had set failed to go off. After such a tragedy we struggle to understand what might have motivated such violence, and a factor discussed was that one of the killers had spent a lot of time playing violent video games, particularly games that involved shooting people who had no means of fighting back. Anderson and Bushman (2001) reviewed the available research to find whether there is a link between violent computer games and increased aggression and violence. They found that the effect is exactly as we would predict based on our knowledge from the literature of TV violence and aggression. Exposure to these violent games is related to increased aggression in children, adolescents, and students; moreover, it is also associated with decreased prosocial behavior.

Anderson and Bushman (2001) found that exposure to violent computer games is related with increased aggression in children, adolescents, and students and is also associated with decreased prosocial behavior.

These findings do not tell us that exposure to violent TV or computer games *causes* the violence we observe in some individuals, but they seem to contribute strongly to an increase in the aggression we observe. The same holds for violent song lyrics (Anderson, Carnagey, & Eubanks, 2003) and any other form of violent media (Anderson, Berkowitz *et al.*, 2003). But what about the question on direction of causality that we raised when considering the very first study conducted by Eron? Does TV violence breed violent behavior or do violent individuals seek out violent programs? This important question has now been addressed in a large-scale study. Boxer, Huesmann, Bushman, O'Brien, and Moceri (2009) compared about 400 juvenile delinquents (a population with high antisocial behavior) to about 400 regular high school students. Aggression and antisocial behavior is not caused by one single factor, but preference for and exposure to violent media are significant in predicting subsequent violence and aggressive behavior, not just in the group of individuals with known violent tendencies but also in the individuals who have very low aggression.

Summary

- Taking into consideration the overall picture generated by the findings reported in this chapter, the evidence is overwhelmingly in support of the idea that human aggression is strongly influenced by the environment. Perhaps the factor that stands out above all is the child's tendency to imitate acts of aggression. When children see television characters behave violently, they are strongly tempted to do likewise. When they observe their parents administering severe physical punishment, once again they follow suit by hitting classmates. Just as children can learn to respond aggressively, so it seems they can learn to respond nonaggressively. The study by Davitz (1952) showed as much, where children learned to react constructively rather than aggressively in the face of frustration. We are able to say with considerable certainty that human aggression is not exclusively due to a hypothesized instinctive lust for violence as suggested by Freud. Instead, Rousseau's suggestion seems more likely to be true, that humans are peaceful creatures by nature, but that society has the potential to make them violent.

Essay Questions

1. Is there enough evidence to suggest that there is a causal link between watching violence on TV and violent behavior?
2. Do children learn to be aggressive?

Further Reading

A more general account of human aggression, going beyond issues of developmental psychology, can be found in Elliot Aronson's book:

- Aronson, E. (2003). *The social animal* (9th edn.). New York: W. H. Freeman.

As for the relationship between television viewing and aggression, there can be no better source than the original:

- Eron, L. D. (1982). Parent–child interaction, television violence, and aggression of children. *The American Psychologist, 37*(2), 197–211.

Glossary

Accommodation: Modifying a scheme to adapt it to a new application.

Adult attachment interview: A systematic interview designed for use with adults to probe the quality of the relationship they had with their primary caregiver when they were children.

Affectionless psychopath: A person who is unable to form an emotional bond with other people.

Alexia: Dyslexia that is acquired, perhaps during adulthood, following neurological damage caused by accident or illness.

Ambiguous message: An utterance that fails to specify a single item uniquely.

Appearance–reality test: A task in which an object has deceptive appearance, as in a sponge painted to look like a rock.

Asperger's syndrome: Having the features of autism but in the absence of language delay.

Assimilation: Applying an existing scheme to a novel task.

Attention-seeking behavior: Misbehavior that attracts a punitive response from an authority figure.

Autism: A developmental disorder affecting about one per hundred of the population. Those with the disorder are impaired in socially connecting with other people.

Behaviorism: A movement in psychology which assumes that it is possible to explain psychological phenomena by focusing only on behavior and the environment in which it occurs, and without reference to the mind.

Binocular parallax: Discrepancy in information received by each eye that varies by degree according to how far away the object of focus happens to be.

Biological preparedness: A genetically determined readiness to learn specific skills, such as how to walk.

Brain plasticity: The capacity for unaffected parts of the brain to assume the activities of damaged parts of the brain.

Capture by meaning: A tendency to overlook fine detail brought about by attention to the global meaning of a stimulus or event.

Cardinal number: The number that determines the size of a set.

Carpentered environment: An environment containing straight lines and 90-degree angles, which is typical in industrialized cultures.

Cerebellum: A structure located at the rear of the brain that has a role in generating fine movements.

Communicative value: The effectiveness of a message in informing a listener.

Conditioning: Controlling behavior by manipulating rewards and various stimuli within the environment.

Confirmation bias: Inappropriately seeking evidence in support of a hypothesis instead of seeking evidence that might falsify a hypothesis.

Connectionism: The idea that cognitive processes can be explained as a result of the interplay between several simple interconnected units.

Constructivism: A theory that knowledge is actively generated by the individual rather than transmitted by another person or through one's genes.

Continuous and discrete variables: Variables that could take on any value in a range are continuous, whereas a discrete variable can only take on certain values such as whole numbers.

Coordination of schemes: Combining schemes to carry out an elaborate task, such as driving a car.

Counterbalancing: A methodological technique for neutralizing order effects in a repeated measures experimental design. Imagine that the participant has to perform under two conditions, A and B. Half the participants will do A followed by B and half will do B followed by A. This manipulation of the order of testing is called counterbalancing.

Crystalized intelligence: A fundamental factor in intelligence that represents the accumulated knowledge of an individual.

Cycle of abuse: Adults who abuse children are likely to have been victims of abuse when they were children.

Decenter: To broaden attention to the various facets of a problem instead of fixating on just one.

Deceptive box task: A test of false belief in which a familiar container, such as a Smarties™ tube, contains something other than its normal content.

Deep structure: An innate grammatical structuring of language that is both universal among humans and unique to humans as a species.

Dizygotic twins: Fraternal twins who share 50% of genetic material because they develop from separate eggs.

DSM: Diagnostic and Statistical Manual of the American

Psychiatric Association. This manual lists features of various psychological disorders.

Echolalia: Meaninglessly repeating words or phrases that you just heard.

Egocentric speech: Speaking in a way that does not respect the informational needs of a listener.

Egocentrism: Difficulty taking on board another person's perspective.

Equilibration: A motivational process that compels us to strive for logical consistency.

Erogenous zone: An area of the body that has sexual focus.

Ethology: The study of animals in their natural habitat.

Executive functions: A process or set of processes located in the frontal lobes of the brain involved in controlling one's own behavior and one's own mental processes.

Experimental noise: Sets of data arising from psychological research seldom or never are pure measures of the phenomenon of interest. Usually, the set of data is composed of a mixture of the thing we want to measure plus other factors that influence the way that research participants (e.g. children) respond. The aspect of the data that is caused by these other unwanted factors is called "experimental noise."

"Feel good" principle: A kind of morality that says an act is justifiable if it yielded positive benefits for the person carrying out the act.

Figure and ground: Objects in the foreground are interpreted as partly or fully occluding objects in the background.

Fluid intelligence: A fundamental factor in intelligence that represents the ability to think and reason on your feet.

Flynn effect: The increase in IQ scores from one generation to the other, which averages about 3 points per generation and cannot be explained by an increase in intelligence in the population.

Frontal syndrome: A condition caused by damage to the frontal lobes of the brain, associated with disinhibition and lack of social sensitivity.

g: General intelligence is the concept of intelligence as a single factor that influences all cognitive functioning.

Gaze following: The ability to follow another person's direction of gaze and to locate and fixate on the object being looked at by the other person. Children normally become highly effective in doing this from 18 months.

Grammar: A set of rules governing language.

Habituation paradigms: Infants are shown a stimulus until they are bored and look away, when a test stimulus is shown. A display of renewed interest shows that infants perceive this as a different stimulus.

High functioning autism: Autism with measured intelligence in the normal range.

Hindsight bias: Believing that you had known something all along even though in fact you only made the discovery recently.

Holophrase: Using a single word, often in combination with a gesture, to express a more complex idea.

Hostile aggression: Aggression that is not instrumental but rather is motivated in an attempt to harm another person just for the sake of it.

Human sense: A term coined by Margaret Donaldson. A task that makes no human sense is one in which children misinterpret the purpose of the experimenter's questions.

Hyperlexia: An unusually large vocabulary, relative to developmental level, especially on a particular topic (e.g. species of dinosaurs).

Imaginary audience: A fantasy that people are watching your actions with great intrigue.

Infant-directed talk: A special style of speech used when talking to infants.

Inference by elimination: Finding the correct answer by ruling out alternatives.

Infinite generativity: The ability to form an unlimited number of utterances from a limited number of words.

Innate: An ability or trait that is with us from birth.

Instrumental aggression: Aggression that is a means to achieve a specific end.

Intellectual realism: The phenomenon of children drawing what they know rather than what they see.

Inter-modal mapping: Mapping from one modality (e.g. information acquired through visual perception) to another (e.g. making a facial expression).

IQ: The intelligence quotient is an index of an individual's intelligence score. It falls on a normal distribution with a mean of 100.

Joint attention: The process of intentionally sharing the experience of observing an object or event through the use of pointing gestures or following gaze.

LAD: The language acquisition device is an innate device for acquiring language.

LASS: The language acquisition support system stresses the contribution of the home environment and culture in children's language learning.

Level 1 perspective-taking: Understanding that an obstacle prevents another person seeing what you can see.

Level 2 perspective-taking: Understanding how an object looks from a vantage point other than your own.

Longitudinal study: A study conducted over a long period of time (months or even years) with the same participants in an attempt to document changes that occur during development.

Mailing procedure: A false belief test in which children mail a picture of the false belief into a mailbox before learning that the belief is actually false; the mailed picture serves as an aide memoir to the false belief.

Maturational unfolding: A genetically determined developmental progression.

Mental imagery: The ability to imagine the existence of things even when they are not directly accessible to the senses.

Mind-minded: A parent who is attuned to her child on a psychological level and not just in terms of physical needs.

Mirror neuron hypothesis: A hypothesis stating that when you observe another person doing something, the same brain areas will be active in you the observer as in the other person doing the action.

Monozygotic twins: Identical twins who share 100% of genetic material because they develop from a single egg and sperm.

Moral dilemma: A dilemma arising from conflict between two moral codes, for example acting in accordance with the law and acting in accordance with one's conscience.

Moral realist: A person who judges moral acts according to the physical consequences of the act rather than according to the intention behind the act.

Moral subjectivist: A person who judges moral acts according to the intention behind the act rather than according to the physical consequences of the act.

Morpheme: Is made up of one or more phonemes and is the smallest unit of meaning in language.

Motion parallax: Discrepancy in apparent movement as we shift vantage point of near and distant objects, depending on the relative distance of those objects.

Motor cortex: A region of the frontal lobes of the outer cortex of the brain that is responsible for volitional control of the muscles.

Nature–nurture debate: A debate on whether abilities and other characteristics are largely the product of our genetic inheritance (nature) or largely the product of our environment and experiences (nurture).

Nonconserving answer: Wrongly judging that quantity has changed just because there is a superficial change in appearance.

Numerical relations: Comparison of the quantity (magnitude or multitude) between things, where one can be greater than or less than the other.

Numerosity: The number of objects in a set.

Object permanence: Understanding that things in the world continue to exist even when you can't sense them directly.

Obsessive-compulsive disorder: A clinical disorder associated with compulsive ritualistic behavior and obsessive cleanliness such as incessant hand-washing and aversion to touching things that have been touched by another person (e.g. coins).

Operational intelligence: The process of solving a problem by working through logical principles.

Overextension: Using a word in a broader context than is appropriate.

Overgeneralization: At one stage in language development children apply the rule for forming the past tense inappropriately to irregular words.

Partial deprivation: Insufficient contact between mother and

baby that brings about negative consequences for the baby's emotional development.

Performative bias: The tendency to respond to a question with an action instead of replying verbally.

Personal fable: A fantasy that you have a privileged position on earth and that you are being watched over and protected by a supernatural being.

Phoneme: The smallest unit of sound making up language.

Placebo: An inert substance that has no active ingredient.

Pragmatic: The form language takes when used in a natural context.

Pragmatic rules: A set of rules that dictates how language is used to communicate; an understanding of pragmatics is often essential to understand what the speaker means.

Prefer to look—preferential looking: Babies prefer to look at novel stimuli, which allows researchers to identify what kinds of things babies do and do not interpret as being novel.

Private speech: Privately talking through a problem in order to arrive at a solution.

Pronoun reversals: Confusion over whether *I* should be denoted as *I* or *you*.

Psychological rejection: Being shunned and ignored by peers and other individuals.

Raven's Standard Progressive Matrices: A nonverbal intelligence test requiring analogous reasoning on geometric shapes and patterns, which was designed to be culture-free.

Reinforcement: Any stimulus that, when following behavior, increases the probability that the organism will emit the same behavior in the future.

Sally–Ann task: A simplified version of the unexpected transfer test of false belief.

Say–mean distinction: Understanding that what people mean might differ in subtle ways from what they actually say.

Scaffolding: Support provided by adults (or more competent other individuals) that helps children to construct knowledge.

Schemes: A mental operation that guides action or allows us to work through a problem in a principled way.

Selection task: A task devised by Wason and Johnson-Laird that reveals illogical reasoning in adults.

Sensitive period: A period in development when learning of a certain kind readily takes place.

Separation anxiety: A state of anxiety experienced by a baby when her mother leaves the room.

Shape constancy: A perceptual mechanism that enables us to appreciate that an object remains the same shape even though it looks different as we take up different vantage points.

Size constancy: A perceptual mechanism that enables us to appreciate that an object remains the same size even though it appears smaller as it recedes into the distance.

Social constructivism: A theory espoused by Vygotsky that emphasizes the role of adults (or other more competent individuals) in supporting the child to construct knowledge.

Social convention: A code of behavior that is based on convention rather than principle.

Social referencing: Babies periodically look at their mother's face for signs of encouragement or anxiety, especially when they are in a novel situation.

Solipsism: Failure to distinguish between yourself and the rest of the universe.

Specificity: A characteristic is specific to a disorder providing that individuals with a different disorder don't have the same characteristic.

Stanford–Binet test: The modern version of the first IQ tests, testing verbal and nonverbal items.

State change: A task employing a box that has characteristic content (e.g. Smarties™ tube) in which the normal content exists to begin with but is then replaced as the child watches with an atypical content.

Strange situation: A task designed to reveal both separation anxiety and the quality of attachment between mother and baby.

Surface structure: The specific grammatical features of a specific language.

Syllogism: All Xs are Ys. John is an X, therefore he must also be a Y.

Syntax: A set of rules that governs how words can be combined into phrases and sentences.

Telegraphic speech: An early style of language, resembling the efficient use of language in telegrams, in which children use few words to get their point across.

The theory of mind hypothesis of autism: A hypothesis positing that autism is explained as impaired theory of mind.

Triad of impairments: Impairments in socialization, communication, and imagination, which are characteristic of autism.

Unexpected transfer test: A test of false belief in which participants observe that an object moves from location A to location B without a protagonist's knowledge.

Universal: A characteristic is universal to a disorder if all individuals diagnosed have the characteristic in question.

Universal grammar: A set of formal structural rules common to all languages.

Usage-based language theory: The idea that there is no specific cognitive module for language learning, but that children learn both vocabulary and rules of language through using it in trying to communicate with others.

Viewer independent: The true dimensions and properties of an object, and not just those that appear from a specific vantage point.

Violation-of-expectation: Understanding of principles and concepts drives expectations about unfolding of events. When babies are presented with unexpected (i.e. impossible) events and look at those longer than at expected (possible) events it indicates that they understand the principle or concept.

Visual cliff: Apparatus designed by Gibson and Walk that formed an apparent precipice for the purpose of testing perception of depth in babies.

Vocabulary: A set of words from a specific language known to a person.

WASI: The Wechsler Adult Scale of Intelligence is the adult version of the WISC and contains the same components.

WISC: The Wechsler Intelligence Scale for children is one of the most widely used IQ tests, split into a verbal and a performance component, which are combined to give a full-scale IQ.

Windows task: A task devised to reveal the kind of mental inflexibility in individuals with autism that could explain their difficulty with tests of false belief.

Wisconsin Card Sort Test: A test devised to reveal mental inflexibility in individuals who have suffered damage to the frontal lobes of the brain.

Yes bias: A bias to answer all questions that require an answer of either "yes" or "no" in the affirmative.

Zone of proximal development: A period in which the child is cognitively ready to acquire a certain kind of new concept.

References

Ackerman, B. P. (1981). Performative bias in children's interpretations of ambiguous referential communications. *Child Development, 52,* 1224–1230.

Ackerman, B. P. (1982). On comprehending idioms: Do children get the picture? *Journal of Experimental Child Psychology, 33,* 439–454.

Ainsworth, M. (1973). The development of mother–infant attachment. In B. M. Caldwell & H. N. Ricciuti (Eds.), *Review of child development research, volume 3.* Chicago: Chicago University Press.

Akhtar, N., Carpenter, M. & Tomasello, M. (1996). The role of discourse novelty in early word learning. *Child Development, 67*(2), 635–645.

Akhtar, N. & Tomasello, M. (1996). Two-year-olds learn words for absent objects and actions. *British Journal of Developmental Psychology, 14,* 79–93.

Anderson, C. A., Berkowitz, L., Donnerstein, E., Huesmann, L. R., Johnson, J. D., Linz, D., Malamuth, N. M. & Wartella, E. (2003). The influence of media violence on youth. *Psychological Science, 4*(3), 81–110.

Anderson, C. A. & Bushman, B. J. (2001). Effects of violent video games on aggressive behavior, aggressive cognition, aggressive affect, physiological arousal, and prosocial behavior: A meta-analytic review of the scientific literature. *Psychological Science, 12*(5), 353–359.

Anderson, C. A., Carnagey, N. L. & Eubanks, J. (2003). Exposure to violent media: The effects of songs with violent lyrics on aggressive thoughts and feelings. *Journal of Personality and Social Psychology, 84*(5), 960–971.

Anisfeld, E., Casper, V., Nozyce, M. & Cunningham, N. (1990). Does infant carrying promote attachment? An experimental study of the effects of increased physical contact on the development of attachment. *Child Development, 61,* 1617–1627.

Antell, S. E. & Keating, D. P. (1983). Perception of numerical invariance in neonates. *Child Development, 54,* 695–701.

Apperly, I. A. & Butterfill, S. A. (2009). Do humans have two systems to track beliefs and belief-like states? *Psychological Review, 116*(4), 953–970.

Axia, G., Bremner, J. G., Deluca, P. & Andreasen, G. (1998). Children mapping Europe: Effects of nationality, age and education. *British Journal of Developmental Psychology, 16,* 423–437.

Baer, L. (2001). *The imp of the mind.* New York: Dutton Press.

Baillargeon, R., Spelke, E. S. & Wasserman, S. (1985). Object permanence in 5 month old infants. *Cognition, 20,* 191–208.

Baird, G., Simonoff, E., Pickles, A., Chandler, S., Loucas, T., Meldrum, D. *et al.* (2006). Prevalence of disorders of the autism spectrum in a population cohort of children in South Thames: The special needs and autism project (snap). *Lancet, 368,* 210–215.

Baldwin, D. A. & Moses, L. J. (1994). Early understanding of referential intent and focus of attention: Evidence from language and emotion. In C. Lewis & P. Mitchell (Eds.), *Children's early understanding of mind: Origins and development* (pp. 133–156). Hove, UK: Psychology Press.

Ball, W. & Tronick, E. (1971). Infant responses to impending collision. *Science, 171,* 818–820.

Bandura, A., Ross, S. A. & Ross, D. (1961). Transmission of aggression through imitation of aggressive models. *Journal of Abnormal and Social Psychology, 63*(3), 575–582.

Bandura, A., Ross, S. A. & Ross, D. (1963). Vicarious reinforcement and imitative learning. *Journal of Abnormal Psychology, 67*(6), 601–607.

Barker, R., Dembo, T. & Lewin, K. (1941). Frustration and regression: An experiment with young children. *University of Iowa Studies in Child Welfare, 18,* 1–314.

Barkley, R. A. (1997). Behavioural inhibition, sustained attention and executive functions: Constructing a unifying theory of ADHD. *Psychological Bulletin, 121,* 65–94.

Baron-Cohen, S. & Ring, H. (1994). A model of the mind-reading system: Neuropsychological and neurobiological perspectives. In C. Lewis & P. Mitchell (Eds.), *Children's early understanding of mind: Origins and development.* Hove, UK: Psychology Press.

Baron-Cohen, S., Leslie, A. M. & Frith, U. (1985). Does the autistic child have a "theory of mind"? *Cognition, 21,* 37–46.

Bartsch, K. & Wellman, H. (1989). Young children's attribution of action to beliefs and desires. *Child Development, 60,* 946–964.

Bates, E., Bretherton, I., Beeghly-Smith, M. & McNew, S. (1982). Social factors in language acquisition: A reassessment. In H. Reese & L. Lipsett (Eds.), *Advances in child development and behavior* (Vol. 16, pp. 8–68). New York: Academic Press.

Baumrind, D. (1967). Child care practices anteceding three patterns of preschool behavior. *Genetic Psychology Monographs, 75*, 43–88.

Baumrind, D. (1997). Necessary distinctions. *Psychological Inquiry, 8*, 176–182.

Beal, C. R. & Flavell, J. H. (1984). Development of the ability to distinguish communicative intention and literal message meaning. *Child Development, 55*, 920–928.

Benton, D. (1991). Vitamins and IQ. *British Medical Journal, 302*(6783), 1021–1021.

Benton, D. & Buts, J. P. (1990). Vitamin mineral supplementation and intelligence. *Lancet, 335*(8698), 1158–1160.

Benton, D. & Roberts, G. (1988). Effect of vitamin and mineral supplementation on intelligence of a sample of schoolchildren. *Lancet, 1*(8578), 140–143.

Bergman, K., Sarkar, P., Glover, V. & O'Connor, T. (2008). Quality of child–parent attachment moderates the impact of antenatal stress on child fearfulness. *Journal of Child Psychology and Psychiatry, 49*, 1089–1098.

Bettelheim, B. (1967). *The empty fortress: Infantile autism and the birth of the self*. New York: The Free Press.

Birch, S. A. J. & Bloom, P. (2007). The curse of knowledge in reasoning about false beliefs. *Psychological Science, 18*, 382–386.

Bloom, P. (2010). How do morals change? *Nature, 464*(7288), 490.

Borke, H. (1975). Piaget's mountains revisited: Changes in the egocentric landscape. *Developmental Psychology, 11*, 240–243.

Bouchard, T. J., Lykken, D. T., McGue, M., Segal, N. L. & Tellegen, A. (1990). When kin correlations are not squared. *Science, 250*(4987), 1498.

Bower, T. G. R. (1965). Stimulus variables determining space perception in infants. *Science, 149*, 88–89.

Bower, T. G. R. (1982). *Development in infancy (2nd edn.)*. San Fancisco: W. H. Freeman & Co.

Bower, T. G. R., Broughton, J. M. & Moore, M. K. (1970). Infant responses to approaching objects: An indicator of response to distal variables. *Perception and Psychophysics, 9*, 193–196.

Bowlby, J. (1965). *Child care and the growth of love (2nd edn.)*. Harmondsworth: Penguin.

Boxer, P., Huesmann, L. R., Bushman, B. J., O'Brien, M. & Moceri, D. (2009). The role of violent media preference in cumulative developmental risk for violence and general aggression. *Journal of Youth Adolescence, 38*, 417–428.

Boyle, C. A., Boulet, S., Schieve, L. A., Cohen, R. A., Blumberg S. J., Yeargin-Allsopp, M., *et al.* (2011). Trends in the prevalence of developmental disabilities in US children. *Pediatrics, 127*, 1034–1042.

Braine, M. D. S. & Rumain, B. (1983). Logical reasoning. In J. H. Flavell & E. M. Markman (Eds.), *Handbook of child psychology, Volume 3: Cognitive development*. New York: Wiley.

Bremner, J. G. & Bryant, P. E. (1977). Place versus response as the basis of spatial errors made by young infants. *Journal of Experimental Child Psychology, 23*, 162–171.

Bremner, J. G. & Moore, S. (1984). Prior visual inspection and object naming: Two factors that enhance hidden feature inclusion in young children's drawings. *British Journal of Developmental Psychology, 2*, 371–376.

Brown, P. & Elliot, R. (1965). Control of aggression in a nursery-school class. *Journal of Experimental Child Psychology, 2*(2), 103–107.

Brown, R. (1973). *A first language*. Cambridge, MA: Harvard University Press.

Brown, R. & Hanlon, C. (1970). Derivational complexity and order of acquisition in child speech. In J. R. Hayes (Ed.), *Cognition and the development of language*. New York: Wiley.

Brown, W. T., Jenkins E. C., Friedman, E., Brooks, J., Wisniewski K., Ragathu, S., *et al.* (1982). Autism is associated with the fragile-X syndrome. *Journal of Autism & Developmental Disorders, 12*, 303–308.

Bruner, J. S. (1983). *Child's talk: Learning to use language*. Oxford: Oxford University Press.

Bryant, P. E. & Kopytynska, H. (1976). Spontaneous measurement by young children. *Nature, 260*, 773–774.

Bryant, P. E. & Trabasso, T. (1971). Transitive inferences and memory in young children. *Nature, 232*, 456–458.

Bushman, B. J., Baumeister, R. F. & Stack, A. D. (1999). Catharsis, aggression, and persuasive influence: Self-fulfilling or self-defeating prophecies?. *Journal of Personality and Social Psychology, 76* (3), 367–376.

Butterworth, G. (1981). Object permanence and identity in Piaget's theory of infant cognition. In G. Butterworth (Ed.), *Infancy and epistemology: An evaluation of Piaget's theory*. Brighton: Harvester Press.

Campos, J. J., Bertenthal, B. I. & Kermoian, R. (1992). Early experience and emotional development: The emergence of wariness of heights. *Psychological Science, 3*, 61–64.

Carpenter, G. (1975). Mother's face and the newborn. In R. Lewin (Ed.), *Child alive*. London: Temple-Smith.

Cattell, R. B. (1987). *Intelligence: Its structure, growth and action*. Amsterdam: North Holland.

Chan, T. W. & Koo, A. (2011). Parenting style and youth outcomes in the UK. *European Sociological Review, 27* (3), 385–399.

Chandler, M., Fritz, A. S. & Hala, S. (1989). Small scale deceit: Deception as a marker of 2-, 3-, and 4-year-olds' early theories of mind. *Child Development*, 60, 1263–1277.

Cheng, P. W. & Holyoak, K. J. (1985). Pragmatic reasoning schemas. *Cognitive Psychology*, 17, 391–416.

Chomsky, N. (1959). A review of B.F. Skinner's verbal behavior. *Language*, 35(1), 26–58.

Chomsky, N. (1975). *Reflections on language*. New York: Pantheon Books.

Clearfield, M. W. & Mix, K. S. (1999). Number versus contour length in infants' discrimination of small visual sets. *Psychological Science*, 10(5), 408–411.

Cohen, D. J. & Bennett, S. (1997). Why can't most people draw what they see? *Journal of Experimental Psychology: Human Perception and Performance*, 23, 609–621.

Cole, K. & Mitchell, P. (1998). Family background in relation to deceptive ability and understanding of the mind. *Social Development*, 7, 181–197.

Cooper, R. G. (1984). Early number development: Discovering number space with addition and subtraction. In C. Sophian (Ed.), *Origins of cognitive skills* (pp. 157–192). Hillsdale, NJ: Earlbaum.

Cooper, R. P. & Aslin, R. N. (1990). Preference for infant-directed speech in the first month after birth. *Child Development*, 61, 1584–1595.

Crombie, I. K., Todman, J., McNeill, G. & Florey, C. D. (1990). Vitamin mineral supplementation and intelligence. *Lancet*, 336(8708), 175–176.

Crook, C. K. (1984). Factors influencing the use of transparency in children's drawings. *British Journal of Developmental Psychology*, 2, 213–221.

Davis, A. M. (1983). Contextual sensitivity in young children's drawings. *Journal of Experimental Child Psychology*, 37, 451–462.

Davis, O. S. P., Haworth, C. M. A. & Plomin, R. (2009). Dramatic increase in heritability of cognitive development from early to middle childhood: An 8-year longitudinal study of 8,700 pairs of twins. *Psychological Science*, 20(10), 1301–1308.

Davitz, J. (1952). The effects of previous training on postfrustration behavior. *Journal of Abnormal and Social Psychology*, 47, 309–315.

De Gelder, B. (1987). On not having a theory of mind. *Cognition*, 27, 285–290.

Dehaene, S. (1997). *The number sense: How the mind creates mathematics*. London: Penguin.

Dehaene, S., Molko, N., Cohen, L. & Wilson, A. J. (2004). Arithmetic and the brain. *Current Opinion in Neurobiology*, 14(2), 218–224.

Denkla, M. B. (2006). Attention deficit hyperactivity (ADHD) comorbidity: A case of "Pure" Tourette syndrome? *Journal of Child Neurology*, 21, 701–703.

Dennett, D. C. (1978). Beliefs about beliefs. *Behavioural and Brain Sciences*, 1, 568–570.

Devlin, B., Daniels, M. & Roeder, K. (1997). The heritability of IQ. *Nature*, 388(6641), 468–471.

Dias, M. G. & Harris, P. L. (1990). The influence of imagination on reasoning by young children. *British Journal of Developmental Psychology*, 8, 305–318.

Dodge, K. A., Coie, J. D., Pettit, G. S. & Price, J. M. (1990). Peer status and aggression in boys' groups: Developmental and contextual analyses. *Child Development*, 61(5), 1289–1309.

Donaldson, M. (1978). *Children's minds*. Glasgow: Fontana/Collins.

Dunn, J., Brown, J., Slomkowski, C., Tesla, C. & Youngblade, L. (1991). Young children's understanding of other people's feelings and beliefs: Individual differences and their antecedents. *Child Development*, 62, 1352–1366.

Eggum, N. D., Eisenberg, N., Kao, K., Spinad, T. L., Bolnick, R., Hofer, C., Kupfer, A. S. & Fabricius, W.V. (2011). Emotion understanding, theory of mind, and prosocial orientation: Relations over time in early childhood. *Journal of Positive Psychology*, 6(1) SI, 4–16.

Eisenberg, N. (1986). *Altruistic emotion, cognition and behaviour*. Hillsdale, NJ: Lawrence Erlbaum.

Eisenberg, N., Fabes, R. A., Miller, P. A., Shell, R., Shea, C. & May-Plumlee, T. (1990). Preschoolers' vicarious emotional responding and their situational and dispositional prosocial behavior. *Merrill-Palmer Quarterly*, 36, 507–529.

Elardo, R., Bradley, R. & Caldwell, B. M. (1975). Relation of infants' home environments to mental test performance from 6 to 36 months—longitudinal analysis. *Child Development*, 46(1), 71–76.

Elkind, D. (1967). Egocentrism in adolescence. *Child Development*, 38, 1025–1033.

Eron, L. D. (1982). Parent–child interaction, television violence, and aggression of children. *American Psychologist*, 37(2), 197–211.

Eron, L. D. (1987). The development of aggressive behavior from the perspective of a developing behaviorism. *American Psychologist*, 42, 435–442.

Fantz, R. L. (1961). The origin of form perception. *Scientific American*, 204, 66–72.

Feigenson, L. & Spelke, E. (1998). Numerical knowledge in infancy: The number/mass distinction. Poster presented at the biennial meeting of the International Conference on Infant Studies, Atlanta, GA. In M.W. Clearfield and K. S. Mix (1999). Number versus contour length in infants' discrimination of small visual sets. *Psychological Science*, 10(5), 408–411.

Feigenson, L., Dehaene, S. & Spelke, E. S. (2004). Core systems of number. *Trends in Cognitive Science, 8,* 307–314.

Fennell, E. B. & Dikel, T. N. (2001). Cognitive and neuropsychological functioning in children with cerebral palsy. *Journal of Child Neurology, 16,* 58–63.

Fischhoff, B. (1975). Hindsight is not equal to foresight: The effect of outcome knowledge on judgment under uncertainty. *Journal of Experimental Psychology: Human Perception and Performance, 1,* 288–299.

Flavell, J. H. (1982). On cognitive development. *Child Development, 53,* 1–10.

Flavell, J. H., Everett, B. A., Croft, K. & Flavell, E. R. (1981). Young children's knowledge about visual perception: Further evidence for the Level 1–Level 2 distinction. *Developmental Psychology, 17,* 99–103.

Flavell, J. H., Flavell, E. R. & Green, F. L. (1983). Development of the appearance-reality distinction. *Cognitive Psychology, 15,* 95–120.

Flynn, J. R. (1984). The mean IQ of Americans— massive gains 1932 to 1978. *Psychological Bulletin, 95*(1), 29–51.

Flynn, J. R. (1987). Massive IQ gains in 14 nations— what IQ tests really measure. *Psychological Bulletin, 101*(2), 171–191.

Flynn, J. R. (1999). Searching for justice—the discovery of IQ gains over time. *American Psychologist, 54*(1), 5–20.

Fogel, A. & Melson, G. (1988). *Child development: Individuals, family and society.* St Paul: West Publishing Co.

Follan, M. & Minnis, H. (2010). Forty-four juvenile thieves revisited: From Bowlby to reactive attachment disorder. *Child Care, Health and Development, 36*(5), 639–645.

Fox, N. (1977). Attachment of Kibbutz infants to mother and metapelet. *Child Development, 48,* 1228–1239.

Fox, T. & Thomas, G. V. (1989). Children's drawings of an anxiety eliciting topic: Effects on the size of drawing. *British Journal of Clinical Psychology, 29,* 71–81.

Frank, M. C. & Tenenbaum, J. B. (2011). Three ideal observer models for rule learning in simple languages. *Cognition, 120,* 360–371.

Freeman, N. H. (1980). *Strategies of representation in young children.* London: Academic Press.

Freeman, N. H. & Janikoun, R. (1972). Intellectual realism in children's drawings of familiar objects with distinctive features. *Child Development, 43,* 1116–1121.

Freud, A. & Dann, S. (1951). An experiment in group upbringing. *The Psychoanalytic Study of the Child, 6,* 127–168.

Friedman, O. & Leslie, A. M. (2004). A developmental shift in processes underlying successful belief-desire reasoning. *Cognitive Science, 28,* 963–977.

Frith, U. (2003). *Autism, explaining the enigma (2nd edn.).* Oxford: Basil Blackwell.

Frith, U., Happe, F. & Siddons, F. (1994). Autism and theory of mind in everyday life. *Social Development, 3,* 108–124.

Gallese, V. (2001). The "shared manifold" hypothesis: From mirror neurons to empathy. *Journal of Consciousness Studies, 8,* 33–50.

Gallistel, C. R. & Gelman, R. (1992). Preverbal and verbal counting and computation. *Cognition, 44,* 43–74.

Gardner, H. (1982). *Developmental psychology (2nd edn.).* Boston: Little, Brown and Company.

Geary, D. C. (2005). *The origin of mind: Evolution of brain, cognition, and general intelligence.* Washington, DC: American Psychological Association.

Gelman, R. & Gallistel, C. R. (1978). *The child's understanding of number.* Cambridge, MA: Harvard University Press.

Gelman, R. & Meck, E. (1983). Preschoolers' counting: Principle before skill. *Cognition, 13,* 343–359.

Gibbs, J. C., Basinger, K. S., Grime, R. L. & Snarey, J. R. (2007). Moral judgment development across cultures: Revisiting Kohlberg's universality claims. *Developmental Review, 27,* 443–500.

Gilmore, C. K., McCarthy, S. E. & Spelke, E. (2007). Symbolic arithmetic knowledge without instruction. *Nature, 447,* 589–591.

Gilmore, C. K., McCarthy, S. E. & Spelke, E. S. (2010). Non-symbolic arithmetic abilities and mathematics achievement in the first year of formal schooling. *Cognition, 115,* 394–406.

Goldfarb, W. (1943). The effects of early institutional care on adolescent personality. *Journal of Experimental Education, 12,* 106–129.

Goldfield, B. A. & Reznick, J. S. (1990). Early lexical acquisition: Rate, content, and the vocabulary spurt. *Journal of Child Language, 17,* 171–184.

Gibson, E. J. & Walk, R. D. (1960). The visual cliff. *Scientific American, 209,* 64–71.

Goldin-Meadow, S. & Mylander, C. (1990). Beyond the input given—the child's role in the acquisition of language. *Language, 66*(2), 323–355.

Golding, W. (1954). *Lord of the flies.* London: Faber and Faber.

Goodlee, F., Smith, J. & Marcovitch, H. (2011). Wakefield's article linking MMR vaccine and autism was fraudulent. *British Medical Journal, 342,* 7452.

Goodnow, J. J. (1977). *Children drawing.* Cambridge: Cambridge University Press.

Goodwin, J. (1982). Use of drawings in evaluating children who may be incest victims. *Child and Youth Services Review, 4*, 269–278.

Gopnik, A. & Astington, J. W. (1988). Children's understanding of representational change, and its relation to the understanding of false belief and the appearance-reality distinction. *Child Development, 59*, 26–37.

Gregory, R. L. (1966). *Eye and brain.* New York: World University Library.

Guralnick, M. J. & Paul-Brown, D. (1977). The nature of verbal interactions among handicapped and non-handicapped preschool children. *Child Development, 48*, 254–260.

Haidt, J. (2001). The emotional dog and its rational tail: A social intuitionist approach to moral judgment. *Psychological Review, 108*(4), 814–834.

Haidt, J. (2003). The emotional dog does learn new tricks: A reply to Pizarro and Bloom (2003). *Psychological Review, 110*(1), 197–198.

Haidt, J. & Joseph, C. (2007). The moral mind: How 5 sets of innate moral intuitions guide the development of many culture-specific virtues, and perhaps even modules. In P. Carruthers, S. Laurence & S. Stich (Eds.), *The innate mind*, Vol. 3. (pp. 367–391). New York: Oxford.

Haidt, J., Koller, S. H. & Dias, M. G. (1993). Affect, culture, and morality, or is it wrong to eat your dog? *Journal of Personality and Social Psychology, 65*(4), 613–628.

Halberda, J., Mazzocco, M. & Feigenson, L. (2008). Individual differences in nonverbal number acuity predict maths achievement. *Nature, 455*, 665–668.

Hamlin, J. K., Wynn, K. & Bloom, P. (2007). Social evaluation by preverbal infants. *Nature, 450*(7169), 557–559.

Hamlin, J. K., Wynn, K. & Bloom, P. (2010). Three-month-olds show a negativity bias in their social evaluations. *Developmental Science, 13*(6), 923–929.

Happe, F. (1994). *Autism: An introduction to psychological theory.* London: UCL Press.

Happe, F. (1995). The role of age and verbal ability in the theory of mind task performance of subjects with autism. *Child Development, 66*, 843–855.

Happe, F. (1996). Studying weak central coherence at low levels: Children with autism do not succumb to visual illusions. *Journal of Child Psychology and Psychiatry, 37*, 873–877.

Harris, P. L. (1974). Preservative search at a visibly empty space by young infants. *Journal of Experimental Child Psychology, 18*, 535–542.

Hauser, M. D., Chomsky, N. & Fitch, W. T. (2002). The faculty of language: What is it, who has it, and how did it evolve? *Science, 298*, 1569–1579.

Haworth, C. M., Wright, M. J., Luciano, M., Martin, N. G., de Geus, E. J., van Beijsterveldt, C. E., Bartels, M., Posthuma, D. *et al.* (2010). The heritability of general cognitive ability increases linearly from childhood to young adulthood. *Molecular Psychiatry, 15*(11), 1112–1120.

Helwig, C. C. & Turiel, E. (2002). Children's social and moral reasoning. In C. Hart & P. Smith (Eds.), *Handbook of childhood social development* (pp. 475–490). Malden, MA: Blackwell.

Herrnstein, R. & Murray, C. (1994). *The bell curve: Intelligence and class structure in American life.* New York: Free Press.

Hirshberg, L. (1990). When infants look to their parents: II. Twelve-month-olds' response to conflicting emotional signals. *Child Development, 61*, 1187–1191.

Hirshberg, L. & Svejda, M. (1990). When infants look to their parents: I. Infants' social referencing to mothers compared to fathers. *Child Development, 61*, 1175–1186.

Hoffman, M. L. (1970). Moral development. In P. H. Mussen (Ed.), *Carmichael's manual of child psychology* (Vol. 2). New York: Wiley.

Hoffman, M. L. (2000). *Empathy and moral development: Implications for caring and justice.* New York: Cambridge University Press.

Hoffman, M. L. (2002). How automatic and representational is empathy, and why. *Behavioral and Brain Sciences, 25*(1), 38–39.

Horn, J. L., Donaldson, G. & Engstrom, R. (1981). Apprehension, memory and fluid intelligence decline in adulthood. *Research on Aging, 3*, 33–84.

Howard, R. W. (2001). Searching the real world for signs of rising population intelligence. *Personality and Individual Differences, 30*(6), 1039–1058.

Huesmann, L. R., Moise-Titus, J., Podolski, C. L. & Eron, L. D. (2003). Longitudinal relations between children's exposure to TV violence and their aggressive and violent behavior in young adulthood: 1977–1992. *Developmental Psychology, 39*(2), 201–221.

Hughes, M. (1975). Egocentrism in preschool children. Unpublished PhD thesis, University of Edinburgh, UK.

Jaffee, S. R., Van Hulle, C. & Rodgers, J. L. (2011). Effects of nonmaternal care in the first 3 years on children's academic skills and behavioral functioning in childhood and early adolescence: A sibling comparison study. *Child Development, 82*(4), 1076–1091.

Jenkins, J. M. & Astington, J. W. (1996). Cognitive factors and family structure associated with Theory of Mind development in young children. *Developmental Psychology, 32*, 70–78.

Jenks, K. M., de Moor J., van Lieshout, E. C., Maathuis, K. G., Keus, I. & Gorter, J. W. (2007). The effect of cerebral palsy on arithmetic accuracy is mediated by working memory, intelligence, early numeracy, and instruction time. *Developmental Neuropsychology, 32*, 861–879.

Jensen, A. R. (1980). *Bias in mental testing*. London: Methuen.

Johnson, W. (2010). Understanding the genetics of intelligence: Can height help? Can corn oil? *Current Directions in Psychological Science, 19*, 177–182.

Kagan, J., Kearsley, R. B. & Zelazo, P. R. (1978). *Infancy: Its place in human development*. Cambridge, MA: Harvard University Press.

Kellman, P. J. & Spelke, E. S. (1983). Perception of partly occluded objects in infancy. *Cognitive Psychology, 15*, 483–524.

Keysar, B., Barr, D. J., Balin, J. A. & Brauner, J. S. (2000). Taking perspective in conversation: The role of mutual knowledge in comprehension. *Psychological Science, 11*, 32–38.

Keysar, B., Lin, S. H. & Barr, D. J. (2003). Limits on theory of mind use in adults. *Cognition, 89*, 25–41.

Kirsh, S. J. (2006). Cartoon violence and aggression in youth. *Aggression and Violent Behavior, 11*, 547–557.

Kohlberg, L. (1981). *The philosophy of moral development: Moral stages and the idea of justice*. San Fransisco: Harper and Row.

Krauss, R. M. & Glucksberg, S. (1969). The development of communication: Competence as a function of age. *Child Development, 40*, 255–266.

Kuppens, S., Grietens, H., Onghena, P. & Michiels, D. (2009). Associations between parental control and children's overt and relational aggression. *British Journal of Developmental Psychology, 27*, 607–662.

Lansford, J. E., Dodge, K. A., Pettit, G. S., Criss, M. M., Shaw, D. S. & Bates, J. E. (2009). Trajectories of physical discipline: Early childhood antecedents and developmental outcomes, *Child Development, 80*(5), 1385–1402.

Lapsley, D. K. & Murphy, M. N. (1985). Another look at the theoretical assumptions of adolescent egocentrism. *Developmental Review, 5*, 201–217.

Leiderman, P. H. & Leiderman, G. F. (1974). Affective and cognitive consequences of polymatric infant care in the East African highlands. In A. Pick (Ed.), *Minnesota symposium on child development, Volume 8*. Minneapolis: University of Minnesota Press.

Leon, M. (1984). Rules mothers and sons use to integrate intent and damage information in their moral judgements. *Child Development, 55*, 2106–2113.

Leslie, A. M. (1987). Pretense and representation: The origins of "theory of mind". *Psychological Review, 94*, 412–426.

Leslie, A. M. & Frith, U. (1988). Autistic children's understanding of seeing, knowing and believing. *British Journal of Developmental Psychology, 6*, 315–324.

Lester, B. M. (1974). Separation protest in Guatemalan infants: Cross cultural and cognitive findings. *Developmental Psychology, 10*, 79–85.

Lewis, C., Freeman, N. H., Kyriakidou, C. & Maridaki-kassotaki K. (1996). Social influences on false belief access: Specific sibling influences or general apprenticeship. *Child Development, 67*, 2930–2947.

Lewis, C. & Osborne, A. (1990). Three-year-olds' problems with false belief: Conceptual deficit or linguistic artefact? *Child Development, 61*, 1514–1519.

Lewis, M., Stanger, C. & Sullivan, M. W. (1989). Deception in 3-year-olds. *Developmental Psychology, 25*, 439–443.

Liebert, R. & Baron, R. (1972). Some immediate effects of televised violence on children's behavior. *Developmental Psychology, 6*, 469–175.

Light, P. H., Buckingham, N. & Robbins, A. H. (1979). The conservation task as an interactional setting. *British Journal of Educational Psychology, 49*, 304–310.

Light, P. H. & Humphreys, J. (1981). Internal relationships in young children's drawings. *Journal of Experimental Child Psychology, 31*, 521–530.

Light, P. H. & Macintosh, E. (1980). Depth relationships in young children's drawings. *Journal of Experimental Child Psychology, 30*, 79–87.

Light, P. H. & Simmons, B. (1983). The effects of a communicative task upon the representation of depth relationships in young children's drawings. *Journal of Experimental Child Psychology, 35*, 81–92.

Lindgren, S. D., Renzi, E. D. & Richman, L. C. (1985). Cross national comparisons of developmental dyslexia inItaly and the United States. *Child Development, 56*, 1404–1417.

LoBue, V., Nishida, T., Chiong, C., DeLoache, J. S. & Haidt, J. (2011). When getting something good is bad: Even three-year-olds react to inequality. *Social Development, 20*(1), 154–170.

Luo, Y. & Baillargeon, R. (2010). Toward a mentalistic account of early psychological reasoning. *Current Directions in Psychological Science, 19*(5), 301–307.

Lynn, R. (1996). Racial and ethnic differences in intelligence in the United States on the differential ability scale. *Personality and Individual Differences, 20*(2), 271–273.

Lyons, M. J., York, T. P., Franz, C. E., Grant, M. D., Eaves, L. J., Jacobson, K. C., Schaie, K. W. Panizzon,

M. S., Boake, C., Xian, H., Toomey, R., Eisen, S. A. & Kremen, W. S. (2009). Genes determine stability and the environment determines change in cognitive ability during 35 years of adulthood. *Psychological Science, 20*(9), 1146–1152.

McCann, D., Barrett, A., Cooper, A. *et al.* (2007). Food additives and hyperactive behaviour in 3-year-old and 8/9-year-old children in the community: A randomised, double-blinded, placebo controlled trial. *Lancet, 370*, 1560–1567.

McClearn, G. E., Johansson, B., Berg, S., Pedersen, N. L., Ahern, F., Petrill, S. A. *et al.* (1997). Substantial genetic influence on cognitive abilities in twins 80 or more years old. *Science, 276*(5318), 1560–1563.

McGarrigle, J. & Donaldson, M. (1975). Conservation accidents. *Cognition, 3*, 341–350.

Main, M., Kaplan, N. & Cassidy, J. (1985). Security in infancy, childhood and adulthood: A move to the level of representation. *Monographs of the Society for Research in Child Development, 50*, 66–104.

Mallick, S. & McCandless, B. (1966). A study of catharsis of aggression. *Journal of Personality and Social Psychology, 4*, 591–596.

Manganello, J. A. & Taylor, C. A. (2009). Television exposure as a risk factor for aggressive behavior among 3-year-old children. *Archives of Pediatrics & Adolescent Medicine, 163*(11), 1037–1045.

Maratsos, M. P. (1974). Preschool children's use of definite and indefinite articles. *Child Development, 45*, 446–455.

Meck, W. H. & Church, R. M. (1983). A mode control model of counting and timing processes. *Journal of Experimental Psychology: Animal Behavior Processes, 9*, 320–334.

Meins, E., Fernyhough, C., Russell, J. & Clark-Carter, D. (1998). Security of attachment as a predictor of symbolic and mentalising abilities: A longitudinal study. *Social Development, 7*, 1–24.

Meins, E., Fernyhough, C., Wainwright, R., Clark-Carter, D., Das Gupta, M., Fradley, E. & Tuckey, M. (2003). Pathways to understanding mind: Construct validity and predictive validity of maternal mind-mindedness. *Child Development, 74*, 1194–1211.

Meins, E., Fernyhough, C., Wainwright, R., Das Gupta, M., Fradley, E. & Tuckey, M. (2002). Maternal mind-mindedness and attachment security as predictors of theory of mind understanding. *Child Development, 73*, 1715–1726.

Meints, K., Plunkett, K. & Harris, P. L. (1999). When does an ostrich become a bird? The role of typicality in early word comprehension. *Developmental Psychology, 35*(4), 1072–1078.

Meints, K., Plunkett, K. & Harris, P. L. (2008). Eating apples and houseplants: Typicality constraints on thematic roles in early verb learning. *Language and Cognitive Processes, 23*(3), 434–463.

Meints, K., Plunkett, K., Harris, P. L. & Dimmock, D. K. (2002).What is "on" and "under" to 15-, 18- and 24-month-olds? Typicality effects in early comprehension of spatial prepositions. *British Journal of Developmental Psychology, 20*, 113–130.

Meltzoff, A. N. & Moore, M. K. (1983). Newborn infants imitate adult facial gestures. *Child Development, 54*, 702–709.

Menig-Peterson, C. L. (1975). The modification of communicative behavior in preschool-aged children as a function of the listener's perspective. *Child Development, 46*, 1015–1018.

Minter, M., Hobson, R. P. & Bishop, M. (1998). Congenital visual impairment and "theory of mind". *British Journal of Developmental Psychology, 16*, 183–196.

Mitchell, P., Currie, G. & Ziegler, F. (2009). Two routes to perspective: Simulation and rule-use as approaches to mentalizing. *British Journal of Developmental Psychology, 27*, 513–543.

Mitchell, P. & Lacohee, H. (1991). Children's early understanding of false belief. *Cognition, 39*, 107–127.

Mitchell, P., Mottron, L., Soulieres, I. & Ropar, D. (2010). Susceptibility to the Shepard Illusion in participants with autism: Reduced top-down influences within perception? *Autism Research, 3*, 113–119.

Mitchell, P., Munno, A. & Russell, J. (1991). Children's understanding about the communicative value of discrepant verbal messages. *Cognitive Development, 6*, 279–300.

Mitchell, P. & Robinson, E. J. (1990). When do children overestimate their knowledge of unfamiliar targets? *Journal of Experimental Child Psychology, 50*, 81–101.

Mitchell, P. & Robinson, E. J. (1992). Children's understanding of the evidential connotation of "know" in relation to overestimation of their own knowledge. *Journal of Child Language, 19*, 167–182.

Mitchell, P. & Robinson, E. J. (1994). Discrepant messages resulting from a false belief: Children's evaluations. *Child Development, 65*, 1210–1223.

Mitchell, P., Robinson, E. J., Isaacs, J. E. & Nye, R. M. (1996). Contamination in reasoning about false belief: An instance of realist bias in adults but not children. *Cognition, 59*, 1–21.

Mitchell, P., Robinson, E. J. & Thompson, D. E. (1999). Children's understanding that utterances emanate from minds: Using speaker belief to aid interpretation. *Cognition, 72*, 45–66.

Mitchell, P., Ropar, D., Ackroyd, K. & Rajendran, G. (2005). How perception impacts on drawings.

Journal of Experimental Psychology: Human Perception and Performance, 31, 996–1003.

Mitchell, P. & Russell, J. (1989). Young children's understanding of the say–mean distinction in referential speech. *Journal of Experimental Child Psychology, 47,* 468–490.

Mitchell, P. & Russell, J. (1991). Children's judgments of whether slightly and grossly discrepant objects were intended by a speaker. *British Journal of Developmental Psychology, 9,* 271–280.

Mitchell, P., Souglidou, M., Mills, L. & Ziegler, F. (2007). Seeing is believing: How participants in different subcultures judge people's credulity. *European Journal of Social Psychology, 37,* 573–585.

Mix, K. S., Huttenlocher, J. & Levine, S. (2002). Multiple cues for quantification in infancy: Is number one of them? *Psychological Bulletin, 128*(2), 278–294.

Moore, C. & Frye, D. (1986). The effect of the experimenter's intention on the child's understanding of conservation. *Cognition, 22,* 283–290.

Morris, S. Z. & Gibson, C. L. (2011). Corporal punishment's influence on children's aggressive and delinquent behavior. *Criminal Justice and Behavior, 38*(8), 818–839.

Mundy, E. & Gilmore, C. K. (2009). Children's mapping between symbolic and nonsymbolic representations of number. *Journal of Experimental Child Psychology, 103,* 490–502.

Nelson, K. (1985). *Making sense: The acquisition of shared meaning.* New York: Academic Press.

Nelson, K. & Grether, J. (1999). Causes of cerebral palsy. *Current Opinion in Pediatrics, 11,* 487–496.

Nicholls, J. G. (1978). The development of the concepts of effort and ability, perception of academic attainment, and the understanding that difficult tasks require more ability. *Child Development, 49,* 800–814.

Nisbett, R. E. (2003). *The geography of thought: How Asians and Westerners think differently … and why.* New York: Free Press.

Noble, C. F., Rowland, C. F. & Pine, J. M. (2011). Comprehension of argument structure and semantic roles: Evidence from infants and the forced-choice pointing paradigm. *Cognitive Science, 35*(5), 963–982.

Nunner-Winkler, G. & Sodian, B. (1988). Children's understanding of moral emotions. *Child Development, 59,* 1323–1339.

Ogbu, J. & Stern, P. (2001). Caste status and intellectual ability. In R. J. Sternberg & E. L. Grigorenko (Eds.), *Environmental effects on cognitive abilities.* Mahwah, NJ: Earlbaum.

Onishi, K. H. & Baillargeon, R. (2005). Do 15-month-old infants understand false beliefs? *Science, 308,* 255–258.

Ozonoff, S., Pennington, B.F. & Rogers, S.J. (1991). Executive function deficits in high-functioning autistic individuals: Relationship to theory of mind. *Journal of Child Psychology and Psychiatry, 32,* 1081–1105.

Parke, R., Berkowitz, L., Leyens, J., West, S. & Sebastian, R. (1977). Some effects of violent and nonviolent movies on the behavior on juvenile delinquents. In L. Berkowitz (Ed.), *Advances in experimental social psychology.* New York: Academic Press.

Parsons, J. E., Ruble, D. N., Klosson, E. C., Feldman, N. S. & Rholes, W. S. (1976). Order effects on children's moral and achievement judgments. *Developmental Psychology, 12,* 357–358.

Pears, R. & Bryant, P. (1990). Transitive inferences by young children about spatial position. *British Journal of Psychology, 81,* 497–510.

Perner, J., Frith, U., Leslie, A. M. & Leekam, S. R. (1989). Exploration of the autistic child's theory of mind: Knowledge, belief and communication. *Child Development, 60,* 689–700.

Perner, J., Leekam, S. & Wimmer, H. (1987). Three-year-olds' difficulty with false belief: The case for a conceptual deficit. *British Journal of Developmental Psychology, 5,* 125–137.

Perner, J., Ruffman, T. & Leekam, S. R. (1994). Theory of mind is contagious: You catch it from your sibs. *Child Development, 65,* 1228–1238.

Piaget, J. & Inhelder, B. (1969). *The psychology of the child.* London: Routledge and Kegan Paul.

Pickles, A., Bolton, P., Macdonald, H., Bailey, A., Lecouteur, A., Sim, C. H. *et al.* (1995). Latent-class analysis of recurrence risks for complex phenotypes with selection and measurement error—a twin and family history study of autism. *American Journal of Human Genetics, 57,* 717–726.

Pinker, S. (1994). *The language instinct: The new science of language and mind.* London: Penguin Science.

Pizarro, D. A. & Bloom, P. (2003). The intelligence of the moral intuitions: Comment on Haidt (2001). *Psychological Review, 110*(1), 193–196.

Plomin, R. & DeFries, J.C. (1980). Genetics and intelligence—recent data. *Intelligence, 4*(1), 15–24.

Plomin, R., Loehlin, J. C. & DeFries, J. C. (1985). Genetic and environmental components of environmental influences. *Developmental Psychology, 21*(3), 391–402.

Plunkett, K. & Marchman, V. (1993). From rote learning to system building: Acquiring verb morphology in children and connectionist nets. *Cognition, 48*(1), 21–69.

Popper, K. (1972). *Conjectures and refutations: The growth of scientific knowledge.* London: Routledge and Kegan Paul.

Povinelli, D. J. & Eddy, T. J. (1996). Chimpanzees: Joint visual attention. *Psychological Science, 7*(3), 129–135.

Pring, L. & Hermelin, B. (1993). Bottle, tulip and wineglass: Semantic and structural processing by savant artists. *Journal of Child Psychology and Psychiatry, 34,* 1365–1385.

Rai, R. & Mitchell, P. (2006). Children's ability to impute inferentially-based knowledge. *Child Development, 77,* 803–821.

Rapp, C. E. & Torres, M. M. (2000). The adult with cerebral palsy. *Archives of Family Medicine, 9,* 466–472.

Reith, E. & Dominin, D. (1997). The development of children's ability to attend to the visual projection of objects. *British Journal of Developmental Psychology, 15,* 177–196.

Rest, J. R. (1983). Morality. In J. H. Flavell & E. M. Markman (Eds.), *Handbook of child psychology: Cognitive development* (Vol. 3). New York: Wiley.

Rizzolatti, G. & Craighero, L. (2004). The mirror-neuron system. *Annual Review of Neuroscience, 27,* 169–192.

Robinson, E. J. & Mitchell, P. (1990). Children's failure to make judgments of undecidability when they are ignorant. *International Journal of Behavioral Development, 13,* 467–488.

Robinson, E. J. & Mitchell, P. (1992). Children's interpretation of messages from a speaker with a false belief. *Child Development, 63,* 639–652.

Robinson, E. J. & Robinson, W. P. (1981). Ways of reacting to communication failure in relation to the development of the child's understanding about verbal communication. *European Journal of Social Psychology, 11,* 189–208.

Robinson, E. J. & Whittaker, S. J. (1987). Children's conceptions of relations between messages, meanings and reality. *British Journal of Developmental Psychology, 5,* 81–90.

Robinson, J. O. (1972). *The psychology of visual illusion.* Oxford: Hutchinson University Library.

Rodriguez, A., Kaakinen, M., Moilanen, I., Taanila, A., McGough, J. J., Loo, S. et al. (2010). Mixed-handedness is linked to mental health problems in children and adolescents. *Pediatrics, 125*(2), e340–e348 (published online 25 January 2010).

Ropar, D. & Mitchell, P. (2001a). Do individuals with autism and Asperger syndrome utilize prior knowledge when pairing stimuli? *Developmental Science, 4,* 433–441.

Ropar, D. & Mitchell, P. (2001b). Susceptibility to illusions and performance on visuo-spatial tasks in individuals with autism. *Journal of Child Psychology and Psychiatry, 42,* 539–549.

Ropar, D. & Mitchell, P. (2002). Shape constancy in autism: The role of prior knowledge and perspective cues. *Journal of Child Psychology and Psychiatry, 43,* 647–653.

Rose, S. A. & Blank, M. (1974). The potency of context in children's cognition: An illustration through conservation. *Child Development, 45,* 499–502.

Roth-Hanania, R., Davidov, M. & Zahn-Waxler, C. (2011). Empathy development from 8 to 16 months: Early signs of concern for others. *Infant Behavior and Development, 34*(3), 447–458.

Rumelhart, D. E. & McClelland, J. L. (1986). On learning past tenses of English verbs. In J. L. McClelland, D. E. Rumelhart & the PDP Research Group (Eds.), *Parallel distributed processing: Explorations in the microstructure of cognition* (Vol. 2). Cambridge, MA: MIT Press.

Rushton, J. P. & Jensen, A. R. (2010). The rise and fall of the Flynn Effect as a reason to expect a narrowing of the Black–White IQ gap. *Intelligence, 38,* 213–219.

Russell, J. (1978). *The acquisition of knowledge.* London: Macmillan.

Russell, J. (1981). Children's memory for the premises in a transitive measurement task assessed by elicited and spontaneous justifications. *Journal of Experimental Child Psychology, 31,* 300–309.

Russell, J. (1982). Propositional attitudes. In M. Beveridge (Ed.), *Children thinking through language.* London: Edward Arnold.

Russell, J., Mauthner, N., Sharpe, S. & Tidswell, T. (1991). The "windows task" as a measure of strategic deception in preschoolers and autistic subjects. *British Journal of Developmental Psychology, 9,* 331–350.

Rutter, M. (1972). *Maternal deprivation reassessed.* Harmondsworth: Penguin.

Saltmarsh, R. & Mitchell, P. (1998). Young children's difficulty acknowledging false belief: Realism and deception. *Journal of Experimental Child Psychology, 69,* 3–21.

Saltmarsh, R., Mitchell, P. & Robinson, E. J. (1995). Realism and children's early grasp of mental representation: Belief-based judgments in the state change task. *Cognition, 57,* 297–325.

Savage-Rumbaugh, E. S., Murphy, J., Sevcik, R. A., Brakke, K. E., Williams, S. L. & Rumbaugh, D. M. (1993). Language comprehension in ape and child. *Monographs of the Society for Research in Child Development, 58,* 1–221.

Saviouk, V., Hottenga, J-J., Slagboom, E. P., Distel, M. A., de Geus, E. J. C., Willemsen, G. & Boomsma, D. I. (2011). ADHD in Dutch adults: Heritability and linkage study. *American Journal of Medical Genetics Part B, 156*, 352–362.

Scaife, M. & Bruner, J.S. (1975). The capacity for joint visual attention in the infant. *Nature, 253*, 265.

Schachner, A. M. & Hannon, E. E. (2011). Infant-directed speech drives social preferences in 5-month-old infants. *Developmental Psychology, 47*, 19–25.

Schaffer, H. R. & Emerson, P. (1964). The development of social attachments in infancy. *Monographs of the society for Research in Child Development, 29*, (No. 3).

Schoenthaler, S. J., Amos, S. P., Doraz, W. E., Kelly, M. A. & Wakefield, J. (1991). Controlled trial of vitamin-mineral supplementation on intelligence and brain-function. *Personality and Individual Differences, 12*(4), 343–350.

Shah, A. & Frith, U. (1983). An islet of ability in autistic children. *Journal of Child Psychology and Psychiatry, 24*, 613–620.

Shatz, M. & Gelman, R. (1973). The development of communication skills: Modifications in the speech of young children as a function of listener. *Monographs of the Society for Research in Child Development, 152*(No. 2), 1–38.

Sheppard, E., Ropar, D. & Mitchell, P. (2005). The impact of meaning and dimensionality on the accuracy of children's copying. *British Journal of Developmental Psychology, 23*, 365–381.

Sheppard, E., Ropar, D. & Mitchell, P. (2009). Autism and dimensionality: Differences between copying and drawing tasks. *Journal of Autism and Developmental Disorders, 39*, 1039–1046.

Siegal, M. & Beattie, K. (1991). Where to look first for children's knowledge of false beliefs. *Cognition, 38*, 1–12.

Siegler, R. S. (1996). *Emerging minds: The process of change in children's thinking*. Oxford: Oxford University Press.

Simon, T. J. (1997). Reconceptualizing the origins of number knowledge: A "non-numerical" account. *Cognitive Development, 12*(3), 349–372.

Simon, T. J., Hespos, S. J. & Rochat, P. (1995). Do infants understand simple arithmetic? A replication of Wynn (1992). *Cognitive Development, 10*, 253–269.

Skinner, B. F. (1957). *Verbal learning*. New York: Appleton-Century-Crofts.

Skuse, D. H., James, R. S., Bishop, D. V., Coppin, B., Dalton, P., Aamodt-Leeper, G., Bacarese-Hamilton, M., Creswell, C., McGurk, R. & Jacobs, P.A. (1997). Evidence from Turner's syndrome of an imprinted X-linked locus affecting cognitive function. *Nature, 387*, 705–708.

Slater, A., Mattock, A. & Brown, E. (1990). Size constancy at birth: Newborn infants' responses to retinal and real size. *Journal of Experimental Child Psychology, 49*, 314–322.

Slater, A., Mattock, A., Brown, E. & Bremner, G. (1991). Form perception at birth: Cohen and Younger (1984) revisited. *Journal of Experimental Child Psychology, 51*, 395–406.

Smith, L. B. (2000). Learning how to learn words: An associative crane. In R. M. Golinkoff & K. Hirsh-Pasek (Eds.), *Becoming a word learner*. Oxford: Oxford University Press.

Smith, L. B., Colunga, E. & Yoshida, H. (2010). Knowledge as process: Cued attention and children's novel noun generalizations. *Cognitive Science, 34*, 1287–1314.

Sodian, B. & Frith, U. (1992). Deception and sabotage in autistic, retarded and normal children. *Journal of Child Psychology and Psychiatry, 33*, 591–605.

Sodian, B., Taylor, C., Harris, P. L. & Perner, J. (1991). Early deception and the child's theory of mind: False trails and genuine markers. *Child Development, 62*, 468–483.

Solley, C. M. & Haigh, G. (1957). A note to Santa Claus. *Topeka Research Papers, The Menninger Foundation, 18*, 4–5.

Sonnenschein, S. (1986). Development of referential communication skills: How familiarity with a listener affects a speaker's production of redundant messages. *Developmental Psychology, 22*, 549–552.

Sonuga-Barke, E. J. S. (2005). Causal models of attention-deficit/hyperactivity disorder: From common simple deficits to multiple developmental pathways. *Biological Psychiatry, 57*, 1231–1238.

Southgate, V., Senju, A. & Csibra, G. (2007). Action anticipation through attribution of false belief by 2-year-olds. *Psychological Science, 18*, 587–592.

Sparrevohn, R. & Howie, P. M. (1995). Theory of mind in children with autistic disorder: Evidence of developmental progression and the role of verbal ability. *Journal of Child Psychology and Psychiatry, 36, 249–263*.

Starkey, P. & Cooper, R. G. (1980). Perception of numbers by human infants. *Science, 210*(4473), 1033–1035.

Stein, A. H. & Friedrich, L. K. (1972). Television content and young children's behavior, Vol. 2: Television and social learning. In P. Murray, E. A. Rubinstein & G. A. Comstock (Eds.), *Television and social behavior*. Washington, DC: US Government Printing Office.

Sternberg, R. J., Grigorenko, E. L. & Kidd, K. K. (2005). Intelligence, race, and genetics. *American Psychologist*, 60(1), 46–59.

Suhler, C. L. & Churchland, P. (2011). Can innate, modular "foundations" explain morality? Challenges for Haidt's moral foundations theory. *Journal of Cognitive Neuroscience*, 23(9), 2103–2116.

Sullivan, K. & Winner, E. (1993). Three-year-olds' understanding of mental states: The influence of trickery. *Journal of Experimental Child Psychology*, 56, 135–148.

Surian, L., Caldi, S. & Sperber, D. (2007). Attribution of beliefs by 13-month-old infants. *Psychological Science*, 18, 580–586.

Svetlova, M., Nichols, S. R. & Brownell, C. A. (2010). Toddlers' prosocial behavior: From instrumental to empathic to altruistic helping. *Child Development*, 81(6), 1814–1827.

Taft, L. (1995). Cerebral palsy. *Pediatric Review*, 16, 411–418.

Taylor, L. & Mitchell, P. (1997). Judgments of apparent shape contaminated by knowledge of reality: Viewing circles obliquely. *British Journal of Psychology*, 88, 653–670.

Thomas, G., Chaigne, E. & Fox, T. (1989). Children's drawings of topics differing in significance: Effects on size of drawing. *British Journal of Developmental Psychology*, 7, 321–332.

Thomas, G. & Silk, A. M. J. (1990). *An introduction to the psychology of children's drawings*. Hemel Hempstead, UK: Harvester Wheatsheaf.

Thomas, M. H., Horton, R., Lippincott, E. & Drabman, R. (1977). Desensitization to portrayals of real-life aggression as a function of exposure to television violence. *Journal of Personality and Social Psychology*, 35, 450–458.

Thouless, R. H. (1931). Phenomenal regression to the real object. I. *British Journal of Psychology*, 21(4), 339–359.

Thouless, R. H. (1932). Individual differences in phenomenal regression. *British Journal of Psychology*, 22, 216–241.

Tomasello, M. (2003). *Constructing a language: A usage-based theory of language acquisition*. Cambridge, MA: Harvard University Press.

Tomasello, M. & Akhtar, N. (1995). 2-year-olds use pragmatic cues to differentiate reference to objects and actions. *Cognitive Development*, 10(2), 201–224.

Tomasello, M. & Barton, M. (1994). Learning words in nonostensive contexts. *Developmental Psychology*, 30(5), 639–650.

Tomasello, M. & Brooks, P. (1999). Early syntactic development: A construction grammar approach. In M. Barrett (Ed.), *The development of language*. London: Psychology Press.

Vaish, A., Carpenter, M. & Tomasello, M. (2010). Young children selectively avoid helping people with harmful intentions. *Child Development*, 81(6), 1661–1669.

Vaish, A., Missana, M. & Tomasello, M. (2011). Three-year-old children intervene in third-party moral transgressions. *British Journal of Developmental Psychology*, 29(Pt 1), 124–130.

Verropoulou, G. & Joshi H. (2009). Does mother's employment conflict with child development? Multilevel analysis of British mothers born in 1958. *Journal of Population Economics*, 22(3), 665–692.

von Frisch, K. (1954). *The dancing bees*. London: Methuen.

Wakeley, A., Rivera, S. & Langer, J. (2000). Can young infants add and subtract? *Child Development*, 71(6), 1525–1534.

Warneken, F. & Tomasello, M. (2006). Altruistic helping in human infants and young chimpanzees. *Science*, 3, 1301–1303.

Wason, P. C. & Johnson-Laird, P. N. (1972). *The psychology of reasoning: Structure and content*. London: Batsford Press.

Wellman, H. M., Cross, D. & Watson, J. (2001). Meta-analysis of theory of mind development: The truth about false belief. *Child Development*, 72, 655–684.

Wimmer, H. & Hartl, M. (1991). Against the Cartesian view on mind: Young children's difficulty with own false beliefs. *British Journal of Developmental Psychology*, 9, 125–138.

Wimmer, H. & Perner, J. (1983). Beliefs about beliefs: Representation and constraining function of wrong beliefs in young children's understanding of deception. *Cognition*, 13, 103–128.

Wimmer, H., Wachter, J. & Perner, J. (1982). Cognitive autonomy of the development of moral evaluation and achievement. *Child Development*, 53, 668–676.

Wing, L. & Gould, J. (1979). Severe impairments of social interaction and associated abnormalities in children: Epidemiology and classification. *Journal of Autism and Developmental Disorders*, 9, 11–29.

Wood, D. J., Bruner, J. S. & Ross, G. (1976). The role of tutoring in problem-solving. *Journal of Child Psychology and Psychiatry*, 17, 89–100.

Woodworth, R. S. (1941). *Heredity and environment: A cultural study of recently published materials on twins and foster children*. New York: Social Science.

Woolfe, T., Want, S. & Siegal, M. (2002). Signpost to development: Theory of mind in deaf children. *Child Development*, 73, 768–778.

Wynn, K. (1992). Addition and subtraction by human infants. *Nature*, 358, 749–750.

Wynn, K. (1996). Infants' individuation and enumeration of actions. *Psychological Science*, 7, 164–169.

Wynn, K. (2000). Findings of addition and subtraction in infants are robust and consistent: Reply to Wakeley, Rivera, and Langer. *Child Development*, 71(6), 1535–1536.

Xu, F. & Spelke, E. (2000). Large number discrimination in 6-month-old infants. *Cognition*, 74, B1–B11.

Yarrow, M. R., Scott, P. M. & Waxler, C. Z. (1973). Learning concern for others. *Developmental Psychology*, 8, 240–260.

Yuill, N. & Perner, J. (1988). Intentionality and knowledge in children's judgments of actors' responsibility and recipients' emotional reaction. *Developmental Psychology*, 24(3), 358–365.

Zafeiriou, D., Kontopoulos, E. & Tsikoulas, I. (1999). Characteristics and prognosis of epilepsy in children with cerebral palsy. *Epilepsy and Cerebral Palsy*, 14, 289–293.

Zajonc, R. B. (1983). Validating the confluence model. *Psychological Bulletin*, 93, 457–480.

Zarbatany, L. & Lamb, M. E. (1985). Social referencing as a function of information source: Mother versus strangers. *Infant Behavior and Development*, 8, 25–33.

Author index

Subject index